The Foreign Economic Policies of Singapore, South Korea and Taiwan

To Mum, Dad, Louise and Charlie...
From a thankful son and brother

The Foreign Economic Policies of Singapore, South Korea and Taiwan

Christopher M. Dent

Lecturer in the Southeast and East Asian Economy, University of Hull, UK

Edward Elgar

Cheltenham, UK • Northampton, MA, USA

Published by
Edward Elgar Publishing Limited
Glensanda House
Montpellier Parade
Cheltenham
Glos GL50 1UA
UK

Edward Elgar Publishing, Inc.
136 West Street
Suite 202
Northampton
Massachusetts 01060
USA

A catalogue record for this book is available from the British Library

Library of Congress Cataloguing in Publication Data
Dent, Christopher M., 1965–
The foreign economic policies of Singapore, South Korea, and Taiwan / Christopher M. Dent.
p. cm.
Includes bibliographical references and index.
1. Singapore—Foreign economic relations. 2. Singapore—Commercial policy. 3. Singapore—Economic policy. 4. Korea (South)—Foreign economic relations. 5. Korea (South)—Commercial policy. 6. Korea (South)—Economc policy. 7. Taiwan—Foreign economic relations. 8. Taiwan—Commercial policy. 9. Taiwan—Economic Policy—1945–
I. Title.

HF1595 .D46 2002
337.51—dc21

2001051263

ISBN 1 84064 838 4 (cased)
Printed and bound in Great Britain by MPG Books Ltd, Bodmin, Cornwall

Contents

Figures and tables

Figures

Tables

Preface

For many years now, I have been fascinated by the economic achievements of East Asia's newly industrializing economies, and particularly Singapore, South Korea and Taiwan – hereafter referred to as the NIE-3. More specifically, I have been intrigued by how they have engaged in the international economic system, and to what extent their success could be attributed to their respective foreign economic policies. This book is the product of a three-year research study on this very subject. Its primary fieldwork involved eight research fieldtrips to the NIE-3 group between May 1998 and November 2000, where 205 people were interviewed in a total of 156 interviews involving 147 agencies. The details of these are provided in the 'Interviewed Agencies' section that follows. I have withheld the names of those interviewed as the vast majority wished to remain anonymous. Nevertheless, I would like to extend my deepest thanks to them all for kindly agreeing to participate in my research interview programme. As the list of interviewed agencies shows, I sought vital insider knowledge from a wide range of foreign economic policy stakeholders covering the government, business, foreign commercial, civil societal, research institute and academic communities.

The first two chapters of this book provide the theoretical and methodological basis on which the main study chapters on Singapore, South Korea and Taiwan are based. Chapter 1 develops a new macro-framework for foreign economic policy analysis that is designed for general application, i.e. beyond the NIE-3. Chapter 2 posits that the 'development context' of the NIE-3's foreign economic policies is grounded in their common *developmental statism* and *semi-peripheralization* – the former being primarily concerned with the *domestic* determination of NIE-3 development while the latter more explicitly considers factors of *external* determination. Chapters 3, 4 and 5 are structured around the macro-framework of Chapter 1 and incorporate the main body of primary and secondary research material. Their long length reflects the comprehensive approach of the research on which they are based. These examine not just the technical aspects and recent events of the NIE-3's foreign economic policies but also changes in underpinning ideologies, values and ideas, and the multi-level contesting 'actor-based' influences exerted over their formation. In addition, central to each of these study chapters is the notion that the pursuit of *economic security* primarily determines the foreign economic policy objectives of the NIE-3. In conclusion, Chapter 6 makes a comparative summary that both highlights this project's most important research findings and draws further direct comparisons between Singapore, South Korea and Taiwan's foreign economic policy experiences.

In addition to my research interviewees, I am extremely grateful to a number of people who helped make this research possible. I would first like to thank the British Academy and EU–China Academic Network for providing facilitative research funding. Robert Ash, Stephen Wilks and Barry Gills offered valuable guidance to me on negotiating through the grant application process. I am also very much obliged to Bruce Chien at the Taipei Representative in London who greatly assisted my efforts in both arranging my first research interviews in Taiwan and finding obscure bits of research data. As in my previous book project, Lizanne Martinez at UNCTAD kindly supplied me with the most up-to-date foreign direct investment data. I would also like to thank Francine O'Sullivan at Edward Elgar for cheerily supporting me through the whole publishing process. Finally, my family again deserve special mention for keeping me generally sane and entertained over the duration of this project. For these and other reasons, I still owe my wife, Ruth, a large number of domestic credits that I hope one day to repay.

University of Hull,
England

Abbreviations

AFTA	ASEAN Free Trade Area
AIA	ASEAN Investment Area
AIE	advanced industrial economy
AMF	Asian Monetary Fund
APBFTA	Asia–Pacific bilateral free trade agreement
APEC	Asia–Pacific Economic Co-operation forum
APROC	Asia–Pacific Regional Operations Centre (Taiwan)
ARATS	Association for Relations Across the Taiwan Strait (China)
ASEAN	Association of Southeast Asian Nations
ASEM	Asia–Europe Meetings
BIT	bilateral investment treaty
BOFT	Board of Foreign Trade (Taiwan)
BOK	Bank of Korea
CBC	Central Bank of China (Taiwan)
CCEJ	Citizens' Coalition of Economic Justice (South Korea)
CEE	Central and East European
CEPD	Council of Economic Planning and Development (Taiwan)
CEPT	Common Effective Preferential Tariff
CFL	Chinese Federation of Labour (Taiwan)
CLA	Council of Labour Affairs (Taiwan)
CMI	Chiang Mai Initiative
CNFI	Chinese National Federation of Industries (Taiwan)
DPP	Democratic People's Party (Taiwan)
EALAF	East Asia–Latin America Forum
EDB	Economic Development Board (Singapore)
EDCF	Economic Development and Co-operation Fund (South Korea)
EFTA	European Free Trade Area
EOI	export oriented industrialization
EPA	Environmental Protection Administration (Taiwan)
EPB	Economic Planning Board (South Korea)
EPZ	export processing zone
EU	European Union
FCIA	Foreign Capital Inducement Act (South Korea)
FDI	foreign direct investment

FEP	foreign economic policy
FETA	Foreign Exchange Transaction Act (South Korea)
FIP	foreign industrial park
FIPA	Foreign Investment Promotion Act (South Korea)
FKI	Federation of Korean Industries
FKTU	Federation of Korean Trade Unions
FPA	foreign policy analysis
FSC	Financial Supervisory Commission (South Korea)
FTA	free trade agreement
FYP	five-year plan
GATT	General Agreement on Tariffs and Trade
GCC	global commodity chain
GDP	gross domestic product
GIC	Government Investment Corporation (Singapore)
GKU	Green Korea United
GLC	government-linked company (Singapore)
GNP	gross national product
HCI	heavy chemical and industry
ICDF	International Co-operation and Development Fund (Taiwan)
ICFTU	International Confederation of Free Trade Unions
IDB	Industrial Development Bureau (Taiwan)
IDP	Import Diversification Programme (South Korea)
IEAT	Importers and Exporters Association of Taiwan
IEO	international economic organization
ILO	International Labour Organisation
IMF	International Monetary Fund
IMSGT	Indonesia–Malaysia–Singapore Growth Triangle
IPE	international political economy
IPR	intellectual property rights
ISI	import substitution industrialisation
JSEPA	Japan–Singapore Economic Partnership Agreement
JTC	Jurong Town Corporation
JTCI	Jurong Town Corporation International
KAIST	Korean Advanced Institute of Science and Technology
KBE	knowledge-based economy
KCCI	Korean Chamber of Commerce and Industry
KCTU	Korean Confederation of Trade Unions
KDI	Korean Development Institute
KFEM	Korean Federation of Environmental Movements
KHIS	Korea House for International Solidarity
KIEP	Korea Institute for International Economic Policy
KIET	Korean Institute for Industrial Economics and Trade

KITA	Korean International Trade Association
KMT	Kuomintang (Taiwan's Nationalist Party)
KOICA	Korea International Co-operation Agency
KoPA	Korean People's Action against investment treaties and the WTO New Round
KOTRA	Korean Trade Promotion Agency
LDC	less developed country
MAC	Mainland Affairs Council (Taiwan)
MAS	Monetary Authority of Singapore
MFA	Ministry of Foreign Affairs (Singapore)
MFN	Most Favoured Nation
MNE	multinational enterprise
MOAF	Ministry of Agriculture and Forestry (South Korea)
MOCAT	Ministry of Culture and Tourism (South Korea)
MOCIE	Ministry of Commerce, Industry and Energy (South Korea)
MOE	Ministry of Environment (Singapore, South Korea)
MOEA	Ministry of Economic Affairs (Taiwan)
MOF	Ministry of Finance (Singapore, Taiwan)
MOFA	Ministry of Foreign Affairs (Taiwan)
MOFAT	Ministry of Foreign Affairs and Trade (South Korea)
MOFE	Ministry of Finance and Economy (South Korea)
MOL	Ministry of Labour (South Korea)
MOM	Ministry of Manpower (Singapore)
MTI	Ministry of Trade and Industry (Singapore)
NAFTA	North American Free Trade Agreement
NGO	non-governmental organisation
NIE	newly industrialised economy
NTB	non-tariff barrier
NTUC	National Trade Union Congress (Singapore)
ODA	official development assistance
ODAC	official development assistance and co-operation
ODM	original design manufacture
OECD	Organisation for Economic Co-operation and Development
OEM	original equipment manufacture
PAP	People's Action Party (Singapore)
PBEC	Pacific Basin Economic Council
PECC	Pacific Economic Co-operation Conferences
PRC	People's Republic of China
PSPD	People's Solidarity for Participatory Democracy (South Korea)
ROC	Republic of China
R&D	research and development
SCC	Singapore Competitiveness Committee

SCI	Singapore Confederation of Industries
SEC	Singapore Environment Council
SEF	Straits Exchange Foundation (Taiwan)
SICC	Singapore International Chamber of Commerce
SME	small and medium-sized enterprise
SOE	state-owned enterprise
SREZ	sub-regional economic zone
TDB	Trade Development Board (Singapore)
TEPU	Taiwan Environmental Protection Union
WTO	World Trade Organisation

Interviewed agencies

SINGAPORE

Government

Economic Development Board (EDB)
- International Policy Division

Government of Singapore Investment Corporation
- Economics and Strategy Dept

Jurong Town Corporation (JTC)

Ministry of Environment (MOE)
- International Environment and Policy Dept

Ministry of Finance
- International Relations Co-ordinator

Ministry of Foreign Affairs (MFA)
- EU and US Affairs Division
- International Economics Division
- Northeast Asian Affairs Division
- Southeast Asian Affairs Division
- Technical Co-operation Directorate

Ministry of Manpower (MOM)
- Deputy Secretary Office
- Labour Relations and Welfare Division

Ministry of Trade and Industry (MTI)
- Trade Policy Division

Monetary Authority of Singapore (MAS)
- Domestic Economy Division

Trade Development Board (TDB)
- Corporate Communications
- Trade Policy Division

Business/Industrial Associations

Bank of America
Exxon Mobil Singapore

Glaxo Wellcome Asia Pacific
Hong Leong Group
Jurong Town Corporation International (JTCI)
Singapore Confederation of Industries (SCI)
Singapore International Chamber of Commerce (SICC)

Foreign Commercial/Official Foreign Offices

American Chamber of Commerce
British Chamber of Commerce
British High Commission
French Business Centre
German Business Association
German Centre for Trade and Industry
German Embassy
Indonesian Embassy
Japanese Chamber of Commerce
Japanese Embassy
Malaysian High Commission
Netherlands Embassy
US Embassy

Academics/Research Institutes

Institute of Defence and Strategic Studies
Institute of Policy Studies
Institute of Southeast Asian Studies
National University of Singapore

- Dept of Economics and Statistics
- Dept of Geography
- Dept of Sociology
- Faculty of Business Administration

NGOs

National Trade Union Congress (NTUC)
Singapore Environment Council (SEC)

Agencies:	45
Interviews:	49
Interviewees:	62

SOUTH KOREA

Government

Bank of Korea (BOK)
- International Finance Planning Team, International Dept

Korea International Co-operation Agency (KOICA)
- Office of Co-operation Policy and Research

Ministry of Commerce, Industry and Energy (MOCIE)
- Europe and Africa Division
- Foreign Investment Promotion Division
- Foreign Policy Division
- Investment Policy Division
- Trade Policy Division

Ministry of Environment (MOE)
- Commercial Affairs Division
- Global Environment Office

Ministry of Finance and Economy (MOFE)
- Economic Analysis Division
- Economic Co-operation Bureau
- International Financial Bureau
- International Investment Division

Ministry of Foreign Affairs and Trade (MOFAT)
- Development Co-operation Division
- Economic Co-operation Division
- Emerging Markets Division
- European Affairs Division
- International Economic Affairs Bureau
- Multilateral Trade Co-operation Division
- North American Affairs Division
- Regional Co-operation Division
- Trade Policy Planning Division
- Trade Affairs Division

Ministry of Labour (MOL)
- International Co-operation Division

Domestic Business/Industrial Associations

Federation of Korean Industry (FKI)
- International Division

Korean Chamber of Commerce and Industry (KCCI)
- Economic Policy Research Dept

Korean International Trade Association (KITA)
- Trade Research Dept

Foreign Commercial/Official Foreign Offices

American Chamber of Commerce
British Embassy
EU Delegation
French Embassy
German Chamber of Commerce and Industry
Japanese Embassy
Netherlands Embassy
US Embassy

Academics/Research Institutes

Institute for Foreign Affairs and National Security (IFANS)
- Dept for Asia Pacific Studies
- International Economy and Trade Affairs

Institute for Global Economics (IGE)
Korea Development Institute (KDI)
Korea Institute for International Economic Policy (KIEP)
- Dept of European Affairs
- Dept of Trade and Investment Policy

Korea Institute of Industrial Economics and Trade (KIET)
- Industrial Policy Division

Kyungwon University
- Dept of Environment Studies

Korea University
- Dept of Economics

Samsung Economic Research Institute
Seoul National University
- Graduate School of International Studies

Yonsei University
- Graduate School of International Studies
- Institute of East–West Studies

NGOs

Citizen's Coalition for Economic Justice (CCEJ)
Federation of Korean Trade Unions (FKTU)
Korean Confederation of Trade Unions (KCTU)

Korean Federation for Environmental Movement (KFEM)
Korea House for International Solidarity (KHIS)

Agencies:	53
Interviews:	56
Interviewees:	66

TAIWAN

Government

Central Bank of China (CBC)
- Economic Research Department
- Balance of Payments Division

China External Trade Development Council (CETRA)
- Marketing Research Dept

Council for Economic Planning and Development (CEPD), Executive Yuan
- Vice Chairman Office

Council of Labour Affairs, Executive Yuan
- Planning and Research Dept

Environmental Protection Administration (EPA)
- Office of Science and Technology Advisors

International Co-operation Development Fund (ICDF)
- Deputy Director Office
- Education and Training Division
- Financial Analysis Division
- Technical Co-operation Division

Mainland Affairs Council (MAC)
- Director's Office

Ministry of Economic Affairs (MOEA)
- Deputy Director-General Office, Board of Foreign Trade
- Trade–Competition Policy Desk, Board of Foreign Trade
- Trade–Environment Desk, Board of Foreign Trade
- Trade–Labour Desk, Board of Foreign Trade
- WTO and Multilateral Trade Affairs, Board of Foreign Trade
- Investment Commission
- International Co-operation Department
- Industrial Development Bureau
- Industrial Development and Investment Centre

Ministry of Finance (MOF)
- Bureau of Monetary Affairs

Ministry of Foreign Affairs (MOFA)
- Dept of East Asia and Pacific Affairs
- Dept of Economic and Trade Affairs
- Dept of European Affairs
- Dept of International Organizations
- Dept of North American Affairs

Business/Industrial Associations

Asea Brown Boveri
Importers and Exporters Association of Taipei (IEAT)
Chinese National Federation of Industries (CNFI)
Institute of Information Industry
Siemens
Taiwan Textile Federation

Foreign Commercial/Official Foreign Offices

American Chamber of Commerce
American Institute in Taiwan
British Trade and Cultural Office
British Chamber of Commerce
European Chamber of Commerce
French Institute, Economic and Commercial Office
German Trade Office Taipei
Japanese Chamber of Commerce and Industry
Japanese Interchange Association
Netherlands Trade and Investment Office

Academics/Research Institutes

Chung-Hua Institute for Economic Research
Institute of European and American Studies, Academia Sinica
Institute of International Relations (National Chengchi University)
Taiwan Institute of Economic Research

NGOs

Chinese Federation of Labour (CFL)
Taiwan Labour Front
Taiwan Environmental Protection Union (TEPU)

Agencies:	49
Interviews:	51
Interviewees:	77

TOTAL

Agencies:	147
Interviews:	156
Interviewees:	205

1. Foreign economic policy: a new macro-analytical framework

1.1 INTRODUCTION

The prime aim of this chapter is to establish a macro-framework for foreign economic policy (FEP) analysis. In doing so, it forms the structure of our study on the FEPs of Singapore, South Korea and Taiwan. However, the analytical framework presented here is designed for general application, and hence may be deployed beyond these three newly industrializing economies (or NIE-3 as we shall collectively refer to them) to other FEP powers both inside and outside East Asia. While this chapter thus outlines the analytical structure of this book, Chapter 2 discusses the specific development context of the NIE-3's foreign economic policies, with particular respect paid to the persisting relevance of developmental statism and semi-peripheralization.

The prime motivation for developing the analytical constructs found in this chapter stems from dissatisfaction with the somewhat vague and disparate approach to FEP analysis that prevails in the international political economy literature. This may be attributed to two main factors. First, there has been scant improvement in the tools of, and perspectives on FEP analysis in recent years. Second, a comprehensive macro-framework for studying the structure, conduct and process of FEP has yet to be ventured. With this in mind, this chapter and text in general endeavours to confront these twin predicaments. The model presented here is based on a multivariate approach to FEP analysis that uses a schematic of interactive functions to demonstrate its analytical workings. Certain key terms of reference are deployed throughout, the most important of which are:

- *FEP protagonists*: relate to actors that are responsible for the directing (political or quasi-political leadership) or managing (bureaucratic leadership) of foreign economic policy. These normally relate to central government representatives but can also include those from sub-state units (e.g. local government), supranational or inter-governmental units such as the EU, and even, in some cases, representatives drawn from business or civil society.[1]

- *FEP powers*: refer to the polities that these protagonists represent. These are typically nation-states, such as South Korea and Singapore, though the latter is more often thought of as a city-state. Whilst Taiwan's own nation-statehood is contested, it is still able to conduct a well defined foreign economic policy and therefore qualifies as a FEP power.
- *FEP formation*: a generic term for the structure, conduct and process of foreign economic policy.
- *Stakeholding FEP constituencies*: relate to any groups with a direct interest in, or even leverage over FEP formation. These can include FEP protagonists themselves, as well as business, civil societal, institutional and other representations and so on.

Before we progress to macro-theorize on FEP analysis, this chapter first examines the development of foreign economic policy scholarship and highlights some analytical problematics that persist.

1.2 CONCEPTUAL DEVELOPMENT AND PROBLEMATICS OF FEP ANALYSIS

Scholarly work on FEP analysis has a long pedigree and has been at least an implicit field of study since the disciplinary origins of international political economy (IPE) itself. There are, however, various unresolved problem areas in FEP analysis. These primarily centre on the definition of an empirical domain, the dominance of 'hegemonic state' (e.g. US) case studies and neglected macro-conceptualization. This section will examine these areas in turn, providing the background context to the main section of this chapter that develops its own macro-analytical framework.

1.2.1 Defining the Empirical Domain

In many ways, FEP analysis is an unwieldy focus of enquiry. Attempts to establish its own empirical domain as either distinct from, or as a subset within foreign policy analysis (FPA) have proved especially problematic.[2] Both types of problem are linked to the growing salience of economic issues in foreign policy practice during the post-Cold War period (Bergsten 1992). This is set against the traditional dichotomy between high politics (political diplomacy, military security) and low politics (economic diplomacy, economic security) becoming increasingly blurred. Given the expanding economic content of foreign policy, we can infer that either FEP analysis is gradually 'stealing the empirical clothes' of FPA or the converse perspective whereby FEP analysis is simply being absorbed into an expanding FPA domain, and subsequently losing its own ontological distinctiveness.

There also exists the problem of untangling the economic from the non-economic in FEP formation. For example, FEP actions may have non-economic objectives just as general foreign policy actions have clear economic consequences. Destler (1980) articulated the same broad point: 'we must ask whether the term [foreign economic policy] excludes any actions, since in this age of interdependence it is hard to find policy actions without some impact beyond US borders and even harder to find actions without significant economic content' (p. 7).[3] Another empirical domain problem concerns distinguishing foreign from domestic economic policy. In an era of advancing globalization and deepening economic interdependence, the externalization of domestic policy becomes increasingly salient, thus creating an 'intermestic' realm (Manning 1977). Furthermore, as linkage theory proposes, maintaining hard and fast boundaries between domestic and foreign policies is difficult when events internally influence events externally and vice versa (Rosenau 1969). We return to this issue in the discussions on neglected macro-conceptualization, and the 'core' and 'associative' technical policy realms of FEP analysis. A further difficulty arises from the foundation of many foreign economic policy studies on idiosyncratic assumptions of what constitutes the empirical domain and general parameters of FEP analysis, thus producing a vernacularization effect in which different dialects of FEP analysis are created. While this diversity of approach has obvious benefits, few attempts have been ventured in establishing a common analytical basis by which meaningful comparative FEP studies may be undertaken.

This latter problem further complicates issues concerning elusive definitions and alternative competing terms of FEP itself. For Cohen (1968), FEP can be defined as government actions intended to affect the international economic environment, while for Destler (1980) it represents the actual impact of government actions on foreign and economic concerns. Baldwin (1986) criticized these somewhat simplistic definitions on the main grounds that they failed to allude to both FEP instruments and the type of effect intended. Matters of FEP definition are further confused by the number of alternative competing terms – such as economic diplomacy, economic statecraft and international economic policy – presenting a lack of consensus over what chosen term we wish to define. Similarly for some analysts, foreign economic policy is more or less synonymous with trade policy (Mercado 1995).

1.2.2 A Hegemony-centric Field of Enquiry?

Another dilemma of FEP analysis is the continued dominance of US case studies,[4] although this is indicative of an IPE scholarship in general. One consequence of this has been a preoccupation of previous FEP analyses with either the Cold War calculus of power politics or managing unilateralist trade policies, with economic sanctions and coercion receiving particular attention in the past.[5] Another has been a preponderance of FEP analyses based on a neo-liberal, hegemonic perspective with some preferring historical studies (Kindleberger 1977, Lake 1983, Pastor 1980). Thus, in one sense, FEP analysis has been defined by American scholarship. However, a challenge to this American quasi-monopoly was evident from the mid-1970s onwards, deriving mainly from studies on West European states or the European Union (EU).[6] Cold War FEP studies on Europe typically examine the political economy of sanctions, embargoes, deepening economic blocism, security-sensitive trade and technology diffusion, and other COCOM[7] issues (Adler and Karlsson 1968; Pinder 1985, Story 1988), whereas more contemporary studies on the EU are often premised on its function as a multilayered, complex system of governance (Smith 1994, Young 1998).[8] There have also been some studies on the Soviet Union and post-Cold War Russia (Drezner 1997, Glaziev 1993, Silvestrov and Filatov 1995, Zyzniewski 1958). Those studies of FEP analysis on East Asia tend to be dominated by Japan (Akao 1983; Bobrow 1985; Calder 1988, 1991; Chapman *et al* 1983; Heginbotham and Samuels 1998; Nester 1991; Nukazawa 1980; Pempel 1978) with very little attention paid to other states in the region (Dent 1998c, 2000; Kokubun 1986). The bias in FEP analyses towards the US and other advanced industrial economies (AIEs) is reflected in the conceptual tools thus far developed in this scholarly field. Although a generically applicable framework of FEP analysis is advanced by this text, it is hoped that its focus on three NIEs will in some way stir interest in new geographic and developmental fields of FEP enquiry.

1.2.3 Neglected Macro-Conceptualization

The empirical and ontological predicaments noted above may also explain the neglected macro-conceptualization evident in FEP analysis over recent years. Up to the 1980s, Pastor (1980) observed that most FEP analysts had been 'narrators of events rather than conceptualisers' and that 'there are few important terms which are used so often and so loosely' (p. 7). While efforts have been made since then to rectify this, FEP analysis remains conceptually impoverished overall with the vast majority of FEP studies lacking the foundation of either a formalized methodology or an analytical construct. This particularly applies to macro-conceptualization, by which I mean a comprehensive approach to FEP analysis that incorporates a holistic range of determining factors and analytical parameters. However, FEP analysis is not without its useful conceptual devices. In their study of US foreign economic policy, Ikenberry *et al* (1988) proposed three broad approaches:

- *System-centred*: where FEP is a function of the attributes or capabilities of one nation-state relative to others, involving the 'prevailing distributions of power, the norms and principles embedded in international regimes, or the imperatives of international economic structures' (p. 219), and where FEP is shaped by the demands and opportunities generated within the international political economy;
- *Society-centred*: where FEP determination either reflects the preferences of the dominant group or class in society, or of the resulting struggle between societal groups to influence it, and thus is essentially a function of domestic politics: that is FEP is shaped by the demands placed upon governments by private groups, sectors and classes within the national political system;
- *State-centred*: where FEP is primarily moulded by the active role of government officials pursuing autonomous goals or the shaping and constraining role of the state organizational structure, thus positing the state as the most important independent and intervening variable in FEP formation.[9]

In applying this system–society–state framework to Katzenstein's (1976) earlier work on AIEs, it could be argued that the prevalence of each approach varies across countries, depending on the nature of the domestic political economy. Thus, a state-centred policy-network dominates in 'centralized' France, whereas the society-centred networks of a 'polycentric' US produce different FEP formation dynamics. Many have been critical of the predominant state-centred strain of FEP analysis (Grossman and Helpman 1995). For Hocking and Smith (1997), society-centred approaches have fewer limitations and 'offer a richer tapestry and recognise that external policy usually reflects a conflict between domestic constituencies rather than societal unity based on an indivisible national interest' (p. 12). Society-centred approaches have also been generally prescribed by radical theorists whereby FEP is ultimately determined by structures of society, and not individuals in position of state power (McGowan and Walker 1981).[10] However, as Chapter 2 explores in some detail, the state-centred approach has traditionally been most relevant amongst the NIE-3, this being primarily attributed to a common developmental state heritage. Yet the other two approaches are becoming increasingly relevant given important societal level changes in recent years, and the more comprehensive engagement of the NIE-3 in the international economic system.

In an evaluative study on trade and foreign economic policy, Odell (1990) identifies another set of prominent theoretical approaches, or perspectives, that overlap with those of Ikenberry *et al* (1988). To Odell, the *market* perspective broadly considers how market conditions affect policy preferences, and is grounded in rational choice and public choice theories. Such conditions may relate to those of an international, industrial or macroeconomic nature. The *cognitive* perspective reflects on the impact of ideas, values, beliefs and ideologies on policy formation, although Odell concedes that establishing their source is a complex task. Moreover, while 'material interests' may affect policy ideas, they are not simply reducible to them. They can also have independent effects on policy content (Goldstein 1989, Odell 1982, Rohrlich 1987), although Ikenberry (1988) contends that 'ideas are never completely disembodied from the complex of professional and governmental institutions within which they emerge' (p. 242).[11] The *institutional* perspective has more direct connections with the state-centred approach articulated by Ikenberry *et al* (1988), where national political institutions are placed before individuals in the hierarchy of influence.[12] Similarly, Odell's *international structure* perspective is akin to the system-centred approach, in which FEP formation is turned outside in, viewing it as a product of international structure of which the state is a unit, or as a response to specific interactions between states. This has particular relevance to our discussion in Chapter 2 on the NIE-3's semi-peripheralization within the world economy.

While the work of Ikenberry *et al* (1988) and Odell (1990) is useful in understanding aspects of FEP formation, both fall short of offering a comprehensive macro-framework as they primarily concentrate on the levels and structures of contesting influence that generally shape foreign economic policy. There is little or no comment on the tangible outcomes of FEP itself: that is what actually constitutes its technical policy and economic diplomacy aspects. Similarly, neither offers a separate analytical device for explaining the orientation of FEP objectives. These deficiencies are also evident in perhaps the most currently influential framework of FEP analysis, this being Putnam's (1988) 'two-level' game model. Although developed for foreign policy analysis *per se*, it has been subsequently applied in various forms to the analysis of foreign economic policy. In a 'two-level' game, the Janus-faced state must simultaneously reconcile both the demands of the international economic system and those of its own domestic constituencies. Resolving conflicts of interest that lie therein may be achieved through striking bargains with other states. These are referred to as 'acceptability sets', a set of deals that are agreeable to other governments (Level I). At the same time, each government must strike a 'win set' that can be defined as the set of all possible Level I agreements which would 'win' the ratification for a given (Level II) domestic constituency. Thus, larger 'win sets' make Level I agreements more likely. In this model, there is no temporal priority or logical sequence to negotiations at any level. Furthermore, greater domestic-level constraints exist in more advanced industrial democracies, for instance because civil society tends to be more active and influential in developed countries in comparison to their developing counterparts – an issue to which we return. In addition, Putnam proposed that while state agents may have their own utility functions or preferences for certain outcomes, these may be constrained by, but are not identical with, those of their domestic constituents.

Putnam's 'two-level' game model of foreign policy analysis lies thus in the tradition of linkage politics, placing the interface between the domestic and the international at its analytical centre. It has been partially extended by Moravcsik (1993) and Risse-Kappen (1995) to include transnational actors in the fray, thus making for a 'three-level' game dynamic, while others have sought to make further analytical refinements or adaptations. While Putnam's model has made a major contribution to foreign economic policy analysis, it was not designed as a full macro-analytical framework. As is apparent from the above, it is mainly focused on both technical processes of FEP formation and the bargaining strategies between FEP protagonists themselves (international level), and those between FEP protagonists and their own constituencies (domestic level). However, there is only secondary consideration of the mediating factors of contesting influence (for example democratization), and again the tangible outcomes of FEP formation are neglected.

While the above conceptual developments have been instructive to FEP analysis, a more holistic conceptual approach has not been forthcoming. Although the intention of this chapter is not to provide universal solutions to the problematics identified above, it does venture a macro-analytical framework as a new heuristic device of FEP analysis. Such a framework may risk constraining the aforementioned parameters of FEP analysis and introduce other rigidities, for example the convenient compartmentalizsation of analytical factors. Yet it is implicitly argued here that to work within loose or vague notions regarding the constructs of FEP analysis constitutes a less satisfactory situation.

1.3 TOWARDS A NEW MACRO-FRAMEWORK OF FEP ANALYSIS

In the macro-analytical framework ventured here, FEP analysis is viewed from the perspective of its various interactive functions that co-exist dynamically within wider 'environment' and 'development' contexts. From this construct, FEP formation can be broadly studied and understood. The interactive functions consist of: cognitive–ideological approaches; generic 'economic security' objectives; *core* and *associative* technical policy realms; economic diplomacy; contesting 'actor-based' influences; and Figure 1.1 presents the schematic framework of FEP analysis being advanced. The diagrammatic arrows indicate the prime transmission of influence (either uni-directional or bi-directional) between the framework's interactive functions, the dynamics of which are either implicitly or explicitly explained throughout this chapter. It will be helpful,

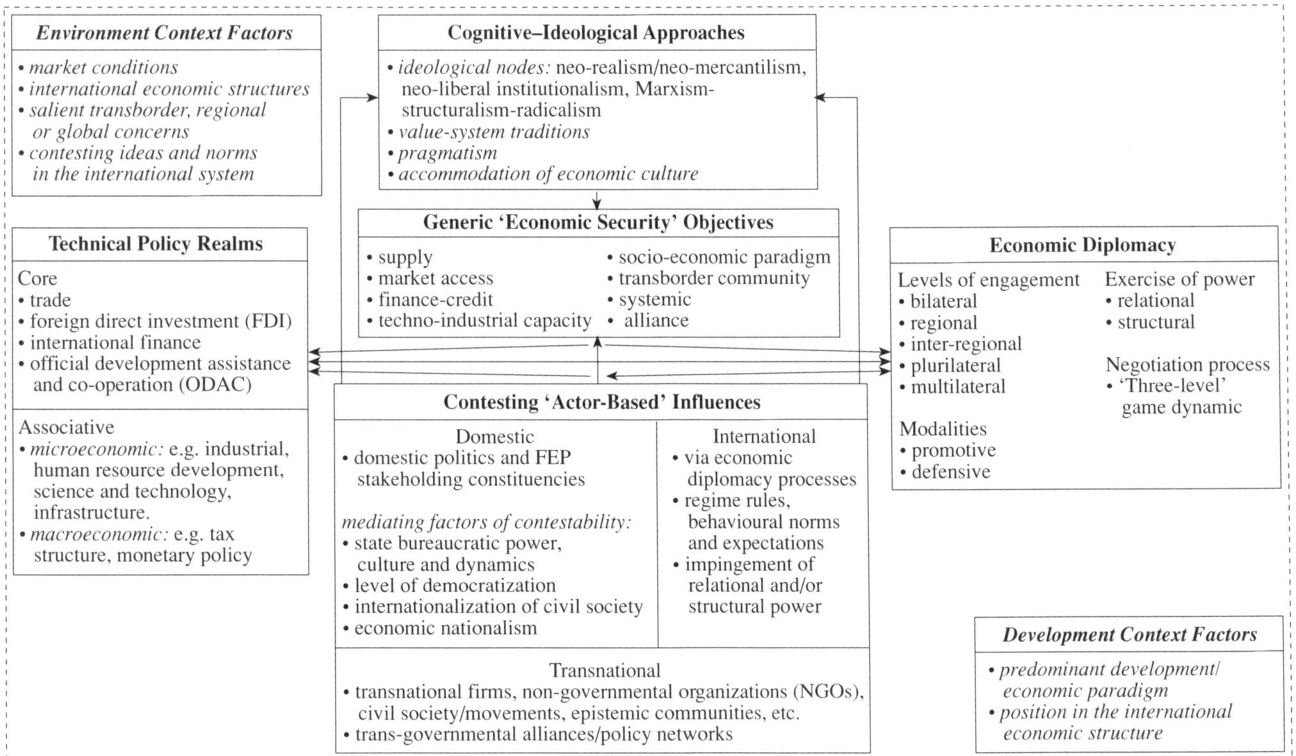

Figure 1.1 Foreign economic policy: a macro-analytical framework

though, to provide a general overview here. The cognitive–ideological approach to foreign economic policy filters through to FEP conduct (i.e. technical policy realms and economic diplomacy) via its influence over the FEP objectives directly pursued by FEP protagonists. Contesting 'actor-based' influences exert themselves both directly and indirectly on all other interactive functions. There are naturally feedback effects between each function, sometimes substantive and sometimes not, and some examples are given later on. Before we examine the interactive functions of the framework, let us first consider the 'environment' and 'development' contexts of FEP analysis.

1.3.1 Environment and Development Contexts

In distinguishing FEP's 'environment' context from its interactive functions, the former analogously represents the biosphere in which the latter exist. Environment context factors can also be perceived as influencing elements – actor-less in form but can nevertheless be shaped by exercises of actor-based power – that are generally beyond the subjugation of FEP protagonists and stakeholding FEP constituencies. Hence, they tend to lie outside the determination of singular FEP powers, especially non-major powers. In our framework, environment context factors comprise:

- *Market conditions*: connected to the neo-liberal notion of the market's primacy of over states. FEP actors adjust their behaviour to changing domestic and international market conditions.[13] The market positions of the FEP power's embedded firms and industries can also affect its policy approach. For example, free market policies may be adopted where these enjoy a strong competitive position in international markets.
- *International economic structures*: including production, finance, technology and knowledge structures, as well as power distributions and alignments in international economic relations. The systemic changes they incur in turn alter the FEP environment context by posing new structural economic conditions and challenges to all FEP actors. Matters of international economic structure also connect to 'development' context factors discussed below.
- *Salient transborder, regional or global concerns*: relating to many 'new' security issues (e.g. ecological, drug trafficking) that are growing concerns of the broad international community, or of a smaller regionalized community in which the FEP power is located, and thus demands an according response from FEP protagonists. These may also include significant exogenous events, such as wars and resource-related disturbances that make their impact systemically or more directly from spillover effects.

- *Contesting ideas and norms in the international system*: which essentially considers the 'battle of ideas' between different parts of the international community. Certain proposed ideas and norms of politico-economic behaviour may prevail or hold sway over others for periods of time. For example, in recent years neo-liberalism has increasingly influenced the mindset of FEP protagonists worldwide, primarily from the strengthening of its 'advocacy channels' (e.g. Anglo-Saxon powers, WTO), the impact of globalization and geo-political changes.

There are naturally overlaps between the above. For instance, there may be a closely correlated development between changes in market conditions and international economic structures. Furthermore, salient transborder, regional or global concerns could originate from changing market or structural conditions. On a more general point, in the current global era where 'world economic processes are increasingly beyond the control of state policy-makers' (Geske 1996: 193), the international environment or context of FEP formation becomes more important: in relative terms, state control has weakened and 'context' factors strengthened. Environment context factors become more critical where the economic and political interdependence between FEP powers is pronounced, owing to the increased sensitivity to external change produced by a denser web of domestic–international linkages (Keohane and Milner 1996). These factors not only then focus on the system-centred approach but also on state and societal responses to the new FEP-related conditions they create.

How the foreign economic policies of Singapore, South Korea and Taiwan are shaped by contemporary environment context factors is either implicitly or explicitly explored in their respective study chapters. While the NIE-3 face similar environment context conditions, their own specific FEP-related responses to them vary greatly, notwithstanding their relative developmental and geographic proximities. Indeed, Chapter 2 discusses at length the commonalities and contrasts of the NIE-3's 'development' context. As this suggests, the development context of our framework is more FEP power-specific, relating to domestic development factors and their interface with the international system. Development context factors broadly comprise the predominant development or economic paradigm of the FEP power in study, and its relative position in the international economic structure or structures (see Chapter 2 for a full discussion). They thus share a connection or overlap with environment context factors. For example, contesting ideas and norms within the international system will bear some influence on the predominant development or economic paradigm of the FEP power. Together, these will affect different aspects of FEP formation, as for example we discuss in Chapter 2 regarding domestic and external sources of neo-liberal advocacy. Furthermore, the level and path of an FEP power's economic development will in some way determine its position in international economic structures, and whose development is conversely affected by changes in those structures, with implications for different aspects of its FEP formation. For example, the continued rise in transnational capital power within the world economy generally will necessitate an FEP power constantly to re-evaluate its development position and economic relationship with regard to multinational enterprises (MNEs). Such an issue is explored from various perspectives in Chapter 4, where the South Korean government is currently seeking a more proactive engagement with foreign MNEs as part of meeting new post-crisis developmental and FEP objectives.

1.3.2 Cognitive–Ideological Approaches

To restate Odell's (1990) *cognitive* perspective on FEP formation, all policy is in some way determined by ideas, values or beliefs. This may occur either through their formation of systematized ideological constructs, or by their development of more personalized or atomistic cognitive views towards FEP formation that often yields a preference for pragmatism. The cognitive–ideological approach adopted by FEP protagonists may also reflect that of stakeholding FEP constituencies through the democratic process, or via other conduits of contesting 'actor-based' influence as indicated in Figure 1.1.

Following the traditional demarcations of ideological approach in IPE, governments may wish to pursue FEP objectives in accordance with one of three main schools of thought: neo-realism (including neo-mercantilism), neo-liberal institutionalism or the Marxist–structuralist–radicalist tradition. However, such classification mostly serves to approximate FEP behaviour. Furthermore, FEP protagonists may concoct mixes of policies that draw upon different ideological sources, for example owing to a natural predilection for pragmatism (as generally prevails in Singapore) or to an ideological transition in progress. While this may lead to capturing the benefits of each approach, it can also produce an incompatible FEP framework where in-fighting between different FEP protagonist groups is commonplace. With respect to the NIE-3, this has been most apparent in South Korea where recent paradigmatic struggles within the country's political economy have been quite pronounced.

These matters notwithstanding, IPE's ideological demarcations still perform the useful function of helping characterize singular, periodic or sustained policy approaches to FEP formation and its objectives, thus acting as *nodal referents* to FEP behaviour. Neo-mercantilism is strongly linked to neo-realism by its prescription of protectionist policies, state promotion of strategic industries and exports.[14] Whereas neo-mercantilism aims at the maximization of the national interest, neo-liberal institutionalism's prime objective is the maximization of global welfare through the promotion of free trade and international co-operation: inter-state alliances of a regional or other kind may be expedient in a world of complex interdependence, but not where these alliances threaten multilateral economic regimes (e.g. WTO, IMF).[15] The acknowledged fusion here of neo-liberalism and institutionalism stems from a mutual recognition of the role performed by international organizations and regimes in supporting co-operation, although some neo-liberals play down the importance of institutionalized co-operation by arguing that 'international organisations are not the causes of co-operation but mechanisms through which co-operation occurs' (Haggard and Moravcsik 1993: 285).

The Marxist–structuralist–radicalist tradition relates to a splintered but related set of ideologies and theories. The Marxist cognitive–ideological approach generally derives from the class-oriented view of a world economy, and adheres to the structuralist view of the entrenched divide between rich capitalist nations (the 'core') and poor underdeveloped nations (the 'periphery'), whereby the latter are subservient to the capital interests of the former. A 'semi-periphery' of middle-income NIEs are also often acknowledged, and the concept of semi-peripheralization is deployed as an analytical device in Chapter 2's discussion on the development context of the NIE-3's foreign economic policies. However, the global retreat of Marxism and the 'socialist market' revolutions of many remaining communist states, as experienced by China and Vietnam, has led to a demise of the Marxist approach in FEP practice. Socialist thought on FEP, based on taming 'economics towards social and political goals of justice and equality' (Buzan *et al* 1998: 96), has constituted the fall back position for many left-wing approaches to FEP which also draw upon the axioms of structuralist dependency theory. The Marxist and structuralist approaches are associated by some IPE scholars with the theoretical and ideological tradition of radicalist thought and its prescription of alternatives to market-oriented pluralist democracy. Radicalism, *inter alia*, embraces environmentalism, pacifism and feminism, with a tendency to emphasize transnational solutions to international economic problems. We shall see in subsequent chapters, though, that the ideological influences to have most affected Singapore, South Korea and Taiwan's FEP formation lie between the nodes of neo-realism and neo-liberal institutionalism.

From a different but related perspective, Rohrlich (1987) argues that there must be a cultural accommodation of particular cognitive–ideological approaches to economic policies. Moreover, a consideration of the prevailing 'economic culture' – which Rohrlich defines as 'the confluence of cultural legacy, historic experience, and contemporary circumstance' (p. 92) – can fill the gaps between government structure and social politics, and between state and society. In addition, different 'value-system' traditions should also be acknowledged in the cognitive–ideological approach, for example the East Asian neo-confucianist,[16] European social democratic, Anglo-Saxon market democratic, and the Middle Eastern socio-religious. These connect foreign economic policy with the 'battle of ideas' between different FEP actors, an illustration being the infusion of neo-liberal values into post-crisis East Asia and its subsequent impact on the FEP formation of the NIE-3. This connects with environment and development context factors discussed earlier in relation to contesting ideas and norms in the international system and development/economic paradigm issues respectively. It is more extensively discussed in Chapter 2, which spends much time examining the Anglo-Saxon neo-liberal challenge to East Asian developmental statism. In that debate, it is argued that developmental statism is embedded within the economic cultures of the NIE-3, and the often slow pace of cultural change infers that developmental statism will remain an important factor in their FEP formation accordingly.

1.3.3 Generic 'Economic Security' Objectives

1.3.3.1 Introduction and context

In this macro-framework of FEP analysis, objective setting is determined by the cognitive–ideological approach of FEP protagonists as well as both indirectly and directly through various contesting 'actor-based' influences discussed later (Figure 1.1). The objectives of FEP are naturally difficult to compartmentalize, made more so by their differential modalities, e.g. tactical, strategic. However, attempts at classification are viable if generic rather than specific[17] FEP objectives are considered. A central principle of this analytical framework is that a broader definition of economic security provides the lowest common denominator basis for FEP's generic objectives. Such a distillation may be viewed as somewhat reductionist, yet this proposed baseline is nevertheless useful and instructive. From another perspective, just as politico-military security has been the prime concern of foreign policy, so economic security concerns provide a derivative basis for analysing FEP objectives.

In general terms, the growing salience of economic security is associated with the respective shifts from geo-politics to geo-economics,[18] from military superpowers to economic superpowers, and hence from politico-ideological competition to economic competition. As Stremlau (1994) contends, 'we are entering an era when foreign policy and national security will increasingly revolve around our commercial interests, and when economic diplomacy will be essential to resolving the great issues of our age' (p. 18). In a similar vein, Reynolds (1993) argued that, 'the definition of national security has changed from the amount of military firepower a country commands to include questions of economic and technological advantage' (p. 31). However, as with FEP, scholarly attempts to conceptualize economic security have lagged behind the supposed practice of it.[19] Recent endeavours, though, have been posited in the larger project of broadening the conceptualization of security itself beyond its traditional politico-military domain (Ullman 1993). Hence, economic security is joined by other 'new' security sectors (e.g. environmental, societal, political) in the creation of a comprehensive security framework. Yet the relative nascence of these sectors has raised familiar problems over defining their empirical domain. For example, Buzan *et al* (1998) ask whether the pursuit of economic security merely represents the securitization of economic issues, and furthermore whether scholars are simply wishing to define it by their attempts to distinguish between politicized economics and security spillovers from the economic sector into others.[20] Moreover, the FEP power's legitimacy to pursue economic security may be questioned when ambiguities exist regarding what exactly is to be protected and from what.[21]

Additional complications also arise from considering other perspectives on the economics–security nexus.[22] For instance, there exist separate discourses relating to the: *economics of security (or security economics)* that concern allocative, productive, techno-industrial, infrastructural and cost–price aspects of resourcing military security capabilities;[23] *subordination of economic policies to security policy interests*, involving the use of FEP to support wider foreign policy objectives, or 'low politics' directly serving the needs of 'high politics'; *subordination of security policies to economic interests*, such as making the world safe for the expansion of capitalist activities with this typically attributed to a hegemonic state's duties, although others have adopted separate approaches.[24]

The substance of *economic security* can nevertheless be differentiated from the above. Security itself relates to guarding or guaranteeing the safety of some entity from extant dangers. In initially determining the economic security of what and of who, we must therefore distinguish between the politico-territorial outline of an economy and an economy's actual physical functions, capacities and interests of its agents (which may be extra-territorial), and also between the individual, the firm and the FEP powers. In both cases, the latter are the most appropriate unit of analysis in the study of foreign economic policy. In pursuing their economic security interests, FEP powers must respond to the changing structural configurations of the IPE and optimize the opportunities and minimize the risks or threats these create (Leech 1993). Most economic security scholars have focused on the latter but some have adopted a more multi-dimensional approach.

For example, Lubbe (1997) perceived economic security as being determined by two key factors, these being: *economic capability*, concerning the ability of FEP protagonists to execute economic and political tasks that delineate the national interest but also help minimize its vulnerability to external pressures and disruptions; and *external environmental*, where large, powerful states that exercise significant structural power can shape the external environment in which economic security objectives are pursued. Strange (1994) defined 'structural' power as the ability of certain international actors to shape and determine the systemic structures within which other actors must also operate. This contrasts with 'relational' power, which relates to the leverage that an international actor can directly exert on the behaviour of, or on decisions made by another. States that are thus not able to influence the external environment must develop 'adaptation abilities' in order to react to environmental or structural change where adaptation is a matter of the 'quality, economic efficiency and technological sophistication of its economy' (p. 64).[25]

This second perspective has links with Lee's (1999a) own thesis that states that have a strong economic structure, stable political system and relatively superior international position are more concerned with an 'outward-oriented' economic security agenda, while those with an inverse profile will be more preoccupied with maintaining internal cohesion and hence an 'inward-oriented' economic security agenda. Here, the former are engaged in winning commercial battles and exerting control or influence over international regimes, whereas the latter are more fixated with mitigating those threats to regime survival and national cohesion. Lee's (1999b) analysis on the economic security issues raised by the recent East Asian financial crisis highlighted such threats. More generally for Lee (1999a), the pursuit of economic security involves 'reinforcing a nation's cohesion, regime legitimacy and world prestige through economic prosperity' (p. 73). In relation to the NIE-3 group, all have been able to concentrate more or less on an outward-oriented economic security agenda given the relative stability of their domestic polities in recent decades. This is not least because they have been characterized by authoritarian, mono-regime politics for most of this period where both state and society have been united in a common developmental purpose, as further discussed in Chapter 2.

We thus have the basis for forming the connection between the pursuit of economic security and the 'power and plenty' objectives of foreign economic policy. As Katzenstein (1976) noted, prosperity represents a neo-liberal core concept while the prime concern of realists is security. The incorporation of a 'prosperity' aspect into the definition of economic security prescribed here forms the basis for some common ground between different schools of thought. Although radicalist thinkers would admittedly question the conventional materialist notions of prosperity, they would not necessarily deny the importance of pursuing some alternative interpretation of it, for example sustainable development.

1.3.3.2 Ideological perspectives

Before we move on to consider a working definition and typology set for economic security, a brief summary of ideological perspectives on economic security would be helpful. In mercantilist thought can be found an early consciousness of the links between economic and military elements of national security, whereby the roles of economic capacity and wealth in upholding state security are stressed. Furthermore, the economic security risks entailed with the surrender to the market are generally unacceptable to the neo-mercantilist position. Counter strategies can involve the mobilization of techno-industrial capabilities as a proactive means to minimize these risks (e.g. the promotion of strategic industries), or the containing of threats from foreign economic interaction, for example regulated or protected trade, arm's-length transactions with foreign markets for capital and technology. This was perhaps best exemplified by South Korea during earlier phases of its developmental statism.

According to the neo-liberal view, capitalism – the dominant economic paradigm – propagates a state of constant insecurity owing to the competitive dynamics it creates. As Buzan (1991) comments, 'capitalism is by definition a competitive system, the whole dynamic of which depends on the interplay of threats, vulnerabilities and opportunities in the market' (p. 235). Thus, neo-liberals generally contend that economic security is a mirage and at best can only be achieved in relative terms, although this is surely a universal predicament that applies to any pursuit of security. Neo-liberals further propose that economic insecurity is not to be feared but embraced insofar as positive responses to foreign competitive threats lead to disciplined improvements in efficiency and productivity. In addition, attempts by losers of this competitive game to 'securitise their plight' merely represent desperation to change the game's rules (p. 109).[26] More generally, neo-liberals tend to subordinate vulnerability issues in the pursuance of 'plenty', which can only be optimized in a free and open global economy. However, the maximization of global welfare is contingent upon the security of the international economic system. It could therefore be argued that maintaining *systemic security* is the *de facto* core economic security concern of neo-liberalism, with systemic support being the neo-liberal FEP power's implicit path to pursuing economic security. Moreover, even ardent neo-liberal FEP powers follow broader economic security aims and strategies (Leech 1993, Mastanduno 1998, Moran 1993, US Council on Competitiveness 1994).[27]

For Marxists and structuralists, economic security concerns arise from significant asymmetries in both global economic development and balances of power within the world capitalist system, from which leads an accordingly uneven distribution of economic vulnerability amongst FEP powers. Those in the periphery and semi-periphery naturally possess higher vulnerability coefficients, their relative weakness making them more susceptible to economic security risks and exogenous threats. This predicament can be linked to Lee's (1999a) argument that the economic security interests of weaker FEP powers are focused on maintaining the internal construction of the economy. Moreover, differences in the economic security interests of FEP powers will prevail in the structure of the IPE in accordance with their position within it. Radicalists tend to connect economic security with other 'new' security sectors, for instance the threat caused by transborder pollution to environmental security.

1.3.3.3 Towards a working definition and typology set

With the above considered, the basis for a working definition of economic security can be ventured, this being *safeguarding the structural integrity and prosperity-generating capabilities and interests of a politico-economic entity in the context of various externalized risks and threats that confront it.* Here, 'politico-economic entity' broadly equates with an FEP power with respect its own territorial economy and extra-territorial (e.g. transborder or transnational) economic interests. Hence, FEP protagonists may work to safeguard the transnational commercial interests of its home-based or hosted foreign MNEs. This is highly relevant to Singapore, South Korea and Taiwan given the importance of transnational capital, albeit in very different ways, in the calculus of their respective FEP formations.

The 'structural integrity' aspect of this working definition essentially relates to maintaining the internal construction of the economy during its interactions in the global economy, and its ability to meet the basic demands of economic agents located therein. Where meaningfully applied, this can be linked to proximate notions of the economy's survival in the international system and thus the prevention of its structural collapse – a rare event in absolute terms as economies invariably recover in a physical sense, albeit sometimes in a new politico-geographically defined form, for example East Germany. The 'prosperity-generating capabilities' aspect broadens the conventional boundaries of the economic security concept beyond its usual attention to minimizing direct and immediate economic vulnerabilities. Safeguarding prosperity-generating capabilities works towards this objective anyway through reducing the future scope for economic security risks, vulnerabilities and threats, constituting a sort of 'insurance policy' or 'preventative medicinal' approach.[28] The development of these capabilities can also be linked to welfare maximization – both localized and global – and the externalization of FEP interests. Also relevant is Lubbe's (1997) distinction between short-term and long-term economic security objectives, with the former concerned with confronting specific challenges (for example unilateral commercial policy threats) and the latter with preserving economic potential and capacity to counteract structural destabilization.

From having established that economic security is not necessarily a loaded ideological concept, we can move on to consider what different typologies of economic security are pursued by FEP powers that orientate their generic FEP objectives. This exercise further develops both the concept and definable pursuits of economic security, as well as the contention that it provides a suitable focal lens for FEP analysis. Again, there are empirical and ontological constraints involved in such an analytical compartmentalization. Moreover, as Lee (1999a) notes, the subjective cognition of economic security interests will naturally vary from state to state. Notwithstanding these points, the economic security typologies outlined below provide further structure to FEP analysis:

- *Supply security*: relating to securing key supply chains involving foreign sources. This is especially important for import-dependent or foreign technology-dependent economies that respectively lack natural resources and indigenous techno-industrial self-sufficiency. Can also apply to securing the supply of international credit and finance, as articulated below, and human resources in short indigenous supply. Supply diversification forms part of a vulnerability management strategy of economic security.
- *Market access security*: concerns securing the best access possible to key foreign markets. This is particularly crucial for export-orientated economies with small domestic markets, although this has become a prime economic diplomacy objective of all FEP powers.
- *Finance-credit security*: ensuring the financial solvency of the FEP power in the international system, as well as its maintenance of access to, or influence or control over sources of international credit. In recent times, this has become an acute economic security concern of developing countries in the context of Third World debt and other countries that have lately required IMF assistance, for example South Korea and Indonesia.
- *Techno-industrial capability security*: preserving and developing the ability of the economy to generate prosperity, productivity and other welfare-creating factors, and involves maintaining the economy's position as close as possible to the technological frontier. This may derive from indigenous or foreign sources, and relate to issues of access and acquisition of foreign technology.
- *Socio-economic paradigm security*: the 'defence' of a society's preferred socio-economic paradigm and its welfare goals where defined.[29] This often entails the resistance of foreign pressure to adapt to new international norms that are associated with a counter-paradigm, as previously highlighted with regard to NIE-3 developmental statism and Anglo-Saxon neo-liberalism. A particularly strong connection may thus be made here with the earlier debate on environment and development context factors.
- *Transborder community security*: regionalized concerns that may either precipitate transborder economic crises or concern localized interdependence issues, for example sub-regional economic integration projects.[30] These often centre on transborder spillovers or externalities that require market failure correction policies, and hence the management of a shared transborder economic space. They may thus also focus on issues from

other security sectors such as pollution, drug trafficking and economic migration.[31] Furthermore, regional architectures for economic security (e.g. in Singapore's case, ASEAN) provide a fall back position if the liberal world economic order is jeopardized.

- *Systemic security*: upholding the integrity of the international economic system, entailing co-operative and concessionary acts to uphold multilateral regimes of systemic governance, facilitate inter-state bargains and maintain overall systemic stability. As previously noted, the *de facto* core economic security concern of neo-liberals.
- *Alliance security*: maintaining and developing international economic partnerships with state and non-state actors in pursuance of the above interests.[32] This may take various forms, ranging from donor–client alliance relationships to looser co-operative or co-ordinative arrangements between relatively equal partners.[33]

There are natural overlaps between these different typologies. The link between supply security and finance-credit security has already been noted, as has the underpinning functions performed by alliance security. Techno-industrial capability security may also be served by supply security where, for example, an infusion of foreign technology through inward FDI or other means enhances the latter. Frictions often arise also between different economic security objectives, for example where fostering certain foreign economic alliances (e.g. bilateral free trade agreements) runs counter to the pursuit of systemic security interests (e.g. upholding WTO multilateralism).

The hierarchy of typologies in any set of generic FEP objectives will be primarily determined by the interaction of contesting influences from different stakeholding FEP constituencies and cognitive-ideological approaches adopted by FEP protagonists. However, the same inherent overlapping of these typologies makes constructing such a hierarchy difficult. In concluding this section, it should also be acknowledged that the power of FEP protagonists to realize economic security objectives is emasculated in an increasingly transnationalized and interdependent world economy where policy control over the domestic economy has become more elusive. Instead, they must co-manage the complex interdependence in the international economic system with their counterpart FEP protagonists from other powers, thus bringing alliance security increasingly to the fore.[34] Yet this essentially neo-liberal institutionalist position must be judged alongside the prevalence of anarchical conflict in international economic relations, hence acknowledging the neo-realist's assessment that, where possible, FEP powers must continue to identify their own distinct economic security interests and undertake suitable FEP measures to address them. As subsequent chapters note, generic economic security objectives remain a salient feature of the NIE-3 foreign economic policy, although their respective

FEP protagonists more implicitly rather than explicitly pursue them. This can be mainly attributed to the preoccupation of Singapore, South Korea and Taiwan's security policy-elites with traditional politico-military concerns.

1.3.4 FEP Conduct: Technical Policy Realms and Economic Diplomacy

In this analytical framework, technical policy realms and economic diplomacy represent FEP conduct, the former being largely concerned with policy content and the latter involved with policy representation in foreign engagements. A close mutual interaction between both FEP functions exists, especially in the simultaneity of technical policy implementation and diplomatic engagement. Moreover, international bargaining often entails synchronous developments between the two, for example in negotiations over trade barrier reductions. Generic 'economic security' objectives in FEP formation set the underlying basis for adjustments to technical policy realm measures, while various contesting influences from domestic, international and transnational sources have their usual pervasive effects over both interactive functions, examples of which are provided later.

Two technical policy realms are presented by this framework, namely the *core* and the *associative*. Both form the basis of an economic statecraft analysis previously advocated by Baldwin (1986), that is the importance of not only considering process but also FEP content and instruments – a critique earlier articulated by this chapter. The *core* technical policy realm of FEP mainly relates to four distinct, yet increasingly overlapping forms of international economic activity, namely: trade; foreign direct investment (FDI); international finance; and official development assistance and co-operation (ODAC). Of these, trade policy is normally afforded greatest priority, although globalization has made FDI and international finance increasingly salient FEP aspects. State ODAC policies, where practised, tend to receive a considerably lower political priority. However, as Chapter 5 examines, Taiwan is a notable exception to this rule, where its ODAC policy is used to nurture diplomatic ties and hence its political legitimacy in the international community. In concluding, the *core* realm could be said to have a cognitive international focus, in that the explicit purpose of its constituent policies is directly connected with foreign economic relations.

In contrast, the *associative* technical policy realm of FEP is concerned with domestic-level policies that either are intended to perform some competitiveness-enhancing function[35] or are allied to *core* realm policies in other ways, for example 'internal' barriers to international trade such as excise duties that discriminate against foreign imported products.[36] This realm can be sub-divided into microeconomic policies (for example industrial, science and technology, human resource development), invariably with a focus on competitiveness, or macroeconomic policies, such as tax incentives. Their 'associative' nature also derives from their usually higher preoccupation with more localized policy objectives. However, the potential breadth of this technical policy realm risks licensing the inclusion of a multitude of traditional domestic-level policies that can demonstrate some supportive connection with FEP's core technical policy realm. Furthermore, such policies may be only implicitly or even unintentionally part of the FEP framework.

Notwithstanding these recurrent problematics of defining FEP's empirical domain, the inclusion of the *associative* technical policy realm into the FEP framework is less tenuous when a neo-mercantilist, developmental statist or *dirigiste* policy approach prevails, with FEP protagonists setting domestic economic policy in a strong international context. Naturally, overlaps or a blurring of the realms arise for the above reasons when technical policy elements from separate realms are either perceived or operationalized in a holistic fashion. Examples include strategic trade policies where a fusing of trade and industrial policies occurs (very evident in the NIE-3), and the use of tax incentives and job creation grants in the policy framework of attracting inward FDI. Nonetheless, the *core-associative* divide remains useful in these circumstances as it helps determine subservient policy relationships, i.e. *associative* technical policy realm measures serving the ends of their *core* technical policy realm counterparts.

The above discussion leads to other important issues regarding FEP management. Both the expanding domestic–international policy interface and the ever enlarging ministerial canvas of trade-related issues raises questions of how the distribution of managerial responsibility is to be organized and co-ordinated across FEP-related ministries, and furthermore what the implications for policy coherency and compatibility are. This can be examined by considering Scharpf's (1994) notions of positive and negative co-ordination in policy formation, where the former is defined as 'an attempt to maximise the overall effectiveness and efficiency of government policy by exploring and utilising the joint strategy options of several ministerial portfolios' (p. 38), while the latter's aim is 'to ensure that any new policy initiative designed by a specialised sub-unit within the ministerial organisation will not interfere with the established policies and interests of other ministerial units' (p. 39). Generally speaking, if FEP protagonists wish to develop a more coherent FEP strategy across technical policy realms then a positive co-ordination approach is required, although more marginal FEP ministries may still defer to their more central counterparts, such as those specifically designated for trade and foreign affairs. In evaluating the NIE-3 on this issue from primary research conducted for this text, Singapore's FEP bureaucracy best exemplified the practice of positive co-ordination, with an impressively coherent management of technical policy aspects between different ministerial units. Conversely, South Korea's FEP bureaucratic management could be largely characterized by negative co-ordination, owing to various inter-ministerial conflicts that persist. As Chapter 4 discusses, many of these have worsened in the recent post-crisis intensification of ideological and paradigmatic struggles within the South Korean political economy.

Foreign economic policy is also conducted within a 'diplomatic space'. The technical policy realm elements discussed above form much of the substantive content of an FEP power's economic diplomacy contact with others. Economic diplomacy itself can be broadly defined as means and parameters within which trade, investment and other international economic relations are conducted between representative agents of different FEP powers. For most FEP protagonists, the practice of economic diplomacy is exercised at multiple *levels of engagement*, ranging from the bilateral to the multilateral (see Figure 1.1). This broad band of economic diplomacy engagement has become increasingly relevant to the NIE-3, as discussed in more detail in subsequent chapters.

As was argued earlier, economic diplomacy can act as a conduit through which international contesting influences originate, thus affecting all other interactive functions. This was particularly argued in regard to *exercises of power*, either relational or structural as defined previously. Moreover, the *modalities* of economic diplomacy concern the use of either promotive or defensive FEP measures, with the former intended to yield collaborative or co-operative outcomes between FEP powers (e.g. a free trade agreement) while the latter are intended to uphold the commercial interests of one FEP power against opposing pressure from a counter-interest power or powers. As Chapter 2 also considers in more detail, diminishing neo-mercantilism in both South Korea and Taiwan has led to progressive moves from defensive to promotive economic diplomacy modalities. Finally, the *negotiation process* of economic diplomacy can be largely understood in the framework of the aforementioned 'three-level' game dynamic, whereby economic diplomacy outcomes are forged by the interplay of domestic, international and transnational contesting 'actor-based' influences. It is this interactive function of our macro-analytical framework we now specifically consider.

1.3.5 Contesting 'Actor-Based' Influences

As previously highlighted, at the root of most scholarly work on FEP analysis lies an examination of the various contesting influences that seek to shape policy formation. The state-centred, society-centred and system-centred perspectives noted earlier have provided the analytical lens through which these influences have usually been studied. The framework presented in this chapter, however, uses an alternative but not incompatible structure to the above, based on the analysis of different 'actor-based' sources of contesting influence, namely the domestic, international and transnational. These geographic-source designations both identify and locate stakeholding FEP constituencies, while also framing the 'three-level' game dynamic advanced by Moravcsik (1993) and Risse-Kappen (1995) as a variation on Putnam's 'two-level' game model. This methodological approach permits us to distinguish between actor-based and aforementioned 'context' factors, as well as to negate some recurrent problematics that arise within the state–society dichotomy of analysis by implicitly acknowledging the two as partially enmeshed.

On a general point concerning FEP protagonists, centralized governments generally lie at the hub of FEP management (i.e. bureaucratic leadership), although there are certain caveats to this rule. As previously noted, the EU member states conduct a Common Commercial Policy through a supranational pooling of sovereignty, which enables the European Commission to manage EU trade policy. However, exclusive competence is not formally conferred to other foreign economic policy areas, for example FDI rules. Sub-state units (e.g. local governments) may also conduct some form of FEP, albeit in a limited sense. Federalized political systems (e.g. US, Canada, Australia, Germany) offer most latitude here, with central governments more willing to devolve 'low' political powers to localized government than entrusting them with matters of 'high' politics. The increasing linkages between the local and international in the global political economy also provide some rationale for 'localizing' FEP, particularly in matters of local export promotion, inward FDI attraction and various competitiveness-enhancing, *associative* FEP measures noted later. These bring their own complexities to the state's overall conduct of economic diplomacy and management of FEP technical policy realms.[37] However, a return to a pre-Westphalian era of city-states, or regional-states (Ohmae 1995) conducting their own 'foreign' policies has been simultaneously countered by central governments seeking to 'extend their powers into areas of local responsibility claiming that these are now legitimate dimensions of external policy' (Hocking 1993: 25), thus connecting to the subsidiarity debate and issues of intra-government bargaining.

The state, or state-like agencies, are often perceived as the central arbiters of contesting influences from domestic, international and transnational sources – this being a core function of FEP protagonists. Yet as Cerny (1995) reminds us, collective actions in the international system do not just centre on the state but on an increasingly plurilateral structure of decision-making agents and processes. Brown's (1995) concept of 'global polyarchy' is also relevant, where state and non-state actors co-exist and interact with each other, forming coalitions in *ad hoc* power plays and bargaining on FEP issues. In relation to our study, FEP formation may still be primarily 'managed' by governments, but FEP 'content' is determined by various non-state influences. Thus, a wider examination of stakeholding FEP constituencies, their degree of influence and their interests is essential. For powerful constituency groups, such as multinational enterprises and industrial associations, this is considerable. Note

Chiquita's prominent role in the transatlantic banana dispute of the 1990s and other examples relating to the 'privatization' of US trade policy. Meanwhile, small non-governmental organizations (NGOs) with only a marginal interest in FEP issues are endowed with weak constituency leverage. These issues will come to the fore in subsequent chapters' analysis of the NIE-3's foreign economic policies, with particular respect to how the prevalent state-centred approach is gradually giving ground to more pluralistic, society-centred contesting influences.

Let us now analyse domestic, international and transnational sources of influences in more detail. In our analytical framework, domestic contesting influences derive from the FEP power's home-based actors and internal mediating factors. Katzenstein (1976) was the first to formally articulate the indispensable role of domestic factors in FEP analysis, focusing on the 'internalisation of international factors' and the 'externalisation of domestic structures' (p. 2). This was previously discussed with respect to the domestic politics function and society-centred approach in FEP analysis. The range of domestic stakeholding FEP constituencies has continued to broaden with the blurring of the domestic–international policy divide (Atkinson and Coleman 1992), most clearly demonstrated by the expansion of the trade-related policy agenda, for example embracing environment and labour standards, and competition policy (Cable 1996, McMichael 2000). Consequently, there has been a wider enfranchisement of the stakeholding FEP constituency base, especially in the socio-cultural sphere, with an increasing number of domestic-level interest groups claiming legitimacy to influence FEP formation. However, new or more legitimacy-empowered constituency groups not only have to compete against one another, but also against powerful incumbents from the business sector. More generally, the predisposition of FEP agendas to domestic-level contestability is contingent upon various mediating factors, primarily relating to:

- *State bureaucratic power, culture and dynamics*: state bureaucrats, and other 'managerial' FEP protagonists, are embedded in society and thus develop their own predilections towards policy objective setting. In strong state-centric societies, the insulation of policy-making elites from societal influences naturally limits the scope of the stakeholding constituencies' own influence over the FEP agenda, although this insulation may derive from organizational factors rather than from socio-cultural determinants. Furthermore, the FEP objectives of ruling politicians and actual policy conduct may be incommensurate owing to the mediating policy interpretations and implementations of FEP bureaucratic cadres. This may be especially evident in developmental states where the politicians 'reign' but the bureaucrats 'rule' (Onis 1991), as further discussed in Chapter 2. Such perspectives are linked to the institutional approach of Ikenberry *et al* (1988) where the state's organizational structure, culture and dynamics provide the main crucible of FEP formation. Yet as previously noted, the preferences of FEP bureaucrats may nevertheless simply reflect the prevailing beliefs, values and normative principles on FEP issues of the society in which they are embedded.

- *Level of democratization*: linked to Putnam's (1988) argument that a wider range of 'two-level' games are more likely in democratic societies where the state policy-making apparatus is open to societal influences, thus permitting greater scope for the contesting influence enjoyed by domestic stakeholding constituencies. Referenda can offer individual citizens the chance to have a direct say on FEP-related issues such as the euro. In authoritarian states, obvious constraints are imposed on societal pressure groups in their endeavours to exert influence.
- *Internationalization of civil society*: in *ceteris paribus* circumstances, inwardly focused societies that exhibit a limited knowledge of the international political economy are less likely to assert their stake in FEP formation due to attributable information gaps and a concomitant lack of articulated interest in FEP issues. This may also explain or reflect a low level of transnationalized civil societal linkages with counterpart groups located in other FEP powers. However, stakeholding FEP constituencies in these societies may nevertheless strongly assert their interests if international forces compel such a response.
- *Economic nationalism*: the previous point above may result from economic nationalist sentiment, where an external threat to the economic security of the FEP power elicits a counter-reaction from domestic societal sources that is often allied with FEP protagonists. Economic nationalism can be defined as the proclivity of the state, firms and individuals for economic actions, decisions or alliance-formation that seek to advance the nation's domestic or international position at the potential expense of foreign national or international interests.[38] The effect of globalization on economic nationalism has been either undermining (by confusing national identity), or reinforcing by coagulating societal resistance to 'foreign' influences further.[39] Of the NIE-3 group, economic nationalism is by far the most pronounced in South Korea.

International contesting influences originate from external sources that impose themselves via economic diplomacy processes (for example trade negotiations), and the rules, behavioural norms and expectations that accompany international regimes[40] (see Figure 1.1). The impingement of relational or structural power from another FEP power can manifest itself through conduits of economic diplomacy. This perspective is intrinsically linked to state-centred and system-centred approaches to FEP analysis by examining the multi-level interactions of different FEP powers within the international economic system. The protagonists of one FEP power will naturally seek to affect the FEP of another in accordance with the latter's position in the former's structure of interests, with a selection of collaborative, co-ordinative or coercive methods chosen depending on the nature of the issue or economic relations between them. Beyond bilateral economic diplomacy, an FEP power is also susceptible to the contesting influences of multi-member economic diplomacy, such as regional and multilateral forms. Here, these influences tend to reflect the norms and principles of the regime framework in which these economic diplomacy engagements are conducted. For example, new WTO members must comply with any global rules on trade and trade-related matters that are subsequently formulated, thus laying open its FEP formation to the influence of an international regime consensus.[41] Moreover, the WTO's Dispute Settlement Body is utilized by those members who wish to bring other recalcitrant members into line with multilateral rules and norms, or settle a persistent trade dispute. Nevertheless, international regimes are likely to be either bypassed or shaped by the respective exertions of relational and structural power. Either way, the foreign economic policies of weak FEP powers must invariably accommodate the FEP interests of the strong.

Transnational contesting influences stem from domestic–international linkages or networks of a cross-border nature, with transnational firms, NGOs, epistemic communities, policy-networks and civil movements being the most prominent actors. These have neither a formal national nor foreign identity but rather one that derives from their transcendence of national borders: they are 'insiders' in the FEP power but with typically commensurate 'outsider' links and interests. Transnational (or multinational) firms located in the FEP power will naturally lobby FEP protagonists to shape policy in accordance with its trade, investment, financial and production interests.[42] Those transnational NGOs with a stake in FEP-related issues will seek outcomes in alignment with the causes they champion. For instance, Greenpeace have been active in lobbying FEP protagonists on issues linking trade with environmental clauses, while the International Labour Organisation is similarly engaged in the issue of trade and core labour standards (O'Brien *et al* 2000). Many of these NGOs represent the formalized interests and concerns of transnational civil society, including those relating to human rights, drug trafficking and sustainable development. According to Geske (1996), 'transnational' citizenship, or 'citizens of the world' syndrome, constitutes a separate layer of citizenship and constituency that seeks to influence the foreign economic policies of different states. Linking to a previous point, the effective degree of this influence is contingent upon the 'internationalization' of the civil society evident within the FEP power.

Epistemic communities relate to co-operative initiatives and linkages provided by professional groups 'that believe in the same cause-and-effect relationships, truth tests to accept them, and share common values; their members share a common understanding of a problem and its solution' (Haas 1990: 55). These are often of a transnational character and may exert considerable influence over FEP formation at various levels through identifying salient policy issues to be addressed, proposing a set of normative and principled beliefs to orientate policy, and by further providing specific expert-centred advice to FEP protagonists. For these reasons, transnational epistemic communities normally have close links with trans-governmental alliances and policy-networks.[43] Risse-Kappen (1995) defines trans-governmental networks as 'state officials in sub-units of national governments, international organisations, and regimes [that] frequently pursue their own agenda, independently from and sometimes even contrary to the declared policies of their national governments' (p. 4). Depending on how large and influential the trans-governmental network, the shared normative principles or cognitive–ideological approach of these actors will have a varying determination on both shaping the FEP preferences of individual FEP powers and on coagulating an international consensus on FEP norms and practice, thus facilitating international policy co-ordination between FEP powers and, at times, the birth of new international institutions.

1.3.6 Interactive Dynamics Between Different FEP Functions

Certain relationships between the interactive functions of our macro-framework of FEP analysis have already been illustrated, either implicitly or explicitly. However, this section affords special attention to these interactions, restating key points and providing examples from the NIE-3's foreign economic policies. Each interactive function is considered in turn, with reference to how it affects other functions and vice versa:

1. *Cognitive–ideological approaches*: are directly determined by contesting 'actor-based' influences. For example, the values, ideas and beliefs that orientate the work of FEP protagonists often cannot be separated from the stakeholding FEP constituencies they represent. Both group sub-sets, especially at the domestic level, may share socio-cultural associations and belong to a similar value-system. In South Korea, for instance, societal economic nationalism has reinforced lingering aspects of bureaucratic economic nationalism, as manifested in the country's resilient neo-mercantilist approach evident in certain aspects of FEP conduct. Furthermore, Chapter 2 discusses in greater detail that external sources of neo-liberal advocacy (the Anglo-Saxon FEP powers, WTO, IMF etc.) have proved an increasingly powerful international contesting influence over the NIE-3's cognitive–ideological approach to FEP formation. The subsequent effect

of this upon the NIE-3's generic 'economic security' objectives is noted below.

2. *Generic 'economic security' objectives*: examples are provided below of how these principally orientate FEP conduct, that is technical policy realms and economic diplomacy. In turn, the NIE-3's economic security objectives are determined by the cognitive–ideological approaches adopted by their FEP protagonists and contesting 'actor-based' influences. In an example of the former, the infiltration of neo-liberal institutional values into the NIE-3's political economies has heightened their attention to systemic security interests, as they accordingly rely more on the WTO and other IEOs to safeguard their commercial interests. Regarding an example of the latter, South Korea's persistent economic nationalism (a mediating factor of contestability) still significantly underpins the attention of the country's FEP protagonists to socio-economic paradigm security.
3. *Technical policy realms*: as noted above, these are primarily oriented by the generic 'economic security' objectives set by FEP protagonists. For example, the pursuit of socio-economic paradigm security could lead to the imposition of certain import restrictions on culturally sensitive products, while techno-industrial security interests may require the adoption of certain technical measures in the NIE-3's foreign direct investment policy. Contesting 'actor-based' influences can also have an indirect (via 1 and 2) and direct effect. In instances of the latter, the NIE-3's closer compliance with the WTO rules and norms, and congruence to the technical prescriptions proposed by trans-governmental policy-networks in which certain FEP protagonists participate have significantly shaped their respective trade policies. Furthermore, as previously stated, a certain simultaneity exists between technical policy implementation and diplomatic engagement, as international bargaining often entails synchronous developments between the two. For example, reductions in the NIE-3's trade or inward FDI barriers may immediately transpire after negotiations with other FEP powers on these issues.
4. *Economic diplomacy*: following on from the above, developments in the NIE-3's technical policy realms will set certain parameters in their economic diplomacy engagements. For instance, the persistence of highly protected or closed *core* technical policy realms will most likely lead to a defensive modality and a narrow 'acceptability' set in negotiation process. As with technical policy realms, generic 'economic security' objectives primarily orientate the goals of economic diplomacy. For example, the pursuit of market access security and supply security interests has often necessitated the NIE-3 to seek commercial concessions from foreign economic partners. Finally, a bi-directional relationship of influence exists between economic

diplomacy and contesting 'actor-based' influences. We noted earlier how the *negotiation process* of economic diplomacy could be understood in the 'three-level' game dynamic framework, whereby economic diplomacy outcomes are forged by the interplay of domestic, international and transnational contesting 'actor-based' influences. In addition, economic diplomacy provides the main originating basis for international contesting 'actor-based' influences themselves. For example, the impingement of US relational and structural power in shaping the NIE-3's foreign economic policies primarily derives from the economic diplomacy function.

5. *Contesting 'actor-based' influences*: the significance of these in the interactive functional relationships of FEP formation has already been articulated above.

1.4 CONCLUSION

This chapter has outlined the macro-framework of FEP analysis that provides the conceptual and methodological structure of this text. It initially considered the conceptual development and problematics of FEP analysis in the international political economy literature before outlining the basis of the macro-analytical framework presented here. Elements of that framework comprise: 'environment' and 'development' contexts, cognitive-ideological approaches; generic 'economic security' objectives; *core* and *associative* technical policy realms; economic diplomacy; and contesting 'actor-based' influences.

It is conceded that this contribution to the FEP analysis debate is not without its limitations. The macro-framework ventured here does not provide an elixir to the problematics of FEP analysis, nor does its strength lie in any startling new perspectives or modelled tools offered. Furthermore, the framework's broadening of the conceptual parameters of FEP analysis to accommodate its general application risks the classification of a lowest common denominator approach. In addition, the compartmentalization of factors portrayed in the framework's schematic may be accused of too neatly disaggregating FEP phenomena. Notwithstanding these shortcomings, the merit of leaving foreign economic policy to mean 'all things, to all people', as is currently the general case, should be questioned. This multivariate but integrated framework does provide some important orientation for subsequent FEP studies by virtue of its eclectic, macro-focused character. The conceptual issues introduced here are further discussed in Chapter 2, which considers the common development context of the NIE-3's foreign economic policies using this macro-framework of analysis.

NOTES

1. Taiwan being an example here.
2. As Tooze (1994) commented, 'the study of foreign economic policy sits uneasily beside the practice of foreign policy analysis; not part of foreign policy analysis, but nominally sharing the same broad empirical referents' (p. 62).
3. However, for Viner (1948) the mercantilist approach to FEP united it with wider foreign policy objectives, where an 'economic' foreign policy and 'political' foreign policy were simultaneously pursued with constant attention to 'power and plenty' as co-ordinate and generally mutually supporting national objectives. Moreover, Cohen (1968) argued that, 'foreign economic policy is part of a country's total foreign policy and to some extent serves the same goals' (p. 1), while Hermann (1982) categorized economic instruments and objectives as one of eight different foreign policy subsets.
4. Amongst the most prominent have been Adams (1984), Cohen (1968, 1977), Cowhey (1990), Destler (1980), Geske (1996), Goldstein (1988, 1989), Hawley (1983), Ikenberry *et al* (1988), Kahler (1980), Katzenstein (1978), Kaufman (1982), Kindleberger (1977), Kreinin (1980), Lake (1983), Mastanduno (1998), McGowan and Walker (1981), O'Leary (1979), Pastor (1980), Price (1981), Randall (1954), and Vernon and Spar (1988).
5. See studies from Amerongen (1980), Barber (1979), Condliffe (1944), Doxey (1980), Kaempfer and Lowenberg (1988), Olson (1979) and Schreiber (1973).
6. Examples have included those on Britain (Blank 1978, Richardson 1936, Wallace 1975), Germany (Hanrieder 1982, Hofhansel 1990, Koopmann 1998), France (Lorot 1998, Mosley 1982), Italy (Bonvicini *et al* 1998), and Western Europe and the EU (Adler and Karlsson 1968; Kenis and Schneider 1987; Marsh 1980; Molle and Mourik 1987; Pinder 1985; Praet 1987; Story 1988; Smith 1994; Tooze 1994; Young 1998).
7. The Paris Co-ordinating Committee that organized trade restrictions on Warsaw Pact countries.
8. The coherence of the EU's foreign economic policy is questionable given this complexity. Nevertheless EU studies raise questions regarding assumptions of statehood as the pre-requisite for FEP formation, an issue of particular relevance to Taiwan.
9. Ikenberry *et al* (1988) also conferred primacy to the institutional setting of FEP formation, where state–society interactions exist within 'institutional structures [that] mediate the interests and capacities of individuals and groups within them' (Ikenberry 1988: 243). Thus, to them, FEP was essentially a state–institutional construct.
10. Furthermore, in the radical instrumentalist model, policy-makers derive from, and defer to, the capitalist class and consequently orientate FEP formation to capitalist values. In addition, policy outcomes tend to reproduce the capitalist features of the domestic and international system, hence acknowledging systemic-level factors of influence.
11. The argument that ideas and values themselves can become institutionalized into law, bureaucratic norms and the guiding principles of organizations is also made by Garrett and Lange (1995), Katzenstein (1978), McGillivray and Smith 1997, and Pastor (1980).
12. As Odell (1990) himself noted, 'institutions establish and defend the particular order and initial distribution of property rights under which market exchange takes place. Individuals' very conceptions of their places and potentials in this social order are learned partly from within their particular historical and institutional environment... At a minimum, the potential behaviour of individuals and industries responds to the constraints and opportunities presented by these institutions' (p. 153).
13. As Moravcsik's (1997) notion of 'commercial liberalism' contends, 'the individual and collective behaviour of states is based on the patterns of market incentives facing domestic and transnational economic actors' (p. 528).
14. Neo-mercantilist studies have frequently centred on East Asia's developmental states, especially Japan, South Korea and Taiwan (Dent 2000, Guerrieri and Padoan 1986, Higginbotham and Samuels 1998, Nester 1990).
15. However, both Heckscher (1955) and Viner (1968) argued that both mercantilists and liberals were concerned with national power and wealth, it was just that their means of achieving this

were different. Viner cites Adam Smith's advocation of Britain's Navigation Acts in their protection foreign markets (or free trade) for the nation's producers.

16. Tu (1984) defines this as 'an amalgam of the family or collectively oriented values of the East and the pragmatic economic goal-oriented values of the West' (p. 110).
17. These may relate to one-off policy projects and initiatives, for example the Taiwanese Government's attempts to establish the island economy as an Asia–Pacific Regional Operation Centre.
18. A broad definition of geo-economics is deployed here that extends beyond its supposed core preoccupation with 'economic warfare' to also embrace the co-operative and more benign competitive aspects of economic relations between the major industrial powers. See Cable (1995), Huntington (1993), Luttwak (1990) and Moran (1993) for more adversarial interpretations of geo-economics.
19. The US government established its own Economic Security Council under the Clinton Administration in the mid-1990s.
20. Buzan *et al* (1998) themselves conclude that the question of economic security concerns the relationship between the political structure of anarchy and the economic structure of the market, and avoid merging security and economy into a single analytical construct.
21. For instance, it has been argued that economic threats in particular are often diffuse and systemic, making it therefore difficult to locate their source (Buzan *et al* 1998, Sperling and Kirchner 1997).
22. The scholarly study of economics and security was first formally undertaken by a number of prominent academics in the 1930s and 1940s, including Jacob Viner, E.H. Carr, Albert Hirschman and Edward Mead Earle. However, the economics–security nexus was surprisingly neglected in the early post-war period despite being a particularly strong feature of US foreign policy (Mastanduno 1998). The global shocks of the 1970s and the emergence of IPE as an academic discipline changed this (Knorr and Trager 1977, Friedberg 1991).
23. In his own analysis, Luciani's (1988) comments that 'to the extent that the dominant consensus and political stability are reinforced by economic prosperity, a deterioration of economic conditions may be perceived as a threat to national security' (p. 154).
24. For example, Heginbotham and Samuels (1998) comment that 'Japan's foreign policy... consistently reflects a more complex calculus, under which the maximisation of military security frequently is subordinated in pursuit of techno-economic security interests' (p. 203). Furthermore, according to Mastanduno (1998) three main factors determine the integration of economic and security concerns, namely: *international structure* where different structures (unipolar, bipolar, multipolar) provide different incentives for integration and separation; *strategic environment* where greater integration can be expected in a more hostile environment; *position in international competition* where a dominant competitive position in the international political economy makes it easier to deploy FEP as a complement to national security policy.
25. Hence a connection with the environmental context factors outlined by our model.
26. Furthermore, Buzan *et al* (1998) state that, 'attempts to securitise economic issues are essentially a part of the politico-ideological policy debate within IPE. In this context, the language of securitisation is a way of taking economic nationalist positions in economic policy debates without having to abandon superficial commitments to the liberal consensus' (p. 115).
27. If the tenets of hegemonic stability theory are applied, the hegemonic state is seen as the systemic guarantor or underwriter motivated by the need to enable its competitive producers to expand into a stable and open global market environment.
28. A link can be made with Stopford and Strange's (1991) notion of the 'new diplomacy' where the creation of wealth in the FEP power's own territory is central to its generic economic security objectives rather than acquiring this wealth by irredentist means.
29. For Alting von Geusau and Pelkmans (1982), national economic security is at stake when external parameters change in such a manner as to cause a breakdown of the preferred socio-economic order, and that economic security is dependent upon the ability of governments to maintain and develop the preferred socio-economic system as its welfare goals.

30. For example, East Asia's 'growth triangles' are based on the development of transborder economic networks or the complementary exploitation of sub-regionally located capital, labour and material resources.
31. See Kulkarni (1995) and Mathews (1989).
32. As Lee (1998) argues, this poses a dilemma for the state in that 'it has to preserve its internal autonomy and economic sovereignty from being exploited by external interference, but at the same time it needs to invite external forces in order to ensure the enhancement of domestic welfare' (p. 21)
33. In her examination of co-operative behaviour in international relations, Milner (1992) argues that co-operation is usually opposed to conflict, competition and unilateral behaviour, and that it concerns goal-directed behaviour that produces mutually shared benefits over and above those yielded by non-co-operative behaviour. Different types of this behaviour include: *tacit co-operation*, which occurs without communication or explicit agreement; *negotiated co-operation*, which derives from an explicit bargaining process; *imposed co-operation*, where the stronger party in the relationship forces the other(s) to enter into co-operative arrangement, its coercive features making this somewhat anomalous although there are clear links to hegemonic stability theory.
34. As Cable (1995) comments, 'contemporary global conditions often call for a co-operative rather than a confrontational pursuit of an economic security that is a shared condition rather than a goal of individual states' (p. 305).
35. For Krugman (1994), the fixation with enhancing competitiveness itself is problematic, not least because competition between nations is not the same as inter-firm competition, a supposed mistake made by Porter (1990). While Krugman acknowledges that enhancing national economic performance is of importance, he adopts the Lockian view in that the pre-occupation with international rivalry is pointless, which runs counter to the Hobbesian view that economic performance is only meaningfully measured in internationally relative terms. This latter realist approach is developed by Gowa (1994) and other national strategists who examine 'power and plenty' objectives in an anarchic international system of states. Furthermore, the value of strategic trade policies are examined by Moran (1996) who argues that 'far from being simply poor students of economics, national strategists have calculated that relative rates of productivity growth, technological innovation, and overall economic expansion determine which states are better able to influence world events, shape and lead common endeavours, manage risks, resist external pressure and counter or thwart antagonistic moves by others' (p. 181).
36. A common example here is the NIE-3's liquor tax rates on whisky and other Western alcohol products.
37. For instance, Cooper (1986) notes how Alberta's 'resource diplomacy' played an important role in US–Canada trade relations during the 1970s and 1980s, with natural gas concessions being offered by the province in return for more open US markets for Albertan cattle ranchers. Moreover, sub-state government representatives from contiguous transborder regions, especially within natural economic territories or 'growth triangle' zones, are often engaged in managing transborder community issues of economic security. In another case, Hong Kong may have seen its political sovereignty transferred to Beijing but it nevertheless still maintains aspects of economic sovereignty, e.g. own currency, separate customs authority.
38. See Baughn and Yaprak (1996), LeviFaur (1997) and Crane (1998) for a wider discussion on economic nationalism.
39. The former effect is associated with Reich's (1991) 'who is us?' issues, in this case where the traditional inter-state bargaining structure of economic diplomacy has been reconfigured by transnational production and its realigning effects on patterns of societal loyalties.
40. Krasner (1983) defines a regime as 'implicit or explicit principles, norms, rules and decision-making procedures around which actors' expectations converge in a given area of international relations' (p. 19).
41. Although derogations to these rules may be secured and many new WTO accords are of a voluntary, plurilateral nature.
42. This may relate to extra-territorial interests as well as those embedded in FEP power. Returning again to the recent transatlantic banana dispute, Chiquita lobbied the US Government not to

secure EU market access for US-based exports but rather for its South America-based export production.

43. At the conceptual level, epistemic communities also share characteristics with 'advocacy coalitions' that Sabatier (1998) defines as 'people from a variety of positions (elected and agency officials, interests group leaders, researchers) who share a particular belief system... and who show a non-trivial degree of co-ordinated activity over time' (p. 115). The Advocacy Coalition Framework developed by Sabatier assumes that the belief system of each coalition is organized into a hierarchical, tripartite structure: the *deep core* of the shared belief system (basic ontological and normative beliefs), *policy core beliefs* (representing a coalition's basic normative commitments and causal perceptions across a policy sub-system) and secondary aspects of a coalition's belief system.

2. The development context: developmental statism and semi-peripheralization in perspective

2.1 INTRODUCTION: THE EAST ASIAN NIE DEVELOPMENT EXPERIENCE

In Chapter 1 we set out a generally applicable, macro-framework for foreign economic policy (FEP) analysis with an initial demonstration of its relevance to Singapore, South Korea and Taiwan – the NIE-3. In this chapter, we specifically consider the development context of these three economies' FEPs as part of that macro-framework. This will serve a number of analytical purposes, the first and foremost being the establishment of shared developmental ground between them (on a collective and sub-set basis) from which common traits in their respective FEPs may be identified. While the political economies of each country exhibit many fundamental differences, there also exist important commonalities between them. As Figure 2.1 suggests, the latter relates to developmental statism, semi-peripheralization, qualification as newly industrialized economies (NIEs), export-oriented industrialization, and key constituents of contemporary East Asian economic dynamism. It is contended that developmental statism and semi-peripheralization deserve particular attention: with the former commonality largely determining the domestic development context and the latter the international structural context of the NIE-3's foreign economic policies. Both commonalities are evolving, however, in response to critical changes in the domestic and international political economy.[1]

Before we examine developmental statism in some detail, we must first acknowledge that it contends with two other main explanatory perspectives on East Asian economic development. The first of these is the market-conforming perspective which proposes that the region's economic miracle principally derived from the implementation of market-friendly policies, that is 'getting the prices right'. According to this view, these created a conducive microeconomic and macroeconomic environment in which dynamic private entrepreneurship flourished and hence high rates of growth were achieved. Examples include realistic exchange rate policies, minimal taxation, selective trade liberalization, and industrial policies that primarily exploited the market-

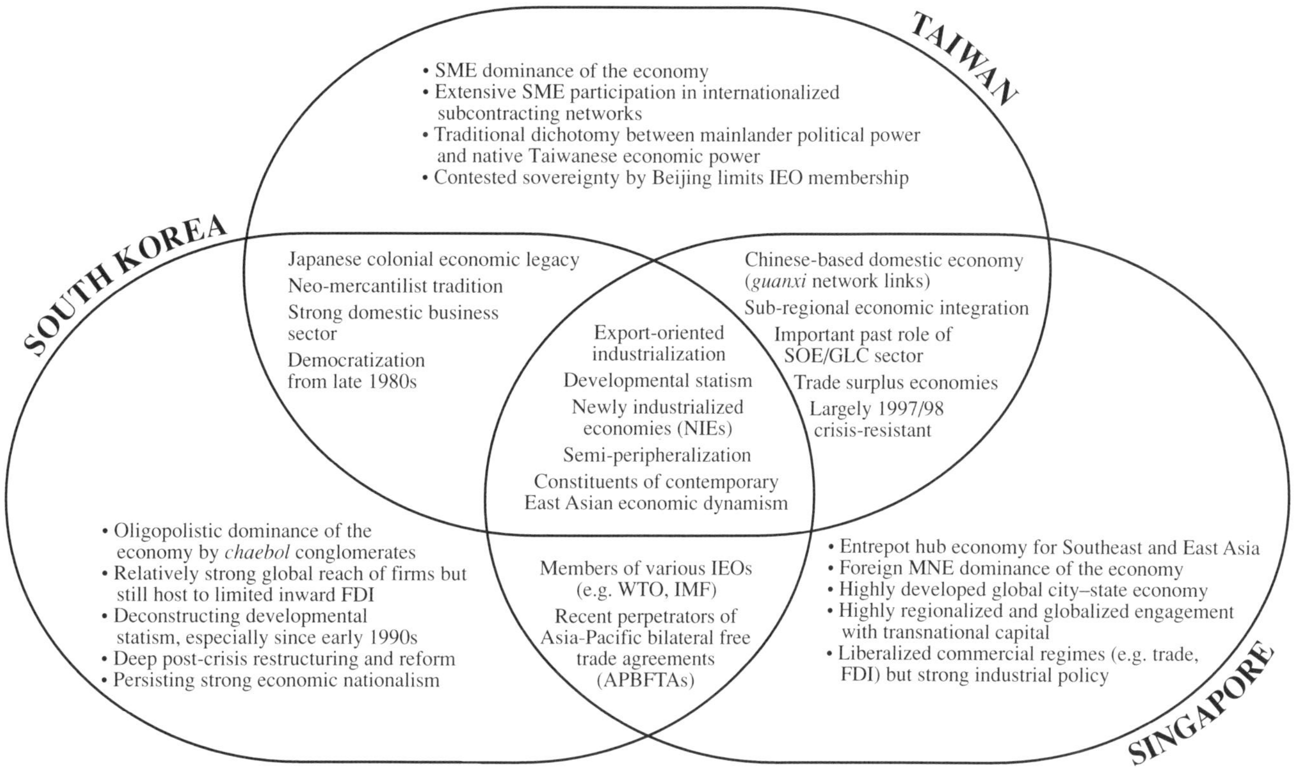

Figure 2.1 Singapore, South Korea and Taiwan: a comparative political-economy overview

exposed comparative trade advantages of the economy (Balassa 1982, Friedman 1988, Krueger 1990). Furthermore, as Chu (1999a) observed, this view tended to 'reduce the question of trade and industrialisation policy... to the purely economic analysis of given comparative advantages and the rational choice of policy-makers acting in the public interest' (p. 287).

Such market fundamentalism was most powerfully articulated in the World Bank's high profile report on the 'East Asian Miracle', although it did indirectly concede the partial relevance of developmental statism (World Bank 1993, Wade 1996). Market-conforming advocates also point to how neo-liberal reform has been required to sustain East Asia's economic dynamism, particularly in the new global era where optimizing the benefits of deepening interdependence within the world economy has necessitated greater market opening of the domestic economy. For example, liberalizing inward FDI regimes has enabled states to capture the benefits of more available, mobile and footloose foreign capital. In addition, as the complexity and size of the NIEs grow, so must the overextended state be substituted by a more decentralized and market-based structure according to this view.

The second contending perspective on East Asian economic development relates to network dynamics. According to this view, the 'state or market' debate creates a false dichotomy of explanations as both constituents are mutually bound within social network linkages (Moon 1999). In the network perspective, state–society vertical relations are concerned with the state's institutional capacity and legal authority to dictate to civil society but these are complemented by a horizontal nexus of ties that constitute both formal (e.g. deliberation councils) and informal organic (e.g. family, localized community) networks. It is the combination of 'vertical' command and 'horizontal' consultative and consensual decision-making mechanisms that best explain East Asia's developmental processes. In other words, it is the network interaction between the state (public sector), market (private sector) and society (civil sector) that has energized East Asian economic development. Furthermore, East Asia is essentially a 'network-based' rather than a 'firm-based' regional economy. This particularly relates to both Chinese *guanxi* networks and Japanese-led transnational production networks connecting different aspects of business activity across the region (Gerlach 1992; Orru *et al* 1997; Whitley 1990, 1992).

In contrast, developmental statism emphasizes the central role of the state as the key determining factor of East Asia's economic miracle. The state's prioritization of growth, productivity and competitiveness; its guidance, discipline and co-ordination of markets and the private sector; its strategic allocation of resources; the utilization of a raft of policy instruments; and the relations fostered with society to realize these ends form the basis of the developmental state model. A distinction is required here between the Western notion of state intervention, wherein government agencies are pitted against powerful private sector interests, and the embedded autonomy of developmental states within key social structures (Evans 1995). In the latter, the state is involved in negotiative and collaborative (rather than arm's-length, antagonistic) relations with strong social actors, notably the domestic economic class, in which a transformative project is commonly pursued. It is this 'relational' aspect of developmental statism rather than its interventionist aspect that has received increasing attention by statist-prescribing academia. In one sense, this suggests a convergence between all three contending perspectives: the developmental state's links with the market and its market-conforming policies have risen in prominence, as have state–society network relations. Aspects of developmental statism are discussed in more detail below. In the last two decades, it has been the most commonly held perspective on East Asian (and especially Northeast Asian) economic development, although post-crisis events and developments in the region have increasingly challenged this position.

2.2 THE DEVELOPMENTAL STATE PARADIGM: CONTENTION AND EVOLUTION

2.2.1 Establishing the Basis of Developmental Statism

While the specified concept of the developmental state has only been around since the early 1980s, its ancestral roots date back much further. Gerschenkron's (1962) 'late industrialization' thesis is usually cited as the earliest proto-theory of the developmental state. In his historical study on economic backwardness, Gerschenkron stressed the key developmental role of the state in mobilizing the necessary resources to reduce the techno-industrial gap between 'late industrializers' and the advanced industrial powers. Drawing mainly upon the experiences of nineteenth century continental Europe and the early twentieth century Soviet Union, Gerschenkron demonstrated the importance of the state's industrial and mercantile policies in gradually strengthening an initially weak domestic business sector in the pursuit of techno-industrial catch up.[2] Moreover, the bigger the gap, the stronger the state-based ideology required to mobilize resources for development. Gerschenkron's typology also strongly suggested that the market will eventually supersede the role of the state as industrialization proceeds, and consequently mercantilism[3] gives way to liberalism as an increasingly independent domestic business sector gradually weans itself from the state. The eventually redundant developmental role of the state in Gerschenkron's thesis is resonant for twenty-first century studies of late industrialization as it emphasizes the ultimately transitional nature of the developmental state, a debate to which we return.

The conceptual lineage of the developmental state is also traceable through the theoretical traditions of Weber (1922, 1947) and Polanyi (1944), who both argued that markets do not exist in isolation of state power or the social relations and organizational dynamics in which they are embedded. This is particularly relevant to developmental states in their creation of specific market structures through various actions, including investment co-ordination, strategic trade and financial regime policies. Later on, Wade (1990) referred to this as the 'governed market' principle, whereby there exists a 'synergistic connection between a public system and mostly market system, the outputs for each becoming the inputs for the other' (p. 5), from which developmental achievement is realized. More specifically, Weber (1922, 1947) argued that the development of capitalism depended on a stable social order maintained by the modern bureaucratic state. 'Technocratic insulation', a key developmental state concept discussed below, draws upon Weberian notions of the virtuous state bureaucracy: meritocratic, coherent and with clear chains of command. Furthermore, Weber contended that it was ultimately in the interest of state bureaucrats to advance the corporate goals of business through both proactive and passive means, the former being most relevant to developmental statism. In elaborating his thesis that market development was socially and institutionally embedded, Polanyi asserted 'the free market was opened and kept open by an enormous increase in continuous, centrally organised and controlled interventionism' (1944: 140).[4]

However, it was not until Johnson's (1982, 1987) studies of Japanese economic development that the notion of the 'developmental state' was first formally proposed and popularized. In outlining his theory, based on an eight year study centred on Japan's Ministry of International Trade and Industry (MITI), Johnson differentiated between the:

- *socialist state*: in which administrative commands substituted for private entrepreneurship and the market mechanism;
- *western capitalist state*: that primarily fulfils a regulatory function and acts as a neutral umpire in the market place;
- *capitalist developmental state*: that seeks to influence private sector decisions by persuasion, coercion and manipulating the parameters of this decision-making process. It is essentially forged from the 'interaction of two sub-systems, one public and geared to developmental goals and the other private and geared to profit maximisation' (Johnson 1987: 141–2).

Johnson contended that the origins of the Japanese developmental state could be traced back to the Meiji period, when the country embarked on a late industrialization drive from the 1860s onwards, and had pioneered developmental statist practices ever since. Wade and White (1984) were also responsible for helping initially to define the conceptual basis of the developmental state, and were followed thereafter by specific country studies (Amsden 1989, Wade 1988) and various comparative studies (Appelbaum and Henderson 1992, Deyo 1987a, Haggard 1990, Chan *et al* 1998, Weiss 1998, Woo-Cumings 1999).[5]

Whilst the developmental statist scholarship subsequently proliferated, a general consensus around Johnston's original definition was more or less maintained into the 1990s. For example, Chang (1999) defined a developmental state as that which 'can create and regulate the economic and political relationships that support sustained industrialisation' and which 'takes the goals of long-term growth and structural change seriously, "politically" manages the economy to ease the conflicts inevitable during the process of such change (but with a firm eye on the long-term goals) and engages in institutional adaptation and innovation to achieve those goals' (p. 192). In the view of Castells (1992), a state is developmental when 'it establishes as its principle of legitimacy its ability to promote and sustain development, understanding by development the combination of steady high rates of economic growth and structural change in the productive system, both domestically and in its relationship to the international economy' (p. 56). The more specific features normally associated with developmental states are as follows:

2.2.1.1 The pursuit of transformative developmental goals

These essentially relate to advancing the (usually long term) techno-industrial capacities of the economy. Weiss (1998) distinguishes between *revolutionary*, *structural* and *sectoral* types of economic transformation. Revolutionary transformation entails breaking with an antecedent economic system, as currently experienced by East European economies in their transition from plan to market. Structural transformation concerns a shift through the primary (e.g. agriculture), secondary (e.g. manufacturing) and tertiary (e.g. services) aspects of the economy. Finally, sectoral transformation involves industrial developments towards a more creative, complex and technology-intensive set of activities. The historical path of most developmental states will have connected at some point with all three transformative typologies. Typically, the transformative project is managed by what Johnson (1982) referred to as the developmental state's 'pilot agency'. In South Korea, this was the Economic Planning Board (EPB), in Taiwan the Council for Economic Planning and Development (CEPD), in Japan the Ministry of International Trade and Industry (MITI) and in Singapore the Economic Development Board (EDB).

2.2.1.2 Technocratic insulation

This is a feature whereby the developmental state's bureaucratic cadres are impervious to rent-seeking influences or interests, in contrast to the patrimonial and clientistic practices of the 'predatory states' where state bureaucrats compromise the pursuit of national developmental goals for personal financial gain. As noted earlier, technocratic insulation is a Weberian ideal of the virtuous state bureaucracy. It relies on the government's ability to recruit and retain the premium managerial talent from society, and moreover on the professional commitment of the bureaucratic cadres to realize the state's transformative developmental objectives.[6]

2.2.1.3 Infrastructural power

This relates to the state's ability to penetrate society, extract resources, and mobilize and co-ordinate social energy (Mann 1986). Thus it is partly a relational concept, concerning the state's linkage with, and influence over different societal groups. It therefore has some overlap with the 'network dynamics' explanation of East Asian economic development as noted earlier. Infrastructural power has a further dimension. As Onis (1991) observed in developmental states, 'the objective of the political elite is to legitimise the actions of the elite bureaucratic agencies and make space for the latter's actions' (p. 111). In other words, 'politicians may reign, but bureaucrats rule', implying that the state bureaucracy's infrastructural power often extends to setting the policy agenda.[7]

2.2.1.4 Embedded autonomy

This is another relational concept of the developmental state. Evans (1995) defines this as the concrete set of social ties that bind the state and society, and provide institutionalized channels for the continual negotiation and renegotiation of (developmental) goals and policies. Whilst the state maintains its technocratic insulation, it also remains sufficiently connected to key economic and social groups. Thus, state–business and state–society links form the basis of various developmental partnerships, with the state at the co-ordinating 'embedded' centre. As Evans further elaborated, embeddedness provides sources of intelligence and channels of implementation that improve the state's policy competence, thus enhancing the effectiveness of its infrastructural power.

2.2.1.5 Authoritarian, 'mono-regime' politics

A common feature of the East Asian developmental state experience has been the predominance of a certain political corps. For Singapore this remains the People's Action Party (PAP), for Taiwan the Kuomintang (KMT) party until 2000, in South Korea the military (up until the early 1990s) and in Japan the Liberal Democratic Party (LDP). The traditional authoritarian, 'mono-regime' basis of developmental states is often defended within the context of late industrialization: the need for a strong state with continuity of developmental purpose to see through the closure of the techno-industrial gap. Developmental authoritarianism has often used the security imperative as self-legitimization in that no other politico-economic modality would have ensured national survival (Moon 1998, Woo-Cumings 1996). However, this position was less defensible after the easing of Cold War tensions. We later consider the pertinent issues arising out of the shift from developmental authoritarianism to developmental democratization.

2.2.1.6 Institutionalized state–business co-operation

Relations between the state and business sector have comprised the prime developmental partnership of the transformative project. State–business policy networks form a key aspect that can include formal policy consultation bodies, deliberation councils, state-sponsored industry associations, and a broad range of more informalized networked contacts and connections. 'Peak' organizations of business (for example large company groups or business associations) also serve an important linkage function. In South Korea, the main peak organizsation is the Federation of Korean Industries (FKI), in Singapore the Singapore International Chamber of Commerce (SICC) and in Taiwan the Chinese National Federation of Industries (CNFI). Manifestations of state–business co-operation have naturally varied in accordance with different national contexts. For example, a once intimate developmental alliance existed between the South Korean state and the *chaebol* conglomerated oligopolies; the Singaporean state has propagated close links with hosted foreign capital; the Taiwanese state has maintained a more arm's-length relationship with the SME-predominant business sector, although both cross-sector (e.g. R&D) and sector-specific (e.g. electronics) co-operation between the state and business remains strongly evident.

2.2.1.7 'Capacity' functions

These provide a more generalized way of viewing the distinctiveness of the developmental state, connecting with most of the above. For Weiss (1998), the developmental state's *transformative capacity* represents its very essence, this being 'the ability of the state to adapt to external shocks and pressures by generating ever new means of governing the process of industrial change' (p. 4).[8] In addition, H.R. Kim (2000a) argues that the developmental state is defined by its managerial, co-ordination and control capacities. *Managerial capacity* concerns how developmental states formulate and implement their economic policies, as well as discharge their functions generally. This requires a cohesive state bureaucracy with technocratic insularity as a fragmented economic bureaucracy emasculates the state's managerial powers over aspects of economic development. *Co-ordination capacity* concerns the institutionalized links between the state and business to govern economic activities, engage in collective decision-making, and mutually address market failures. Lastly, *control capacity* is strongly related to the concept of 'infrastructural power', for example concerning the extent of state control over key economic resources such as finance that has enabled state–business investment co-ordination to be practised across various sectors of the economy.[9]

It is contended here that the political economies of Singapore, Taiwan and South Korea from the 1960s onwards have all exhibited significant degrees of developmental statism. An initial comparative observation is perhaps useful at this stage. Firstly, some question whether Singapore qualifies as a developmental state, mainly because of the dominant foreign rather than domestic business community in the economy, and the more arm's-length, persuasive rather than coercive manner in which the state has attempted to steer capitalist development towards developmental goals (Low 1998). Furthermore, both Singapore and Taiwan's development statism has traditionally lacked the ardour of South Korea's, although ironically it is the latter that has recently succumbed most to the eroding forces of neo-liberalism. It is to the neo-liberal challenge to developmental statism that we now turn.

2.2.2 The Challenge of Neo-liberalism: Extinction or Evolution of the Developmental State?

As noted in Chapter 1, the ascendancy of neo-liberalism has considerably affected the environment context of contemporary foreign economic policy, and thus in turn has permeated the interactive functions of FEP formation. To understand neo-liberalism's impact upon the FEPs of our three developmental states in study, it is initially necessary to consider the sources of its advocacy. From the mid-1970s onwards, there was a broad shift in the West to 'new right' policies, as embodied by Thatcherism and Reagonomics and the neo-liberal fundaments on which these were based. Consequently, the mixed economy axioms of Keynesianism were substituted by those of market economics, that together with liberal democracy formed the ideological basis of what later become known as the 'Washington consensus', as espoused by the US and other Anglo-Saxon powers. To a large extent, it was no coincidence that many East Asian developmental states embarked on their first phase of liberalization of economic policy during the early 1980s, as evident in the realms of trade, FDI and international finance. However, we must distinguish between domestic and external sources of neo-liberal advocacy in examining their effect upon developmental statism.

Domestic sources of neo-liberal advocacy derive from two main factors. The first of these relate to what Woo-Cumings (1991) refers to as 'ideological osmosis', whereby the domination of Japanese-trained technocrats in Northeast Asia's economic bureaucracies and policy think tanks, imbued with neo-mercantilist values, have been gradually replaced by US-trained economics graduates who are invariably inculcated with neo-liberal values. This process is most evident in South Korea, the country in study to have moved furthest in recent years to embracing the neo-liberal paradigm, at least in terms of rhetorical politics (Kim, Y.T. 1999, Moon and Rhyu 2000). The second concerns the democratization process in which the emergence of a more pluralistic society and the polycentric distribution of power undermined the authoritarian basis of the developmental state. This can be partly explained by the so-called 'grave-digger' hypothesis of the developmental state, whereby the state's nurturing of the business sector creates an increasingly empowered bourgeoisie that in turn seeks greater political power and a more liberal policy agenda. In both Taiwan and South Korea, the onset of democratization from the late 1980s onwards saw the empowerment of their respective business sector's political influence over policy formation. Even Singapore's powerfully entrenched but also highly pragmatic PAP Government has acknowledged the benefits of pluralistic debate on matters of politics and economics. Furthermore, democratization has to a lesser degree strengthened the political influence of East Asian civil society, although this has often proved a counter-pressure to neo-liberalism as illustrated by events during and since the World Trade Organisation's (WTO) 1999 Seattle Ministerial Meeting (McMichael 2000, Chakravarthi 2000).

Meanwhile, external sources of neo-liberal advocacy (especially deriving from the Anglo-Saxon imbued variant) have also softened the mercantilist practices of East Asian states. A deepening participation in international economic organizations (IEOs) – such as the WTO, International Monetary Fund (IMF), Organisation for Economic Co-operation and Development (OECD) and World Bank – has further conditioned them to neo-liberal norms and values, the implicit core ideological basis of these institutions. For example, concessions made by South Korea to enter the OECD group and by Taiwan in its accession into WTO membership required both to make preparatory liberalizations of their commercial regimes during the 1990s. Furthermore, greater engagement in IEOs has fortified the channels by which proponents of the aforementioned 'Washington consensus' (especially the US) can assert their own neo-liberal advocacy. The US's active utilization of the WTO's disputes settlement mechanism and its influence in shaping the new trade agenda testify to this.

Moreover, globalizing forces, as with democratization at the domestic level, provide additional compelling pressures upon East Asia's developmental states to liberalize. This has particularly occurred in the finance sector, where the region's governments have removed controls that hindered home firms' access to new global sources of capital. The growing engagement of these same firms in transnational business activity has further required the opening up of trade and FDI regimes in order to reduce the associated costs of such activity. In Taiwan, liberalization and internationalization were the twin slogans of government used to push through its neo-liberal policy reforms from the early

1980s onwards. In the 1990s, the South Korean Government deployed its *Segyehwa* (globalization) programme to achieve similar ends, whilst the Singapore Government pursued a 'regionalization' strategy as a means to liberalize the transnational space of its domestic and hosted foreign firms more effectively beyond the city-state's territorial borders.

To what extent, then, are neo-liberalism, globalization and democratization challenging the current purpose and hence longevity of developmental statism in the NIE-3? Our discussion so far suggests a path to eventual extinction, thus complying with the Gershenkronian view that developmental states are essentially transitional configurations whose fate is sealed by their own limitations and inherent contradictions. However, while some dismantling of the developmental state apparatus is indisputably evident across East Asia, it is argued here that evolution rather than extinction best describes the path of developmental statism. The general case for this hypothesis is as follows.

We noted earlier that authoritarian, mono-regime politics had been a defining feature of East Asian developmental statism, providing the continuity and strong state powers required to sustain the transformative project. However, the irresistible pressures of democratization created by a bourgeoisie and other societal groups that progressively aspire and gain in economic and political power eventually rupture this status quo. Both liberals and Marxists agree on this, as do modernization theorists who contend that with economic prosperity come social mobilization, that is urbanization, mass communication and education, and an expanding middle class (Deutsch 1961, Lipset 1959, Cutright 1963). Democratization thus empowers and diversifies the range of stakeholding constituencies that seek influence over, and potential deviation to developmental statist policies. It undermines the developmental state's traditional authoritarian basis and thus the state's ability to pursue coercive policy measures without negative political feedback. Democratization also brings political competition, giving rise to new governments and hence regularized changes to economic ideology and policy orientation.

The question is therefore, can a shift from developmental authoritarianism to developmental democratization be achieved whilst maintaining the integrity of the developmental state, or is the democratic developmental state an oxymoron (Jomo 2000, Kim, Y.T. 1999, Kuo 1998, Moon and Rhyu 2000, White 1998)? However, the strengthening of domestic contesting influence over the economic policy-making process from both business and civil societies does not necessarily infer a weakening of developmental state capacity but rather a rebalancing of one of its integral elements. As Weiss (1995, 1998) has argued in the context of 'governed interdependence', the transformative capacity of the developmental state works optimally under the conditions of 'strong state, strong society'. While an empowered business community could admittedly use its strengthened position of influence to pursue rent-seeking interests *vis-à-vis* state officials, its role in a more 'bottom-up' style corporatism could lead to more effective and rational goal-setting within state–business policy dialogues, not least because of business representatives' generally more informed knowledge of domestic and international market conditions.

Moreover, the democratization-induced shift from state corporatism to societal corporatism allows for a greater penetration of societal interests in economic policy formation, thus broadening the scope for negotiation and re-negotiation of economic policy goals. The stronger engagement of civil groups in this process bestows upon the state new ideas on how to meet new developmental challenges. For example, as the twenty-first century progresses, the techno-industrial advancement of Singapore, South Korea and Taiwan will increasingly be judged less in terms of pure economic growth and more by alternative developmental criteria. These include environmental virtuosity, improving welfare services, and creating healthier working conditions for their people. Thus, while the NIE game of techno-industrial 'catch-up' still focuses on higher-tech economic development, it also looks to close other gaps elsewhere. In doing so, the twenty-first century developmental state needs to draw upon the expertise of civil society if it is to establish a new developmental paradigm that is both welfare enhancing and environmentally sustainable. Thus, while democratization may change the developmental mentality of both state and society in East Asia, it does not necessarily follow that the mentality itself will consequently diminish.

With more direct regard to politics, Evans (1997) contended that the rise of civil society should not necessarily lead to a corresponding weakening of state power, making the point that civil groups are often closely associated with effective public institutions. Moreover, as Putnam's (1993) study on 'social capital' argued, just as modern markets are embedded in social institutional frameworks, so civic engagements flourish when a competent public sector functions as an interlocutor between private citizens and those stakeholding constituencies now better able to work effectively alongside the state. More generally, democratization should not undermine other defining features of the developmental state, such as technocratic insulation, and may actually enhance some: for instance, it could elicit more effective responses from society to exercises of infrastructural power. In sum, democratization has brought both palpable threats and opportunities to the developmental state, and may simply re-orientate the state's developmental objectives to achieving more sustainable and welfare enhancing ends. As subsequent chapters discuss, the FEPs of our three case study economies increasingly reflect this.

Finally, it is by no means assured that globalization will bring eventual neo-liberal normalization across the international system, or that increasing degrees of globalization lead to corresponding diminishments of state power (Gore 2000, Higgott 2000, Smith 1999). As Evans (1997) and Weiss (1998, 1999,

2000) assert, states may seek to harness globalizing forces to suit their own policy objectives: in other words, 'globalization is able to make of the state only what the state is able to make of globalization' (Weiss 2000: 338). For example, the Singapore Government works in close collaboration with hosted foreign multinationals within the framework of its own competitiveness strategy. As we shall discuss in the following section, the turbulent events of 1997/98 led East Asian governments to establish better and not less governance of markets. Indeed, the view that the 1997/98 East Asian financial crisis was the first real crisis of globalization is pervasive in the region (Higgott 1998). Thus, the neo-liberal advocacy of free markets has been treated with increasing caution in post-crisis East Asia after having experienced the associated risks of unfettered global capital flows (Bhagwati 1998, Mastanduno 2000). The extent to which certain developmental state capacities have been consequently strengthened in Singapore, Taiwan and South Korea, and the implications for their respective FEPs, is the subject of subsequent debate. Furthermore, it is noted how in many cases a persistent and considerable divide exists between the espoused neo-liberal rhetoric of East Asian politicians and actual FEP practice.

2.2.3 The Impact of the 1997/98 East Asian Financial Crisis

The 1997/98 East Asian financial crisis marked a critical point in the region's contemporary economic development. In the chapters that follow, the significance of the crisis and post-crisis developments for Singapore, Taiwan and South Korea's respective FEPs is discussed in some detail. In this chapter, rather than concentrating on the causes of the crisis, we shall pay most attention to its general consequences, especially with regard to its impact on the development context of FEP formation. The causal themes of the crisis are now well documented: debt-driven development, state over-activism, weak corporate and policy governance, speculative asset bubbles, crony capitalism, disruptive global capital flows, multilateral institutional failure, Western conspiracy, and so on. From an even more reductionist perspective, one can adopt the view that the crisis was caused by either too much state regulation or by too little. Adherents to the former view, for instance, argue that the regulatory excesses of the state and its misconceived industrial policies produced the accumulative market distortions in the economy that precipitated the crisis. Meanwhile, those holding the latter view point to, amongst other things, the actual lack of supervisory regulation and monitory mechanisms in the region's financial sectors. Moreover, by pursuing the neo-liberal path of deregulation and liberalization, many East Asian governments overlooked the need for compensating regulatory reform and support (Feldstein 1998, Prakash 2001, Sachs 1998, Stiglitz 1998, Wade and Veneroso 1998). Hence, domestic banks and firms could acquire freer access to global capital without the incurred financial flows being adequately supervised or monitored. More specifically, this process allowed South Korea's newly unshackled *chaebols* from the state's investment co-ordination framework to overextend their industrial portfolios into each other's core sectors, as exemplified by Samsung's foray into the automobile market. This occurred when most *chaebols* were experiencing overcapacity problems, and it was the subsequent accumulation of non-performing loans owed mainly to foreign banks that precipitated the country's crisis (Chang 1998, Lee and Kim 2000).

What emerged from the crisis, though, was a series of subsequent paradigmatic struggles pertaining to what future direction East Asian economic development should take. The crisis did much to strengthen the position and channels of neo-liberal advocacy in the region. For domestic neo-liberal advocates, the crisis exposed the structural rigidities inherent in the (developmental) statist paradigm that had for too long constrained the market and entrepreneurial dynamics of the economy. Thus, the 'old' paradigm was a time-bomb waiting to go off, despite the preceding neo-liberal reforms they had secured prior to the crisis. In the most crisis-affected countries (i.e. South Korea, Indonesia, Thailand, Malaysia and the Philippines), enough economic, political and social distress was caused for there to emerge a broad societal consensus for paradigmatic change. To varying degrees, this too was evident across less crisis-affected areas of the region, Singapore and Taiwan included. Hence, the crisis both empowered and expanded domestic sources of neo-liberal advocacy.

New changes to economic policy reflected this, but in South Korea, Indonesia and Thailand much of this change was imposed by an external source of neo-liberal advocacy, namely the IMF. The liberalization of South Korea's trade and FDI regimes – a condition to receiving IMF 'bailout' funds – is documented in Chapter 4.[10] Suffice to quote here the statement from Lawrence Summers, then US Deputy Treasury Secretary speaking in February 1998, that 'the IMF has done more to promote America's trade and investment agenda in Korea than 30 years of bilateral trade talks' (from Weiss and Hobson 2000: 68). Indeed, as has been argued elsewhere, the US used both the IMF's interventions and the crisis more generally to its own advantage (Belo 1998, Higgott 1998, Wade 1998). The insistence of US Congress that any extended American aid to the IMF 'bailout' packages came attached with conditions that recipient states introduce far reaching market reforms was indicative of such American opportunistic behaviour.[11] Furthermore, some have argued that the US's slow response to the crisis, at least relative to the 1994 Mexican peso crisis, was deliberate: its own neo-liberal advocacy for market reform in East Asia could best be exploited after the crisis had caused significant damage (Weiss and Hobson 2000).[12] As Belo (1998) contended, the US saw the crisis of an opportunity to 'achieve what it has been trying to push over the last decade, with little success: the free market transformation of economic systems that are best described as state-assisted capitalist formations' (p. 434). Certainly, key US policy-makers[13] were highly active in selling the neo-liberal, 'free market' brand of capitalism to East Asia as the elixir to the region's problems.

However, to many the Western neo-liberal paradigm remains unpalatable and inappropriate to East Asia, especially to those that perceived the intrusions of the IMF, the US and other external sources of neo-liberal advocacy as 'foreign meddling'. Indeed, the sharp recovery evident in many parts of crisis-torn East Asia from 1999 onwards (most notably South Korea) suggested to some that the events of 1997/98 were more akin to a recession rather than a crisis, and more importantly it was the fundamental strengths of the 'old' paradigm rather than neo-liberal reform that was primarily responsible for the recovery. Within the group of three case economies, the crisis-related paradigmatic struggle has been most ardent in South Korea, mainly because its developmental statism was once the strongest and also because it was by far the most crisis-affected of the NIE-3. This is therefore a central theme of Chapter 4 as new directions in South Korea's FEP can be mostly understood in this context.

In contrast, Singapore and Taiwan only suffered a phase of shallow economic growth during 1997/98, and moreover their apparent relative immunity to the crisis can at least be partly attributed to developmental statist responses (Prakash 2001). While both had liberalized their financial sectors during the 1990s, this was accompanied by re-regulation, thus maintaining the developmental state capacity to govern this important aspect of the economy adequately. When the crisis came, the Singapore and Taiwan governments were therefore able to introduce effective counter-measures. For example, prior to the crisis the Central Bank of China (CBC – Taiwan's central bank) negotiated with other government agencies that it should develop contingency powers over foreign exchange transactions in case of financial crisis. These were used to effect during the turbulent course of events over 1997/98 when it intervened to discipline international speculative capital. Although financial deregulation had been implemented in certain areas from the late 1980s onwards, the opening up of Taiwan's capital market was accompanied by new regulatory controls and co-ordinative powers (Weiss 2000). An instance of this was the need for Taiwanese firms raising foreign currency loans for domestic use having to invest in new plant facilities and not stocks and real estate, thus avoiding the speculative asset bubbles that had precipitated many of Southeast Asia's financial market instabilities leading up to the crisis. According to Weiss (2000), this was typical of the Taiwanese economic bureaucracy's synchronous 'liberalization with re-regulation' approach, a more general prescriptive argument developed by Vogel (1996). Meanwhile, the Singapore developmental state brokered a tripartite agreement between government, business and labour to cut employers' contributions to the Central Provident Fund (the state-run savings scheme) by 5% to provide a cost competitiveness boost to the economy.

Even in South Korea, where the crisis was used to legitimize the further dismantling of the developmental state, achieving this in real terms proved elusive. Strong path dependence may be associated with developmental states whereby they become embedded within the national meta-economic culture that they have also helped create. As such, they cannot easily be wrenched from their multilayered engagement with the institutional, business and civil networks of the economic society which they inhabit. Thus, the apparent neo-liberal erosion of the developmental state is counteracted by various structural relationships and socio-cultural factors that maintain degrees of integrity, a point emphasized in Pempel's (1999a) 'developmental regime' concept detailed below. For example, the state–*chaebol* nexus in South Korea has once again demonstrated its resilience after attempts by a new President to cut the government's links with business (Gills 1999). As Chapter 4 discusses, Korean economic nationalism remains a formidable force in both shaping the economic policy preferences and determining the success of new policy initiatives. Societal responses to the South Korean Government's recent FDI policy are a case in point, with the country's trade unions supporting *chaebol* rather than foreign multinational (MNE) takeovers of ailing domestic firms.

Notwithstanding the above points, we must in conclusion recognize that the crisis had a profound impact on both the nature and debate on developmental statism. An important consequence was a spur to new or alternative concepts of the developmental state, some key examples of which include:

- *Transformative states* (Weiss 1998, 2000): set within the context of 'governed interdependence', which is defined as 'a negotiated relationship in which public and private participants maintain their autonomy, yet which is nevertheless governed by broader goals and monitored by the state' (Weiss 1998: 38). Moreover, the effective transformative state depends on the 'strong state, strong society' equation noted earlier, whereby 'the state is well insulated and industry highly organised and linked into a policy-making framework in a robust negotiating relationship' (Weiss 1998: 38). In this model, the state continues to depend on strong economic groups at the societal (business and civil) level to be able to respond to its transformative objectives. This infers a compatibility with democratic developmentalism in which the state–industry 'negotiating relationship' becomes more enfranchized and consensual rather than elitist and coercive. In one sense, it constitutes a maturing of developmental state or 'statism' from its 'strong state, weak society' origins, and thus a counter-thesis to the 'grave-digger' prediction on the demise of the developmental state. Overall, the state continues to upgrade its transformative objectives commensurate with new techno-industrial developments.

- *Enterprise associations* (Cotton 2000): these are purpose-governed communities in contrast to civil associations, i.e. a body of individuals governed by rules and norms that regulate their conduct but which is not committed to any particular or identified purpose. Here, the enterprise is understood as an undertaking, hence a connection with the 'transformative project' ideal proposed by mainstream developmental statism.
- *Regulatory states* (Jayasuriya 2000): these have evolved in the contextual shift towards the authoritarian liberalism that facilitates the emergence of the regulatory state with the primary purpose of both safeguarding and regulating the market. As Jayasuriya comments, 'pivotal to authoritarian liberalism is the existence of dualistic state: a strong state combined with a liberal market economy' (p. 319). Markets are insulated from political interference but still depend on strong and effective regulatory institutions for their optimal functioning, thus making a connection to Polanyi's thesis noted earlier. Jayasuriya draws upon the role of central banks as examples of such institutions. His thesis suggests not the decline but rather the reconstitution of the developmental state into a new metamorphosed form, in other words a state with a range of regulatory capacities.
- *Social capital* (Fine 1999): the developmental state in transition formed part of a wider global trend of recomposing capitalist forms by the millennial eve. Drawing mainly from a new Keynesian approach to economic organization, the concept of 'social capital' essentially examines the role of non-economic, or non-market factors that make the economy work better. More specifically, organized societal communities with high levels of social capital are needed to work with strong, sophisticated state bureaucracies to yield more effective state–society synergies. However, Fine's thesis is based on a view that the developmental state literature has evolved within the 'political school' (read 'statist') but predicts that this domain will be subsumed into the 'social capital' debate as part of broader confluence of social science discourses. Fine makes connections to various other prominent social capital theorists, such as Evans (1996), Fukuyama (1995) and Putnam (1993).
- *Developmental regime* (Pempel 1999a): the preference for this term derives from its capture of not just state-related (i.e. government) aspects but also socio-economic conditions and international relations in East Asian economic development. This requires looking 'beyond the state as a reified concept separate from society' and 'a sensitivity to the interactions between "state" and "society", as well as a sensitivity to domestic and international conditions' (p. 156). A 'developmental regime' thus embodies a 'sustained fusion among the institutions of the state, particular

segments of the socio-economic order, and a particular bias in public policy orientation' (p. 157). Pempel even goes so far as to argue: 'there is no sharp dichotomy between state and society. The presence of semi-permanent socio-economic conditions closely linked to state institutions make such a reified bifurcation meaningless' (p. 160). By emphasizing the broader relational framework of developmental statism, Pempel implicitly makes a case for its embedded resilience. In other words, deconstructing the developmental state requires more than simply dismantling the state policy and institutional apparatus of the past. It depends also on a radical reconstitution of the structural relationships that it has both spawned and in which it is subsequently embedded, a point raised previously. As a fundamental essence of these relationships is socio-cultural, the penetration of 'Western' neo-liberal norms is constrained.[14]
- *Neo-developmental states* (Amsden and Hikino 2000): more a restatement of developmental statism than a new conceptualization of it. Amsden and Hikino argue that the developmental state's latitude for neo-mercantilist manoeuvre remains considerable in the contemporary global economic order. Although the WTO is cited as a pillar of global neo-liberalism, its rules still permit late industrializing states to 'subsidise new industries where necessary and to ensure that subsidies are result-oriented through the imposition of performance standards' (p. 110). Amsden and Hikino further contend that it is informal political pressures exerted by North Atlantic economies in favour of radical market opening that in reality dissuade such states from pursuing this developmental path rather than formal legal constraints imposed by the WTO. Although not amplified by these scholars in their work, this argument has significant FEP implications.

The contention of the evolution and adaptation rather than extinction of developmental statism in the NIE-3 has important implications for their foreign economic policies, as we analyse in later chapters. Let us now, though, examine the NIE-3's development context in a more international setting.

2.3 THE NIE-3: BEYOND SEMI-PERIPHERALIZATION?

The contemporary techno-industrial advancement of the NIE-3 has been startling. In the 1950s, their level of economic development was on a par with many African states. By the twenty-first century each had become a major world manufacturer and exporter in key technology-intensive industry sectors,[15] and had surged ahead of other developing countries in terms of income per capita. The importance of the developmental state paradigm in achieving these outcomes has already been acknowledged, but to what extent could the NIE-3's techno-industrial advancement be characterized as 'dependent development' (Cumings 1984; Evans 1979, 1987; Lim 1985; D.A. Smith 1997, 1999; Smith and Lee 1990)? In other words, how much of their economy's development is attributed to foreign firms and sources rather than their indigenous equivalents?[16] This is critical to our analysis insofar as it posits the development context of the NIE-3 more firmly in the international (or world) economic system. It therefore follows that understanding how their contemporary economic development has been determined by their position in this system helps us in turn understand many behavioural aspects of the NIE-3's foreign economic policies. Thus, whereas our analysis on developmental statism was primarily concerned with the *domestic* determination of NIE-3 development, this section more explicitly considers factors of *external* determination and its international context. Some link can be made here with the *system-centred* approach introduced in Chapter 1, whereby FEP formation in some way reflects international systemic structures, norms and other relational factors. This point is elaborated further below.

As already hinted in Chapter 1, the notion of 'dependent development' is usually associated with the *structuralist* perspective of international political economy that draws together dependency theory and world-system theory, amongst other analytical strands.[17] It places great emphasis on the importance of economic, political and social structures in explaining the nature of the world economic system (Wallerstein 1978, 1979; Chase-Dunn 1989). In terms of international *economic* structures, we must particularly refer to those of production, finance, technology and knowledge. Its analysis of economic history stresses the particular division of labour that has evolved in the world economy based on the growth of capitalism as the dominant form of production. In analysing the structure of the world economic system, structuralism draws upon dependency theory to explain the persisting gap between developed and developing country areas. According to this theory, the *core-periphery* divide between advanced industrialized regions (the 'core', i.e. the advanced industrial economies, or AIEs, of North America, West Europe, Japan and Australasia) and under-developed regions (the 'periphery' consisting of less developed countries, or LDCs) is sustained by a subservient economic relationship in which the latter remain dependent upon the former for capital, technology, finance and trade. This relationship of 'unequal exchange' endures because it is in the interests of dominant capitalist forces (for example state policy-makers from developed countries and MNE executives) to maintain the status quo.

While not intending to prescribe to structuralism *per se*, I do utilize one of its analytical devices to examine a key aspect of the NIE-3 developmental experience. This relates to the world system theorist's proposition that the NIE-3 form part of the *semi-periphery*. As such, semi-periphery economies or states, as their name suggests, are situated somewhere between the core and periphery. The concept of semi-peripheralization first acquired prominence in the late 1970s, arising out of the critique of dependency theory's rather simplistic core-periphery dichotomy (Wallerstein 1978). By this time, the bleak prediction that developing countries would always remain marginalized within a capitalist world economy became increasingly untenable, especially given the evidence of East Asia's dynamic economic development. The region's advanced NIEs (the NIE-3 plus Hong Kong) in particular offered a strong case to acknowledge a semi-periphery tier of development (So and Chui 1995).

However, world system theorists retained similar dependency theory assumptions in their treatise on semi-peripheralization. Wallerstein (1978, 1979), their leading protagonist, proposed that their intermediate position within the world economy was based on extracting surplus value from the periphery while simultaneously yielding surplus value to the core. He also emphasized the state's role in creating the conditions for semi-periphery development and engagement in the world economic system, and thus a passing (probably unintended) acknowledgement to developmental statism and 'late industrialization'. While Wallerstein's thesis attracted some acclaim, it has also been heavily criticized, particularly for concentrating almost exclusively on market processes and adopting a somewhat reductionist approach to key factors such as socio-economic structure and technological change (Taylor and Thrift 1981). Furthermore, the national boundary demarcations deployed in his core–semi-periphery–periphery analysis often look dubious given that transnational regions of specific development (e.g. East Asia's 'growth triangles', West Europe's 'blue banana') are increasingly evident and thus a 'zonal' approach being more relevant. In addition, as Arrighi (1990) points out, the semi-periphery is not a heterogeneous entity, making only relative generalizations possible about its characteristics. He further argued that core economies can possess semi-periphery features, while semi-periphery economies can possess features of their core counterparts.

Notwithstanding these caveats, the categorization of semi-periphery development serves a useful analytical purpose, allowing us to refer to an economy's *structural position* in the world economy and its *historical process* of development from the periphery to the semi-periphery within the global economic system. According to O'Hearn (1994) semi-periphery economies are more 'adaptive' responders to change in contrast to the 'creative' responsiveness of the core. This can be applied to new developments in technology, finance and other related domains of economic activity, as discussed below. While this does infer some degree of core–semi-periphery dependency, this should not be overplayed. Moreover, I generally concur with Haggard's (1986) view that dependency is less a determinant international structure and more a set of mercurial constraints within which individual economies have room to manoeuvre. In other words, the dependent development of the NIE-3, and their associated foreign economic relations, do not negate the fluidity of both in today's fast-changing global economy. By broadening our discussion further, semi-peripheral economies can be said to possess the following general characteristics with relevance to FEP analysis:

- *Persistent dependence on the core for sources of technological development*: stemming from an underdeveloped autonomous capacity to generate new high technology products and processes. For example, even South Korea's large *chaebol* remain heavily reliant on foreign 'core' MNEs for key technologies, e.g. Daewoo's dependence on General Motors for design and component technology. Technology licensing, reverse engineering practices, high-tech inward FDI and other technology transfers remain critical to the semi-periphery's economic development (D.A. Smith 1997, 1999). Indeed, the 'Triad' of core powers (US, EU and Japan) currently maintain between a 90–95% triopoly of new technology patents (Dent 1997). However, this weakness should not overshadow the semi-periphery's capacity to assimilate new technologies once developed by the core.
- *Substantial reliance on the core for sources of finance capital:* while the NIE-3 have proved successful at domestically generated capital provision, the semi-periphery in general maintains a considerable reliance on 'core' banks and other financial institutions for finance capital. South Korea's foreign debt problems predate the 1997/98 crisis, though these never reached the stratospheric heights of the Latin American semi-periphery's debt. To many, the financial crises experienced by the semi-periphery in the 1990s (i.e. in Mexico, East Asia, Russia and Brazil) exposed a shared periphery vulnerability to 'core-centred' international finance[18] (Onis and Aysan 2000). However, Singapore and Taiwan's more robust domestic financial capacity make them somewhat an exception.[19]
- *Often participating as a subservient link in global commodity chains (GCCs)*: according to Gereffi (1998), the East Asian NIEs' situation in both producer-driven and buyer-driven GCCs is central to explaining their economic development, with the main task of their state's developmental strategy being to exploit their semi-periphery position in transnational production systems to increase productivity, competitiveness and welfare. Certainly, much of Taiwan's SME-based economy is plugged into international sub-contracting networks where they essentially perform a manufacturing service for foreign 'core' MNEs. Singapore's own reliance on transnational production is even more conspicuous, with hosted foreign MNEs dominating its economy. The relative GCC position of the South Korean economy, itself the source of *chaebol*

transnational capital, is more contentious (D.A. Smith 1997). Finally, NIE-3 firms are invariably the minor or more dependent partners in the international strategic alliances they forge with foreign 'core' MNEs.

- *Assisters of AIE techno-industrial restructuring:* concerning the core's relocation of more mature technology industries to the semi-periphery to exploit the triple combination of lower cost production, fast developing technological capability and new emerging markets. This has particularly applied to Singapore and Taiwan from the NIE-3 group who have much higher inward FDI ratios than South Korea, although the latter has begun to close the gap with Taiwan since the 1997/98 crisis.
- *Emerging competitive challenges to the AIEs:* owing mainly to the first two factors of the 'triple combination' identified above. Moreover, the semi-periphery's competitive challenge to the core is often politically-sensitive as its export strengths invariably lie in relatively labour-intensive industrial sectors experiencing structural decline in core power areas such as textiles and steel. Subsequently, semi-periphery economies are frequently confronted by protectionist barriers erected by the core, a main issue in the foreign economic policies of the NIE-3.
- *Potential mediators between the core and periphery in matters of economic diplomacy:* semi-periphery states simultaneously possess recent 'developing country' origins and emerging 'developed country' features, providing them with the opportunity to mediate between the contesting interests of the core and periphery. International tensions over the 'new' trade issues present a good example. Many core powers are currently advocating closer links between trade rules and environmental standards, labour standards and so on, a move strongly resisted by periphery states wary of the hidden protectionist agenda this may carry. Semi-periphery states can empathize, to varying degrees, with both positions and therefore can perform a diplomatic mediation between the two, with brokering a core–periphery compromise agreement a possible outcome.
- *The predicament of 'sandwiched competition'*: semi-peripheral producers must simultaneously compete with AIE rivals in higher technology sectors and LDC rivals in lower technology sectors. As Martin (1990) commented, 'the semi-periphery bears the burden of a modern Janus: facing oligopolistic and political pressures from core zones and economic competition from the periphery below' (p. 8). Whilst semi-periphery states must thus tackle competitive pressures on these twin fronts, this can also spur their firms and governments actively to develop competitive-enhancing solutions across a range of economic activities. In the NIE-3, this has provided some rationale for a strong 'associative' technical policy realm of FEP, particularly in the linking of industrial and trade policies.

In sum, rising semi-peripheral economies are pulling away from a characteristically dependent past but the legacy of this still lingers. Moreover, some semi-peripheral states have proved effective at 'negotiating dependency' (Deyo 1987b, Smith 1999). As Deyo (1987b) contended, 'state mediation of dependency involves the institutional channelling of most external linkages through bureaucratic agencies that are thereby enabled to introduce strategic criteria into the construction of foreign market, technology, and capital relationships' (p. 237). This is relevant to how, in different ways, the NIE-3's developmental state capacity harnessed foreign capital to meet transformative objectives whilst generally resisting any predatory or rent-seeking interests pursued by foreign firms. Examples include Singapore's developmental relationship fostered with its hosted foreign MNEs, and South Korea's 'arm's-length' use of foreign loans up to the 1990s, with the state positioning itself between foreign lenders and local capitalists (Smith 1999). As is argued throughout this book, a strong *state-centred* approach to FEP formation prevails amongst the NIE-3 group. This is notwithstanding the aforementioned emergence of *society-centred* contesting influences and – with specific respect to the semi-peripheralization context – the fact that a structuralist interpretation of the *system-centred* approach remains highly relevant. Yet this study also contends that it is the NIE-3 developmental state's generally successful working within a series of semi-periphery constraints on one hand, while exploiting semi-peripheral opportunities on the other, that continues significantly to define their respective foreign economic policies.

The East Asian region has a rich seam of semi-peripheral economies, with the NIE-3 forming the highest grade of these. Some comment on the conducive international conditions for the semi-periphery development of the NIE-3 should also be noted. Although these varied to some degree across the group, as subsequent chapters make clear, there are nevertheless a number of general conditions that link them. During the Cold War period, the US was particularly active in supporting the industrialization of the NIE-3, at least whilst they did not pose a competitive industrial threat to American firms. The US had a strong geo-political interest in consolidating East Asia's fledgling capitalist societies as part of resisting the advance of communism in the region. American support took various forms, including financial aid, technical assistance programmes and acting as a 'market of last resort'.[20] The global expansion of trade from the 1950s to the early 1970s, largely facilitated by the US's own free trade advocacy and policy, created new opportunities for the then increasingly export-oriented NIEs. However, with the receding of the Cold War, and the associated communist threat, the US was less inclined to absorb high levels of East Asian NIE exports. Moreover, the burgeoning trade deficits maintained with these economies turned Washington's priorities to advocate neo-liberal reform and negotiate the dismantling of the NIE's neo-mercantilist regimes.[21] South Korea and Taiwan – both comparatively ardent practitioners of neo-mercantilism – were particularly targeted for such treatment.

However, the decline of US support was compensated by two other main developments. The first concerns Japan's own economic resurgence, and pivotal role in East Asia's regional economic development (Akamatsu 1962, Blomqvist 1996, Cumings 1984, Lim 1995, Mendl 1995). The start of a transborder expansion of Japanese trading companies and SMEs into developing East Asia was evident from the early 1970s onwards. After the 1985 Plaza Accord, when the Japanese Government conceded to an appreciation of the yen to ease tensions in trade diplomacy, Japanese companies embarked on large-scale relocation exercises in which East Asia's NIEs were major beneficiaries. Consequently, the NIE-3's techno-industrial development was spurred by infusions of Japanese technology transfers and investment capital. This issue can be explored further by considering the 'flying geese' model of regional economic development, whereby the region's core economy (i.e. Japan) lies at the apex of a multi-tier, interdependent development relationship with its neighbours. The NIE-3 form the second tier of a region-level restructuring in which they, in turn, assist the techno-industrial development of the neighbouring lower-grade semi-periphery (e.g. Malaysia and Thailand) and periphery (e.g. Vietnam) by shifting their own more labour-intensive production to these locations. Thus, there is a strong regional dimension to the NIE-3's economic development, with them experiencing relatively fast changing roles in both the regional division of labour and regional economic diplomacy. In relation to the latter, there are greater expectations from less developed East Asian countries upon the NIE-3 as sources of investment capital, prospering markets, financial aid and other forms of development assistance.

The second factor relates more generally to globalization itself, whose integrative forces have presented the NIE-3 and other semi-periphery economies new commercial opportunities in terms of market access, capital acquisition and technological assimilation. The following chapters explore how the developmental states of South Korea, Singapore and Taiwan have in their own ways been astute at exploiting different aspects of economic globalization. Finally, world system's theory proposes that the semi-periphery may ascend to the core just as core powers may be relegated to the semi-periphery, as history has previously demonstrated. The NIE-3 have achieved a successful 'pathway from the periphery' to the semi-periphery (Haggard 1990), so what chance of their progression to advanced industrial nation status? The strong post-crisis recovery of each, and accompanying return to high rates of economic growth, suggests that this may well transpire within a few decades. South Korea became an OECD member in 1996, and Taiwan and Singapore would also be eligible if economic development alone was the sole criterion for membership.[22] The larger two NIEs have income per capitas approaching poorer EU member states, while Singapore's now approximates that of Germany.

Each NIE-3 economy is also developing a more independent capacity to generate new high technology product and processes, albeit frequently working with foreign 'core' capital in a (more balanced) strategic alliance framework. As a consequence, the technological gap between the NIE-3 and many core powers is narrowing across a range of industrial activities. Furthermore, the group have become increasingly important capital providers to some core and many periphery countries alike. As with developmental statism, the evolutionary nature of the NIE-3's semi-peripheralization has had a profound impact on their foreign economic policies. Moreover, the group's FEPs have been deployed to the purpose of moving beyond the semi-periphery itself.

2.4 CONCLUSION

This chapter has examined the development context of the NIE-3's foreign economic policies. It has particularly highlighted the importance of the NIE-3's developmental statism and semi-peripheralization in this respect. The former is especially relevant in the domestic determination of their foreign economic policies, whilst the latter is particularly relevant with respect to external determining factors. Although both the developmental state and semi-peripheralization are increasingly contested concepts, with some arguing that they have become redundant terms of reference, this chapter has made a case for their persisting analytical relevance and value in seeking to understand aspects of the contemporary global economy. In the chapters that follow, we discuss how this dyadic development context has common implications for the NIE-3's foreign economic policies.

NOTES

1. As Pempel (1999a) argued, 'because a fundamental goal of the developmental state is the improvement of its economic conditions relative to other states, any country aspiring to development must choose its strategy within the broader context of regional and international power balances' (p. 147).
2. This follows a similar line of argument previously advanced by nineteenth century mercantilist thinkers such as Friedrich List (1841) and the importance of developing the productive powers of the state. Furthermore, Schumpeter (1950) had argued before Gerschenkron that the uncertainties and costs of techno-industrial catch-up legitimized a role for the state in socializing risk and arranging entrepreneurial profits.
3. According to Anderson (1974), 'mercantilism was precisely a theory of the coherent intervention of the political state into the workings of the economy, in the joint interests of the prosperity of the one and the power of the other' (p. 36).

4. The case for examining both the state and market in a broader social environment is made by Clark and Chan (1994). Structuralist development theory, the conventional wisdom in development studies during the early post-war years, provided some vindication for developmental state practice by contending that pervasive market failure in developing countries created an *a priori* need for state 'corrective' measures. For its part, the regulatory school could have perceived developmental statism as a mode of social regulation to counterweight the emerging capitalist 'accumulation regime' in developing countries. A possible reason why this was never formally articulated is because of the development state's connections to both socio-political and capitalist actors.
5. In geographic terms, East Asia, and especially Northeast Asia, remains the main focus of developmental state studies, although countries from other regions have also been discussed (Levifaur 1998, Woo-Cumings 1999). Grabowski (1994) went so far as to contend that all effective or 'hard' developmental states originate from East Asia, as opposed to 'soft' developmental states evident elsewhere.
6. As Chan *et al* (1998) commented, 'by implication, a developmental state is staffed by agents of change who are unified by a common purpose and technical orientation' (p. 2).
7. According to Onis (1991) this is in contrast to 'despotic' power, which he defines as 'highly centralised and authoritarian states in which the state elites extensively regulate economic and political activity but at the same time take decisions without routine, institutionalised negotiations with groups in civil society' (p. 123).
8. Moreover, Weiss, a prominent state apologist, argues generally that, 'state institutions can offer the most encompassing organisational complex for overcoming a number of widely recognised obstacles to change, including problems of collective action, bounded rationality and short-term horizons, as well as unprecedented time compression in technological transformation' (p. 6).
9. As Chapter 4 discusses, South Korea's capacity has been particularly weakened here, moving from a position where the state's control over credit allocation was used extensively to develop the nation's export industries during the 1960s and 1970s to that where the state has liberalized its financial regimes and cut the *chaebol's* dependence on the state in this domain.
10. According to Feldstein (1998), the IMF view that the South Korean, Thai and Indonesian Governments would not be able to service their debts unless a broad programme of structural reform is implemented only served to undermine investor confidence still further, resulting in bond-rating agencies downgrading South Korean debt to junk bond status. He further argued that the IMF's macroeconomic austerity measures killed off both sick and healthy firms alike.
11. The US's considerable influence over the IMF is widely acknowledged. In a broader context, Bhagwati (1998:11) made the observation that, 'Wall Street's financial firms have obvious self-interest in a world of free capital mobility since it only enlarges the arena in which to make money. It is not surprising therefore that Wall Street put its powerful oar into the turbulent waters of Washington political lobbying... [Moreover]... Wall Street has exceptional clout in Washington for the simple reason that there is a definite network of like-minded luminaries among the powerful institutions – Wall Street, The Treasury Department, the State Department, the IMF and the World Bank... This powerful network... is unable to look much beyond the interest of Wall Street, which it equates with the good of the world. Thus the IMF has been relentlessly propelled toward embracing the goal of capital account convertibility'.
12. The US's response to the crisis contrasted much with Japan's own very immediate proposal to establish an Asian Monetary Fund (AMF). This was first suggested in August 1997 to help resolve Thailand's financial difficulties, the original spark that lit East Asia's wider crisis. The AMF was intended as a temporary arrangement to deal with this one-off event, but the cascade of financial crises in other East Asian countries led to talk of institutionalizing such a fund. However, the US scuppered the AMF plan, not least because it feared the redeployment of Japanese surplus capital from supporting the US's debtor position ($350bn worth of Japanese money invested in US treasury bills by this time) to the ailing East Asian neighbours. The US was also wary of any compromise to the IMF's multilateral legitimacy and competence to deal with international financial problems.

13. Amongst them Charlene Barchevsky (US Trade Representative), Jeffrey Garten (Under-Secretary of State for Commerce) and Robert Rubin (Treasury Secretary) and Larry Summers (Treasury Under-Secretary).
14. Indeed, many discourses on the 'state' in general consider additional attributes that extend beyond the primarily executive nature of the 'government', for example by embodying a continuous administrative, legal, bureaucratic system that can also incorporate a varied set of social relations involving both public and private domains (Stepan 1978, O'Donnell 1993).
15. For example, South Korea in autos, Taiwan in IT peripherals and Singapore in wafer microchips.
16. More specifically, Evans (1979) defined 'dependent development' as, 'a special instance of dependency, characterised by the association or alliance of international and local capital. The state also joins the alliance as an active partner, and the resulting triple alliance is a fundamental factor in the emergence of dependent development' (p. 32).
17. Including Marxist and Gramscian analysis.
18. For example, in the 1997/98 East Asian financial crisis it was European, American and Japanese banks that provided much of the loan capital to the crisis-affected countries that subsequently became non-performing loans.
19. This derives primarily from regular trade and fiscal surpluses.
20. South Korea received $13bn and Taiwan $5.6bn in US financial and military aid, respectively amounting to $600 and $425 in per capita terms (Cumings 1984). Furthermore, Pempel (1999b) comments that, 'no other West European, African, Australasian or Middle Eastern countries bear any comparable levels of single market dependence for their exports' (p. 380).
21. Strategic trade theory has provided the main intellectual rationale for neo-mercantilism, based on the assumptions of strategic game behaviour in imperfectly competitive markets (Brander and Spencer 1985, Krugman 1986). It prescribes the use of industrial subsidies and investments to enable firms to expand production, hence achieving scale economies and to gain market share at the expense of foreign rivals. The protection of strategic industries from the compromising effects of foreign competition assists this process. Apart from facilitating the exploitation of oligopoly–monopoly rents within imperfect markets, these policies also yield positive externalities, such as technological spillovers into other related industrial sectors and the wider potential realization of scope economies. For example, this can be seen in the application of electronics technology and componentry in the automobile sector (as exploited by Korean *chaebols* such as Hyundai) and the interaction between the underlying technologies in the chemical and petrochemical sectors. Moreover, in the 'promotive' aspect of neo-mercantilism the state provides a raft of competitiveness-enhancing measures (e.g. export subsidies) as well as proactively supporting the development of strategic export production. Neo-mercantilism's 'protectionist' aspect aims to insulate domestic producers from injurious foreign competition, especially where it may compromise export capacity in new technology sectors. South Korea and Taiwan have actively practised both aspects of neo-mercantilism. While the Singapore state has practised its 'promotive' aspect, its liberal trade policies make even its partial association with neo-mercantilism problematic.
22. Here, Taiwan's contested international status is problematic, while according to one research interviewee Singapore is reluctant to apply for OECD membership because it may be obliged to sign the Kyoto Protocol, and thus comply with substantially reducing its CO^2 emissions – Singapore's per capita levels of which are the highest in the world.

3. Singapore: the FEP of a global city-state

3.1 INTRODUCTION

Perhaps in no other economy is the disaggregation of foreign from domestic economic policy so problematic as in Singapore. The city-state is arguably the most internationalized economy in the world, possessing extremely high ratios for both trade and foreign direct investment (FDI) to GDP. As a small entrepot economy, it is highly trade focused, and around 80% of this trade stems from hosted foreign multinational enterprises (MNEs) that both dominate the Singapore economy and plug it into various international production and distribution chains. The further blurring of the domestic–foreign divide stems from Singapore's internationally-focused state, whereby its many 'domestic appearing' economic policies have a close associative link with the city-state's foreign economic policy (FEP). Moreover, as one interviewed Singapore Government official commented, 'much of Singapore's foreign policy is driven by economic necessity, and thus it is difficult to draw the distinction where the economics ends and the politics starts'.[1] These caveats notwithstanding, this chapter deploys the macro-framework of foreign economic policy analysis outlined in Chapter 1 to explore the parameters and development of Singapore's FEP.

On the whole, Singapore maintains a highly activist foreign economic policy that is driven at the centre by the state. It is positively engaged in various levels of economic diplomacy. For example, Singapore was a founding member of the Association of Southeast Asian Nations (ASEAN) where it has long advocated the strengthening of its economic dimension. In its bilateral, regional and multilateral economic relations, the city-state ardently promotes the cause of free trade. Yet the Singapore developmental state also retains a predilection for guided market development, as for instance demonstrated in its FDI and international finance policies. As with its NIE-3 counterparts, Singapore's advanced semi-peripheral position in the international economic system is another important determining feature of its FEP. This particularly relates to its pronounced dependence on foreign capital, technology and investment, as well as its intermediatory role performed between core and periphery economies in matters of economic diplomacy and international production.

Despite its small size – population 4 million and GDP of $92.2bn in 2000 (Table 3.1) – Singapore was the world's 16th largest trader in 1999, ahead of much larger economies such as Russia, Brazil, India and Australia. This is attributable to the important entrepot role Singapore performs in East Asia, and accounts for the fact that trade often reaches 300% of the city-state's GDP. More than 10 000 companies use Singapore as their distribution hub for Asia-Pacific markets, while around 5000 foreign companies have based their regional production and service facilities there. Singapore also possesses financial strengths with virtually zero foreign debts and the world's sixth highest level of foreign exchange reserves at $76.8bn in April 2001. In the section that follows, we chart how Singapore progressed from a 'third world' to 'first world' country within four decades (Lee, K.Y. 2000), and hence key 'development context' features of its foreign economic policy.

3.2 SINGAPORE'S DEVELOPMENT CONTEXT

3.2.1 A Brief Economic History up to the 1990s

From its very beginning, Singapore's *raison d'etre* was essentially commercial. In 1819, Thomas Stamford Raffles established a colonial trading post on the small, more or less uninhabited island[2] of Singapore as part of further expanding British imperial interests in Southeast Asia. Singapore was chosen for its strategic location at the southern entrance to the Straits of Malacca, and thus along one of two sea-routes between the Indian Ocean and South China Sea. The island also possessed a superb natural harbour, and it was here that Raffles' administration created a free trade port. According to Huff (1987), Singapore's natural resource endowment and geographic position offered three logical possibilities for its early development, namely as a port of call, an entrepot for China trade, and an entrepot for the Malayan region. It was the latter that became Singapore's earliest prime commercial function. Later on, though, after the opening of the Suez Canal in 1869, the island's harbour became the region's chief port of call. From this date until the end of the 19th Century, Singapore's trade grew more than six-fold, this being mainly concentrated in primary products such as tin, rubber, tropical produce and petroleum. Commercial diversification ensued, and by the 1870s a number of European banks had established branches in Singapore, largely serving the interests of trade facilitation. Singapore's rapid trade development continued under British colonial rule in the early 20th Century. Yet as Huff (1994) argued, Singapore remained largely similar in its economic development up to 1939 to many major port cities across Asia, Latin America and Africa, and thus was not that developmentally unique or especially advanced.

Table 3.1 Key economic indicators of the Singapore economy (1995–2000)

Year	GDP[1] (S$m)	Per Capita GDP[1] (S$)	GDP[1] (US$m)	Per Capita GDP[1] (US$)	Exports (US$m)	Imports (US$m)	Current Balance (US$m)	Exchange Rate (S$/US$)	Official Foreign Reserves (US$m)
1995	118,195	35,022	83,388	27,992	118,268	124,507	14,436	1.4174	68,673
1996	128,727	36,735	91,289	30,900	125,014	131,338	12,822	1.4101	76,796
1997	140,466	39,924	94,603	31,035	124,985	132,437	17,927	1.4848	71,392
1998	138,529	38,418	82,773	26,672	109,895	104,719	20,334	1.6736	75,208
1999	143,981	39,721	83,846	26,976	114,689	111,060	21,751	1.6949	77,176
2000	159,042	42,212	92,233	24,486	137,958	134,680	21,797	1.7239	80,362

Note: 1. Current price figures

Source: Singapore Department of Statistics

In the post-war deconstruction of the British Empire, Singapore became a constituent part of the newly independent Malayan Federation in 1959. Hereafter, as Huff (1994) observed, Singapore increasingly became a government-directed society under the charismatic leadership of Lee Kuan Yew and his People's Action Party (PAP). In 1961, a UN Industrial Survey Mission formulated a programme for Singapore's own industrialization based on an import substitution industrialization (ISI) strategy that aimed to resolve a growing unemployment problem.[3] The expansion of its infant industries within a pan-Malayan market was steered by the state's newly established Economic Development Board (EDB), which became the key pilot agency of the Singaporean developmental state. However, Singapore's separation from the Malayan Federation in 1965 required a new developmental strategy for the now wholly independent city-state. That chosen by Lee Kwan Yew's Administration centred on promoting Singapore as a regional export platform for foreign multinational enterprises (MNEs). American electronics manufacturers were particularly courted for their inward FDI, and they were attracted by Singapore's combination of cheap but skilled and disciplined labour, industrial infrastructure, and low taxation.[4] The motives behind this developmental strategy had a strong security focus: embedding American commercial interests in Singapore through FDI significantly enhanced the US's stake in the city-state's own political survival and stability, and hence created a deterrent to invasion from either Malaysia or Indonesia. This was a distinct possibility during the turbulent mid-1960s when military tensions in the regional locale reached near boiling point.

The full switch in the Singapore Government's ISI strategy to export-oriented industrialization (EOI) occurred in late 1967. Given Singapore's small domestic market this was the natural course for its industrial strategy to take. Around this time, the British government announced it would close down its military bases by 1971, the expenditure from which had accounted for between 20 to 25% of the city-state's GDP up until the mid-1960s. This added further impetus to attract foreign MNE investment, and the state achieved progressive success with this policy. By the early 1970s, Singapore became a principal location for the offshore assembly activities of the American and European semiconductor industries, and a major regional centre for electrical and electronics goods production. As a consequence of these and other developments, the total stock of inward manufacturing FDI in Singapore rose significantly from $303m in 1967 to $2659m by 1973. Meanwhile, real gross domestic product (GDP) grew at a compound rate of 13.0% per annum over the same period.[5]

According to Soon and Stoever (1996) the first systemic attempts at upgrading the Singapore economy occurred over 1973–1978. With the attainment of full unemployment, the focus of the government's industrial strategy shifted from labour-intensive to higher value-added activities. Consequently, greater emphasis was placed on the skill, quality and technological content of Singapore's production activities. This was followed by a period of economic restructuring (1979–1984) brought on by the impact of the 1970s oil crises. It was also accompanied by a decline in energy-intensive activities, such as petrochemicals, and a corresponding shift towards 'cleaner' industries such as telecommunications, computer components and peripherals, and financial services. This formed the basis of Singapore's so-called 'Second Industrial Revolution' that further entailed both a substantial increase in wage levels designed to shift more labour-intensive production offshore, as well as compensatory enhancements in skill and productivity levels designed to attract higher technology FDI. The EDB had the responsibility of overseeing the city-state's 'high growth, continual upgrading' strategy, with industrial diversification also becoming an increasingly important focus of state policy.

By the early 1980s, the Singapore economy was highly dependent on foreign MNEs – a central feature of its semi-peripheralization. In 1981, around a third of all firms operating in the city-state had some participating foreign ownership, and by 1984 its stock of manufacturing inward FDI had risen to $12.2bn. Moreover, the government began to promote Singapore more actively as the ideal regional headquarters location for foreign MNEs. Such a dependence on transnational capital was not perceived by the state as that significant a risk at this time. The onset of recession in 1985, however, compelled Singapore's leaders to re-examine the need for stronger indigenous entrepreneurship, and according policy measures duly followed. In another response to the recession, the Government created an Economic Committee in which the advice of business representatives was sought to assess the new strategic economic environment and directions for the economy. As we later note, other formal state–business channels of consultation were to emerge within the evolving framework of Singapore's developmental state.

In the mid-1980s, Singapore's economic competitiveness was being eroded by a combination of rising labour costs, an appreciating currency and other inflationary pressures. However, both the appreciation of the yen and techno-industrial upgrading helped offset these problems.[6] Part of the EDB's strategy to improve techno-industrial capacity entailed establishing institutes of technology with the co-operation of the Japanese, German and French governments, these being primarily designed to upgrade the skill-base of Singaporeans in the electronics and engineering fields. Meanwhile, increasingly higher value-added FDI flowed into the economy whilst labour-intensive production shifted offshore, especially in the borderland areas of the emerging Indonesia–Malaysia–Singapore 'Growth Triangle' (IMSGT).

With Goh Chok Tong replacing the long-serving Lee Kuan Yew as Prime Minister in October 1990, many expected the style of Singapore Government to become more relaxed and *laissez faire* under its new younger leadership. However, the continuity of state activism in the economy soon became apparent.

In 1991, the Goh Administration introduced its Strategic Economic Plan that provided a new developmental vision for the Singapore economy in the 1990s. More specifically, the newly established National Science and Technology Board (NSTB) joined the EDB in steering Singapore's course of techno-industrial upgrading. As the decade progressed, the EDB placed more emphasis on industry cluster development aimed at fostering new capabilities in electronics, engineering, chemicals and exportable services. In January 1999, it launched its Industry 21 strategy, a 10-year plan to 'develop Singapore as a vibrant and robust global hub of knowledge-driven industries'[7] and part of a wider vision to create a knowledge-based economy (KBE).

The Industry 21 initiative provided an important focus for techno-industrial development in the aftermath of East Asia's 1997/98 financial crisis. Although Singapore did not experience its own domestic crisis (unlike South Korea) it was nevertheless affected by the turbulence of the wider region, recording only a 0.4% growth rate in 1998.[8] The Government was quick to respond to crisis-related events. It avoided recourse to a currency devaluation, but decided instead to engineer a tripartite response to reduce business costs. This was achieved through cuts in employers' contributions to the Central Provident Fund (CPF)[9] – the state's mandatory saving scheme – and wage rate reductions negotiated through the National Wage Council (NWC)[10] that varied between 5 to 8%.[11] In addition, the Government provided a fiscal boost to the economy by accelerating development of a number of large-scale infrastructure projects (e.g. its light rail network), increased spending on education and training, and measures and investments to enhance Singapore's role as a centre for e-commerce and R&D.[12] These policies proved generally successful and the Singapore economy recovered strongly in 1999, attaining a 5.4% growth rate for the year and 9.9% for 2000. Moreover, as both domestic and foreign research interviewees commented, the crisis was in many ways beneficial to Singapore in the long run by further strengthening its reputation as a haven for economic and corporate stability in Southeast Asia. As one interviewee commented, 'the Government took advantage of this, promoting Singapore as a risk averse location for inward investment'.[13] The crisis nevertheless exposed some of Singapore's inherent semi-periphery frailties. At the time, the Government was seriously concerned about the possible flight of foreign capital from the economy on which it so fundamentally depended. In addition, many of Singapore's local SMEs integrated into international sub-contracting networks were badly affected by the crisis and have either gone bankrupt or have yet to fully recover.

The negative impact of the 1997/98 regional financial crisis notwithstanding, Singapore over the longer term is one of the 20th Century's economic success stories, having transformed itself from a third world port city into a highly developed city-state economy. In 2000, it was the second richest state in Asia (after Japan) and the fourth richest in the world, attaining an income per capita level of around $30,000 by the mid-1990s. Other key aspects of Singapore's development context are now considered.

3.2.2 A Global City-State in the Southeast and East Asian Region

Singapore is often described as a global city-state in the commercial tradition of ancient Greek or medieval Italian city-states, for example Venice. It has developed into a modern trading centre and regional hub that maintains relatively high degrees of commercial innovation and economic freedom. Yet as the Singapore state's economic bureaucracy is keen to stress,[14] the city-state's comparison with other global city economies (for example London, New York, Tokyo) rather than with national economies is more appropriate when judging its relative economic development and prosperity. Furthermore, Singapore is a 'trading state'[15] in that its economy's export-orientation and entrepot function[16] form an underlying basis of its FEP. In acknowledging Singapore's aspirations of global city-statehood, Foreign Minister Rajaratnam commented in February 1972 that: 'We draw sustenance not only from the region but also from the international economic system to which we as a Global City belong and which will be the final arbiter of whether we prosper or decline'.[17] This resonates of both the overt regional and global dimensions of Singapore's FEP, in that whilst it seeks to exploit economic synergies with its Southeast Asian neighbours – as demonstrated by the IMSGT arrangement and active participation in the ASEAN Free Trade Area (AFTA) project – the city-state has simultaneously positioned itself a key node in the global economy. Indeed, as is discussed throughout this chapter, the predominance of foreign capital in the Singapore economy is a prime factor in the FEP calculus. Furthermore, while the Singapore state's regionalization and globalization strategies are intended to be mutually reinforcing, they often set off counteracting forces within its FEP framework, as will be later discussed at some length.

Traditionally, Singapore's commercial role in the region has centred on its entrepot trade function.[18] In more recent times it has become the pre-eminent centre for global capital in Southeast Asia, acting as a crucial regional node for various global networks of production, finance, marketing and increasingly research and development (R&D), as well as trade itself. It is ultimately Singapore's embrace of economic globalization that underlies the basis of its global city-statehood. The city-state has a strong case for being considered the world's most globalized economy. Foreign MNEs dominate Singapore's industries, exports, investment and technological development. Along with Hong Kong, it has the world's highest trade-to-GDP ratios. Moreover, Singapore's FEP protagonists continue ardently to promote the city-state as the ideal export platform for high value-added activities in East Asia.

Understanding Singapore's position in the regional economy, and its intermeshing with the global, is also critical. Initial policy attempts to develop Singapore's economic engagement in the regional locale began in the late 1980s with the IMSGT project. Here, Singapore acts as the core of a transborder sub-regionalized economy, promoting the integration of its business activities with the neighbouring provinces of Johor (Malaysia) to the north and Riau (Indonesia) to the south and southwest (Perry 1991). As part of this development, Singapore's first foreign industrial parks (FIPs) were established at Batam and Bintan Islands in Indonesia's Riau province during the early 1990s (see Table 3.2). Singapore's prime economic motives behind the IMSGT were to assist the process of techno-industrial restructuring in the city-state, promoting the shift of lower tech production to Johor and Riau and thus making room for more higher tech activities in the city-state.

In 1995, the Government formally introduced its 'Regionalisation 2000' strategy that added further momentum to these developments and had three main objectives, these being: (i) the extension of its FIP policy to more distant Asian locations, e.g. China; (ii) enhancing Singapore's role as a 'value-adding' gateway to the Asia Pacific for foreign MNEs; (iii) establishing stronger linkages with regional economies to further develop its manufacturing and service sectors. Hence, by the mid-1990s, Singapore's economic regionalization objectives had broadened from the sub-regional focus of the IMSGT to the pan-regional geographic focus of the Asia-Pacific. As Yeoh and Willis (1997) commented around the time on this strategy, "going regional" is seen as a primary strategy to transcend Singapore's domestic constraints of land and labour as well as capitalise on the rapid economic development and industrialisation of the Asia-Pacific region' (p. 184). During the early years of Singapore's regionalization drive there was a significant increase of its outward FDI into neighbouring countries. Over the years 1993 to 1995, the stock of Singapore's FDI in China rose five-fold from S$444m to S$2.4bn, whilst that in Indonesia grew six-fold from S$517m to S$3.4bn.

These figures partly reflected the increasing internationalization of Singapore's local companies, albeit mostly within the East Asian region. The Government's motives for promoting such internationalization largely derive from concerns over the 'crowding out' of local firms by foreign MNEs in the Singapore economy (Lee, W.K.M. 1997). Various attempts have been made by the state to address the apparent marginalization of local entrepreneurship. In 1978, the Government introduced the Product Development Assistance Scheme to assist indigenous manufacturers to develop new product and process capabilities, and to enhance their international competitiveness. This was followed in the 1990s by the Local Industries Upgrading Programme, whereby both foreign MNEs and Singapore's government-linked companies, or GLCs, were encouraged to transfer technology and know-how to their local subcon-

Table 3.2 Summary profile of selected Singaporean Foreign Industrial Parks (FIPs)

FIP	Start-up Year	Size	No. of investors	Investments	Nationality of investors
Batam, Indonesia	1991	500 ha	87	$306m	Japan 48%, S'pore 26%, Europe 13%, US 5%, others 8%
Bintan, Indonesia	1992	4 km^2	25	$88m	S'pore 74%, Japan 22%, others 4%
Suzhou, China	1994	70 km^2	85	$2,860m	US 34%, S'pore 27%, Europe 15%, Japan 14%, others 10%
Wuxi, China	1995	1 km^2	48	$585m	Japan 37%, Asia 31%, Europe 17%, US 15%
Ho Chi Min, City, Vietnam	1997	500 ha	25	$312m	S'pore 56%, Japan 16%, Europe 12%, others 16%
Bangalore, India	1997	100 ha	16	$167m	Europe 43%, India 28%, S'pore 18%, Japan 10%, US 1%

Source: Singapore Investment News, May 1998

tractor firms. Later that decade, the Government launched its Promising Local Enterprises scheme that was specifically designed to develop 100 local enterprises into S$100m sales firms by 2005. While these schemes have achieved some success, Singapore's developmental paradigm continues to depend heavily on hosted foreign capital (Low 1998).

3.2.3 A Developmental City-State

The origins of the Singapore developmental state date back to the independence of the city-state itself. On assuming power, Lee Kwan Yew and his fellow PAP leaders recognized the need for state-guided development given the Singapore's domestic economic and international circumstances. Squeezed between their volatile neighbours (i.e. Malaysia and Indonesia) and presiding over an underdeveloped and weak local business sector, the newly independent Singapore Government was confronted with the fundamental challenge of ensuring economic and political survival. One of the PAP's first economic policies was to establish the EDB, which was given the responsibility of spearheading Singapore's 'late industrialization' drive. The EDB was designed as a multi-functional organization with divisions on financing, industrial facilities, and technical consulting services, as well as being a general one-stop agency for industrial promotion. It remains the state's main partner agency to those foreign MNEs attracted to Singapore's industrial estates. In 1968, the EDB was rationalized, seeing its financial division delegated to the newly formed Development Bank of Singapore, and its industrial development and management arm forming the basis of the new Jurong Town Corporation (JTC),[19] which oversaw Singapore's premier industrial estate to the south west of the island.

As Asher (1994) observed more generally, 'the state has acted as strategist, planner, regulator or enforcer, manager and administrator, entrepreneur, social engineer, and a direct participant in economic activities' (p. 795). State strategic planning still aims to improve the techno-industrial capacity of the economy to keep up with the new demands of the global market (Ermisch and Huff 1999, Huff 1995a, Ramesh 1995). This has most recently focused on transforming Singapore into a knowledge-based economy, or KBE. Other aspects of Singapore's developmental statism are strongly apparent. The state's bureaucratic cadres have long exhibited strong technocratic insulation, and have drawn upon the best managerial talent of Singapore's impressively educated population. Moreover, as discussed later in the chapter, a high degree of ministerial coherence and co-ordination is evident in the Singapore state's bureaucratic machinery.

The state-owned enterprise policy of the Government forms another important feature of 'Singapore Inc.'. This primarily relates to two main types of public enterprise, namely statutory boards and government-linked companies

(GLCs). Statutory boards are autonomous organizations established by Acts of Parliament but which come under the aegis of relevant government ministries. For example, both the EDB and Trade Development Board (TDB) – responsible for promoting Singapore's trade – are affiliated to the Ministry of Trade and Industry (MTI). In contrast, GLCs are state-owned enterprises intended to fill strategic gaps in the economy.[20] High profile examples include Neptune Orient Lines (shipping), Intraco (trading), Singtel (telecommunications), the Development Bank of Singapore and Singapore Airlines.[21] Just as in Taiwan, Singapore's state-owned enterprises have been used to extend the economy's regional and global reach. On the whole, this has proved a relatively successful venture into public entrepreneurship, and an important element of the Singapore state's transformative economic capacity.

One of the more unique features of Singapore's developmental statism is the state's choice of developmental partnership with foreign rather than domestic capital, and therefore in contrast with South Korea and Taiwan. In addition to the aforementioned security motivations behind this early developmental strategy was the PAP's decision to counter-check the political influence exerted by the local business sector. The state's subsequent relationship nurtured with foreign capital has been central to understanding Singapore's dynamic economic development (Rodan 1989). Another key feature concerns the special nature of state–society relations in Singapore. In one sense, Singapore's civil society has made a developmental bargain with the state, or more specifically with the consistently ruling PAP, in that it has proved largely willing to trade-off limited civil rights against the progressive levels of prosperity delivered by the same soft authoritarian political regime that has held sway for over 40 years. It is the PAP Government's economic success that thus maintains high levels of public support for its policies, and that also constitutes an important binding of Singapore Inc.

In sum, the Singapore state may well be a comparatively autonomous policy-making unit with a high level of technocratic insularity, yet it maintains various dialogue channels with representations from business and civil society, hence being consistent with Evans' (1995) concept of the embedded autonomy of developmental states. The transnational business community in particular provides useful information via consultative interaction that assists the state in making rational strategic decisions in shaping Singapore's future developmental path. As research interviews confirmed, foreign MNEs in particular view the Singapore state itself as a strategic alliance partner in their international business operations. Thus, developmental statism remains strongly evident in the Singapore political economy (Huff 1999, Low 1998, Perry *et al* 1997). As with its NIE-3 counterparts, Singapore's developmental statism is evolving in accordance with a fast changing global economic environment. Part of this process has entailed a shift to the objectives of 'new developmentalism', as discussed previously in Chapter 2. One especial area of interest here concerns the Government's recent endeavours both to develop the city-state's cultural amenities and to foster creative thinking amongst Singapore's citizens. While this is intended to improve the quality of public life in the city-state, it is more importantly an attempt to develop the socio-economic fabric and human resources required to sustain the future development of the KBE. To conclude, Singapore's developmental statism and its advanced semi-periphery position in the world economy form a critical development context to the city-state's foreign economic policy. As this chapter reveals, this particularly relates to its function as a regional platform and hub for foreign capital.

3.3 COGNITIVE–IDEOLOGICAL APPROACHES

What is apparent when analysing the cognitive–ideological approach of Singapore's FEP is its multi-faceted nature, and how seemingly opposing ideologies can co-exist with each other. This must be considered, though, alongside the often argued line that the study of 'isms' in Singapore's political economy is redundant as the city-state's leaders have never been tied to any dogmatic values and beliefs, and if anything have pursued a non-ideological approach to economic policy. As Huff (1994) commented, 'the clear policy lessons of Singapore's achievement of economic development were adaptability to world conditions, pragmatism and a relative absence of ideology' (p. 369). The ideological origins of the PAP itself were rooted in the leftist tradition but it is its own blend of home grown ideology, customized to the city-state's geopolitical and geoeconomic circumstances, that is most discernible.

To generalize, Singapore's leadership has adopted a neo-realist worldview in matters of geopolitics and traditional security issues. Lee Kuan Yew speaking in October 1966 remarked that 'in the last resort it is power which decides what happens and, therefore, it behoves us to ensure that we always have overwhelming power on our side'.[22] As Leifer (2000) argued, the PAP Government's prescription to the neo-realist paradigm in matters of core foreign policy has persisted, as revealed by Foreign Minister S. Jayakumar comments in July 1997 that 'the dynamics of international relations bear a striking resemblance to the laws of the jungle: not all creatures are created equal and only the fittest survive'.[23] According to one research interviewee, this constant view of Singapore's foreign policy-makers derived from an 'ideology of survival' long perpetrated by the PAP, in that from the earliest days of independence its leaders have been wary of the city-state's fundamental vulnerability.[24] As another interviewee observed, 'Singapore first faced the communist threat, then the ethnic threat of being a Chinese-based community in a Malay sea, and with the crisis it faced the threat from regional economic breakdown'.[25] Moreover, Perry *et al* (1997) contended that the PAP's persistent reminder to fellow Singaporeans of the city-state's inherent vulnerability in the international system served the Party's own purposes, in that 'maintaining a permanent state of insecurity has helped keep the state free from the challenge of alternative agendas' (p. 6).[26]

Yet this apparent neo-realist approach in Singapore's core foreign policy must be reconciled with the neo-liberalism that is strongly evident in its core FEP. As discussed in Chapter 1, the overlap between the empirical domains of foreign policy and foreign economic policy, as well as that between the geopolitical and the geoeconomic, is invariably considerable and often hotly contested. More to the point, Singapore's policy elite has demonstrated that two seemingly opposite ideological nodes can co-exist and indeed be mutually reinforcing within this overlap. The neo-liberalism of Singapore's FEP protagonists specifically relates to their free trade advocacy, which in turn is a function of the city-state's entrepot position in the international economy. The technical policy realms of its FEP maintain highly liberalized commercial regimes. It is from Singapore's free market approach to trade and FDI, as well as the pro-business disposition of the state, that the neo-liberal basis underpinning its economic policy formation was asserted (Friedman 1988). However, this was liberalism with a realist or even mercantilist purpose. As Singapore's Finance Minister, Richard Hu, articulated in his 1997 budget statement, 'we have no choice but to be open and to compete in the world market to *survive and prosper* (my emphasis). We can grow faster by taking advantage of global markets and advanced technology... Adapting nimbly to changes in the environment and staying relevant to global demand remains fundamental to Singapore's survival'.[27] Hence, the imperatives of remaining both economically open to the global market and competing effectively within it are closely associated in the minds of Singapore's FEP protagonists. As with its NIE-3 counterparts, the state's attention to upgrading Singapore's techno-industrial competitiveness remains a perpetual high priority. We later examine in the technical policy realm of Singapore's FEP how the 'promotive' (but not 'protectionist') aspects of a neo-mercantilist approach – e.g. state promotion of strategic industries and exports – are still very salient. In returning to the issue of 'survival' ideology to further developing this point, Yeung (2000) revealingly commented that the 'discourse of survivalism and competition has sustained Singapore's competitiveness in the face of global competition' (p. 146).

Further connections between neo-realism and neo-liberalism within Singapore's survival ideology are closely linked to the 'global city' concept first proposed by Foreign Minister Rajaratnam in 1972, whereby he suggested that for the city-state to survive it must establish relationships based on economic interdependence in the rapidly expanding global economic system.[28] As we discuss later, Singapore's highly internationalized economy depends greatly on the maintained stability and security of that system, and the city-state's highly effective FEP protagonists have thus sought where possible to promote a stable balance of power between major economies in both regional and global contexts. This is particularly exemplified in our study on Singapore's economic diplomacy with respect to the city-state's catalytic alliance-building role. Thus, Singapore's active participation in 'managed' economic interdependence (a neo-liberal institutionalist concept) is compatible with the survival ideology (essentially a neo-realist concept) still ardently adhered to by the PAP Government. It is in this cognitive–ideological crucible that Singapore's FEP is forged.

As Regnier (1991) contended, the various external challenges facing Singapore required such a pragmatic and adaptable approach to state policy, and political dogmatism would have only limited the state's room for policy manoeuvre in a fast changing and unpredictable regional–international environment. There are also other cognitive–ideological facets that demand comment, especially regarding the accommodation of economic culture. Unlike their Malaysian counterparts, references made by Singapore's FEP protagonists to 'Asian values' have been used more as a rhetorical device in regional economic diplomacy than an actual basis for FEP conduct. Nevertheless, the Singapore state still produces technocrats who identify strongly with Confucianist ethics, and thus an administration that believes society should 'conform to the rules of good social conduct defined by the elders' (Regnier 1991: 241). This also legitimizes in their minds the need for a strong state-centric approach to foreign economic policy. In 1991, the Government introduced a Confucian-based national ideology known as 'shared values' aimed at reinforcing Confucianist 'group ethic' values amongst Singaporeans. Such a move could be interpreted as a counter-measure to the infiltration of Western values in the highly internationalized city-state, especially with regard to maintaining the integrity of Singapore's paternalistic Confucian state and its core values – an important basis of its developmental statism. Indeed, as Rahim (1998) argued, 'democratic developments in many Northeast Asian societies such as Taiwan and South Korea have made it intellectually problematic for the PAP Government to sustain its conservative interpretation of Confucian ideology' (p. 63). Yet while Singapore's citizens remain willing to make the aforementioned trade-off between civil liberties for economic prosperity, the PAP's core values, and the strong state-centric approach to foreign economic policy in general, are likely to prevail.

The 'distant horizon', strategic approach of Singapore's FEP protagonists constitutes another key cognitive–ideological facet for consideration. This relates to both the long-term and strong geoeconomic perspectives that inform the city-state's FEP formation, which in turn are largely attributable to developmental statism. The Singapore Government expends a great deal of technocratic effort and resources to develop its foresight capacity, not just in terms of anticipating

Singapore's own future development but also in trying to anticipate future trends in the global economy.[29] It is such attention to longer-termism inherent in this 'distant horizon' approach that shapes many aspects of Singapore's foreign economic policy, as subsequent sections of this chapter illustrate.

3.4 GENERIC 'ECONOMIC SECURITY' OBJECTIVES

Commensurate with the preceding debate on the PAP's adherence to a 'survival ideology', Singapore has maintained a strong security complex ever since its attained independence. As Leifer (2000) commented, 'Singapore is a state whose foreign policy is rooted in a culture of siege and insecurity which dates from the traumatic experience of an unanticipated separation from Malaysia in August 1965' (p. 4). The political continuity of the PAP in government has helped sustain this view, and moreover Leifer argued that the city-state's security crisis is not just contemplated in terms of political survival but also in terms of defending its sustained economic achievement. Thus, safeguarding Singapore's economic prosperity has broad security connotations, and moreover the pursuit of economic security objectives is born largely from the high level of security-consciousness evident in Singapore. Like its NIE-3 counterparts, however, it is the strong implicit pursuit of economic security objectives rather than their definitive explicit pursuit by Singapore's security policy-makers that is most relevant.[30] There are signs that a more explicit pursuit of economic security will emerge in time, with Singapore's Minister of Defence Tony Tan becoming increasingly interested in new security sectors (MINDEF 2000).[31]

More generally, Singapore's economic development strategy is generally acknowledged to have been subservient to a broader security strategy – a common NIE-3 theme. This, for example, is evident in both the assiduously cultivated techno-industrial edge over neighbouring rivals and the nurtured stake of Western multinationals in Singapore's future. Furthermore, as Chin (1998) noted, there has been 'a repeated official emphasis on economic performance as a basis to national security' (p. 307). This issue is highly politicized in the sense that a strong motivation behind this strategy has been to ensure the longevity of the ruling PAP regime, with which most Singaporean citizens attribute the dual achievement of delivering economic prosperity and national security over the last four decades.

Singapore's size, one of world's smallest of any state, heightens its sense of foreign enclosure, and is exacerbated by its generally unpredictable relations maintained with its much larger neighbours, namely Indonesia and Malaysia. In this sense, Singapore's pursuit of economic security has focused on extending beyond its borders in search of what Minister of Trade and Industry, George Yeo, referred to as "multidimensional space" – the kind that is created by diplomacy, economic alliances, overseas investments and international networking'.[32] This currently relates to Singapore's endeavours to develop a 'second' or 'external' wing to its economy, with particular respect to the IMSGT and the various FIPs that Singapore has propagated around East Asia (Table 3.2). Moreover, in this respect the Singapore state has not just sought to develop its hub economy function confined to the regional locale but rather that of a prime node within the circuitry of global economy. The city-state's FEP protagonists are also highly conscious of the economy's semi-peripheral fragility. For example as Wilson (2000) comments, 'Singapore is potentially very vulnerable to a fall in export earnings, short-term and long-term capital outflows, gyrations in international interest rates, and imported inflation, given its heavy dependence on imports and MNEs and its financial openness' (pp. 117–8). Our following analysis confirms that Singapore's pursuit of economic security objectives involve a broad spectrum of FEP challenges.

3.4.1 Supply Security

In one respect, Singapore's fundamental supply security interests are reducible to this predicament: it is a small trading state with virtually no natural resources and no indigenous economic hinterland that must sustain the material demands of a highly industrialized and developed territory. Given this acute dependence on strategic industrial materials such as energy fuels and water, maintaining channels to their access is a key FEP concern for Singapore. Of course, it is not the only industrialized state to feel strategically vulnerable when their supply of oil or other foreign fuels become compromised, or the prices of which rise sharply as experienced in the latter half of 2000. However, Singapore's supply vulnerability is more critical than most, as perhaps best demonstrated by its dependence on foreign neighbouring sources for much of its water.

Singapore relies on Malaysia for about half of its total freshwater requirements. The city-state's expanding techno-industrial base and increasingly prosperous population have over time added greater demand pressure upon Malaysian water supplies. If the Malaysian authorities ever decided to cut off this supply, Singapore's industry and society would grind to a halt. In 1962, Singapore negotiated an accord with Malaysia in which it agreed to supply water to the city-state for 99 years (i.e. until 2061).[33] The first third period of this contract had not expired before the Singapore Government sought further assurances from Malaysia and from the mid-1990s onwards, Singapore has been pressing Malaysia to commit to a new 100-year agreement ending in 2161. The city-state even made an abortive offer of financial assistance to Malaysia during the 1997/98 East Asian financial crisis in return for securing a new water deal.

This whole issue exposes two key features of Singapore's foreign economic policy. First, it reveals the 'distant horizon' strategic thinking of its FEP protagonists previously noted. There are very few governments currently engaged in foreign economic negotiations over a contract that expires in 60 years' time. Second, the water supply issue demonstrates the emerging interdependence within that same calculus. Whilst Malaysia declares a reluctance to allocate too much land as water catchment areas in the Johor province because of competing pressures for developed land usage, it remains in its own economic interests to supply water to Singapore's industry to maintain Johor's own economic development on track. In other words, by compromising Singapore's own economy it compromises that of a key economic region of Malaysia. Another aspect of this interdependent relationship concerns Singapore selling treated water back to Johor, although Malaysia's development of its own water treatment capacity gradually attenuates this technological and supply dependence. Similar themes are discussed later regarding Singapore's trans-border economic community security.

Indonesia also figures in Singapore supply security interests, with particular respect to its supply of natural gas to the city-state. We later discuss under economic diplomacy two important Indonesian gas supply deals signed by Singapore in 1999 and 2001. Suffice to say here that the Singapore Government is looking to use these projects to develop a future trans-ASEAN gas pipeline, which although wrought with many technical challenges could help diminish the city-state's energy resource dependency on Indonesia alone. Since the early 1990s, Singapore has also approached Indonesia concerning increasing its raw water supplies from the neighbouring Riau Islands.[34] Both Singapore and Indonesia are also party to an agreement with Malaysia concerning the safety of maritime navigation within the Straits of Malacca, one of the world's busiest shipping routes and of great commercial importance to Singapore given its regional entrepot role.[35] More generally, Singapore co-operates quite closely with Malaysia and Indonesia within the Federation of ASEAN Shipping in concerted attempts to tackle piracy problems in the Straits. Singapore and Japan have also more recently announced their intentions to address this issue, motivated by similar supply security objectives.[36] Any significant threat to these supply routes constitutes a threat to Singapore as a trading state, and hence maintaining their integrity is of prime FEP priority.

Finally, Singapore's supply security predicament has increasingly extended into the domain of human resource shortages. This particularly relates to supply of foreign workers to fill human resource gaps at both the high end (e.g. techno-preneurs) and low end (e.g. construction workers) of the labour market.[37] The former is a more recent development, where the Singapore state's 'foreign talent' policy has involved brokering contracts with foreign business schools to establish campuses in the city-state as a means to propagate the human capital required to sustain the emerging knowledge-based economy, or KBE. These and other incentives are intended to act as a regional magnet for the best young managerial and technical talent to study,[38] and hopefully thereafter reside and work, in Singapore. Like other supply security issues discussed, Singapore's economic diplomacy in this respect is essentially problematic insofar as its strong gravitational pull for economic resources – whether they be natural or human – risks appearing like a mini 'black hole' to its regional partners. By sucking in a growing proportion of Southeast Asia's finest young talent in pursuit of its own economic security interests, Singapore's actions will undoubtedly cause notable disquiet within certain quarters of ASEAN's membership. As with the water issue, Singapore FEP protagonists are compelled to exercise considerable sensitivity when negotiating with its lesser-developed neighbours, especially regarding any perceived rapacious nature of its economic demands. Moreover, the city-state's dependency on these critical resource supplies provides both Malaysia and Indonesia with potentially important leverage in their relations with Singapore.

3.4.2 Market Access Security

As noted in Chapter 1, upholding market access security interests is a particular priority for small trading states given their comparative dependence on foreign markets to generate prosperity domestically. Cutting off Singapore's access to key foreign markets would effectively cripple its export-based, entrepot-functioning economy. Hence, Singapore not only practises free trade but also ardently promotes it within every audience of its economic diplomacy. At the regional level, it has been a vocal advocate of the AFTA initiative from the very start, with Southeast Asia still representing a large market for Singapore's exports (see Table 3.3). For similar reasons, it has strongly backed the trade liberalization and facilitation endeavours of the Asia–Pacific Economic Co-operation (APEC) forum, whose membership are committed to create a free trade and investment zone across the Asia–Pacific by 2020. As is discussed in more detail under systemic security, Singapore also keenly supports the World Trade Organization (WTO) regime and upholding multilateral trade order in general. Recent trading missions made by TDB delegations have covered an ever wider geographic spread of 'emerging markets', embracing Africa, Central Asia, Latin America, Central and Eastern Europe, and the Middle East (Yeung 2000). This active targeting of export markets that still constitute little commercial value to Singapore is indicative of both the 'distant horizon' approach of its FEP protagonists and the fuller global dimension to the city-state's foreign economic policy being currently fostered.

Table 3.3 Geographic breakdown of Singapore's international trade (percentage per trade partner, 1960–1999)

	1960		1970		1980		1990		1997		1998		1999	
	Imports	Exports	Imports	Exports	Imports	Exports	Imports	Exports	Imports	Exports	Imports	Exports	Imports	Exports
Japan	7.3	4.5	13.5	7.6	18.0	8.1	20.1	8.8	17.6	7.1	16.2	6.6	16.7	7.4
China	3.4	2.5	5.1	1.5	2.6	1.6	3.4	1.5	4.3	3.2	4.6	3.7	5.1	3.4
Asian NIEs[1]	2.7	2.7	4.7	5.6	3.2[2]	9.2[2]	10.2	12.3	10.3	17.0	9.3	15.0	10.6	15.7
ASEAN	57.1	39.5	28.7	34.7	20.7	27.8	19.9	24.8	22.5	27.8	22.6	23.9	23.8	25.8
United States	3.8	7.0	10.8	11.1	14.1	12.5	16.1	21.3	16.9	18.4	17.9	19.9	17.1	19.2
Canada	0.3	1.4	0.5	1.2	0.5	0.7	0.6	0.9	0.5	0.3	0.4	0.5	0.4	0.4
Australasia	2.8	5.4	5.1	3.8	2.6	5.8	2.2	2.9	1.5	2.7	1.4	3.2	1.5	3.1
EU15	15.8	20.6	16.4	17.8	12.6	14.4	13.8	15.0	13.4	13.9	13.5	15.8	12.7	15.2
Middle East	3.1	1.2	9.3	2.3	22.6	6.4	11.0	2.5	7.7	1.6	6.3	2.0	7.1	1.6
Africa	0.5	1.7	1.5	3.5	1.0	4.4	0.7	2.0	0.5	1.1	0.6	1.1	0.4	1.0
Latin America[3]	0.1	3.0	0.9	1.7	0.8	2.6	1.2	1.3	1.0	1.7	1.1	1.7	1.0	1.7
Other	3.1	10.5	3.5	9.2	0.5	6.5	0.8	6.7	3.8	5.2	5.1	6.6	3.6	5.5

Notes:
1. Hong Kong, South Korea and Taiwan;
2. Excludes Taiwan for this year;
3. Includes the Caribbean states.

Source: IMF Direction of Trade Statistics, various editions

Singapore has certain advantages on its side in the pursuit of market access security. First, its liberal commercial regimes have made its trade partners more conducive to opening up their markets to Singapore exports. Owing to its non-protectionist trade regime, Singapore faces no reciprocated protectionist constraints on its own exports, either of a sectoral or cross-sectoral nature. Second, around 80% of its export production is attributable to hosted foreign MNEs and much of this eventuates as intra-firm trade, whereby the MNE is simply exporting intermediate products to other nodes in their transnational production chains. It is invariably in the economic interests of other node-importing countries to ease the flow of this trade to permit their own domestic efficiencies to be captured. Moreover, MNEs are able to deploy their own techniques, such as transfer pricing, to offset most constraints imposed upon their intra-firm trade flows. Third, MNEs make powerful allies in many instances of market access diplomacy, allying the 'economic logic' of globalization to neo-liberal arguments concerning the benefits of trade liberalization. While Singapore's FEP formation remains essentially state-centred, we later discuss under 'contesting influences' how the Government has nevertheless fostered a close consultative relationship with the hosted foreign MNE community in which, *inter alia*, issues of market access are constantly discussed. More generally, the global trend towards liberalized markets has alleviated this particular economic security concern of Singapore, notwithstanding recent problems experienced in both the WTO and APEC's[39] trade liberalization programmes.

Partly in response to these problems, Singapore has actively engaged in the correspondent emerging trend of Asia–Pacific bilateral free trade agreements (APBFTAs). By 2001, it had signed a free trade agreement with New Zealand, undertaken formalized negotiations for similar agreements with Japan, the US, Australia and Mexico, and initiated joint feasibility studies with Chile,[40] Canada and the European Free Trade Area (EFTA).[41] South Korea is also participating in this APBFTA trend that is helping propagate this parallel form of 'lattice regionalism' within APEC's membership. Singapore's prime motivations for doing so are strongly related to market access security concerns, both in terms of lending what it perceives as much needed momentum behind APEC's trade liberalization process,[42] and as part of a fall back position if this process regresses. Positive gains in market access from the bilateral FTA signed with New Zealand were apparent soon after the agreement came into force on 1 January 2001. During the first two months after this date, Singapore's exports to New Zealand rose by 54% on a year-on-year basis.[43] However, we later discuss how this particular pursuit of market access security could prove counter-productive to Singapore's other economic security interests, with especial regard to systemic security.

3.4.3 Finance–Credit Security

Singapore is one of East Asia's most prominent financial centres. In 1968, the Government established an Asian Dollar Market, the Asian counterpart of the Eurodollar market, the objective being to mobilize the pool of US dollars for lending to Asian borrowers. During the rapid expansion of this market in the 1970s, Singapore also sought to attract international financial institutions (e.g. banks) to the city-state in an attempt to develop its position as a diversified financial centre, and hence to rival Hong Kong. In the 1980s, the Singapore International Monetary Exchange was created for similar motives, establishing the primary centre for foreign exchange transactions in Southeast Asia. While these and other developments in Singapore's financial centre industry have generated substantial profits for the city-state, the transactions conducted here largely concern externalized foreign capital and hence only augment Singapore's own finance–credit security position to a limited degree. As the 1997/98 East Asian financial crisis demonstrated, foreign capital flight in the era of financial globalization can be both sudden and dramatic. Nevertheless, Singapore's development as an international financial centre has been partly driven by the motive of enhancing confidence in the city-state's broad finance–credit status amongst foreign investors.

Interesting parallels can be drawn between Singapore and Taiwan regarding both their response to the 1997/98 crisis and their financial robustness. Whilst many other East Asian states (for example South Korea and Thailand) had spent the 1990s deregulating and liberalizing their financial sectors without due attention to buttressing supervisory and monitoring mechanisms, Singapore and Taiwan's respective monetary authorities – the Monetary Authority of Singapore (MAS) and the Central Bank of China – had not made the same mistake. When the crisis struck, both had in place strong supervisory and regulatory capacities in their international finance policy regimes, undertaking appropriate actions both before and during the crisis to ensure relative stability.[44] Indeed, the MAS continues to closely monitor the actions of currency speculators transacting in the Singapore dollar.[45] As MAS Chief, Lee Hsien Loong, remarked in March 2001: 'we are not against currency speculation *per se*… However, given that the exchange rate is our main policy instrument, we must be able to manage the exchange rate. Hence, we would not feel comfortable with speculators taking very short positions against the Singapore dollar and funding them through local banks'.[46] Such reluctance to relinquish control over a key aspect of financial policy is consistent with a developmental statist approach to finance–credit security, in that it upholds the state's capacity to where possible mediate the economy's (or in this specific case, the currency's) engagement in the international financial system. In addition, both Singapore and Taiwan have amassed a considerable stock of foreign exchange reserves, primarily generated by consistent trade surpluses and representing an important contingency resource when confronted by international financial crisis. However, unlike Singapore, Taiwan cannot rely on the systemic support of the International Monetary Fund (IMF) owing to its marginalized diplomatic status. Yet Singapore joined many other East Asian states in calling for systemic improvements in the governance of international finance after the IMF regime's failure to contain the outbreak of the region's 1997/98 crisis. While Singapore's amassing of foreign exchange reserves to ensure finance–credit security remains a critical objective, strengthening the institutional capacity of IMF and other international financial arrangements (e.g. within the new 'ASEAN Plus 3' framework) is of equally important interest to its FEP protagonists.

Another source of Singapore's financial strength stems from the Government Investment Corporation (GIC), established in 1981 to manage Singapore's accumulated fiscal surpluses and general foreign reserves in excess of foreign exchange management. The GIC's original mission in the 1980s was firstly to diversify the state's assets, and secondly 'interpenetrating Singapore in the core financial and industrial networks of the advanced economies' (Castells 1988: 32). By the 1990s, though, a further objective was added, namely to realize financial profits from the GIC's regional investments so as to expand Singapore's financial reserves. The GIC currently invests its accumulated fund of over $100bn in a long-term oriented portfolio of globally spread assets in over 40 markets, and in real estate mostly located in advanced industrial countries.[47] No funds are invested in Singaporean assets owing to any conflict of interest that may arise, and they have not been drawn upon for short-term purposes. The GIC's role in Singapore's foreign economic policy relates not just to its managed global spread of domestically generated funds, but also in safeguarding a strategically critical contingency fund for use during future unforeseen emergencies.[48] This latter function is again indicative of the 'distant horizon' approach of Singapore's FEP protagonists and the extent of the city-state's vulnerability complex, insofar that a fund of this considerable magnitude be hypothecated to underwrite such a long-term economic security 'insurance policy'.

3.4.4 Techno-Industrial Capacity Security

Singapore's post-independence economic development has largely depended on its ability to attract foreign MNEs to locate increasingly technology-intensive export production activities within its well-organized and serviced industrial estates. As previously noted, the strength of perceived connection between techno-industrial development and the wider spectrum of national security interests has been perpetuated in the minds of the ruling PAP elite. Furthermore, successfully sustaining this developmental edge confers Singapore with greater economic diplomacy options, for example by participating in fora with other high-income, industrialized nations. For these and other reasons, maintaining a strong techno-industrial capacity – most recently centred on cultivating the KBE – is of critical importance to Singapore's broad strategic interests in the international system.

It is under this security theme that the distinction between domestic and foreign economic policy is especially blurred. The Singapore state has adopted various human resource development and infrastructural policies that have successfully enhanced the economy's techno-industrial capacity. Other domestic-level policies designed to enhance Singapore's industrial competitiveness are highly *associative* with those at the FEP technical *core*, for example inward FDI policy. Indeed, Singapore's inward FDI policy has long been synonymous with its industrialization policies given the persisting dependence of the city-state's techno-industrial capacity on hosted foreign MNEs (Lee, W.K.M. 1997). However, such is the sophistication of this capacity that the Singapore state, via the EDB, often exercises a high level of selectivity in choosing only those inward investments best able to construct the knowledge-based economy.[49] It is this ability to attract high-technology inward FDI, and hence high-technology transfer and assimilation, which remain critical to Singapore's long-term economic security. This critical role performed by Singapore's FDI policy therefore continues to rank as an FEP priority objective, and has been used to diversify the city-state's export production base. Like its NIE-3 counterparts, Singapore's exports are concentrated in a few industrial sectors, with office machines, electronic products and telecommunications equipment accounting for 62% of its merchandise exports in 1999. As an additional final comment, Singapore's engagement in the IMSGT has played some part in assisting the techno-industrial restructuring of its economy, by the transborder relocation of mature technology production that has made way for higher-technology production within its industrial estates, as well as helping to secure access to key industrial resources.

3.4.5 Socio-Economic Paradigm Security

For a state with virtually no trace of economic nationalism, defending the integrity of Singapore's socio-economic paradigm as part of its FEP may appear highly incongruous. On the one hand, there have been Lee Kwan Yew's much touted 'Asian value' apologetics, the aforementioned Confucianist 'shared values' promoted by the Goh Chok Tong Administration since the early 1990s, and more recent efforts to develop a distinct 'ethno-national' identity (e.g. the 'Speak Mandarin' campaign) insofar as this is permissible in a multi-racial society. On the other hand, the global culturization of Singapore society and highly internationalized nature of the economy suggests a state that has actively embraced foreign influences, synthesizing or simply accommodating best practices from overseas in order to enhance the city-state's prosperity-generating capabilities. Malaysia certainly offers a better example of a state using its FEP to resist foreign pressure to assimilate 'foreign' norms associated with a counter-paradigm, for example 'Western' neo-liberalism.

While, though, Singapore has openly embraced many aspects of globalization, it has also resisted others. In an age of diminished state responsibilities, Singapore's FEP formation remains highly state-centred. As previously mentioned, the Government may be pro-business but most importantly it works in close developmental partnership with hosted foreign MNEs in ultimate accordance to state-determined interests and policy blueprints. Moreover, its own brand of economic liberalism is a variant hybrid of deregulation and re-regulation, as seen in Singapore's international finance policy. This, as well as more *dirigiste* economic policies maintained by the state, is strongly connected to the 'inward-looking' economic security agenda of the PAP in that the defence of Singapore's developmentalism equates with the defence of the domestic political regime. Sustained prosperity-enhancing improvements delivered by the PAP to Singaporean citizens form the bedrock of its mono-regime legitimacy. Thus, although Singapore's liberal commercial regimes have deflected pressures of neo-liberal advocacy encountered by its East Asian counterparts in their economic diplomacy, the PAP – whilst it remains in power – may be expected to ardently resist any externalized threats to Singaporean developmentalism.

3.4.6 Transborder Community Security

Given Singapore's small size, geographic location and geopolitical position, its susceptibility to transborder community factors and associated spillovers, is quite pronounced. Surrounded by two much larger states with which political tensions still simmer, Singapore has sought to emphasize the economic dimension of 'border management' with both Malaysia and Indonesia. The IMSGT forms the centrepiece of this strategy and plays an important part in safeguarding the city-state's economic security interests. For example, the fostering of a more prosperous development at Singapore's borders achieves three main objectives in this respect, as it: (i) strengthens the industrial capacity of its own transborder economic hinterland; (ii) attenuates politico-economic tensions born from marked developmental divides apparent just beyond Singapore's borders; (iii) develops Malaysia and Indonesia's own stake in Singapore's continued economic prosperity and development. More generally, Singapore has used the IMSGT to reinforce perceptions of a transborder 'natural economic zone' existing in the sub-regional locale, with itself at the organizing centre, managing the localized economic interdependence.

However, endeavours to construct an IMSGT-based transborder economic community can only achieve so much. Firstly, it is more a bipedal than a triangular arrangement owing to the still underdeveloped economic linkages between Johor and Riau, and hence undermining the notion of widespread transborder interaction within the IMSGT zone. Secondly, many Singapore-based companies have not been lured by the economic advantages and incentives that accompany relocation in Johor and Riau. Other low-cost locations, such as China, are proving increasingly more attractive in comparison. Thirdly, Singapore's IMSGT partners can only assist its techno-industrial restructuring process to a certain degree. Further infrastructural and human resource development investments are required from both Malaysian and Indonesian sources before future phases of restructuring can be engaged.[50] There is a current feeling that the IMSGT is losing its dynamics and momentum, for the above and 1997/98 crisis-related reasons.[51] As previously noted, since the crisis the Singapore Government has placed more emphasis on the global dimension of foreign economic policy relative to its sub-regional and regional dimensions.

Nevertheless, other transborder community security issues still demand much of the Singapore state's attention. These relate to prior discussed examples under the theme of supply security (e.g. safeguarding maritime supply routes in the Straits of Malacca, freshwater security) and others such as economic migration, post-crisis economic and political instability in Indonesia, and pollution. Regarding the penultimate of these latter issues, Singapore is watching current events in its giant southern neighbour very closely as a possible Balkanization of Indonesia carries with it potentially very significant and wide ranging transborder economic spillovers. It has therefore been in Singapore's interests to assist Indonesia's smooth transition to a new politico-economic paradigm since the 1997/98 crisis.

Forest fire haze constitutes another critical recent transborder community security issue for Singapore, and provides an example of economic security's overlapping with another 'new' security sector, namely environmental security. The economic content of this security concern primarily relates to the substantial damage incurred by forest fire haze pollution to Singapore's tourist and airline industries, as well as to health costs.[52] Singapore, Malaysia and Indonesia collaborate particularly closely within the ASEAN Regional Haze Action Plan, introduced in December 1997 to tackle this transborder externality concern, with Singapore making mostly a technological contribution in the form of satellite monitoring equipment that locates initial forest fire 'hot spots'.

3.4.7 Systemic Security

As an aspiring global city-state, Singapore's interest in upholding the integrity of the international economic system is of fundamental economic security importance. Its export-oriented, inward FDI-based, entrepot functioning economy is highly dependent upon systemic stability, and explains Singapore's strong advocacy of multilateral economic regimes such as the WTO and IMF. Hence, there exists a firm consensus amongst the city-state's FEP protagonists that supporting WTO-led trade liberalization remains Singapore's most important trade diplomacy objective. Moreover, they prescribe to the 'bicycle theory' of multilateral free trade negotiation in that a critical momentum must be sustained, otherwise collapse ensues.[53] Indications of systemic frailty at the millennial eve were thus a cause of much disquiet in Singapore. The twin emergence of a more 'complex multilateralism' and stronger global civil society movement poses a potentially significant economic security threat to the city-state. The encroachment of controversial 'new' trade issues (e.g. labour and environment clause linkage) onto the WTO agenda and the civil society assault on the WTO's institutional foundations have recently posed a destabilizing threat to the multilateral trade order. However, Singapore is placed in a semi-periphery predicament: it must reconcile its shared circumspection with its developing East Asian neighbours regarding 'new' trade issue linkage with its ever closer association to fellow developed countries, many of which actively promote this linkage.

In the meantime, Singapore's APBFTA strategy is intended to keep the flame of trade liberalization alive within the Asia–Pacific region,[54] the partial importance of which derives from APEC's own past demonstrated utility for enhancing multilateral free trade at the WTO level.[55] However, promoting the APBTFA trend may prove counter-productive in the longer-run by bypassing both APEC and WTO channels for trade liberalization, and possibly exposing further the institutionalized weaknesses of these regimes. A similar contradiction of interests may arise in relation to the IMF and international finance. We noted under finance–credit security the importance to Singapore of strengthening the institutional capacity of the IMF, especially after East Asia's 1997/98 financial crisis had revealed the organization's shortcomings in certain areas. Owing partly to a lack of subsequent progress here, Singapore has participated in the new 'ASEAN Plus 3' framework involving Southeast and Northeast Asian countries in developing regional-level financial governance mechanisms, which is discussed in more detail later in the chapter. Promoting regionalized solutions in the face of multilateral-level inertia may, as with the WTO, prove a risk-laden strategy.

3.4.8 Alliance Security

Small, outward-oriented economies like Singapore afford especial priority to nurturing foreign economic relations. Singapore's alliance-building endeavours, and attention to alliance economic security in general, form part of a multi-faceted economic diplomacy that is becoming a defining feature of its foreign economic policy. In recent years, its FEP protagonists have proved effective alliance initiators and catalysts, particularly in the field of inter-regional relations. The Asia–Europe Meetings (ASEM), East Asia – Latin America Forum (EALAF), and ASEAN-Mercosur Agreement all originated from Singaporean diplomatic proposals. Furthermore, Singapore is a key perpetrator of the recent APBFTA trend within the Asia-Pacific, cementing new level ties between it and fellow APEC members. Another important aspect of augmenting closer economic relations with regional partners is its FIP policy in which part of the Singaporean economic paradigm has been transposed onto designated industrial plots across Asia (Table 3.2). These multi-level economic linkages are essentially subordinate to realizing Singapore's various economic security interests, such as those pertaining to supply, market access, techno-industrial capacity and transborder community.

However, recent developments in Singapore's FIP policy reveal some problems of alliance-overreach. We discuss later the associated costs of the Suzhou IP failure in China to Singapore in both financial and reputational terms, with the credibility of Singapore FIP policy suffering some considerable damage. If nothing else, it has provided Singapore with a lesson on the frequently complex interaction between domestic politics and international negotiation. At another level, Singapore's proclivity for alliance-initiation on the broader international stage may compromise its systemic security interests by catalysing bilateral and inter-regional economic partnerships that potentially deflect recourses to various multilateral interactions. Hence, Singapore's strong urge to economic alliance-building must be duly tempered by a systemic risk analysis within the calculus of its economic diplomacy.

The Singapore state's long-standing alliance with transnational capital forms another defining characteristic of its FEP. The symbiotic nature of this state–business relationship has proved highly successful in a commercial sense. Government agencies such as the EDB have developed effective export-production and hub-service platforms for foreign MNEs in the region in return for widespread technology transfer and other high value-added contributions towards meeting Singapore's economic security objectives, especially regarding techno-industrial capacity. This pro-(foreign) business approach of the Singapore state, combined with its liberal commercial regimes, largely explains the generally harmonious bilateral economic relations it enjoys with most trade partners, and to some extent the greater inclination of foreign powers to consider its alliance-initiation schemes in comparison to others.

There is also a strong semi-periphery context to Singapore's alliance diplomacy. As a high income, capital-intensive economy, Singapore's economic interests are arguably more aligned to the core than the periphery. Certainly, its alliance-building with less developed countries (LDCs) remains comparatively weak. For example, we later note how Singapore maintains a relatively modest official development assistance and co-operation (ODAC) programme whose conferred resources to LDCs are almost purely technical and non-financial. This is largely because there exist limited economic security motivations for acting more generously, except in the case of conferring financial assistance to pressing matters of a transborder economic community nature. For these reasons, ASEAN will remain the main focus of Singapore's economic alliance security interests with lesser-developed countries.

3.5 TECHNICAL POLICY REALMS

In the analysis that follows we shall see how there are various approaches at work within the technical policy realms of Singapore's FEP framework. A high degree of continuity is also apparent in terms of each realm's underlying policy principles, which can be at least partly attributed to the PAP's own continuity in government. Other even more enduring factors are also relevant especially in relation to trade policy, which continues to be driven by the requirements of an entrepot functionality that dates back to the 19th century. A liberal, open approach is generally prevalent in the *core* technical policy realm of Singapore's FEP but this is also combined with different forms of state guidance and regulation. For example, the city-state's FDI policy is highly liberalized but as noted under techno-industrial security, the Government is often highly selective in which foreign investments it permits. We later examine in international finance policy how new international financial markets have developed in Singapore largely owing to the Government's open and promotive approach, yet also how the MAS retains measures to negate currency speculation in the Singapore dollar in accordance with its finance–credit security interests. Furthermore, in the *associative* technical policy realm an ardent state activism remains strongly evident. Whilst there has been continuity in policy principle, Singapore's FEP protagonists have by and large adapted their range of technical policies with considerable effect to the changing international economic environment. As is argued throughout this book, this is indicative of the NIE-3's evolving and adaptive developmental statism.

3.5.1 Trade Policy

Entrepots such as Singapore need a liberalized trade policy in order to minimize the transaction costs of its international trading services. It is this entrepot function that primarily explains why Singapore has one of the world's most open trade regimes, with applied tariff levels at or approaching zero percent.[56] Moreover, Singapore-based firms are less dependent on the small domestic market and rely far more on export market demand. To remain cost-competitive, export trading firms need access to low cost imported inputs, and hence a low import tariff regime. For these reasons, Singapore's trade policy is amongst the world's least complex, and by far the least complicated of the NIE-3 group. Nevertheless, Singapore does maintain certain trade restrictions, primarily for health and safety and environmental reasons. For example, imports of automobiles that are at least three years old are banned, and this is in addition to the already stringent environment regulations imposed on cars in Singapore. The import of rice is also licensed on the grounds of food security. In addition, a number of excise duties are applied on alcoholic products, automobiles, motor spirits, and motor oil – products that are largely imported. Furthermore, Singapore had an average bound tariff rate of 9.7% in 1999 (projected to decline to 6.9% by 2005), with almost 30% of lines left unbound, thus providing some degree of uncertainty to its overall tariff regime (WTO 2000a).

Such is the comparative simplicity of Singapore's trade policy that it is often made synonymous with trade diplomacy. A corollary of this is that as foreign trade partners face virtually no barriers to trade with the city-state they are invariably preoccupied with its promotive trade policy and diplomacy initiatives. This is evident at all levels of economic diplomacy. For example, Singapore's highly liberal trade policy regime makes it a natural perpetrator of bilateral FTAs as its trade partners can avoid drawn out negotiations about market access in the city-state. Moreover, Singapore's compliant trade policy adjustment to the demands of its bilateral FTA partners is in most cases minimal. Indeed, its trade policy technocrats working in this area have mostly been busy with attaching other 'promotive' measures to these agreements, such as on investment and finance, and hence connect trade policy to other technical policy aspects of Singapore's FEP.[57] At the regional level, Singapore has pursued further trade policy liberalization, and its wider advocacy therein, through APEC's Early Voluntary Sectoral Liberalization and Accelerated Tariff Liberalization schemes, as well as within the ASEAN Framework Agreement on Services. At the multilateral level, it recently signed the Fourth Protocol (Agreement on Telecommunications Services) and the Fifth Protocol (Agreement on Financial Services) to the WTO's General Agreement on Trade in Services. We note later how Singapore remains sceptical of the so-called 'new' trade issues (e.g. labour and environment standard linkages with trade policy) and the potential scope for trade protectionism they present.

3.5.2 Foreign Direct Investment (FDI) Policy

The fundaments of Singapore's FDI policy still lie in the PAP's original economic development strategy of promoting Singapore as a production and services platform for hosted foreign MNEs. It is both a highly liberal technical policy realm with simultaneously high degrees of state guidance. We have already noted the EDB's central role performed here in attracting foreign investment since the earliest days of Singapore's independence. A few years later the 1967 Economic Expansion Incentives Act introduced important new fiscal incentives to encourage foreign investment, primarily tax concessions on profits. In April 1973 the then Finance Minister, Hon Sui-Sen, announced a two-prong approach to attract higher value-added FDI, these being: intensified efforts to attract more technology-intensive manufacturing investment, such as petrochemicals, machine tools, precision engineering, and sophisticated electronics; and assistance to existing industries to upgrade their skill and technological content. This set the general 'upgrading' theme of the FDI policy development that followed in Singapore.

Moreover, Singapore's FDI policy is to some extent synonymous with its industrialization policy in that the core of Singapore's techno-industrial development has derived primarily from the contributions of hosted foreign MNEs. Hence the state, through its various FDI policy initiatives and strategies, has guided transnational capital's development of the Singapore economy. Over time, general policy measures have comprised a raft of fiscal and structural incentives available to foreign firms, such as: tax incentives for 'pioneer' industrial activity, export enterprises, foreign loans, foreign technology, R&D activities; duty-free importation of machinery and equipment; industrial estates served with high quality amenities and infrastructure; industrial training subsidies (Chen 1983, Chia 1986, Huang 1989, W.K.M. Lee 1997, Lim and Pang 1991, Soon and Stoever 1996).

Furthermore, Singapore's FDI policy remains highly liberal in many aspects. For example, there are extremely limited stipulations and restrictions concerning local content, the exporting and importing activities of foreign firms, and foreign ownership of local company assets. Inward FDI is permitted in most sectors of the economy, with some restrictions maintained in comparatively few service sectors (e.g. insurance, real estate), and even these are being gradually liberalized. For example, the 40% limit on foreign investment in any locally incorporated banks was abolished in 2000, and in the same year all remaining restrictions on foreign investment in the telecommunications sector were also removed (WTO 2000a). Singapore participation in the Framework Agreement of the ASEAN Investment Area (AIA), which will extend national treatment in investment to investors from ASEAN countries by 2010 and subsequently to all investors by 2020, has further liberalized its FDI policy.

The EDB remains at the centre of Singapore's FDI policy formulation and implementation. In terms of policy approach, it now places more emphasis on creating a more effective FDI environment (e.g. infrastructural development, tax exemptions) rather than direct financial inducements, such as job creation grants. For the first few years of the EDB operations, it welcomed almost any inward FDI project. However, as previously noted, it is now far more selective about what foreign investments it permits, affording current priority to those projects that will enhance Singapore's KBE development capacity. This hence more specifically dovetails the city-state's FDI policy into the overarching techno-industrial upgrading strategy of the state. The range of tax incentives deployed to encourage foreign investment in selected industries is thus integral to the Singapore developmental state's own ongoing transformation project.

3.5.3 International Finance Policy

As earlier discussions on Singapore's finance–credit security suggest, international finance has traditionally been amongst the Government's priority policy areas. In close comparison to its Taiwanese counterpart, the Singapore state has adopted a 'guided' liberalization approach to international finance by gradually opening up and developing financial market functionalities whilst retaining strong elements of state capacity in governing them. More specifically, this entailed directing the liberalization process down a particular open market path whilst avoiding another. This approach has evolved in accordance with Singapore's developmental statism and aforementioned economic security objectives. Furthermore, government initiatives in banking and financial services liberalization have essentially aimed at improving Singapore's competitive advantages (Leifer 2000). Interviewed MAS and Ministry of Finance (MOF) officials themselves confirmed that recent financial sector restructuring has been undertaken with this aim in mind.[58] The MAS is the state's key agency in this technical policy realm, and its current policy framework is based on three stated principles, namely:

- *self-governance*: whereby the MAS has taken several initiatives to encourage good corporate governance, rigorous internal controls and effective risk management in Singapore's banks and financial institutions;
- *market discipline*: centring on the imposition of external incentives on banks and financial institutions to conduct business in a sound and effective manner, partly by fostering great information disclosure and through encouraging the adoption of international accounting standards;
- *official oversight*: this in turn comprises of three aspects, these being *regulation*, *supervision* and *surveillance*. Regulation concerns establishing industry-wide rules of behaviour, such as setting capital requirements, prudential limits and permissible activities. Supervision mainly relates to monitoring and inspecting individual institutions to ensure compliance to regulation, as well as assessing the adequacy of risk management

activities. Lastly, MAS surveillance involves monitoring events and developments in the industry for possible systemic risk.[59]

Historically, the MAS has depended heavily on official oversight, and to a lesser extent on self-governance as prime guiding principles on policy. More recently, however, much greater emphasis has been placed on promoting market discipline. Furthermore, within the scope of official oversight there has been a shift away from high regulatory measures towards more risk-focused supervisory policy instruments and the tighter surveillance of markets. This should be understood in the context of financial globalization, and how the move away from monolithic regulation towards a more customized supervisory approach provides greater policy flexibility. In the MAS's own words, 'Shifting the emphasis away from regulation does not imply diminishing its importance. On the contrary, it places a higher premium on regulation being sound. Sound regulation provides the framework for risk-based supervision and surveillance; it also facilitates the effective functioning of... self-governance and market discipline'.[60] The same March 2001 press release later notes how regulation needs to be essentially 'risk-focused', as well as 'responsive and adaptive to changing market conditions'. Such retained state capacity helped steer Singapore through the turbulent waters of the 1997/98 East Asian financial crisis (Weiss 1999).

Developments in exchange rate policy help illustrate the above. From 1907 to 1967, Singapore's currency was fixed to the pound sterling. The 14.3% devaluation of sterling against the US dollar in 1967 prompted the Singapore authorities to peg the currency to the more steadfast US dollar, although sterling was retained as the official intervention currency given Singapore's large stock of sterling reserves. This, however, changed in June 1972 when the US dollar became the city-state's official intervention currency. Further change came in June 1973, when in more general response to the collapse of the Bretton Woods international exchange rate system and the subsequent weakening of the US dollar, Singapore moved to a floating exchange rate system (Peebles and Wilson 1996). This policy regime, which persists today, was never based on a pure floating system, and the Singapore dollar is currently managed within undisclosed target bands set by the MAS in relation to an undisclosed basket of major trading currencies. Moreover, since 1981 the MAS has pursued a policy of allowing the Singapore dollar to strengthen against major currencies. This was recently affirmed in April 2001 when an MAS press release stated that the authority continues to 'stand ready' to intervene in the currency markets to maintain the currency within its policy band.[61]

To maintain this policy, and moreover the state capacity to manage it, the Government has sought to prevent the internationalization of the currency – a process that provides scope for foreign currency speculators significantly to affect the Singapore dollar's exchange rates. Non-internationalization was achieved by imposing a withholding tax on interest earned by non-residents on Singapore dollar holdings, and in addition by MAS directives that restricted the banking system's S$-denominated loans to non-residents or residents for use outside the city-state to the sole purpose of financing Singapore's external trade. In accordance with the MAS's 'guided' liberalization approach, it first began to loosen up its non-internationalization policy in late 1998, allowing foreigners to list S$-denominated shares and issue S$ bonds, as well as transfer currency swap proceeds out of Singapore. It later fully liberalized the market for over-the-counter interest-rate derivatives products, and lifted the S$20m consultation limit for repurchase transactions in Singapore Government Securities and S$ bonds with non-residents.

Most recently under Notice 757 promulgated in December 2000, the MAS announced two further key changes. First, banks could now lend Singapore's currency to non-residents for capital investment purposes in the city-state, and could also extend S$ credit facilities to non-residents to fund offshore activities, so long as the S$ proceeds were changed into foreign currency. The stated policy objective here was to broaden the investor base for Singapore dollar assets whilst effectively cutting off routes to currency speculation. Second, banks could now transact in S$ currency options with other banks and financial institutions in Singapore, thus facilitating the use of currency options for hedging purposes.[62] Consistent with the finance–credit security objectives previously discussed, the primary policy goals of this liberalization policy were, in the words of MAS Managing Director Koh Yong Guan, 'to limit borrowing by non-residents for currency speculation, and to discourage the development of an offshore S$ market'.[63] Thus, the MAS had liberalized Singapore's international finance markets with a developmental purpose in mind, and moreover down a particular route of liberalization but avoiding another.

In other developments, the Government further liberalized Singapore's direct insurance market in March 2000, lifting the 49% restriction on foreign ownership of local insurers. An open market entry policy for insurance brokers was also adopted, adding to previous partial liberalizations that occurred in 1984 and 1990. In March 2001, the MAS introduced further measures designed to add greater liquidity to Singapore's currency exchange market, especially targeting those offshore banks in the city-state wishing to engage in exchange transactions of foreign currency with non-bank organizations. At the same time, the MAS sought to attract foreign fund managers to Singapore to expand its investment base, involving both the MAS and GIC in outplacing funds to external asset managers.[64] However, Singapore's currency exchange market is relatively illiquid owing mainly to the relative lack of Singaporeans who want to change US dollars and other prime currencies for Singapore dollars. This in turn, combined with MAS rules on discouraging the internationalization of the Singapore dollar, has constrained the growth of Singapore's debt (or S$ bond) market.[65]

Some note is also required on the GIC's role in Singapore's international financial policy. This may be characterized as either *passive* or *clandestine*, depending upon your interpretation. It is *passive* in the sense that the GIC mainly accumulates and invests the Singapore Government's globally spread, long-term financial assets without actually initiating policy measures as such. The Corporation is essentially a fund manager working in the service of the state, and whose operations are generally obscured from public scrutiny and knowledge – hence the *clandestine* tag. Returns from the GIC's international investments are ploughed back into its fund portfolio (around $100bn by 2001), with legislation only permitting portfolio funds to be used in extreme emergency cases.[66] The GIC may even be conceived as performing an economic diplomacy function insofar as it establishes financial ties with Singapore's international economic partners.

3.5.4 Official Development Assistance and Co-operation (ODAC) Policy

Singapore itself received foreign technical assistance from the 1950s right up to the late 1970s. Like its NIE-3 counterparts, the Singapore Government began to develop its own ODAC programmes some time before its recipient status ended. Various low-key technical missions from the city-state were despatched from the late 1960s onwards. Its ODAC capacity gradually developed over the years, and in 1992 all programmes were brought together under the Ministry of Foreign Affairs' (MFA) control within its Technical Co-operation Directorate (TCD). The TCD is one of 14 directorates within the MFA and further draws upon the expertise of other government agencies such as the TDB and EDB.

The prime emphasis of Singapore's ODAC policy is on technical assistance rather than financial dispensation, such as grants and loans. Moreover, the MFA prefer to use the term 'development partner' rather than 'donor' in its dealings with recipient countries. The TCD works to a relatively modest $10m annual budget that funds around 250 ongoing projects. In research interviews with MFA officials on this matter, the phrase 'it is better to teach a man how to fish rather than simply give him fish' re-occurred in legitimizing this self-help approach.[67] While this may be laudable, Singapore has been criticized for not offering more extensive and systematic financial aid programmes.[68] It is the richest of the NIE-3 group and yet, based on its technical aid budget, Singapore has a substantially lower ODA/GDP ratio than either South Korea or Taiwan at a mere 0.0001%. Certainly the city-state possesses the financial reserves to be more obliging. However, the Singapore Government has on occasions provided very generous 'one-off' aid packages to developing countries. Examples of such offers to fellow ASEAN members have been previously noted, as also has Singapore's technical contribution to tackling Southeast Asia's forest fire haze problem. Furthermore, an MFA political directorate also dispenses additional humanitarian aid worth around $30m annually, a recent singular instance being the $50,000 worth of emergency supplies it sent in January 2001 to the victims of the Indian earthquake.[69]

All developing countries are eligible for Singapore's ODAC programmes but their main recipients are concentrated in the Asia–Pacific and South Asia regions. The centrepiece of the Government's ODAC policy is the Singapore Co-operation Programme (SCP), established in 1992 and bringing together various technical schemes into a unified operational framework. By 2001, the SCP had sponsored Singapore-based training programmes for over 13 000 officials from some 130 developing countries. Its Bilateral Technical Assistance Programmes (BTAPs) are delivered directly on a government-to-government basis, whereas its Third Country Training Programmes (TCTPs) are offered in conjunction with another country or international organization. In the BTAP scheme, recipient country representatives are invited to Singapore itself where its courses are run. There are a number of separate sub-schemes that operate here, including the Singapore-ASEAN Training Awards and the Singapore Technical Assistance Programme for Sustainable Development. These cover a multitude of training themes, including communications, transport, economic development and trade promotion, environment, healthcare, information technology, management and productivity. Amongst BTAP's most notable successes are the Botswana National Productivity Centre co-developed with the Botswana Government and opened in August 1995, and the Vietnam–Singapore Technical Training Centre set up in June 1999 in a venture within Singapore's FIP at Ho Chi Min City.

The TCTP is run in partnership with 11 countries (Australia, Canada, Denmark, Germany, Japan, Luxembourg, Norway, South Korea, Thailand, the Vatican and the UK) and 11 international organizations, such as the IMF, World Bank and WTO. High profile examples of its work are: the Japan–Singapore Partnership Programme launched in 1994 to offer joint training courses to participants from the Asia–Pacific and Africa (from May 1997); the IMF–Singapore Regional Training Institute established at Singapore in September 1997 to provide courses in financial management in developing countries. The TCTP's fields of training cover similar ground to the BTAP, and include port and airport management, productivity enhancement, civil service practice, information technology assimilation, financial services, and environment-related services.

Another element of the SCP – the Singapore Scholarship scheme, set up in 1999 – has a direct link to the city-state's supply security interests, where the Government seeks to attract students with outstanding academic talent from other ASEAN countries to study in Singapore. The scheme has drawn some criticism from Singapore's neighbours for reasons discussed under supply security. These relate to the perceived rapacious demands of its 'foreign talent' policy whereby the city-state is creaming off the best young managerial talent from Southeast Asia to help meet its own transformative economic objectives. However, it is too early to judge how many of these students will decide to stay in Singapore after graduating.

3.5.5 The Associative Technical Policy Realm

As noted in this chapter's introduction, many aspects of Singapore's domestic economic policy have an *associative* link with its FEP. For example, the state's high expenditures on education are perceived as a critical factor in underpinning international economic competitiveness.[70] Over time the state has shifted its concentrations of education expenditure in accordance with the progressive phases of Singapore's techno-industrial development. Hence, there was an early emphasis on primary education, and then later on secondary-level technical education, and since the late 1980s on improving tertiary education provision. As an extension of this latter trend, and in the context of supply security, the Government has sought to attract up to ten foreign world-class academic institutions to collaborate with Singapore's own universities and polytechnics, the main intention being to address the city-state's skills shortages.[71] By 2001, the French business school INSEAD had established a $16m campus in partnership with the Singapore Government, with others – such as the University of Chicago, Johns Hopkins University, Harvard Business School and Cornell University – following suit. Developing partnerships with foreign university franchises was also used as a short-term strategy. In addition, the Ministry of Manpower's (MOM) 'Contact Singapore' scheme was devised to attract foreign talent at the high end of the labour market.

We have already established both the state's continued activism in guiding Singapore's techno-industrial development and the strong competitiveness-enhancing focus evident in most economic policies. As with the NIE-3 group as a whole, competitiveness remains one of the highest policy priorities of the Singapore Government and it has achieved considerable success here. According to the 2000 World Competitive Yearbook, Singapore was the second most competitive economy in the world after the US that year, and in 1999 the world's most competitive according to the Global Competitiveness Report. Moreover, Singapore Government policies were deemed the most competitiveness enhancing from a study of 50 leading economies undertaken by the World Economic Forum over 1997–1999.[72] Further in keeping with the NIE-3 norm, Singapore retains an extensive industry policy that is designed to upgrade export production capacity as well as to attract high value-added inward

FDI. This currently centres on the state's Industry 21 strategy, which contains six corporate programmes, these being:

- *Cluster Development*: fostering the growth of key industry clusters (e.g. biotechnology, IT) as central to developing a knowledge-based economy;
- *International Business*: tapping into global and regional hubs for ideas, capital, technology, resources and markets;
- *Promising Local Enterprise (PLE) and World Class Company (WCC) schemes*: to respectively promote the internationalization and growth of local companies and embed world-class foreign companies in Singapore;
- *Headquarters*: to attract foreign companies to establish their regional headquarters in Singapore in order to expand the economy's regional and global reach;
- *Innovation*: various R&D and innovation schemes encouraging the development of new knowledge-driven capabilities and activities;
- *Resource Development*: or more specifically human resource development, with schemes designed to create a 'flexible workforce which is continuously educated and trained in core skills needed for the new millennium', as well as attracting the necessary foreign talent to complement local human resources.[73]

As part of the EDB's main thrust to transform Singapore into a dynamic exporting, knowledge-based economy, it also identifies key technology-intensive industries for development. For example, during the late 1990s it specifically designated industrial estate space to develop Singapore's production capabilities in wafer fabrication (high-tech microchips) and petrochemicals. The recent development of Singapore's FIPs across East Asia also marks an externalization or internationalization of its industrial policy. Jurong Town remains the city-state's premier 'satellite platform' industrial district for technology-intensive export production, and has provided the basic model for these FIPs. In one way they are a transplantation of the Singapore industrial development experience and are constituent to the Singapore economy's 'external' wing. Moreover, this international extension of Singapore's industrial policy has an important economic diplomacy dimension that we consider in more detail later in the chapter.

Another key industrial policy development concerns the Government's attempts to move Singapore's techno-industrial base beyond simply acting as an export production base for hosted foreign MNEs to developing it into a global centre for R&D activity, especially in the biotechnology and life science fields. The overarching aim here is the consolidation of one integrated global research and production complex through combination of inward foreign investment and state directed development. To help lever in foreign MNE investment, the Government announced in October 2000 a near 50% expansion of its R&D funding under its new National Science and Technology Plan 2005, amounting to $4bn over a five-year period. Singapore has begun to achieve some notable successes with this policy: for instance, Hewlett Packard recently developed an R&D facility in the city-state to complement its huge production facilities already located there, these being the company's second largest outside the US. Furthermore, in March 2001 two high profile biotechnology firms, SurroMed and Affymetrix, announced that they would be establishing multi-million dollar research and production centres in Singapore, developing leading edge techniques for identifying and measuring genetic material and proteins. Singapore's ability to attract further foreign R&D investment depends on a series of *associative* technical policies, but particularly industrial, infrastructural and human capital policies.

3.6 ECONOMIC DIPLOMACY

For such a small state with comparatively limited technocratic resources, Singapore maintains a highly effective set of economic diplomacy linkages[74] and conducts a notably activist economic diplomacy *per se*. This is especially apparent in its aforementioned catalysing of bilateral and inter-regional economic partnerships, as well as its vocal advocacy of international economic organizations. While Singapore's mini-statehood ultimately constrains the ability of its FEP protagonists to shape important developments in the international economic system, it is able to draw upon a reputational influence – primarily based on technocratic competence, foresight capabilities and economic achievement – that enables it to initiate key events successfully. As an interviewed MFA official commented, 'Singapore does not take a leading role but rather takes diplomatic initiatives that others often follow'.[75] Yet Singapore also faces serious economic diplomacy challenges. These especially concern its economic relations with neighbouring Southeast Asian countries, as well as reconciling certain actions and strategies at different levels of economic diplomacy (e.g. bilateral and multilateral) with the other countries.

3.6.1 Bilateral

In comparison with other East Asian states, Singapore has presided over a much less adversarial set of bilateral economic relations with the Western powers. This can be mainly attributed to Singapore's liberal commercial policies and the state's cultivated partnership with foreign capital. Trade diplomacy conflict has been further avoided by Singapore's extremely limited 'sensitive' industry production, for example textiles and agriculture. Its bilateral FTA strategy added another important partnering feature to its economic diplomacy. According to an interviewed MTI official, this was not only a 'messy but practical' approach to maintaining the momentum of Asia–Pacific trade liberalization but in addition 'a means to fortify Singapore's bilateral links with strategic foreign partners'[76] – the fuller intent of which we examine below. Singapore's small size is to its geo-economic advantage here in that it poses little cost or challenge for a fellow APBFTA partner, thus representing a litmus test or 'practice swing' for others (e.g. Japan, New Zealand) before proceeding to more challenging and larger free trade partners. A potential problem for Singapore is that its APBFTA appeal is strongest to first-timers for the same reason, and that long active counterparts in the same game, such as South Korea, have little incentive to sign with Singapore owing to its small market and virtually open market access. Hence, Singapore has tended to include other measures to entice partners into agreement, as shown by those negotiated with New Zealand and Japan.

Singapore's economic relations with the advanced industrial economy (AIE) powers – the 'core' – have been largely cordial and well developed, largely owing to the obliging semi-peripheral function the city-state is willing to perform for them. However, Singapore's economic relations with its immediate neighbours (Malaysia and Indonesia) have in comparison proved inherently problematic and complex. Much of its current bilateral tensions with these two countries owe much to the legacy of the nation-building conflicts of the early 1960s. Singapore achieved self-governing status in June 1959 but instead of proceeding to full independence it became a state of the Malaya Federation in September 1963. In August 1965, Singapore broke away from the Federation due to a mixture of ethnic and political factors, and against a backdrop of ensuing military conflict between Malaysia and Indonesia. Partly as a demonstration of its new independence, Singapore imposed a series of licensing and quota arrangements on Malaysian products, provoking an immediate retaliation and a subsequent short-lived tariff war between the two neighbours.

Tensions in Singapore–Malaysia economic relations owed much to the uneasy peace between the respective political leaderships of each state, yet both sides still meet regularly to discuss key bilateral issues. Most recently those of an economic diplomacy nature included water supply, transport linkages, the withdrawal of CPF monies by West Malaysians, and the so-called 'CLOB' issue.[77] In the corporate sphere, the Singapore–Malaysia Business Forum provides a vehicle for developing closer business linkages between the two states. A further positive contribution to bilateral relations is the economic complementarity between Singapore and the Johor province of Malaysia. The IMSGT project was specifically designed to exploit this, and has helped develop promotive aspects of their bilateral economic diplomacy. Although the IMSGT has recently waned, Malaysia's economic importance to Singapore was reconfirmed in trade statistics for 2000 that showed Malaysia had overtaken the US to become the city-state's largest trade partner. This was a general consequence of strong post-crisis recoveries in both countries and a surge in trade-inducing FDI from Singapore into Malaysia, a reflection of the production-based integration between the two economies especially evident in electronics manufacture.

The same economic interdependence brings its own complexity to Singapore's economic relations with Malaysia, as exemplified by the freshwater supply issue. Singapore currently receives between 200–350 million gallons of freshwater daily (mgd) from Johor sources. The government estimates that the city-state will require 750 mgd from Johor in 160 years' time. This is based on assumptions that by 2161, Singapore's population will hit 7 million (currently 4 million) and will consume a total of 950 mgd. However, Malaysia has contested these figures, arguing that they overestimate both the future consumption and population growth of Singapore. Moreover, Malaysia's negotiators argue that Johor's future population growth will continue to outstrip Singapore's, thus progressively increasing demand for its own freshwater supplies. Under existing agreements, Singapore pays Johor three Malaysian sen (approx. 1 US cent) per 1000 gallons of raw water. Around 30 mgd of Singapore treated water is sold back to Johor at 50 sen per 1000 gallons, leading to Malaysian accusations of profiteering by the city-state's authorities. In November 2000, however, Malaysia informed Singapore that it would stop buying its treated water in 2003. This is because Johor's new $200 million water treatment plant at Semanggar will become operational by late 2002, producing 35 mgd of treated water. Hence, Singapore will be relieved of the burden of supplying treated water back to Johor, permitting more to be channelled to its own development purposes. In Singapore's round of bilateral talks with Malaysia held in February 2001, both sides were again unable to come to any firm agreement on the water supply issue.

Another more fundamental problem in Singapore's economic diplomacy with Malaysia is the perception that their economic interdependence is based more on a principal–agent relationship rather than that of equal partners. This is founded on the city-state's superior techno-industrial capacity, orienting role in the IMSGT and growing demand for Malaysia's resources. Malaysia has also expressed some disquiet over Singapore's bilateral FTA strategy and its potentially adverse effect on the integrity of AFTA. In February 2001, Malaysia's Prime Minister Mahathir expressed specific concern about the trade deflection problem of semi-finished products from bilateral FTA partners entering Singapore, then being fully completed in the city-state and thereafter securing 'back door', zero tariff entry into the wider AFTA market.[78] His trade minister, Datuk Seri Rafidah Aziz, further stated that Malaysia would oppose any moves by Singapore to advocate the extension of AFTA to Australia and New Zealand, through a trilateral FTA arrangement with Singapore or otherwise.[79] In reply, Singapore's MTI stated that its local content laws did not permit such trade deflection to occur, implying that Singapore-made exports were sufficiently locally sourced to legitimately qualify for access to the AFTA market.[80] Moreover, Goh Chok Tong later argued that Singapore's BFTA strategy ensured that key partners outside Southeast Asia remained engaged in ASEAN.[81]

Singapore's economic relations with Indonesia have proved equally challenging, and there exist certain similarities with Malaysia's relations with the city-state. For example, Singapore–Indonesia economic diplomacy is shaped significantly by political factors, and furthermore managing the economic interdependence between Singapore and Indonesia has broadly occurred through the IMSGT relationship and certain supply security issues, for example gas and freshwater. The two recent gas supply deals have been particularly important in improving Singapore–Indonesia economic relations. In January 1999, Singapore signed an $8 billion agreement with Indonesia's state-owned Pertamina oil company to supply natural gas through a 640 km pipeline from the West Natuna Sea to Jurong Island over the next 22 years. This was the first agreement of its kind, and this supply line became fully operational on 15 January 2001. Just four weeks later on 12 February 2001, a second gas supply deal with Indonesia worth $9 billion was signed after three years of negotiation. In this agreement, Singapore would import 150 million standard cubic feet of natural gas daily through a 500 km pipeline from the Asamera gas fields in South Sumutra, and would become fully operational in July 2003.

The economic development of Indonesia's Riau province has been especially stimulated by Singapore's imperative demands for resources and techno-industrial restructuring. By 2000, induced investments from the city-state in the Riau Island's industrial parks (i.e. Bintan and Batam) amounted to $4 billion, having also created 100 000 Indonesian jobs and generated $2.5 billion in export revenues in the same year. An estimated 3000 jobs will be created in the province by supplying natural gas to Singapore.[82] Interestingly, though, Singapore Government's continued reluctance to produce statistics for its trade with Indonesia indicates concern over revealing just how dependent the city-state's economy is on Indonesia, whose own published trade statistics would suggest it ranks as Singapore's fifth or sixth largest trade partner.

There are, though, more palpable economic diplomacy concerns amongst Singapore's FEP protagonists regarding Indonesia. As discussed under the theme of transborder community security, the 1997/98 financial crisis-induced strains placed upon Indonesia's political economy posed significant spillover risks for the city-state, and the Singapore Government has responded in various ways to this potential economic security threat. During the latter months of 1997, Goh Chok Tong paid multiple visits to Indonesian President Suharto in

Jakarta in failed attempts to persuade him to co-operate more resolutely with the IMF in order to restore investor confidence in the economy. Goh also offered a pledge from Singapore of US$5bn towards an IMF bailout programme, while the MAS meanwhile intervened in the currency markets to support the Rupiah–Dollar exchange rate. Later on in January 2000, Goh Chok Tong announced a $698m aid plan, including a $400m trade assistance package, to help promote Indonesia's economic recovery. Singapore may yet offer more assistance to Jakarta as part of an economic security approach to transborder management. Indonesia's political leadership, though, have proved somewhat reluctant to receive support from the city-state, reflecting unease about demonstrating its own economic dependence on Singapore.

As with Singapore's relations with Malaysia over 1997 and 1998, crisis-induced pressures within the Southeast Asian international political economy brought simmering tensions to the fore in Singapore–Indonesia diplomacy. Then Indonesian President Habibe threateningly referred to Singapore as a 'little red dot' amongst a sea of Indonesian green on the regional map.[83] For a short while, bilateral relations improved somewhat with the inauguration of Indonesia's new President Abdurrahman Wahid – the country's third leader over the space of a year. Although Wahid formally acknowledged Singapore's generous economic assistance, offered during his country's recent turmoil, he soon followed in his immediate predecessor's footsteps by unleashing a vitriolic outburst on the city-state. At the annual ASEAN informal summit convened in November 2000, the Singapore Government proposed its 'Initiative for ASEAN Integration', aimed primarily at developing human resources in Cambodia, Laos, Myanmar and Vietnam. Perhaps interpreting Singapore's proposal as an attempt to exploit its lesser-developed ASEAN partners, Wahid commented that, 'they just look after themselves; all they look for are profits'. Drawing upon his country's own supply security leverage over the city-state, Wahid further remarked that Indonesia and Malaysia should collaborate to 'teach a lesson' to Singapore by cutting off its water supply.[84] A few months later, some cordiality was restored to Singapore–Indonesia bilateral relations after Singapore's Senior Minister Lee Kwan Yew became a member of the Indonesian Government's International Advisory Panel. In attending his first meeting in February 2001, Lee discussed with other members how to accelerate Indonesia's economic recovery. He also expressed the opinion that Singapore's bilateral ties with Indonesia, just as those with Malaysia, must focus on the long-term. While this was partially intended to deflect attention from recent tensions between the respective leaderships of Singapore and Indonesia, it also reminded both sides of the complementarity that exists between their economies from which a more promotive economic diplomacy should be cultivated.

While Singapore's economic diplomacy with Indonesia is likely to move along a similar uneasy, unpredictable and heavily politicized path as that conducted with Malaysia, its economic relations with other key foreign partners have mostly proved far less problematic. Like many East Asian states, Singapore has a strong strategic interest in fostering close economic ties with the US. In late 2000, both sides initiated negotiations on establishing a bilateral FTA to be concluded most likely by the end of 2001. Singapore was chosen as the US's first bilateral FTA partner from Asia mainly because of its liberal commercial policies. During the 1990s, American economic diplomats had had to deal with very few problem issues in the city-state, and these were relatively minor. These included intellectual property rights (IPR) cases over pirated software[85] and certain export controls[86] maintained by the Singapore Government.[87] More importantly, it is issues of promotive economic diplomacy that dominate bilateral negotiations between the two sides. Apart from bilateral FTA talks, Singapore's FEP protagonists have been exploring new ways to link up the city-state to the US through networked 'new economy' linkages. This forms part of Singapore's Technopreneurship 21 scheme, chaired by Defence Secretary Tony Tan that, *inter alia*, aims to link start up companies in the US's high-tech industrial districts such as Silicon Valley to those based in Singapore, e.g. Jurong Town.

There is a similarly strong semi-periphery context to Singapore's economic relations with the EU. The Government frequently looks to both the US and EU for advice on financial sector matters.[88] A similar interest in developing a stronger strategic partnership with Europe is demonstrated by Singapore's ASEM proposal, announced in October 1994 by Goh Chok Tong, as well as its approaches toward both the EU and the EFTA group in late 2000 and early 2001 respectively to sign bilateral FTAs. While the much larger EU group gave a lukewarm response to the idea, the EFTA countries were far more receptive and agreed to commence negotiations in July 2001.[89] As with the US, the EU's commercial disputes with Singapore mainly concern minor technical problems relating to Singapore's trade policy. High rates of domestic alcohol taxes remain an issue for British and French producers in particular, and high tax rates on cars and tobacco are another minor issue for the EU.[90] More generally, though, EU solidarity on matters of economic diplomacy with Singapore is not required as, unlike in Taiwan and South Korea, the US and Japan have not enjoyed preferential market access over their European counterparts.[91] This is a consequence of Singapore's liberal commercial tradition that leaves limited scope for such differentiated advantages to arise, but also reflects Singapore's endeavours to maintain positive economic relations with its key foreign capital partners. In 1999, the EU was Singapore's third largest export market for Singapore and fourth largest source of imports (Table 3.3). It also represented Singapore's second largest source of inward FDI in 1999 (Table 3.4), and the UK and Netherlands are Europe's biggest investors in the city-state.

Table 3.4 Singapore's inward FDI by geographic source, percentage of cumulative total

	–1987	–1992	–1997	–1999
Japan	15.3	23.3	18.1	21.2
Malaysia	4.3	3.9	4.2	3.8
Hong Kong	6.5	6.1	3.4	3.3
Other Asia	2.1	2.3	11.5	6.7
US	26.6	23.1	23.3	24.5
Canada	6.9	4.1	3.3	2.9
EU	20.8	17.0	19.4	21.8
Other West Europe	5.9	4.6	3.3	2.2
Aus/NZ	5.7	5.5	3.0	4.6
Other	5.9	10.1	10.5	9.0

Source: UNCTAD database.

Singapore's economic diplomacy with Japan has centred on similar issues to that of its 'Triad' counterparts. Japanese corporate interests in the city-state are well developed in terms of foreign investments, regional headquarters location and trade flows. For some time, Singapore has cultivated these interests in keeping with its economic alliance security objectives, particularly in relation to the strategic counterweight that Japan's commercial stake in Singapore provides to the city-state regime. Some hint of this, albeit in a wider context, was revealed in Lee Kuan Yew's acknowledgment in 1979 that, 'Japanese investments and transfer of technology to ASEAN countries and the promotion of two-way trade are Japan's best contribution in the security and stability of the region'.[92] Like the NIE-3 group generally, Japan also offered some managerial lessons to Singapore, especially with respect to developmental statist practice.

Notwithstanding similarities in their developmental tradition, tensions between both Singapore and Japan have tended to derive from different paradigmatic perspectives on certain issues. There are two main aspects to this. Firstly, Singapore's leadership is often perturbed about how Japan's hegemonic practices in East Asia impact upon regional and multilateral orders. For instance, it expressed notable scepticism about Japan's proposal to create an Asian Monetary Fund (AMF) in response to the outbreak of the 1997/98 financial crisis, mainly because this posed a potential threat to the IMF's multilateral competence and integrity, and hence could possibly undermine confidence in the international financial order.[93] Moreover, it remains in Singapore's economic security interests to maintain the US's comprehensive engagement in the region, and the AMF proposal could have 'locked out' Washington from an important development in East Asia's regional political economy. One may read Singapore's reluctance to enter into a bilateral currency exchange agreement with Japan under the Chiang Mai Initiative (CMI), stemming from the new ASEAN Plus 3 framework, as partly attributable to such concerns.[94] This is not to suggest that Japan purposely seeks to upset the regional and multilateral balance of order, nor marginalize American interests in East Asia. Rather, Japan's post-crisis hegemonic foray into the sphere of regional financial governance is a cause of some disquiet amongst Singapore's FEP protagonists insofar as it could disrupt the equilibrium of interests between the Asia–Pacific's great powers – an equilibrium that is perceived to best serve the city-state's economic security interests.[95] Moreover, recent developments suggest that Singapore still adheres more strongly to the multilateral paradigm of international economic governance than Japan. Notwithstanding these points, we argue later how Singapore's overall support of ASEAN Plus 3 derives from the contemporaneous weaknesses of other regional and multilateral regimes, these specifically being the IMF, WTO, APEC and ASEAN. Singapore's FEP protagonists nevertheless remain circumspect of Japan's hegemonic salience within ASEAN Plus 3 for the reasons stated above.

Secondly, Japan's neo-mercantilist paradigm – a defining feature of its post-war political economy – is somewhat at odds with Singapore's liberal commercial policies and advocacy of free trade. While its once ardent neo-mercantilism has been significantly tempered, Japan's various structural barriers to trade and inward foreign investment remained a key issue for Singapore's trade diplomats during the 1990s. This, though, is set to change quite dramatically with the signing of a bilateral FTA between the two countries. Negotiations on the agreement commenced in January 2001 with the intention of concluding by the end of that year. The Japan–Singapore Economic Partnership Agreement (JSEPA), as it is formally known, not only covers trade but also FDI, financial services and various other commercial matters.[96] This is notable diplomatic success for Singapore, not just because JSEPA is the first free trade agreement Japan has ever signed but also because it strengthens one of Singapore's key strategic axes in East Asia.

Another bilateral strategic axis that Singapore has sought to develop is with China. Singapore's leadership has long perceived the country as a 'kinship' state and enjoys relatively intimate relations with Beijing (Leifer 2000). Deng Xiaoping visited Singapore in November 1978 just as his inaugural economic reforms in the People's Republic were being introduced. He had admired Singapore's model of economic development and political economy, not least because it demonstrated the compatibility of rapid economic development with tight government control (Yuen 1999). Singapore has also provided a source of modern technology and guidance on economic zone development in China. Following Deng's visit in 1978, both sides signed a trade agreement the following year that proved a spur to their bilateral trade and economic co-operation. In addition, Singapore has often performed a diplomatic mediating role in China–Taiwan relations, with the city-state hosting the first official Cross-Straits talks in April 1993. However, Singapore is not involved significantly in the commercial mediation between the Chinese and Taiwanese economies, this being mostly conducted through Hong Kong (see Chapter 5).

Like many other FEP powers, Singapore views China's new commercial frontier as a rich seam of economic opportunities but also as one carrying notable risks. This has been best exemplified by Singapore's FIP experience in the People's Republic. As Table 3.2 shows, the city-state authorities had established industrial parks in Suzhou and Wuxi in the mid-1990s, the former being the largest yet undertaken covering 70 km^2 and involving nearly $3bn worth of initial foreign investment. The Suzhou Industrial Park (SIP) experience, though, proved a commercial disaster and an eventual liability in Singapore's economic diplomacy with China. Formally launched in May 1994, the Singapore–Suzhou Township project, as it was formally called, was spearheaded by the Keppel Corporation – one of Singapore's major GLCs – that led a consortium of 24 Singapore firms with the Singapore Government taking a leading political and organizing role in its establishment. The Singapore consortium held a 65% stake against the 35% stake held by its Chinese counterpart. It was thought the project would take between 20–30 years to complete and would create employment for around 360 000 people. The SIP was also the first transfer of Singapore's economic management 'software' beyond its sub-regional locale, and thus carried considerable political as well as financial risk, with the reputation and credibility of the 'Singapore way' at stake. However, the whole project fell victim to various problems from the start. The Chinese consortium was reluctant to proceed as they could not expect to make short-term profits, and the initial momentum of the project was hindered by the region's 1997/98 financial crisis. Furthermore, from the very beginning the SIP was competing with a pre-existing competitor, the Suzhou New District, that had been established in 1989 and which attracted a diversion of attention and resources from the local municipal government. These problems were further exacerbated by the local government's preference for the incumbent industrial park, which it duly developed during the course of events, as well as Singaporean and other foreign investors having to acclimatize to the lack of rule by commercial law in the Chinese business environment. Facing these setbacks and the consequent haemorrhaging of investment funds, the Singapore authorities decided to cut their losses. In June 1999, Lee Kuan Yew announced that Singapore would complete just one sector of the project with the rest left for China to develop.[97] Prime Minister Goh visited Beijing in April 2000 in part to smooth over ensuing economic diplomacy tensions arising from the Suzhou project, and on 1 January 2001 the Chinese authorities assumed majority ownership and management control of the SIP. The whole experience was a somewhat unexpected culture shock for Singapore, and demonstrated that China's 'kinship' link with the city-state was only useful in certain diplomatic circumstances.

3.6.2 Regional/Inter-Regional

Regional economic diplomacy has long been a salient feature of Singapore's FEP. Many of its important economic security interests connect to economic relations with Southeast and East Asian countries. Singapore has furthermore proved remarkably active in perpetrating inter-regional economic alliances. The Government's 'regionalization' strategy of the 1990s, largely founded on its FIP policy is another key area for analysis. Yet it is the city-state's economic diplomacy within ASEAN that deserves special mention. At the time of ASEAN's launch in 1967, Singapore's leaders were generally sceptical about the regional organization's political aims, having just broken off from the Malaysian Federation and seeing more advantages in allying with powerful Western states and their markets. These factors largely explain why Singapore has been a strong advocate of developing ASEAN's economic dimension from the very beginning. In 1969, the then Foreign Minister Rajaratnam suggested that the regional organization should remain mostly concerned with promoting economic co-operation rather than resolving military and territorial disputes.[98]

It was not, though, until the end of the Cold War that ASEAN's firmer economic rationale developed, as geopolitical competition gave way to new geo-economic imperatives. Singapore was a keen supporter of the AFTA project, first proposed in January 1992 and currently the centrepiece of ASEAN economic diplomacy. The geo-economic context behind AFTA's emergence at the time broadly related to the following:

- *As a response to external pressures:* both prolonged delays in the GATT's Uruguay Round and intensified regionalist activity in both the developed and developing world during the early 1990s presented a future possible scenario of entrenched protectionism and trade bloc proliferation. Furthermore, many of ASEAN's economic rivals could anticipate preferential access to important regional markets: Mexico to NAFTA and the central and East European economies to the Single European Market.
- *To make ASEAN's voice louder in international economic negotiations*: by using its collective market of over 400 million prospering Southeast Asians as a bargaining chip.
- *Offset the diversion of trade and investment to China*: as was becoming increasingly apparent from the late 1980s onwards.
- *Internationalizing ASEAN's business community*: by learning first to compete with local regional rivals before progressing to compete globally.

The main technical mechanism of AFTA is the Common Effective Preferential Tariff (CEPT) scheme, designed to reduce intra-ASEAN tariffs on trade in manufactures and processed agricultural products. In the first phase, the tariffs on 85% of products (numbering 38 400 lines) falling into this 'Inclusion List' were reduced to between 0–5% by 2000. Targets for expanding the Inclusion List's coverage to 90% by 2001 and to all products by 2002 were further set. By late 2000, the average CEPT tariff rate was 4.4% compared to 12.8% at AFTA's launch in 1993. Singapore, Brunei, Indonesia, Malaysia, the Philippines and Thailand (the ASEAN-6) are all fully engaged in the mainstream AFTA process. However, more recent members have longer to comply. Vietnam has over 1999–2006 to implement AFTA trade liberalization, Laos and Myanmar 2001–2008, and Cambodia 2003–2010. More generally, unprocessed agricultural products comprising the 'Sensitive List' are given a longer period for integration into AFTA, although Singapore has no items listed here owing to its virtually non-existent agriculture sector. In addition, the commitment to remove quantitative restrictions and non-tariff barriers is extended until 2010 for the ASEAN-6, 2013 for Vietnam, 2015 for Laos and Myanmar, and 2017 for Cambodia. There is also a 'General Exception List' comprising products that are permanently excluded from AFTA for reasons of national security, environmentalism, cultural-sensitivity, and so on. Interestingly, Singapore has included 109 items on this list, by far the highest amongst the ASEAN-6 group,[99] and most of these related to demerit goods such as alcohol.

Creating a free trade area in Southeast Asia is seen by many as serving a higher end, this being to promote the region's efficiency as an export-production location so as to attract further inward investment from outside countries. This is referred to as the ASEAN Investment Area (AIA) concept, which runs parallel to AFTA but is currently more a marketing device than a substantive programme of measures, although this may soon change. Not surprisingly Singapore's FEP protagonists have taken a particular interest in AIA given its potential to enhance the Government's regionalization strategy. As Southeast Asia's primary hub for transnational corporate operations, Singapore has much to gain from schemes that create a more conducive business and regulatory environment for foreign investment in the region. Notwithstanding the substantial progress made by the AFTA project, significant problem issues remain. These mainly comprise:

- *Asymmetric tariff rates within ASEAN:* being comparatively high in Thailand, Indonesia, the Philippines and Malaysia but notably low in Brunei and virtually non-existent in Singapore. There has, therefore, been much debate about the relative distribution of AFTA's benefits within the group. For example, Singapore stands to gain to a proportionately high degree not just because of its comparatively liberal tariff regime but also owing to its highly internationalized production interests in Southeast Asia.

- *Low intra-ASEAN trade:* at just over 20% is relatively modest for a prospective free trade area, and even this low figure drops quite dramatically if Singapore's ASEAN trade is left out of the equation. Moreover, during 1997–1999 intra-ASEAN trade fell from $85.4bn to $74.4bn, although a slight reversal in this trend was evident by 2000. Nevertheless, the expected trade creation gains from manufacturing tariff liberalization are small.
- *Post-crisis tensions at the domestic level:* the political and economic fallout of the region's 1997–98 financial crisis has somewhat averted the attention of certain ASEAN member states from their AFTA obligations. This particularly concerns Indonesia, the group's largest country and economy, which has lately been preoccupied with maintaining national cohesion. Singapore's economic diplomacy with Indonesia thus has a strong regional dimension.
- *Competition with other local regionalist forms:* A long-standing concern has been AFTA's 'concentric circle' relationship with APEC forum, a larger and more ambitious trade liberalization arrangement into which AFTA's membership broadly falls. Hence, AFTA's significance may simply be subsumed by APEC when the latter's 'free trade and investment zone' is completed between 2010 and 2020. Furthermore, at the November 2000 ASEAN Plus 3 summit in Singapore, the region's leaders talked of creating a future East Asia Free Trade Area (EAFTA), although this would essentially be an extension of AFTA into Northeast Asia. Finally, AFTA must increasingly compete with the APBFTA trend in which an increasing number of Southeast Asian countries may soon be participating.[100]

At the November 2000 ASEAN Plus 3 summit, Goh Chok Tong himself commented that working towards an EAFTA over the longer-term would prove a valuable exercise in fostering regional cohesion between Southeast and Northeast Asia.[101] Despite the commercial advantages this offers the city-state, Singapore is unlikely to advocate EAFTA's development against vocal opposition from the US for reasons previously discussed. Similarly, whilst Singapore participates in the ASEAN's own currency swap agreement with the four other member economies, we noted earlier that it does not participate in the separate bilateral agreements with Japan under the Chiang Mai Initiative.[102] Although Singapore has welcomed such developments in regional economic diplomacy, there remains concern over its impact on APEC and the signal that a more exclusive East Asian economic regionalism sends to Washington.[103]

Both are inter-connected as APEC is perceived by Singapore's leadership as a crucial device of economic diplomacy to strategically engage the US in the region. As hinted earlier, APEC is seen also to have significant multilateral utility in that it aims to promote global free trade and underpin the WTO regime generally. Whether this is actually the case is a moot point (Dieter 1997).

Singapore's active involvement in other inter-regional economic diplomacy linkages are based on the similar common motivation of reconciling regional and multilateral orders, although as already discussed in this chapter this risks bringing systemic and alliance economic security interests into conflict with each other. Goh Chok Tong's 1994 proposal to create the ASEM framework, duly realized two years later, was followed up by the East Asia–Latin America Forum (EALAF), another inter-regional initiative proposed on his state visit to Chile in October 1998. Building on the precursorial ASEAN–Mercosur Agreement of 1996 (another Singapore initiative), Goh then conceived the EALAF as a 'multi-dimensional dialogue' between the countries of both regions that also includes Oceania.[104] The inaugural meeting of EALAF senior officials was convened in Singapore over 1–3 September 1999, with a second meeting hosted by Chile over 16–18 August 2000. No real substantive projects have been initiated, such as trade agreements, and Singapore accepts that the traditionally weak linkages between the two regions will take some time to strengthen. However, Mexico and Chile's FTA projects with Singapore and other West Pacific rim countries provide some useful foundation for further development.

Singapore's FIP policy constitutes another important feature of its regional economic diplomacy, albeit based on a series of bilateral linkages. Notwithstanding the troublesome experience of the Suzhou IP project, where Singapore was caught in a conflictual alliance partnership with China's central and local government authorities, other FIP projects have generally proved successful exercises in promotive economic diplomacy. Although Singapore's FIPs work to a commercial rather than political rationale, they possess an important politico-diplomatic dimension, helping to cement ties with regional partners such as China, Vietnam, Philippines, Indonesia and India.

3.6.3 Plurilateral/Multilateral

The significant priority afforded by Singapore's FEP protagonists to systemic economic security places plurilateral and multilateral economic diplomacy high on their policy agenda. Singapore both actively engages in these levels of economic diplomacy and promotes their development generally. In a symbolic acknowledgement of this by its foreign economic partners, Singapore was conferred the honour of hosting the WTO's First Ministerial Meeting, convened in December 1996. The Singapore Government has ardently supported the

WTO's trade liberalization agenda on both plurilateral and multilateral fronts. By 2001, it had concluded negotiations with 40 other WTO members on the Information Technology Agreement in which tariffs on IT products are eliminated. Singapore also signed up for similar plurilateral WTO accords on telecommunications, financial services and e-commerce, and has also been a vocal advocate of the WTO's New 'Millennium' Round of multilateral trade talks. The aborted launch of the Round at the WTO's Seattle Ministerial Meeting in December 1999, and its continued stalling into 2001, caused much consternation amongst Singapore's leadership.[105] In response, the Government has taken every opportunity in various channels of economic diplomacy to promote the Round's earliest possible launch. As previously established, its stalled launch poses an economic security threat to the city-state insofar as it undermines confidence in the multilateral trade order, the health of which its commercial interests so heavily depend upon.

While Singapore's position on multilateral trade diplomacy is relatively clear-cut, we noted earlier the dilemma of its semi-periphery predicament with regard to 'new' trade issues. On the one hand, it has a common interest with the US, EU and other advanced industrial powers in pushing forward a more sophisticated multilateral trade agenda given its similar trading profile to the AIE 'core'. On the other hand, Singapore shares the position of many developing countries, including East Asian neighbours such as Malaysia, that the incorporation of both labour and environment clause linkage to that same agenda is inherently problematic. Although concern is shared with the LDC 'periphery' over the negative impact of cost competitiveness through complying to labour and environment clauses, much of the anxiety of Singapore's FEP protagonists lies elsewhere: not only do such polemical issues drive a wedge between sections of the WTO membership but they also act as both a drag on, and distraction to advancing trade liberalization itself. This view was adamantly expressed in all the interviews I conducted amongst MTI, MFA, TDB and other Government agencies over 1999–2000. As an official from Singapore's Ministry of Manpower (MOM) indicatively commented, 'together with other ASEAN members, we have argued strongly against any trade–labour linkage as we are concerned that such linkage is likely to be used for protectionist purposes detrimental to the causes of both trade liberalisation and global economic growth'.[106] Singapore's demonstration of ASEAN solidarity and semi-periphery advocacy of neighbouring LDCs on the trade–labour issue is thus driven by contrasting motivations.

According to an interviewed Ministry of Environment (MOE) official, a similar situation applies to the trade–environment linkage, where Singapore's position 'can be attributed not so much to ASEAN solidarity but rather more to a series of coincidently aligned national positions'.[107] By and large, Singapore remains highly sceptical of any trade restrictions incorporated into multilateral environmental agreements, although it strictly complies with its Montreal Protocol obligations on CFC trade. More generally, Singapore's performing of a semi-periphery mediating role between core and periphery countries on these contentious multilateral issues is also increasingly evident. For example, on the trade–labour controversy it has lent its support to a plurilateral route to linkage, proposing a voluntary compliance to higher standards by countries willing to undertake it rather than a strict regulationist application of trade–labour rules. Yet this falls short of proposing a formal plurilateral accord at the WTO for fear of proving the thin end of a protectionist wedge. Singapore is also against the International Labour Organization's (ILO) linkage with the WTO, and for debate on the trade–labour issue remaining at the ILO.

Thus, Singapore strongly supports the development of multilateral trade diplomacy but not in a direction that steers the WTO off its primary path of trade liberalization. The incorporation of 'value-based' issues into the international trade agenda is seen to throw sand into the WTO's wheels, as well as disturb the balance of the multilateral trade order. The attention to similar systemic economic security interests can be witnessed in international finance, where Singapore's relatively lukewarm reception to the Chiang Mai Initiative owes much to concern over how this and similar developments within the ASEAN Plus 3 framework might undermine the IMF's multilateral competence. Yet as we have seen, Singapore's FEP protagonists like to develop dual-function positions at bilateral and regional economic diplomacy levels that may either underpin endeavours at the multilateral level or provide a fallback position if this falters. Singapore's perpetration of the APBFTA trend is the exemplar here by both seeking to keep trade liberalization on the international agenda whilst also developing an insurance policy during a period of WTO inertia. We discussed earlier, however, the potential conflict of economic security risks inherent in this dualistic approach.

3.7 CONTESTING 'ACTOR-BASED' INFLUENCES

3.7.1 Domestic

While the foreign economic policies of the NIE-3 group remain essentially state-centric in formation, Singapore's is most resolutely so in comparison. It has not witnessed the same progressive democratization as experienced in South Korea and Taiwan since the late 1980s, and hence FEP formation remains more impervious to societal contesting influences. As Chong (2001) comments, 'Singapore's original success has been built upon the austerity and discipline of a political economy of authoritarian corporatism, enabling a unified voice in foreign policy presentation' (p. 35). Moreover, it has traditionally been a high elitist circle within the state that sets foreign policy objectives. Leifer (2000) argued that the management of Singapore's foreign policy has never been that complex, and that in the beginning it was more or less shaped by three central figures, namely Lee Kuan Yew, Foreign Minister Sinnathamby Rajaratnam and Defence Minister Goh Keng Swee. While the calculus of domestic-level contesting influences over Singapore's FEP is comparatively straightforward, there nevertheless exists a series of nuanced relationships to analyse between the state, society and business community.

3.7.1.1 Domestic stakeholding FEP constituencies

The domestic determination of Singapore's FEP stems mostly from state bureaucratic power and processes. Whereas the state's developmental partnership with foreign capital has long been a salient feature of Singapore's FEP, its relationship with local private entrepreneurship remains comparatively stunted. As in Taiwan, many key industries are dominated by state-owned enterprises, or GLCs as they are commonly known in Singapore, as part of the state's strategy of deliberately constraining the growth of private domestic oligopoly–monopoly capital as a potential rival power centre. Consequently, the contesting influence of the domestic business community in Singapore is both crowded out by that of foreign capital and circumscribed by the state's control of many 'commanding heights' of the economy, for example in transport and telecommunications. This domestic stakeholding constituency is not, though, completely shut off from the FEP formation process. As with transnational capital, the Singapore Government maintains various channels of communication with the domestic business sector via peak organisations like the Singapore Confederation of Industries (SCI).[108] Furthermore, the EDB works closely with the SCI in certain FEP-related matters such as the Promising Local Enterprises scheme, and in fostering supportive network links with hosted foreign companies. Indeed, the proliferation of these links implies that the contesting influence of Singapore's domestic business community is significantly entwined with that of the transnational capital it serves.

Despite the strong state-centricity in Singapore's FEP formation, the Government's own propagated concept of Singapore Inc. suggests that an inclusive, team-working approach prevails within the domestic political economy. In this context, the state identifies 'political leaders and government, institutions and academia, chambers of commerce and trade associations, industrialists and labour, foreign investors and local companies, [and] the people' as the nation's stakeholders, and that: 'Together, these stakeholders form Singapore Inc, working together like entities in a large corporation. Each responsible for a specific aspect of Singapore's value chain. Each working as a team to support and add value to our business partners'.[109] Thus, while policy-making processes in Singapore are very much controlled at the state's centre, it also outreaches to various stakeholding constituencies for their views and opinions. This defining feature of the city-state's FEP formation is clearly seen in the Government's relationship with domestic civil society.

Ooi and Koh (1998), two researchers working at Singapore's Institute for Policy Studies (a government sponsored think tank), define 'civil society' as 'the public sphere that mediates between the state and the individual where members spontaneously and voluntarily join together to pursue independently-identified mutual interests' (p. 98). They concede that organized civil society in Singapore is not really that independent from the Government, has very limited contesting influence in general, and is essentially subservient to the developmental mindset of the state. A substantial part of voluntary life in Singapore emerged out of PAP initiatives to create a sense of community, including the establishment of grassroots, para-political organizations that may be financially or administratively supported by the Government and linked to the PAP. The leaders of these organizations are appointed by the Prime Minister's office, and are also accountable to capture local political debate and channel community-level views back to the government (Perry *et al* 1997). In sum, Singapore's 'people sector' comprises spontaneous civil society and state-initiated voluntary organizations. The somewhat oxymoronically termed 'state-related NGOs' fall into this latter category, e.g. the Singapore Environment Council (SEC) and National Trade Union Congress (NTUC), whilst the former are more marginalized within the Singapore polity (Chua 2000, Leong 2000).

3.7.1.2 State bureaucratic power, culture and dynamics

The Singapore state's rational and effective economic policies derive from a rationally organized and effective state economic bureaucracy. Numerous factors can be attributed to this. Firstly, 'Singapore Inc.' is rooted in the state itself, as demonstrated by the deep cohesion evident in the FEP bureaucracy. In my research interviews conducted across various Government agencies, a strong sense of teamwork and consensus was generally manifest. Each agency knew its place in the FEP managerial division of labour, and no significant conflict of interest or unclear demarcation of policy competence was discernible. The degree of inter-agency collaboration and consultation is also impressively extensive, as the analysis that follows illustrates. Secondly, Singapore's FEP bureaucrats are imbued with the same core cognitive–ideological values (e.g. 'survival ideology', technocratic virtuosity) and are driven by a common developmental purpose. This owes much to the political continuity provided by successive PAP governments. Thirdly, Singapore's city-state dimensions are conducive to managing a compact circuitry of relations and controls from the state's policy-making centre, and from here it is able to shape the parameters of contesting influence more definitively. Furthermore, there are no different regional interests to reconcile, or tensions within a domestic centre–periphery divide to resolve, and Singapore's small size also brings each stakeholding FEP constituency into close geographic proximity with the state and with each other. Fourthly, the effectiveness of Singapore's FEP bureaucracy owes much to its strong technocratic competence. The Government is still able to recruit the top managerial talent from Singapore society based on a combination of associated societal cachet and generous remuneration.

In the past, FEP management was mainly the shared responsibility of the Ministry of Finance (MOF) and the MTI's precursor, the Department of Trade, which then presided over the TDB and EDB (Leifer 2000). While the MOF's importance in the state's FEP management has waned, the MTI is currently the most important state agency in this respect. It maintains responsibility for Singapore's trade policy functions and works very closely with the MFA on matters of trade diplomacy. The MTI also delegates certain policy operations to its statutory boards (whose budgets it controls), the most important in the FEP context being the EDB and TDB. The EDB's main foreign economic policy function relates to FDI policy where it administers a range of policy incentives and regulations. It is also heavily involved in the associative technical policy realm, for instance being the key agency managing the Government's Industry 21 strategy and spearheading its FIP policy. Given the EDB's traditional role of pilot agency of the Singapore developmental state, it enjoys a high degree of policy latitude in comparison to other statutory boards. Like the MTI itself, though, it is plugged into an extensive network of consultative relationships with other state agencies discussed hereafter. To generalize the EDB's role, and citing its own words, it 'plays a significant role in planning and implementing economic strategies for the development of manufacturing and exportable services sectors'.[110]

The TDB was established in 1983 primarily to develop and promote Singapore's trade and other commercial interests. It explores new markets and business niches for Singapore's exports but also has responsibility for making Singapore a more attractive base for international traders, as well as helping Singapore-based companies invest overseas. While the MTI provide the TDB with well-defined policy blueprint parameters, it is permitted to take its own initiatives (e.g. on trade diversification projects in Latin America) although these need the MTI's endorsement.[111] There is strong private sector representation within the TDB with three quarters of its board of directors drawn from the business community, and the rest from the Government. The EDB and TDB work very closely together themselves on trade-related investment issues and joint promotional projects, for example despatching commercial missions to emerging markets. They also maintain close channels of consultancy with the MTI and the MFA through both formal and informal policy networks, for example the MFA's commercial attaches are often ex-TDB staff.[112]

The MFA is generally responsible for issues of high politics in Singapore's foreign policy management but is also involved in crucial aspects of FEP formation. Singapore's chief WTO negotiator is from the MFA not the MTI, and the Ministry's officials are engaged in most levels of economic diplomacy. As noted earlier in the chapter, the MFA is responsible for Singapore's ODAC policy, which is administered by the Ministry's Technical Co-operation Directorate. In general, the MFA adopts a more political perspective to FEP-related issues in contrast to the MTI's more commercial perspective. Having said this, the MFA's foreign missions bring it into frequent contact with Singapore-linked MNEs.

Another key FEP state agency is the Monetary Authority of Singapore (MAS), the city-state's central bank and a statutory board of the MOF. We noted earlier how the MAS works in a relatively autonomous fashion from the MOF, though is not independent from the state as many other central banks such as the US Federal Reserve and European Central Bank. It is conferred prime responsibility for managing Singapore's international financial policy, and its International Relations Department works with international organizations, such as the IMF and Bank of International Settlements, in multilateral finance diplomacy. In addition, the MAS sends representations to ASEAN, APEC and ASEM financial ministers meetings,[113] while its External Economic Division monitors and assesses financial developments in regional economies and the OECD group. Close consultative links are maintained with the MOF on various policy measures and initiatives, and the MAS also works with MTI, EDB and TDB officials on foreign exchange related matters.[114] More specifically on the foreign exchange issue, the MAS operates its own reserves to manage Singapore's exchange rate policy, while the Government Investment Corporation (GIC) acts as a resource bank to safeguard the city-state's foreign reserves, an important component of its public funds (Peebles and Wilson 1996). Furthermore, the MAS conducts regular dialogue with foreign banks, finance-related firms and other representations from private sector finance. We should finally note that the MAS's own standing in the state's framework of FEP management is significantly augmented by the fact that its Chairman – the highly respected Lee Hsien Loong and son of Lee Kwan Yew – is currently being groomed as Singapore's next Prime Minister.

The MOF's main policy competence lies in domestic financial policy but it also performs a comparatively minor role in the Singapore state's FEP management. For example, its International Relations Department liaises with development finance organizations such as the World Bank and Asian Development Bank. In addition, MOF officials work with their EDB counterparts on tax incentives for inward FDI, and with the TDB on procurement of goods and services.[115] We discussed earlier in the chapter how the GIC is involved in even more key aspects of Singapore's FEP, especially regarding the management of the city-state's globally spread, long-term financial assets. Central banks are usually conferred this responsibility in other countries, and most of these invest in shorter-term assets by comparison. The GIC is not a statutory board nor a government-linked company but rather an autonomous private company[116] whose singular client is the Government; this relationship is mediated through the MOF who technically own it. Government ministers also comprise half the GIC board of directors (Lee Kwan Yew is its Chair) with the other half deriving from the private sector.

As in other governments, the encroachment of new trade issues onto Singapore's FEP agenda has brought additional state agencies into the managerial framework. According to research interviewees from all sides, there is a long-established collaboration between the MTI and the Ministry of Environment (MOE) on trade–environment issues, and with the Ministry of Manpower (MOM) regarding issues of trade–labour linkage. The MFA is also involved to some extent in this sub-realm of trade policy, especially where WTO diplomacy is at stake. Moreover, such collaboration within Singapore's state executiveship is deepening as these issues become increasingly salient within the global political economy. Although the MOE did not despatch its own representation to the WTO's Seattle Ministerial Meeting in December 2000, it did consult extensively with the MTI's own delegation before it departed. By its own admission, the MOE's role is largely deferential towards the MTI, by and large complying with the latter's position on trade–environment issues, this being that the new trade issues mostly obstruct the path to global free trade. Moreover, MOE officials still only participate in *ad hoc* meetings with their MTI counterparts and seem generally less active in the new trade issue debate in comparison with the MOM.[117] At International Labour Organization (ILO) meetings on trade–labour linkage, the MOM has sent its own delegations to represent the Singapore Government's position, and furthermore works on a more regularized consultative basis with the MTI on this issue.[118]

3.7.1.3 Level of democratization

Singapore is the least democratized of the NIE-3 group. As Chua (2000) observed, the city-state is still characterized by a centralized power structure and a closed and elitist policy-making structure dominated by the PAP. The PAP regime permits no opposition from interest groups outside the Parliament, and presides over control of local media and the regulation of foreign news publications. Political debate is channelled through government-controlled agencies or officially registered political parties, though these are not conferred the same opportunities as the ruling PAP. Singapore's Internal Security Act upholds a series of constraints on civil activities, while the Societies Act requires regularly-meeting groups of more than ten people to register formally with the Registrar of Societies, and moreover prohibits such registered organizations to engage in most forms of political activity. Singapore's civil society is further circumscribed by so-called 'out-of-bound markers' on political commentary and activity, which clearly demark where the lines of transgression lie. We noted earlier the Government's shepherding of Singapore's civil movements into its own herd of 'state-related' organizations. To Chua (2000), this forms part of a wider trend of the PAP absorbing greater segments of domestic society to identify and associate with itself. Moreover, Government's preference to promote 'civic society' instead of 'civil society' development is revealing insofar as the former evokes the duties and responsibilities of citizens rather than the rights of citizenship.

In sum, the primary role of domestic societal stakeholders in FEP formation is essentially affirmative rather than influential, and their views and opinions are channelled through government-sanctioned mechanisms. For example, the Government's Feedback Unit was created in 1984 to gather views from society on a variety of issues, yet it does not mediate contesting influence over the policy-making process but rather provides rhetorical feedback to pre-determined policy strategies and initiatives. All this provides the Singapore developmental state with a considerable degree of infrastructural power and embedded autonomy that in turn has enabled it to improve various technical aspects of foreign economic policy through societal feedback and mobilized social energy. While, then, the relative lack of democratization in Singapore ultimately restricts the scope of independent contesting influence from domestic stakeholding constituencies over FEP formation, they are nevertheless made to feel *involved* in the policy-making process, albeit at the mutually acknowledged margins. In keeping with Weiss' (1998) 'strong state, strong society' thesis, the Government desires a societal response on FEP-related issues, if nothing else to demonstrate the operational functionality of Singapore Inc.

The Singapore Government's relations with domestic civil society regarding new trade issues provide good illustration on the above. Both the NTUC and SEC are essentially state constructs, formed as the main official representative organizations in their respective fields of labour and environment. Tripartism is a well-established feature of Singapore's labour relations, consistent with the state's corporatist approach toward civil society. As Chong (2001) comments, 'labour management relations were codified into an umbrella doctrine of tripartism where empathetic partnership and mutual compromise was encouraged through government guidance as an alternative to confrontational bargaining on the streets with regard to wages, bonuses and working conditions' (p. 36). The NTUC is managed by state-linked officials and furthermore does not have to formally lobby the Government as such because its Secretary General is a Minister without Portfolio.[119] In interviews with both NTUC and MOM officials, both sides commented that although there has not been much direct dialogue between the two organizations on trade–labour issues, their views were essentially the same, this being the promotion of open trade and investment owing to the positive employment effects and social progress this generates.[120] A similar relationship exists between the SEC and MOE. Indeed, the SEC was initially part of the MOE but became organizationally independent in 1995. Like the NTUC, the SEC can be classified as a state-related NGO. The MOE has representation on its Board of Directors and also ultimately sets the parameters of its permitted activities. As we discuss in the next section, both have co-ordinated their actions on certain FEP-related matters.

3.7.1.4 Internationalization of civil society

One may expect that a by-product of Singapore's small highly internationalized economy would be a relatively internationalized culture and society that is tuned in to contemporary global issues. To some extent this is true, especially in comparison to South Korea and Taiwan's own experience, although across the NIE-3 group the younger generation tend to be most international in outlook. It is nevertheless often difficult to tell whether Singapore civil society's involvement in FEP-related issues is simply a sanctioned extension of state policy. Like the Government, the NTUC is a free trade advocate and in principle against trade–labour clauses. At the 1999 WTO Seattle Ministerial, the NTUC delegation did not participate in the civil society demonstrations, and issued a public statement expressing their disappointment over the aborted launch of the New 'Millennium' Round. Both the International Confederation of Free Trade Unions (ICFTU) and ILO took another NTUC delegation to task over its lack of support on labour standards in the trade arena.[121] While the NTUC's official line is that trade should not be held hostage to the labour standard issue, it does support ratification of well-supported ILO conventions, for example on forced labour. The NTUC's pro-commerce stance also extends to its strong support for inward FDI, and closely observes its impact on techno-industrial restructuring so as to adapt its various reskilling programmes offered to its members.

The SEC is also involved in various FEP-related issues, albeit generally contained to a more localized, sub-regional level. Furthermore, it often works in partnership with the MOE, a good example being on the forest fire haze issue where the SEC added its voice of 'civil society' to that of the MOE's own in pressuring Malaysia and Indonesia into action. Later on, SEC officials worked with the MOE in developing the ASEAN Regional Haze Action Plan. The SEC has been more independently active, however, on other fronts. In its shark's fin campaign, SEC representations actively lobbied the Government – and the MOE, Primary Production Board (PPB) and TDB in particular – to adopt measures to curb trade in this commodity. From the mid-1990s, it has also lobbied the PPB to address Singapore's wildlife transit trade, and continues to press the Government to sign the Kyoto Protocol on carbon dioxide emissions. The SEC sent a delegation to the 1996 WTO Ministerial convened in Singapore itself, and at the 1998 WTO Ministerial in Geneva, but was not invited to the 1999 Seattle Ministerial. It is not engaged to a great extent in the trade–environment standards debate owing to its own self-confessed lack of cognisance and technical expertise on the issue. Even if the SEC viewed the trade–environment linkage positively, the extent of its advocacy is ultimately constrained by the MOE. More generally, its view on the environmental credentials of Singapore's trade policy is positive, mainly because of the economy's miniscule primary sector and its gradual upgrading to less resource-intensive production.[122]

3.7.1.5 Economic nationalism

Whereas economic nationalism runs very deep in South Korean society, it barely registers in Singapore. From previous readings of this chapter, this should come as no surprise. To recap, Singapore is a highly internationalized and open economy with a very small domestic market and a substantial dependence on hosted foreign capital. Moreover, it is a multi-racial, multi-cultural society whose resident population contains a large proportion of non-Singaporean nationals. Given these circumstances, economic nationalism serves no rational commercial or socio-cultural purpose in the global city-state, and consequently is virtually absent as a mediating factor of contestability in its FEP formation. Indeed, most sections of Singapore society openly embrace globalization and foreign influences in general, and are therefore quite willing to accommodate the state's open policies on trade and FDI. This even applies to the domestic civil movement, often a source of economic nationalism. But as an interviewed IPS researcher commented, 'you'd be hard pressed to find any anti-globalisation sentiment in Singapore's civil society'. Notwithstanding recent attempts by the Government to foster a stronger sense of cultural nationalism (e.g. through the 'Speak Mandarin' campaign), Singapore's commercial foundations mean that economic nationalism serves no real purpose to any stakeholding FEP constituency.

3.7.2 International and Transnational

An important feature of Singapore's FEP formation is that its protagonists seek a general congruence with international and transnational contesting influences. As our analysis on bilateral economic diplomacy indicated, this especially applies to those deriving from the great economic powers. In particular contrast to neo-mercantile South Korea, Singapore has long embraced economic globalization and its accompanying conduits of foreign influence. Here, Singapore is very susceptible given the highly internationalized nature of its economy, small economic size, deep participation in many regional and multilateral regimes, advocacy of liberal commerce and associated natural disposition towards neo-liberal regime rules, norms and expectations. From this we should not assume, however, that Singapore's FEP protagonists are essentially acquiescent to the demands of foreign capital interests and their buttressing of international institutional structures, such as the WTO. As argued earlier in the chapter, the Singapore state's robust technocratic insulation and capacities have helped foster an effective developmental partnership with hosted foreign MNEs. Moreover, its nurtured alignment of commercial interest with the US, EU and Japan has created a conducive environment for promotive economic diplomacy to flourish. This consequently mediates most exertions of AIE relational and structural power upon the city-state. While Singapore's FEP has deliberately adapted and evolved in accordance with an international economic system that has been shaped by more powerful countries and their interests, Singapore's close developmental partnership with these interests implies that most exertions of structural power are seen in either a neutral or positive perspective rather than negatively. For example, the US and EU's collective influence over WTO norms and rules that govern international trade is considerable but these generally suit Singapore's own economic interests; this influence has been significant in helping to liberalize trade in sectors key to the city-state's techno-industrial development. Moreover, hosted American and European firms account for a large proportion of the city-state's own trade, and thus provide another linked interest. More generally, this brings relevance to the *system-centred* approach of understanding Singapore's FEP formation, yet mostly with regard to how the Singapore developmental state has worked with the grain of international systemic norms and power structures. As Chapter 4 examines, Western advocacy of global free trade has elicited a quite different set of responses in South Korea. Yet as our preceding discussion on socio-economic paradigm security suggested, the Singapore state is quite willing and able to defend its developmental state-influenced FEP in the face of global neo-liberalist pressures to diminish state activism *per se*.[123]

The Singapore state's developmental partnership with hosted foreign MNEs means that transnational contesting influences are a key issue in its FEP formation. Unlike South Korea and Taiwan, it is the Government's relations with the transnational rather than domestic business community that are most prominent. This relationship is based on three main features. The first of these concerns the *extensive and varied range of consultative frameworks and channels created by the state*. While these have long existed between the state and transnational capital in Singapore, such linkages became more formalized after the 1985/86 recession. The Singapore Economic Review Committee, set up in response to the recession and chaired by Lee Hsien Loong, provided an important benchmark for subsequent developments in the Government's dialogue with foreign MNEs. More recent high profile frameworks for consultation include the EDB's International Advisory Council (IAC) established in January 1995 (currently consisting of 14 top MNE executives and chaired by DPM Tony Tan) and the Singapore Competitiveness Committee (SCC) that was set up in May 1997. The former is permanent in nature and advises the EDB on its international strategies, providing an important point of contact between the Singapore state and the transnational business community, while the latter was project-based and designed to offer the Government a wide-ranging business perspective on how to improve both price and qualitative competitiveness, particularly concentrating on the KBE paradigm. The SCC was disbanded in 1998 after making its published recommendations in November that year. Partly in response to these, the Government initiated programmes such as Industry 21, as well as new tax incentives to encourage inward FDI in higher value-added activities.[124] Outside such structured frameworks, foreign MNEs tend to engage with the Government on a specific issue basis, hence lending to a more atomistic influence of the transnational business over aspects of Singapore's FEP. In the words of one interviewed foreign MNE representative, the transnational business community enjoys a 'symbiotic and consultative relationship' with the Government. According to another, the Government actively seeks 'honest feedback' from hosted foreign MNEs, and this can be 'forthright, honest and brutal but non-political'.[125]

Furthermore, these consultative relations are based less on the state's links with Singapore's peak business organizations and more on those nurtured with executive personalities from foreign MNEs, which have also generally intensified after the 1997/98 regional financial crisis at the behest of the state.[126] This being said, the role performed by peak business organizations is still important. The Singapore Federation of Chambers of Commerce and Industry has traditionally been the city-state's main umbrella organization representing the business community. In turn, the Singapore International Chamber of Commerce (SICC) is its largest constituent and a conduit through which the state's relations with transnational business are partly managed. The SICC is Singapore's oldest and most powerful industrial lobby, representing 70% of its hosted foreign firms. It engages in structured consultative processes with the Government on FEP-related matters through various working committees and advisory boards. An important SICC function here is to survey and then dovetail the lobbying demands of separate foreign chambers of commerce to government agencies. In addition, the SICC enjoys wide and direct access to Singapore's FEP-related ministries.

The second main feature centres on the *state's pre-drafted policy blueprints*. In approaching transnational business representatives for advice, the Government does not come with a 'blank page' but rather with an extensively pre-planned and sophisticated policy framework. In their dealings in such matters, interviewed business representatives all confirmed that the Government mainly consults with them for fine-tuning advice and ultimate endorsement of their policy strategies. Thus, Singapore's hosted foreign MNEs 'do not directly shape the Government's economic policies' but are rather invited by the state to 'sit around the strategic table to supplement the Government's own thinking'. Moreover, 'change is very much government-led' and 'the state combines its own industrial intelligence with that of transnational firms based here'.[127] Similarly, IAC representatives do not exert any discernible independent leverage over Singapore's economic policy-makers, at most suggesting minor amendments to the state's pre-designed policy blueprints and strategies. For example, at the 6th IAC meeting convened in February 2001, its business members largely approved the EDB's longer-term economic strategy on attracting foreign talent, developing stronger links to global markets and other FEP-related matters.[128] Consistent with the 'distant horizon' approach of Singapore's FEP protagonists, one interviewee particularly lauded the strategic developmental capability of the government, citing its 25-year industrial plan to develop Jurong Island's world-class petrochemical facility.

The third and last main feature concerns *state provision of customer-oriented services to enhance transnational business operations in and from Singapore*. This in turn primarily relates to earlier analysis on the technical policy realms of Singapore's FEP, and how the EDB and other agencies approach foreign MNEs to ascertain what they require in order to realize the state's transformative developmental objectives. Yet as above, this only permits transnational contesting influence over Singapore's FEP formation within well defined state-determined parameters.

Other modes of transnational contesting influences also deserve comment. Singapore's involvement in the IMSGT project has required some degree of transnational policy-making with neighbouring Malaysian and Indonesian authorities but not to a very significant level. Moreover, the 'growth triangle' dynamic has been principally driven from Singapore's hub centre. The Government's participation in trans-governmental policy networks (e.g. within APEC fora) is extensive but its own strong independent capacity for foreign economic policy-making and strategizing somewhat moderates the extent of its contesting influence. Finally, Singapore society's participation in transnational civil movements is generally very weak, not least because of the Government's very cautious stance towards them. For example, by 2001 it continued to refuse both Greenpeace and Friends of the Earth from registering in Singapore. Thus, the contesting influence of such organizations over Singapore's FEP formation is virtually non-existent.

3.8 CONCLUSION

Any analysis on Singapore's FEP must centre on the highly internationalized nature of its economy. Singapore's extensive entrepot linkages, its regional hub function performed for transnational capital in Southeast and East Asia, and emerging centre for global financial operations comprehensively integrates the city-state into the international economic system. While actively engaged in the commercial interactions of its regional locale, Singapore aspires to be a global city economy in the same league as London, New York and Tokyo. Thus, extending the global reach and reputation of the Singapore economy is an important aspect of the city-state's FEP. This chapter also contended that despite its impressive level of techno-industrial development, Singapore's semi-peripheralization remains a distinctive characteristic of its economy and FEP formation. It maintains a fundamental dependence on foreign capital, investment and technology, and furthermore plays an often salient intermediating role between core and periphery countries in both international production chains and economic diplomacy. In addition, developmental statism remains key to understanding the domestic context of Singapore's FEP formation. The Singapore state's developmental partnership fostered with hosted foreign capital figures highly in the calculus of its foreign economic policy, while the ruling People's Action Party (PAP) regime's setting of transformative economic objectives continue to orientate many aspects of FEP formation.

This chapter has also explored the multi-faceted nature of the cognitive–ideological approach to Singapore's FEP. Its most prominent feature is the 'ideology of survival' perpetrated by the PAP since the earliest days of independence, and is based on a pragmatic blend of neo-realism and neo-liberalism. Long wary of the city-state's fundamental vulnerability, Singapore's FEP protagonists have paid neo-realist attention to national survival when confronted with externalized threats (mainly localized in Singapore's case) whilst simultaneously subscribing to the neo-liberal view that improved prosperity comes from a positive and open engagement in an ever interdependent world economy. Furthermore, the Singapore state still produces technocrats who identify strongly with paternalistic Confucianist ethics, which accordingly legitimizes in their minds the continued need for an ardent state-centric approach. In addition, a strategic 'distant horizon' approach forms another key cognitive–ideological dimension to Singapore's FEP, whereby long-termist views are corporately manifest.

It has been further contended that a multifarious pursuit of economic security interests generally determines Singapore's generic FEP objectives. As a small trading state with virtually no natural resources and no indigenous economic hinterland, Singapore's supply security objectives mostly concern sustaining the material demands of a highly industrialized and developed territory. We also noted that given Singapore's export-based, entrepot-functioning economy, and its pronounced dependence on foreign markets to generate prosperity domestically, market access security objectives are particularly prioritized within the FEP framework. In matters of finance–credit security, the Singapore state upholds its capacity to, where possible, mediate the economy's engagement in the international financial system, as demonstrated in its current non-internationalization policy. Singapore's amassing of foreign exchange reserves to ensure finance–credit security also remains a critical FEP objective. Attention to techno-industrial capacity security is of further critical importance to Singapore's FEP protagonists, especially in terms of attracting high-value added foreign investment on which developing a knowledge-based economy (KBE) so depends. In addition, Singapore's small size, geographic location and geopolitical position afford significant FEP priority to matters of transborder community security. While Singapore has often sought to catalyse change to suit its economic security interests, as exemplified by its bilateral FTA strategy, this approach simultaneously gives rise to potential frictions between different economic security objectives (e.g. alliance and systemic) as discussed.

Examining the technical policy realms of Singapore's FEP reveals a high degree of apparent continuity in each realm's underlying policy principles. The city-state's long-standing entrepot and export production platform functionalities still determine the technical foundations of its trade policy. A liberal, open approach remains generally evident within the *core* technical policy realm, yet this is combined with different forms of state guidance and regulation. For example, although Singapore's FDI policy is highly liberalized, the Government has become increasingly selective in choosing foreign investments that enhance the KBE. In international finance policy, the Government has furthermore adopted a 'guided' liberalization approach, whereby it has gradually opened up and developed financial market functionalities whilst retaining strong state capacity in governing them. This approach has additionally involved directing the financial liberalization process down a particular open market path whilst avoiding another, as seen by the state's efforts to negate speculative trading in the Singapore dollar. In ODAC policy, we noted the Singapore Government's preference for sponsoring the principles of self-help and independent development capacity amongst its LDC recipients rather than systematically dispensing financial aid. In the *associative* technical policy realm, it was contended that an ardent state activism remains manifest, driven by a still fervent zeal to constantly upgrade Singapore's techno-industrial competitiveness.

Regarding economic diplomacy, we highlighted how Singapore's comparatively limited technocratic resources have been deployed to impressive effect.

The city-state has proved adept at both developing extensive economic diplomacy linkages, and more specifically at catalysing of bilateral and inter-regional economic partnerships. Singapore's penchant for bilateral FTAs had become a key feature of its economic diplomacy by the early 2000s, and a natural extension of its free trade advocacy. While the city-state maintains very promotive economic diplomacy links with AIEs, it conducts a 'guarded' economic diplomacy with its two much larger neighbours of Malaysia and Indonesia: these relations are crucially important to Singapore yet remain highly politicized and unpredictable. Singapore's highly active economic diplomacy is also evident at the regional, inter-regional and multilateral levels. It has positively engaged in AFTA and APEC, and has provided the vision and initiative behind new inter-regional arrangements such as ASEM and the EALAF. Singapore also remains a vocal supporter and advocate of the WTO and IMF in both the East Asian region and the wider international community. Yet Singapore must strike a critical balance between different levels of economic diplomacy activism at a time when the foundations of the multilateral economic order have been significantly shaken.

The dominant power of the PAP in Singapore's political economy has ensured the prevalence of a strong state-centric approach in FEP formation. Hence, the domestic determination of Singapore's foreign economic policy stems mostly from state bureaucratic power and processes. Moreover, Singapore's FEP bureaucracy exhibits high levels of cohesive management and collaboratively interacts within clearly defined divisions of ministerial labour. Yet while Singapore's FEP formation is very much controlled at the state's centre, it nevertheless seeks the views and opinions of various stakeholding constituencies as part of a 'Singapore Inc.' framework designed to foster an inclusive, team-working approach to addressing the city-state's future challenges. This being said, the Government sees the main role of non-state stakeholding constituencies in Singapore's FEP formation as being essentially affirmative rather than influential. In the comparatively undemocratized Singapore, organized civil society is largely state-sanctioned and consequently wields extremely limited independent contesting influence over FEP-making processes. A similar principle applies to the state's relationship with transnational capital, in that its extensive consultative channels developed with hosted foreign MNE representations act primarily as a conduit for 'fine-tuning' advice and ultimate endorsement of the state's largely pre-determined policy blueprints and strategies. Thus, despite Singapore's seeming susceptibility to international and transnational contesting influences owing to the highly internationalized and open nature of its economy, this is mediated by the state's impressive technocratic and developmental capacities to harness the forces of globalization to its own advantage. This, if anything, remains *the* defining feature of Singapore's FEP formation.

NOTES

1. Interview with Ministry of Foreign Affairs official, November 1999.
2. A fishing village of some 200 people existed at this time on Singapore's 225 square miles of land.
3. More specific measures included the control of wage costs and workforce behaviour; provision of serviced industrial estates proximate to available labour; the upgrading of technical education; taxation incentives and the free remittance of capital.
4. For example, the Pioneer Industries Ordinance No. 1 act provided significant tax reductions (from 40% to 4% for a five year period) on profits from 'pioneer' industry exports.
5. In addition, manufacturing's share of GDP rose from 16.0% to 22.3% over 1996–73, while direct exports' share of total manufacturing sales increased from 43.3% to 54.9%, and gross domestic capital formation's share of GDP from 21.0% to 40.0%.
6. In 1988, the EDB identified five key high-tech industries promoted for growth: information technology, biotechnology, robotics, microelectronics, and laser technology.
7. See www.sedb.gov.sg.
8. In local currency, inflation-adjusted terms.
9. These contributory payments were cut from 20% to 10% until November 1999, and were thereafter raised by 2% to 12% with additional 2% annual increases henceforth until a restoration of the 20% rate was achieved.
10. The NWC was set up in 1972, a tripartite forum comprising officials from government, business and organized labour. Over time, it has enabled the state to exert downward pressure on wage inflation, consequently allowing Singapore's unit labour costs to rise at a comparatively slow rate from the 1970s to 1990s. By 1993, Singapore's rates here were comparable to those of Taiwan and South Korea, despite being at least twice their level in 1975 (Huff 1995b).
11. According to one research interviewee, the Government was especially concerned about maintaining price competitiveness of Singapore's electronics exports, a key sector of the economy and one facing particularly intense global competition. Interview with British High Commission official, November 1999.
12. *Straits Times*, 30 June 1998.
13. Interview at the British Chamber of Commerce, November 1999.
14. Taken from comments in research interviews at the Ministry of Trade and Industry (MTI) and Ministry of Foreign Affairs (MFA), November 1999 and September 2000.
15. Rosecrance, R. (1986) *'The Rise of the Trading State: Commerce and Conquest in the Modern World'*, Basic, New York.
16. The Singapore Straits are at the southern end of the Strait of Malacca, which is considered the westernmost limit of the Pacific Ocean and the key sea traffic choke point in Asia. At its narrowest point, the Phillips Channel, the sea lane is only 1.5 miles wide. 1999 estimates by the US Department of Energy are that more than 50,000 vessels transit the Strait of Malacca each year, and their cargoes include 10.3 million barrels of oil per day.
17. The full version of this speech is reprinted in Chan and Obaid (1987).
18. Over 1965 to 2000, Singapore's re-export ratio to GDP varied between 200 and 370%, and was at 300% by the end of this period. Its domestic exports ratio to GDP varied between 75 to 90% over 1985 to 2000. Moreover, the import content of these exports is very high, and the expansion in Singapore's intra-industry trade has caused import penetration generally to increase. In addition, as Sandlands and Tan (1986) note: 'Re-export trade is important to Singapore not only in the narrow sense of conventional entrepot trade but also because of the great extent to which imported intermediate inputs are re-exported after some degree of local processing' (p. 34).
19. The JTC currently runs over 30 other smaller industrial parks around the city-state hosting nearly 6000 companies.
20. GLC ownership was transferred in 1970 to Temasek Holdings, a private holdings company but working in the service of the Government.
21. There were, however, plans to privatize some GLCs in the 2000s, including Singtel.

22. 'We Want to be Ourselves', speech delivered at the National University of Singapore, 9 October 1966.
23. Ministry of Information and the Arts, *A Bimonthly Selection of Ministerial Speeches (Jul–Aug 1997)*, p. 50.
24. Interview at the Institute of Policy Studies (IPS), November 1999.
25. Interview at Bank of America, September 2000.
26. As another research interviewee commented, 'the PAP still maintain a crisis rhetoric tailored for domestic consumption', and like all other interviewees quizzed on this matter, he did not foresee much change here.
27. *Ministry of Finance Press Release*, 10 July 1997.
28. From speech reprinted in Chan and Obaid (1987), pp. 223–31.
29. An exemplar of this approach is embodied in the 'strategic pragmatist' culture of the EDB (Schein 1996).
30. Interview with Institute of Defence and Strategic Studies (IDSS) official, September 2000. At the IDSS, Singapore's main security policy think-tank, the explicit examination of economic security-related issues currently remains a low priority. For example, in late 2000 there was only one IDSS researcher currently active in examining economic security-related issues, and this specifically centred on developments in regional financial co-operation within the new ASEAN Plus 3 framework.
31. Also confirmed by interview with IDSS official, September 2000.
32. *Straits Times*, 9 February 1992.
33. More specifically, Singapore was assured access to Tebrau River sources until 2011 and Johor River sources until 2061.
34. In July 2000, the Singapore Government announced plans for a $1.5 billion project to realize this objective by 2005. This would involve the construction of two undersea pipelines totalling 450 km in length, and thus prove far more expensive than drawing upon the considerably more proximate Johor water supplies. Most recently, Singapore's Trade and Industry Minister, George Yeo, made a four-day visit over 12–15 February 2001 to Indonesia's Riau Province, where he proposed another water deal that would involve Singapore importing between 50–100 mgd from Bintan Island. However, there have been no firm commitments from the Indonesian side regarding this proposal.
35. Singapore intersects with almost 400 shipping lanes and has links to over 600 ports worldwide.
36. *Straits Times*, 10 January 2001.
37. The initial findings of Singapore's 2000 census revealed that 19% of the total population were neither citizens nor permanent residents. This compared to 1990's figure of 10%.
38. This includes the Singapore Scholarship scheme discussed later under ODAC policy.
39. In relation to APEC, see Ravenhill, J. (2000) 'APEC Adrift: Implications for Economic Regionalism in Asia and the Pacific', *Pacific Review*, Vol 13(2), pp. 319–33.
40. With which it was negotiating a trilateral FTA along with New Zealand.
41. EFTA membership comprises Switzerland, Norway, Iceland and Liechtenstein. (*Financial Times*, 21 November 2000).
42. As acknowledged in a speech made by Minister for Trade and Industry, George Yeo, at the Institute for International Economics, Washington DC, 14 March 2001. *MTI Press Release*.
43. *Straits Times*, 17 April 2001.
44. For example, both have maintained close monitoring and supervision over the level and type of foreign debts incurred by their firms.
45. *Straits Times*, 7 December 2000.
46. *Business Times*, 14 March 2001.
47. Some Middle East oil-rich states possess similar funds.
48. Disclosed in various research interviews.
49. Interviews at EDB, November 1999.
50. Moreover, there is growing concern that Johor may rival Singapore as a regional hub economy, with Port Klang's facilities actively promoted and developed by the Malaysian Government with this objective in mind.

51. This was acknowledged in many research interviews with government, business and academic representatives. One research interviewee even proclaimed that 'the IMSGT is dead'.
52. Hon (1999) placed the estimated economic cost caused by recent Indonesian forest fire hazes to Singapore's tourism industry and health services at between $69.3m and $78.8m. In another report, the Singapore-based Economy and Environment Programme for Southeast Asia estimated that Singapore suffered a loss of around $104m for 1997 alone, with the tourist and airline industries losing $81.8m and $9.1m respectively while health costs amounted to $12.5m. *Straits Times*, 16 March 1998.
53. An interviewed MTI official even used the 'bicycle theory' concept to explain Singapore's trade diplomacy position, November 1999.
54. See Prime Minister Goh's comments in 'Leapfrogging the Region', *Straits Times*, 26 January 2001.
55. WTO accords on IT and telecoms trade being prime examples, both being 'pre-cooked' within APEC.
56. Only four tariff lines on alcoholic products actually had non-zero rates by 2001.
57. As confirmed by interviewed MTI officials, September 2000.
58. Interviews at MAS and MOF, November 1999.
59. MAS website.
60. *MAS Press Release*, 21 March 2001.
61. *MAS Press Release*, 10 April 2001.
62. *MAS News Archive*, 6 December 2000.
63. *Straits Times*, 7 December 2000.
64. *MAS Press Release*, 15 February 2001.
65. This had nevertheless expanded to S$14.3bn worth of non-government Singapore dollar issues by 2000. *MAS Press Release*, 3 April 2000.
66. Dual key access to GIC funds are held by the President (Singapore's Head of State) and the Government.
67. Interviews at the TCD and other MFA directorates, November 1999 and September 2000.
68. From interviews with representatives from the Institute of Southeast Asian Studies and IDSS, September 2000.
69. Various efforts were made by the author to find locate Singapore's annual overseas financial aid statistics, including through various contacts with the MFA. However, the TCD's budget figures were the only information disclosed by the Government.
70. This has proved very effective, with Singapore workers having been consistently rated the world's best skilled from 1981 to 2001 by the US-based Business Environment Risk Intelligence organization. *MTI Press Release*, 8 May 2001.
71. *The International Herald Tribune*, 15 February 1999.
72. See www.weforum.org.
73. See www.sedb.com.sg.
74. Singapore has diplomatic relations with 158 states, although limited human resources currently permit full overseas missions to only 37 states and international organizations.
75. Interview, September 2000.
76. Interview, September 2000.
77. Around 200 000 Singaporeans had collectively invested billions of dollars in Malaysian shares but these assets were frozen after Malaysia's imposition of credit controls in September 1998, enacted in response to the regional financial crisis.
78. *Straits Times*, 26 February 2001.
79. *Straits Times*, 22 February 2001. Malaysia also criticized Singapore's willingness to exclude agriculture from its BFTA negotiations with Japan and inclusion of measures linking trade to labour and environmental standards in similar negotiations with the United States owing to its endorsement of the developed country position within the multilateral trade order. *International Herald Tribune*, 22 February 2001.
80. *Straits Times*, 5 March 2001.
81. *Straits Times*, 16 May 2001.
82. *MTI Press Release*, 12 February 2001.

83. *The Asian Wall Street Journal*, 4 August 1998.
84. *Asiaweek*, 27 November 2000.
85. From 1997 to May 2001, Singapore was placed on the US's Special 301 watch-list on this matter. The Singapore Government responded positively to American pressure by passing copyright and trademark law amendments, making more vocal commitments to IPR protection to safeguard its international reputation, and launching a public education campaign.
86. This was a particular problem for the US owing to its Helms-Burton Act, which is supposed to penalize foreign companies that trade with pariah states such as Cuba, Libya and Iran. The volume of Singapore's re-export trade – about 40% of its total – makes identifying trans-shipped products destined for these countries extremely difficult, especially as Singapore is the agent and not the principal actor.
87. Interviews with Singapore-based US Embassy officials, November 1999. In addition, negotiating access to Singapore's retail banking sector is likely to be the most significant issue for the US in its bilateral FTA talks with Singapore.
88. Interview with MAS and MOF officials, November 1999.
89. *MTI Press Release*, 4 May 2001.
90. Interviews at the French Business Association and British Chamber of Commerce, November 1999.
91. Interviews at the British Chamber of Commerce and Netherlands Embassy, September 2000.
92. *Business Times*, 23 October 1979.
93. As confirmed in interview with GIC official, November 1999.
94. *Straits Times*, 12 May 2001. This is in contrast to South Korea, which, along with Malaysia and Thailand, has signed such an agreement with Japan under the Chiang Mai Initiative launched in October 2000. See Chapter 4 for more details.
95. These currency exchange deals would, though, only be activated in tandem with IMF supervised reforms, thus allaying potential US concerns. However, ASEAN Plus 3 leaders stated it would review this by 2004.
96. *MTI Press Release*, 27 April 2001.
97. *Straits Times*, 10 June 1999.
98. *The Mirror*, Singapore, 29 December 1969.
99. Indonesia was second highest of the ASEAN-6 group with 65 items. However, Singapore's total was less than that for Cambodia (134), Vietnam (196) and Brunei (202).
100. Singapore's involvement notwithstanding, Thailand was beginning to explore its APBFTA options by early 2001.
101. *Straits Times*, 19 January 2001.
102. According to an interviewed IDSS official, Singapore generally supports the CMI but cannot foresee the need to draw upon Japanese financial assistance of this kind, unlike many other ASEAN Plus 3 economies.
103. Interviews with MTI and MFA officials, September 2000.
104. The EALAF's 27-country membership includes the ASEAN-10, Japan, China, South Korea, Australia, New Zealand, Argentina, Bolivia, Brazil, Chile, Columbia, Ecuador, Mexico, Panama, Paraguay, Peru, Uruguay and Venezuela.
105. *Straits Times*, 15 December 1999.
106. Interview with MOM officials, September 2000.
107. Interview with MOE official, September 2000.
108. The SCI mainly represents Singapore-owned manufacturing companies, with 80% of its members falling into this category.
109. From www.singapore-inc.com.
110. From EDB website: www.sedb.gov.sg.
111. Interview with TDB officials, November 1999.
112. From interviews with EDB and TDB officials, November 1999.
113. These are also attended by its MOF counterparts.
114. Interview with MAS officials, November 1999.
115. Interview with MOF officials, November 1999.

116. The GIC technically comprises three separate companies, namely the Government of Singapore Investment Corporation Pte Ltd, the GIC Real Estate Pte Ltd, and the GIC Special Investments Pte Ltd.
117. Interview with MOE official, September 2000.
118. Interview with MOM officials, September 2000.
119. The NTUC official I interviewed in September 2000 was himself a Junior Minister of State.
120. A certain degree of dissonance between the NTUC and the Government's positions is, though, sometimes apparent. For example, the NTUC took the view in a recent ILO conference that sanctions should be imposed upon Myanmar for violating the forced labour convention, while the Singapore Government took a different view and voted against the sanctions. Interview with NTUC official, September 2000.
121. Interview with NTUC official, September 2000. See also www.icftu.org.
122. Insights from this paragraph derive from interview with SEC official, September 2000.
123. The Government's continued use of measures to guide the techno-industrial development of the economy in spite of signals of concern expressed at the WTO level provides an instance of this (WTO 2000a).
124. The SCC was divided up into various sub-committees, each producing a set of policy recommendations that were duly implemented in the most part. In sum, the SCC channelled around 500 business executives' views through the dialogue process. Interview with participating foreign MNEs representative, September 2000.
125. Interviews with foreign MNE representatives and SCC members, September 2000.
126. Ibid.
127. Ibid.
128. *EDB Press Release*, 7 February, 2001.

4. South Korea: the FEP of a deconstructing developmental state

4.1 INTRODUCTION

South Korea has experienced perhaps the most profound political economy transformations amongst the NIE-3 group, and this may be attributed to two main interrelated factors. First, the institutional and policy apparatus of South Korean developmental state – once the most extensive of any East Asian NIE – has been gradually deconstructed since the 1980s. Consequently, the sharp edges of the country's neo-mercantilist FEP have been rounded, and in some cases totally blunted. Second, South Korea's 1997/98 financial crisis had a significant catalytic effect on accelerating this deconstruction, and furthermore marked what many believe was a critical turning point in the country's economic history. After decades of exhibiting many characteristics of a closed economy, the new South Korean Government under the leadership of Kim Dae-jung has endeavoured to convert the country into an 'open trading nation', thus further reversing the neo-mercantilist practices of the past. This new openness in South Korea's FEP can be witnessed across most technical policy realms, with especial regard to trade, inward foreign direct investment (FDI) and international finance regimes. It can also be seen in South Korea's economic diplomacy. For example, in an historic precedent, it has sought to partner free trade agreements with other Asia–Pacific countries. Such moves have been strongly supported by various sources of domestic and external neo-liberal advocacy, which themselves were significantly fortified by the 1997/98 crisis.

The post-crisis context of South Korea's FEP is much stronger than that of Taiwan or Singapore. This chapter will illustrate that point extensively, demonstrating how the 1997/98 crisis brought important new factors into the calculus of South Korea's FEP formation. However, this chapter will also show how there has been strong resistance to crisis-induced change, mainly originating from the inter-locking structural relationships and modes of socio-economic behaviour spawned by developmental statism. It will be particularly argued that certain institutional and socio-cultural features of South Korean developmentalism remain a strong defining feature of the country's political economy, with implications for the current and future formation of its foreign economic policy.

As we argued in Chapter 2, deconstructing the developmental state requires more than simply dismantling certain state policies and aspects of the institutional apparatus that sustained it in the past. It also requires a radical reconstitution of the structural relationships that the developmental state has both spawned and in which it is subsequently embedded. As a fundamental essence of these relationships is socio-cultural, the penetration of 'Western' neo-liberal norms is constrained. This especially relates to aspects of societal and state bureaucratic economic nationalism, the state–*chaebol* nexus, South Korea's 'export-orientation' culture, and matters of national economic security, all of which indicate the embedded nature of the country's broadly conceived neo-mercantilism. Thus, it is contended that recent developments in South Korea's FEP have been shaped by powerful forces of both change and continuity.

4.2 SOUTH KOREA'S DEVELOPMENT CONTEXT

4.2.1 A Brief Economic History to 1961

While the Korean nation has a long and ancient history, its experience of modern industrial development is very recent. For many centuries it remained an agrarian-based, feudal economy and society dominated by the *yangban* (landed gentry) of the Choson Dynasty (1392–1910). Moreover, it was frequently subject to interference from powerful neighbours. While unsuccessful attempts were made by France and the US to open up Korea to international trade during the 1860s, both Japan and China forced Korea to accept their own one-sided commercial treaties in the latter quarter of the 19th century. China urged other countries to do the same in an endeavour to counter Japanese influence. Yet it was Japan that prevailed, first defeating China in the 1894–95 Sino-Japanese War and later securing victory in the 1904–5 Russo-Japanese War to emerge as Northeast Asia's undisputed hegemonic power at the start of the 20th century.

In 1905, Korea became a Japanese protectorate and then was fully annexed five years later. During 1910 to 1945, Japan exercised an aggressive and exploitative colonial rule in Korea: the Korean people were forced to learn Japanese, endure other forms of cultural imperialism and suffer general economic hardship, while the economy became subservient to the material demands of the Japanese economy (Kwak and Lee 1997). At the same time, Korea benefited from investments made in its infrastructure and education systems, a codification of modern civil laws, increased monetarization of the economy, the introduction of a new financial system and the development of the country's export sector. Hence, like Taiwan, Korea's first real steps towards industrialization occurred under Japanese colonial rule. Although Korea's rural and urban workers alike experienced considerable socio-economic misery during this period, with agrarian and industrial surpluses siphoned off by their colonial masters, the Japanese set in place a framework for modern industrial development to be subsequently built upon from 1945 onwards.

However, much of the industrial capital and infrastructure left by the Japanese was concentrated in the north, and what remained in the south was destroyed during the Korean Civil War of 1950–1953. After the conflict ending in stalemate, the newly formed states of North Korea and South Korea[1] were consolidated and respectively led by the communist Kim Il Sung and US-backed Rhee Syngman. Both emerged as leaders on the crest of anti-colonial, independent struggles against the Japanese that provided a spur to both communist and nationalist movements (Lie 1998). This mutual penchant for self-reliant development manifested itself in Kim Il Sung's *juche* ideology and economic policies,[2] and the Rhee Government's somewhat haphazard, yet generally effective import substitution industrialization (ISI) policies of the late 1950s. Like most ISI strategies, this aimed to insulate domestic producers from foreign competition whilst simultaneously promoting indigenous techno-industrial development, particularly in food and textile sectors (Lee 1996, Song 1994, Soon 1994). South Korea's economy also benefited from large inflows of foreign aid, primarily from the US, hypothecated to South Korea's reconstruction.[3] In April 1960, Rhee's Government collapsed after a period of widespread civil disquiet born from a combination of political corruption, repressive acts and the effects of an economic slowdown (Oh 1999). The replacement administration, led by Chang Myon, was not able to deliver quick solutions to problems generated by an ill-managed economy and subsequently fell victim to a successful *coup d'etat* organized by Major-General Park Chung-hee in May 1961.

4.2.2 The Emergence of the South Korean Developmental State

The ascendance of Park Chung-hee to power marked a key turning point in South Korean economic development. It was from 1961 onwards that the country emerged from the periphery into the semi-periphery, and the date from which the construction of South Korea's developmental state formally began (Amsden 1989). The new Park Government drew upon Japan's developmental state model as a partial template for South Korea's own. For example, the introduction of a Five Year Plan (FYP) economic framework was based partly upon Japan's sector-based rationalization plans of the 1950s, with the former representing a more comprehensive attempt to state-orchestrate the country's economic development[4] (Bridges 1993). In the corporate sphere, the South Korean state fostered the development of large conglomerate enterprises – the *chaebol* – so as to acquire the same scale production advantages achieved by Japan's pre-war *zaibatsu* and post-war *keiretsu* company groups[5] (Kim, H.R. 2000a). Indeed, the state–*chaebol* nexus became the key structural relationship of the South Korean developmental state.

Broader lessons and legacies from the Japanese developmental experience are also relevant. Both Rhee and Park built on the authoritarian political foundations left by Japanese colonial rule, underwritten by the US to consolidate capitalist state resistance against the advance of communism in Northeast Asia (Kim, Y.T. 1998). Furthermore, as Lie (1998) comments, 'the sheer geographic proximity and the lure of Japan's booming economy, not to mention common language and at times shared school ties, influenced the architects and engineers of South Korean development' (p. 183). Thus, for various reasons, Japan's developmental statism – which as Chapter 2 noted could be traced back to the late 19th century – had some considerable bearing upon South Korean post-war developmentalism, especially from the early 1960s onwards.

In another departure from the previous administrations, the Park Government implemented a transition from ISI policies to an export-oriented industrialization (EOI) strategy during the early 1960s – a relatively early switch in comparison to most other developing country counterparts but one also undertaken by Taiwan and Singapore. The Government's maxim of 'nation building through exports' galvanized the country into meeting new development objectives, with export targets set for business and sanctions imposed if these were not met. Indeed, it was trade that clearly dominated the country's FEP agenda at this time, the objectives of which were relatively well defined and articulated within the South Korean state's FYP framework. Export-based growth was to be the engine to progressively advance the country's position amongst the international community of nations. This was partly achieved by the cult of growth and expansion propagated by the state in South Korean society, hence reinforcing the civic sense of economic nationalism (Koo 1992).

The apparatus and practice of South Korean developmental statism reached its zenith in the late 1970s. Much of the country's rapid industrialization and economic growth[6] derived from the 'developmental alliance' of the state–*chaebol* nexus. The Government's economic ministries, and in particular the Economic Planning Board (EPB) – the key pilot agency of the South Korean developmental state[7] – provided cheap credit and discretionary incentives for the *chaebol* to help develop new techno-industrial capacities[8] (Cho and Kim 1995). More generally, the *chaebol* spearheaded South Korea's techno-industrial restructuring and export-drives, largely in accordance with the transformative developmental objectives set by the state's technocratically insulated economic bureaucracies. Representatives from the EPB in particular worked closely with their *chaebol* counterparts through a series of informal and formal channels, through which the state's strategies for techno-industrial transformation could be perpetrated. These dialogue channels and other functions of state capacity (e.g. managerial, co-ordination, control), such as its FYP framework, provided the state with its infrastructural power within South Korea's 'big business' community. The concentration of corporate power within a handful of business organizations, together with an active engagement with peak associations, such as the Federation of Korean Industries (FKI) and the Korean Chamber of Commerce and Industry (KCCI), assisted the above processes by facilitating a relatively narrow span of administrative control (Song 1994). Moreover, the South Korean state enjoyed a considerable degree of embedded autonomy, being sufficiently insulated from any predatory, rent-seeking corporate interests yet significantly connected to the business community and other economic groups.

4.2.3 The Origins of Deconstruction

Analysts generally chart the beginnings of the deconstruction of the South Korean developmental state from the early 1980s onwards. South Korea entered into a period of economic and political crisis around this time, after both the assassination of President Park Chung-hee in October 1979 and pressures exerted upon the economy by the global 'shocks' of the early 1980s (i.e. oil price hikes, currency and interest rate fluctuations) that exposed various structural rigidities in the domestic economy. Furthermore, while South Korea's developing country status and structural trade deficit position had enabled the Government to effectively defend its neo-mercantilist policies, foreign trade partners were by this time applying considerable bilateral pressures upon the country both to open up its emerging domestic markets and to act in a more responsible manner within the multilateral trading system. Faced with this combination of factors, the new Chun Doo-hwan (1980–1987) Administration introduced various deregulatory and liberalizing measures within the Fifth FYP (1982–1986) designed to inject more flexibility into the economy. However, the subsequent progression of neo-liberal reform through the early to mid-1980s was slow and piecemeal. This trend was continued by the Sixth FYP (1987–1991), whose inauguration coincided with the receding of military governance under the new Presidency of Roh Tae-woo (1988–1992).

South Korea entered the 1990s at a critical economic and political juncture. Deepening democratization, especially after the 1987 election, brought constitutional and social reforms that empowered both capital and labour interests. Consequently, the business community's influence over economic policy-making strengthened, whilst new wage-level hikes significantly eroded Korean export competitiveness, converting much prized trade surpluses into deficits (see Table 4.1). Within the South Korean Government, the neo-liberal decomposition of the developmental state was increasingly evident. For Kim, Y.T. (1999), the most important origin of this decomposition lay in the transition from the Park Chung-hee's Administration to Chun Doo-hwan's, whereby Chun allied himself with neo-liberal economists and bureaucrats, appointing them to strategic command positions in key economic bureaucracies.[9] Hence, there began a change of guard with those Japanese-trained incumbents loyal to Park – and thus imbued with developmentalist, neo-mercantile values – gradually giving way to more neo-liberal minded personnel. This 'ideological osmosis', as Woo-Cumings (1991) refers to it, manifested elsewhere within the South Korean developmental state. For example, a similar infiltration of neo-liberal advocates occurred in the state's research institutes and think tanks: by the 1990s, the research staff of the Korean Development Institute (KDI) – the country's most prestigious research institute with a substantial influence over economic policy – were all PhD graduates from American universities.[10]

Moon and Prasad (1994) argued that by the early 1990s, the South Korean developmental state had lost much of its past coherence. The ideological struggle between statist and neo-liberal bureaucrats over economic policy formation exacerbated pre-existing inter-ministerial conflicts, themselves also fuelled by profound changes to the internal configuration of the state structure. A defining moment of this trend occurred in December 1994, when the developmental state's key pilot agency, the EPB, was merged with the Ministry of Finance to form the new Ministry of Finance and Economy (MOFE), thus emasculating the EPB's once powerful bureaucratic potency. Furthermore, Moon and Prasad contended that democratization had made the South Korean developmental state increasingly prone to particularistic interests of business and societal groups,[11] testing its technocratic insularity and the country's propensity for democratic developmentalism (see contesting 'actor-based' influences section).

As with most of its predecessors, the new Kim Young-sam Government (1993–1997) brought with it an ambitious agenda of economic reform.[12] In 1993, a key element of the South Korean developmental state – the FYP framework – was curtailed in favour of a '100 Day Plan for the New Economy'.[13] In addition, South Korea's commitment to uphold Uruguay Round and World Trade Organization (WTO) accords further extended the scope of liberalization to other areas, such as agriculture, government procurement, retail and financial services. The Government was also compelled to liberalize South Korea's capital markets to meet the membership criteria for joining the Organization for Economic Co-operation and Development (OECD), to which it acceded in October 1996. Notwithstanding an initial fervour and exogenous pressures upon it to undertake far-reaching policy reforms, the Kim Young-sam Administration made only limited progress with economic liberalization. Both the state's imperative to support South Korea's techno-industrial upgrading and its compulsive neo-mercantilist urges remained prime bases of economic policy. Such continuity can be linked to the sources of resistance to change in South Korea's post-crisis FEP analysed later.

Table 4.1 Key economic indicators of the South Korean economy (1955–2000)

Year	GDP (W bn)	Per Capita GDP (US$)	Exports (US$m)	Imports (US$m)	Current Balance (US$m)	Import Liberalization Rate (%)	Exchange Rate (W/US$)	Foreign Exchange Reserves (US$m)	Average Tariff Rate (%)
1955	115	65	18	341	–36	1.0	30.2	96.1	25.4
1956	152	66	25	386	–23	3.6	50.0	98.6	–
1957	197	74	22	442	–3	6.6	50.0	115.6	30.3
1958	205	80	17	378	38	6.4	50.0	146.5	–
1959	218	81	20	304	16	4.8	50.0	147.3	–
1960	245	79	33	344	13	5.1	62.8	157.0	–
1961	294	82	41	316	33	4.7	127.4	207.0	30.3
1962	356	87	55	422	–56	5.6	130.0	168.6	39.9
1963	503	92	87	560	–143	0.4	130.0	131.5	–
1964	716	98	119	404	–26	2.0	214.2	136.4	–
1965	806	105	175	463	9	6.0	266.3	146.3	38.9
1966	1,037	125	250	716	–103	9.3	371.3	245.2	–
1967	1,281	142	320	996	–192	60.4	270.5	356.6	–
1968	1,658	169	455	1,462	–440	57.6	276.6	391.0	39.1
1969	2,155	210	722	1,823	–549	55.1	288.3	552.9	–
1970	2,788	253	835	1,983	–623	54.3	331.6	609.7	–
1971	3,419	289	1,068	2,394	–848	55.0	347.2	568.1	–
1972	4,191	319	1,624	2,522	–371	50.9	392.9	739.7	–
1973	5,376	396	3,225	4,240	–309	52.1	398.3	1,094.4	31.5
1974	7,597	542	4,460	6,582	–2,023	50.7	404.5	1,055.7	–
1975	10,135	594	5,081	7,274	–1,887	49.1	484.0	1,550.2	–
1976	13,913	803	7,715	8,774	–314	51.0	484.0	2,960.6	–
1977	17,807	1,012	10,047	10,811	12	49.9	484.0	4,306.4	29.7
1978	24,002	1,396	12,711	14,972	–1,085	61.3	484.0	4,937.1	–
1979	30,802	1,644	15,056	20,339	–4,151	67.6	484.0	5,708.1	24.8
1980	36,750	1,592	17,505	22, 292	–5,321	69.1	607.4	6,517.4	–
1981	45,528	1,734	21,254	26,131	–4,606	74.4	681.0	6,891.0	23.7
1982	52,182	1,824	21,853	24,251	–2,551	76.6	731.1	6,983.7	–
1983	61,722	2,002	24,445	26,192	–1,524	80.4	755.8	6,909.7	–
1984	70,084	2,158	29,245	30,631	–1,293	84.8	806.0	7,649.6	21.9
1985	78,088	2,194	30,283	31,136	–751	87.7	870.0	7,748.6	–
1986	90,599	2,505	34,715	31,584	4,709	91.5	881.4	7,955.2	–
1987	106,024	3,110	47,281	41,020	10,058	93.6	822.6	9,192.9	–
1988	126,230	4,127	60,696	51,811	14,505	94.7	730.6	12,378.3	18.1
1989	141,794	4,994	62,377	61,465	5,360	94.7	671.5	15,245.2	12.7
1990	171,488	5,659	65,016	69,844	–2,003	96.3	707.8	14,822.4	11.4
1991	215,734	6,745	71,870	81,525	–8,317	97.2	733.4	13,733.0	–
1992	240,392	6,988	76,632	81,775	–3,943	97.7	780.7	17,153.9	10.1
1993	267,146	7,484	82,236	83,800	990	98.1	807.6	20,262.4	8.9
1994	305,970	8,467	96,013	102,348	–3,867	98.6	803.8	25,672.4	7.9
1995	351,975	10,037	125,058	135,119	–8,508	99.0	771.1	29,351.2	–
1996	402,821	10,543	129,715	150,339	-23,005	99.3	804.8	29,414.0	–
1997	423,007	10,550	136,164	144,616	–8,618	99.9	1,696.3	8,873.6	–
1998	394,710	7,088	132,313	93,282	40,365	99.9	1,208.1	48,510.3	7.5
1999	436,798	8,680	144,745	119,750	24,476	99.9	1,138.0	74,105.3	–
2000	475,236	9,628	172,621	160,492	11,044	99.9	1,265.4	96,198.2	–

Note: All figures relate to year-end positions.

Sources: Sohn *et al* (1998); Bank of Korea Monthly Statistical Bulletin, various editions; MOCIE website.

Despite the lack of progress on economic reform, the Kim Young-sam Administration presided over a period of substantive techno-industrial restructuring in Korea that involved the continued replacement of heavy and chemical industry (HCI) activity with emerging knowledge-intensive sectors. Part of this restructuring process concerned the extension of the *chaebol* group's division of labour across Southeast Asia and China based on the low-end production of their main manufacturing activities (Park 1996, Suh 1993). Moreover, the *chaebols*' globalization strategies[14] marked the beginning of a shift from internal internationalization (export-based) of the South Korean economy towards external internationalization (FDI-based). Partly in response to this, South Korea's FEP-makers introduced the *Segyehwa* (globalization) policy framework in the mid-1990s that, *inter alia*, aimed to support the *chaebols*' multinational activities but also to liberalize some of South Korea's own trade and foreign investment barriers exposed by globalization (Gills 1996, Kim K.S. 1997, Kim S.S. 2000a, Moon and Mo 1999, Rowley and Bae 1998). As we later discuss, this proved a key turning point in the cognitive–ideological approach to South Korea's FEP.

4.2.4 The 1997/98 Financial Crisis and Beyond

South Korea's 1997–98 financial crisis has been the subject of much academic study.[15] While there is conflicting debate surrounding the distribution of blame for the crisis, there is a general consensus that its root cause lay in the country's high-debt model of development. Signposts to a full-blown crisis included worsening macroeconomic conditions over 1996 and early 1997.[16] Presiding over a growing trade deficit, the Kim Young-sam Administration decided against currency devaluation in Summer 1996, backed by a strong alignment of South Korean business interests dependent upon heavy foreign borrowing: devaluation would incur higher repayments and carry the political risk of pushing the country's GDP per capita below the psychological $10 000 level. By the end of 1996 the current account deficit reached $23.0bn, or 4.6% of GDP (Table 4.1). In the corporate sector, Hanbo Steel, a major manufacturer, announced its insolvency in January 1997. Later that October, Kia Motors was nationalized after banks refused the company further loans. The fragility of other *chaebols*' highly geared financial structures also became increasingly exposed by this time[17]. South Korea's liquidity problems were further exacerbated by both the widespread practice of its banks borrowing short-term capital to finance long-term investment[18] and the unravelling of a wider financial crisis across East Asia. By November 1997, South Korea was experiencing a foreign exchange crisis in which a rapid and drastic depreciation of the won[19] created an economy-wide liquidity crunch, leaving the country on the verge of bankruptcy.[20] The Kim Young-sam Administration's failure to provide a convincing policy solution to these problems precipitated both the intervention of the IMF and the election of Kim Dae-jung as President in December 1997. Attached to the IMF's $58bn financial assistance package came the condition that South Korea's new Government must introduce far reaching economic reforms. These became collectively known as the IMF 'bailout' programme[21] and comprised five main areas:

- the tightening of monetary and fiscal policy aimed at reducing South Korea's trade deficit-induced external debt;
- a comprehensive restructuring of the financial and banking system based on a firmer exit policy, increased competition and strong market and supervisory discipline;[22]
- a timetable to liberalize various aspects of trade policy in accordance with commitments set by the WTO;
- wider foreign access in Korea's finance and capital markets;
- a more flexible labour market, including the lifting of restrictions on lay-offs and strengthening employment insurance.

The new Kim Dae-jung Administration readily embraced the IMF's policy prescriptions and subsequently initiated wide ranging neo-liberal reforms. Perhaps most significantly, Kim Dae-jung intended to dismantle much of the state–*chaebol* nexus, thus upholding the recent tradition set by newly inaugurated South Korean Presidents.[23] The *chaebols*' bad debts, bloated commercial empires and cronyist links with state bureaucrats were widely perceived as a central cause of South Korea's crisis. In matters of corporate governance, the new Government introduced rules aimed at abolishing the practice of cross guarantees, whereby profit-making *chaebol* subsidiaries were heavily subsidizing their loss-making counterparts within the group. The *chaebols* were also forbidden to enter new business sectors. These reforms were intended to dissolve the conglomerate structures of the *chaebol*. Furthermore, strict prudential regulations on debt–equity ratios were introduced, with the *chaebol* given the target of reducing these to 200% by 2000. The collapse of Daewoo,[24] one of the 'big five' *chaebols*, lent further exigency to the government's corporate governance reforms. However, this reform area was problematic owing to both the aforementioned *chaebol* recalcitrance and an old political impasse: both sides of the state–*chaebol* nexus recognized the top *chaebols*' pivotal role in the economy and thus could ultimately depend on policy latitude and compromise from the government.[25] Deadlines for the elimination of cross-guarantees and debt–equity realignments were extended or fudged, while loop-holes in rules concerning the latter were expertly exploited by the *chaebols*. Many *chaebols* also resisted to some extent the Government's 'big deals' policy of pan-*chaebol* restructuring which revived the previous Kim Young-sam Administration's efforts of focusing *chaebol* activity on core sectors. In addition, the financial affiliates of the biggest *chaebols* intensified their oligopolistic–monopolistic dominance in South Korea's capital market and non-bank financial sector.[26] Furthermore, in March 2001 the Government extended financial assistance to troubled divisions of the Hyundai group (Engineering and Construction; Electronics), with Finance Minister Jin Nyum vindicating this policy decision by stating, 'the Government can't keep its hands off. The market was not working'.[27] This action was criticized by the US who saw the move as a violation of its IMF and WTO commitments.

Notwithstanding ongoing inertia on corporate governance reform, South Korea's 1997/98 financial crisis represented a watershed in the country's economic development and history. Neo-liberal advocates particularly likened South Korea to an 'economy in transition', experiencing a parallel ideological conversion to that confessed by their Central and East European (CEE) counterparts, albeit from a different developmental background (i.e. communism rather than developmental statism) and in a pre-gradualistic manner. Just like many of these CEE countries (e.g. Hungary, Poland), the transition process to a market-oriented economy had begun some time before crisis-events accelerated its pace. As Lee, D.H. (1999) comments, pre-crisis South Korea was clinging 'to methods that were incompatible with trends in global development' (p. 109), a similarly neo-liberal assessment that could be applied to the CEE countries during the Cold War.

In various post-crisis speeches, high-level government officials talked in terms of creating a 'new paradigm' in South Korea, based on the Kim Dae-jung Administration's three stated governing principles of *democracy*, *market-orientation* and *productive welfare*.[28] This was further presented in the rhetoric of moving from an 'industrial society to information society', and of 'embracing the global economy'.[29] In the field of deregulation, the Government eliminated 70% of the more than 11 000 government regulations by September 2000 that existed two years previously.[30] In the context of South Korea's rapid economic recovery in 1999/2000, it also keenly stressed the structural nature of required economic reform rather than the counter-cyclical. In articulating the Government's approach, Trade Minister Han Duck-soo proposed that South Korea's new development strategy be based on the 'mobilisation of national commitment to the cause of development', and that 'only democratically generated national commitment will make the development process sustainable and successful'.[31] Yet achieving this 'mobilization' may nevertheless require recourse to the state's prevailing 'infrastructural power' wielded over domestic economic agents, especially if political pluralism makes such a consensus unattainable.

As argued in Chapter 2, South Korea's shift from developmental authoritarianism to developmental democratization still leaves considerable latitude for state capacity in national economic management. South Korea may be moving more towards a liberal regulatory state, but this chapter will show how certain structural economic, institutional and socio-cultural factors form the basis of a resilient developmental statism, with critical implications for the future development of the country's FEP. Indeed, the crisis necessitated that the South Korean state increase its command authority in many areas of the economy.[32] For instance, new government agencies such as the Planning and Budget Commission (PBC) and the Financial Supervisory Commission (FSC) were created to deal with South Korea's emergency economic conditions. As Kang (2000) comments, 'although these entities were meant to bypass entrenched interests in government bureaucracies, some argue that these new entities, with sweeping powers, may end up reinforcing a key pillar of the developmental state' (p. 98). In another example of resilient developmental statism, the Kim Dae-jung Government selected ten major industries for comprehensive reorganization, legitimizing this interventionism by the critical need for sectoral restructuring. As part of this process, a consortium of aircraft and part manufacturers was created in order to maintain a strategic industrial capacity in this sector after the crisis had passed.

The crisis also reminded South Korea of its semi-periphery fragility, particularly regarding both its independent weakness in resisting external market forces and the extent of its dependent development. While it remains the third largest economy in Asia and the thirteenth largest in the world – with a GDP of $457.4bn in 2000 – the country was brought to the point of bankruptcy by the countervailing powers of global finance. Yet just as globalization may be partly culpable for South Korea's crisis, so it also contributed to its remarkable recovery with exports playing a major role in the country's economic rebound over 1999 and 2000. Like its NIE-3 counterparts, the South Korean economy remains highly trade-oriented with total trade accounting for 36.4% of its GDP in 2000 (see Table 4.1). The fundamental export-orientation of the economy and South Korea's sense of 'trading statehood', underpinned by the common developmental resolve demonstrated by the South Korean people through the crisis, were key factors in the recovery. After the 6.7% contraction of the South Korean economy in 1998 a 10.9% economic growth rate was registered in 1999 and 8.8% in 2000, although South Korean economy's predicted growth rate for 2001 was around 5% at time of writing, at least partly owing to the slowdown in the US economy. From a previous run of trade deficits, South Korea recorded trade surpluses of $39bn in 1998, $24bn in 1999, and $11.8bn in 2000. Consequently, the country's foreign exchange reserves bounced back from their nadir of $3.9bn during late 1997 to a record high of $96.2bn by the end of 2000, making South Korea the world's fifth largest retainer behind Japan, China, Taiwan and Hong Kong. The nation had also maintained its ranking as the world's second largest shipbuilder, fourth largest steel producer and seventh largest automobile manufacturer. While there remains much outstanding post-crisis restructuring in the short-to-medium term, South Korea's longer term fixation of closing the developmental gap with the core industrial powers prevails, albeit with a much altered fusion of statist and neo-liberal approaches.

4.3 COGNITIVE–IDEOLOGICAL APPROACHES

Of the NIE-3 group, the battle of economic ideas and values within South Korea over the last decade or so has been the most intense. As the previous section discussed, the cognitive–ideological basis of South Korea's FEP until the 1990s was founded on strong neo-mercantilist principles. Moon and Ko (1999) talk of 'the long-term socialisation of mercantilist ideas and practices in South Korea' (p. 201) that was ingrained not just in the country's economic bureaucrats but also across the broad populus. By the mid-1990s, neo-mercantilist values still ran deep within South Korean society. A 1995 opinion poll found that 24.4% of South Koreans identified trade conflicts with advanced industrial economies (AIEs) as the most serious threat to national security. Another conducted a year later found 52.3% of South Koreans felt that enhancing international economic competitiveness was the most important priority of government policy.

Moreover, the cognitive–ideological links between South Korea's developmental statism and neo-mercantilist FEP have been strong. As we discuss later, it is particularly those developmentalist-minded bureaucrats that have resisted moves towards a more neo-liberal economic policy paradigm. Likewise, many stakeholding FEP constituencies from the business and civil sectors have expressed unease at both the state's disposing of the South Korean developmental model and its embrace of 'open market' globalization. Such suspicions were evident before the crisis, as demonstrated by attitudes towards the government's *Segyehwa* (globalization) programme. Before the *Segyehwa* policy was formally announced in the Sydney Declaration of 17 November 1994, Foreign Minister Han Sung-joo had given prior signals of the South Korean state's embrace of global neo-liberalism (Gills and Gills 2000). In May 1994, he noted the importance of South Korea's 'striving for globalisation, trying to induce foreign investment, liberalising its financial market and preparing to join the OECD'.[33] This formed part of South Korea's 'new diplomacy', based on globalism, diversification, multi-dimensionalism, regional co-operation, and future orientation.

In January 1995, the Presidential *Segyehwa* Promotion Commission (PSPC) was created with a mandate to see through a gambit of related policies. Kim Young-sam's *Segyehwa* initiative was holistic in design with the intention of fostering economic, political, social and cultural open-mindedness (Ha 1999,

Kim S.S. 2000b, Lee Y.S 1997, Moon 1995). Yet as Gills (1999) commented, it transpired to be 'more rhetorical than substantive, more of a slogan than a coherent policy' (p. 8). Moon (1999) was similarly critical, stating that 'its actual implementation has been tarnished by erratic variations of opening and closure, regulation and deregulation, and intervention and non-intervention' (p. 211). In an earlier work, Gills (1996) explored the tension between Kim Young-sam's twin *Segyehwa* policy objectives, concluding that the imperative of supporting *chaebol* global strategies proved stronger than that of economic liberalization, and that replacing statist, neo-mercantilist forms with 'competitive capitalism' in South Korea's political economy was inherently problematic. This was partly due to the profound socio-political changes that would be required to facilitate this, a recurrent theme of this chapter.

Notwithstanding such inertia and resistance to embrace neo-liberal globalization, the influence of both domestic and external neo-liberal advocates upon the ideas driving new South Korea's FEP initiatives had gained supremacy by the time of the 1997/98 crisis. The 'ideological osmosis' noted earlier that had permeated the ranks of the economic bureaucracies created a swelling faction of neo-liberal minded FEP protagonists holding key policy-making positions.[34] Whilst there was bureaucratic inertia to implementing new market-based policies, in the broader perspective the cognitive–ideological tide was turning against the statists. At the apex of this change was the Presidential Office itself. In a rallying proclamation, Kim Dae-jung stated in August 1998 that 'Korea must shed its blind nationalism to meet the challenges of globalisation'.[35] This constituted a reinvigoration of the *Segyehwa* ethos and an endeavour to 'de-nationalize' South Korea's economic culture, with the creation of new economic cultural constructs (e.g. 'market democracy', 'productive welfare') intended to help engineer a paradigm shift in South Korean society's economic thinking, and thus laying the popular basis for a more open, neo-liberal economic policy approach.

Furthermore, many used the 'transitionary logic' of Gershenkronian late industrialization to legitimize the gradual deconstruction of the South Korean developmental state from the 1980s onwards, and with it developmentalist and neo-mercantile policies (see Chapter 2). They argued that as the complexity and size of the South Korean economy grew, so must the overextended state be replaced with a more decentralized, market-based economic structure. Accordingly, this required new ideas and directions in state economic policy, or as Kim (1997) more specifically proposed a shift from neo-mercantilism to globalism, i.e. a cognitive–ideological approach oriented by neo-liberal and multilateral norms. External neo-liberal advocates lent considerable support to this process. During the early 1980s, the emerging neo-liberal faction within the South Korean polity worked closely with both World Bank and IMF officials on the restructuring loan provided to the country at this time. Under the more recent IMF 'bailout' programme similar ties flourished to a far greater extent, helping substantively to fortify a growing neo-liberal consensus within the state economic bureaucracy. As well as training most of the government's post-graduate recruits, and hence its young elite, the US's unremitting bilateral pressure upon South Korea to adopt a more neo-liberal policy paradigm had various reinforcing effects.

However, despite the extensive neo-liberal inroads apparent within the South Korean polity at the millennial cusp, neo-mercantilism remains a resilient cognitive–ideological fundament of the country's FEP. This can be partly attributed to South Korea's resilient developmental statism itself, as well as numerous other 'embedded' factors that maintain the relevance of the neo-mercantilist approach. As contended earlier, national advancement remains a prime FEP objective: the game of techno-industrial 'catch-up' has yet to run its course, and hence South Korea's strong urge to move beyond the semi-periphery strata. There thus remains a compulsion to close the developmental gap, and hence maintain a relatively strong 'associative' technical policy realm of FEP as discussed later. Similarly, South Korea's structural trade deficit, born from a continued dependence on strategic import supplies, infers that export-oriented industrialization will remain an important element of the FEP calculus. Evidence of a persisting neo-mercantilist approach is also apparent, as for example revealed by the government's interest in accumulating substantial foreign exchange reserves, underpinned by continued public anxiety over trade deficits, and the government's and public's preoccupation of maintaining export industry competitiveness.[36] This is further augmented by FEP protagonists' continued accommodation of a strong 'nationalist' economic culture. As we discuss in greater detail later on, the enduring strength of economic nationalism has blunted the lead edge of neo-liberalism's advance in South Korea.[37]

Indeed, there were many South Korean policy-makers who before the crisis had wanted to introduce more overt neo-liberal measures but feared both socio-cultural and bureaucratic resistance. This group therefore welcomed the IMF-prescribed economic reforms and new neo-liberal paradigm they would help consolidate in South Korea. Nevertheless, post-crisis developments revealed that the aforementioned resistance remained substantial. Bureaucratic cadres that adhered to the neo-mercantilist ideological approach provided a source of considerable inertia on policy reform. This resistance derived mainly from low-level bureaucrats who, in comparison to ministerial executives, were far more politically distanced from the Presidential Office. Their apprehensions over reform generally centred on the technical dismantling of the developmental state (e.g. moves towards smaller government, privatization sales, removing the levers of state control and guidance over the economy) and thus an emasculation of their infrastructural power. Bureaucratic resistance to FEP reform was manifest in various areas in the crisis aftermath. For example, the

Government's rationalization plan to merge the Ministry of Commerce, Industry and Energy (MOCIE) and the Ministry of Information, Communication, Science and Technology failed due to strong bureaucratic opposition from those agencies to be disbanded or merged with others.[38] FEP bureaucrats also stalled the revision of many inward FDI policies, arguing that the inflow of foreign investment funds was generating upward pressure on the won exchange rate at the expense of South Korea's exports. This argument was supported by the *chaebols* whose increased export production had helped lift the South Korean economy out of the crisis by 1999.[39]

As part of this lingering economic nationalism, Kim Dae-jung has faced some strong public criticism over his readiness to embrace globalization at the apparent sacrifice of South Korea's national interest. Moreover, in the words of one research interviewee, 'most Koreans accept the need to embrace globalism but many are not actually willing to do it in practice'.[40] However, as our more detailed analysis on this subject later observes, economic nationalistic impulses at both the bureaucratic and societal levels are gradually diminishing. A 1999 KDI survey found that 66.9% of the South Korean public were generally favourable to foreign investment, with the younger generation providing more positive 'globalist' responses to this and similar questions. Yet, while another research interviewee stated that 'economic nationalism is giving way to pragmatism in South Korea, and more so than in Japan', she also insightfully commented that 'South Korea will never do things the Western way. The ends maybe Western but their methods will remain Korean'.[41] Thus, the cognitive–ideological basis of South Korea's FEP may well be aligning more closely to a neo-liberal approach, but this does not infer a template adoption of the Anglo-Saxon or other Western neo-liberal norms. Instead, a new South Korean brand will emerge based on an accommodation of its own economic culture currently experiencing a phase of considerable flux.

4.4 GENERIC 'ECONOMIC SECURITY' OBJECTIVES

South Korea entered the 21st century with its security agenda still dominated by the issue of North Korea, with which it still shares a highly charged military border. As Moon (1998: 222) observed, 'the enduring military threat from North Korea… still remains the primary existential security problem' for South Korea, and while this threat remained it was unlikely that Seoul would alter its hierarchy of national security interests. Nevertheless, indications of a more pluralistic approach – including economic security issues – became evident from the early 1990s onwards, partly owing to the transition from military to democratic rule (Moon and Lee 1995). It is later argued how such pluralism will continue, especially as the prospect of Korean reunification brings with it important economic and other 'new' security domain challenges for South Korea.

As with their NIE-3 counterparts, South Korea's security policy elites have paid little explicit attention to economic security issues, its FEP protagonists pursuing strong implicit rather than explicit economic security objectives. To paraphrase a ministerial interviewee, the rare occasions of the latter have tended to concentrate on immediate economic concerns (e.g. critically short fuel import supplies), although another stated that 'safeguarding the capacity for long-term prosperity has always been a central element of the post-war Korean mindset'.[42] Some prominent South Korean academics have also developed a growing interest in economic security issues. For Moon (1998), the essential goals of South Korea's economic security are prosperity, stability and welfare against externalized threats derived from trade protectionism and international economic stabilities. He further cites three specific external challenges or threats to South Korea's economic security, these being growing foreign pressure to liberalize the economy – especially from the US and liberal international economic organizations (IEOs) – intensified competition from China and Southeast Asia's NIEs, and the nation's exposure to systemic changes within the global economy.

Meanwhile, Lee D.H.'s (1999) more neo-realist conceptualizations of economic security are posited in an economic diplomacy context and involve three constituent aspects, namely: (1) securing national economic welfare, which includes 'protecting its economic sovereignty against external challenges brought on by changes in the international economic environment and maximising its economic interests by solidifying economic relations with other nations' (p. 113); (2) fortifying national security through the utilization of economic power; (3) securing a certain level of technological expertise to ensure a required level of military power. The overt neo-realist approach of Lee, a scholar at MOFAT's Institute of Foreign Affairs and National Security, reflects the deeper retention of traditional security interests within the South Korean policy-network elites. However, both Lee (1999) and Moon (1998) are critical of deficient 'new security' thinking in South Korea's security policy formation. Indeed, Lee goes so far as to suggest that the lack of explicit economic security consciousness was partly to blame for the country's 1997/98 financial crisis.

As we discuss below, the instabilities and uncertainties generated by the crisis brought South Korea's economic security interests into sharper focus. In the words of one interviewed MOFAT official, 'the crisis heightened the country's attention to economic survival'.[43] Critical issues regarding South Korea's trade balance, import-supply dependency (especially on fuels) and foreign exchange reserve management all came to the fore, with 'crisis-prevention' forming an important underlying principle of South Korea's FEP in the aftermath. Amongst other issues, these new post-crisis developments in the country's economic security interests and objectives are now considered.

4.4.1 Supply Security

With a shared NIE-3 paucity of natural resources, South Korea maintains a high degree of import dependency on foreign raw materials. This is most pronounced in imported fuels, where its industrial transformation has made it the world's sixth largest oil importer and even more dependent than Japan or Taiwan on foreign energy sources. Over 1987 to 2000, South Korea's dependence on imported energy materials rose from 80.0% to 97.3%, and its reliance on oil as an energy fuel from 43.7% to 52.1%. As oil must be paid for in dollars, the country's terms of trade and exchange rate policy have been closely implicated, partly explaining why South Korea had for many years tied the won closely to the dollar to attain some imported oil price predictability. Furthermore, the country's balance of payments was hit hard during expensive oil price periods, with repercussions elsewhere in the technical policy domains such as trade.

Furthermore, South Korea fuel-supply security interests have oriented certain objectives in the domain of economic diplomacy. The geo-political concentration of South Korea's imported oil sources during the 1960s to 1980s was located in the Middle East. In associated efforts to develop closer economic relations with Middle Eastern states, South Korean governments helped progressively to direct considerable levels of outward FDI to the region, particularly in the construction sector where the *chaebols* built new offices, factories and infrastructure in conjunction with the state's 'alliance' economic security objectives (see Table 4.2). During the 1980s South Korea began to diversify its oil source supply, Southeast Asian countries becoming increasingly important in this respect with Indonesia and Brunei acting as its major, more localized suppliers. By 1994 more than 22 countries supplied South Korea with oil, consequently reducing its dependency on the Middle East from a 1980 peak of 98.9% to 76.6% (Moon 1998). The sharp decline in oil prices over the late 1980s to early 1990s altered the economic security calculus, with for example outward FDI policy objectives shifting focus to matters of market access security where the *chaebols'* strategic competitive position within the emerging Triad market structure (i.e. East Asia, Europe and North America) demanded increasing attention. However, the return of high oil price volatility in late 2000 caused the Government to introduce new measures in February 2001 aimed at strengthening overseas resource development by South Korean companies in Southeast Asia, the Russian Far East oil and gas fields, and the Middle East.[44]

Table 4.2 South Korea's outward FDI by geographic destination, percentage of cumulative total

	1968–1980	–1987	–1997	–1998
East Asia	31.5	24.5	44.5	41.4
North America	24.4	41.6	29.9	29.5
Europe	3.9	2.5	15.1	16.4
Middle East	16.6	19.5	1.2	3.0
Africa	18.8	1.2	4.8	2.2
Latin America	3.5	1.7	2.2	5.0
Oceania	1.3	9.0	2.3	2.5

Source: Bank of Korea, UNCTAD database.

South Korea's persisting techno-dependence upon Western and Japanese firms extends its supply security interests to safeguarding key foreign sources of strategic industrial products, e.g. intermediate componentry and high-tech capital goods. In 1999, 59.8% of South Korea's imports from the US – the country's most important trade partner – were in capital goods, and around two thirds of these were utilized for export production. Similar ratios apply to South Korea's imports from Japan: more than 80% of South Korea's total imports from Japan are comprised of parts and production materials.[45] More generally, South Korea's export production maintains a high dependence on capital good imports from AIEs, especially in high-technology lines (Yang and Kim 2000). As is further discussed below, recent South Korean governments have gradually moved from the 'arm's-length', foreign technology licensing approach to that of induced technology transfer through inward FDI as a means to realize this supply security objective.

4.4.2 Market Access Security

Given South Korea's 'trading state' tradition and the enduring export-orientation of its economy, market access security interests remain a strong FEP priority. Expanding the export outlets for domestic production is still seen as critical to advancing South Korea's techno-industrialization and economic prosperity. With the US no longer willing to act as its 'market of last resort', European and burgeoning East Asian markets were increasingly targeted by South Korea's FEP protagonists and exporters from the 1980s onwards (Table 4.3). The then anticipated tripolarization of world economy reinforced this 'Triadic' strategy, with trade and FDI promotion delegations dispatched from Seoul to explore new market opportunities and foster more promotive economic diplomacy ties (Dent 2000). In Europe, the surge of inward South Korean FDI experienced during the early 1990s was partly driven by market-access motivations in that acquiring such 'insider' status would both permit the *chaebols* more effectively to exploit the benefits of the EU's 'Single Market' and circumvent various trade barriers facing home-based export production (Dent and Randerson 1996, Park 1995). The contemporaneous increase in *chaebol* FDI in the US can be attributed to similar circumstances *vis-à-vis* the North American Free Trade Agreement (NAFTA). South Korea's aforementioned techno-dependency on the core Triadic powers (US, Japan, EU) provided additional imperative here.

As the 1990s progressed, Kim Young-sam's *Segyehwa* programme initiated a wider global search for new emerging markets in what seemed then to be areas of marginal commercial interest to South Korean firms (e.g. Central Asia, Latin America), and this strategy was intensified under the Kim Dae-jung Administration (see the trade policy section). As other chapters indicate, both Singapore and Taiwan have also conducted similar market access strategies over recent years, sending their own trade delegations to the same relatively unfamiliar market destinations.

While South Korea's trade negotiators continue to prove formidable, the corresponding shifts from neo-mercantilism to neo-liberalism in trade policy, and from defensive to promotive economic diplomacy has altered the way in which market access security objectives are pursued. The 1997/98 crisis was highly catalytic in this respect, accelerating the at least rhetorical conversion of South Korea's FEP protagonists to free trade advocacy. Consequently, there is a closer alignment between market access security and system security objectives, where greater faith has been placed in the WTO and multilateral processes *per se* to realize South Korea's FEP objectives. The more comprehensive opening up of its own domestic markets is now accepted as part of the same process, and as an important 'leap of faith' in this respect. Most of South Korea's domestic business community, so long enjoying varying degrees of insulation from foreign competition, accept this paradigm shift in government policy.[46] However, the more ardent support of global market access co-exists with the new exploration of institutionalized bilateral market access, as demonstrated by various bilateral free trade agreement projects initiated in the post-crisis period with fellow members of the Asia–Pacific Economic Co-operation (APEC) forum. The number of Asia–Pacific bilateral free trade agreement (APBFTA) partners is likely to increase as East Asia's post-crisis recovery deepens and the region's markets restore their attractiveness. This issue is discussed further under alliance security issues. Thus, while the crisis may not have changed South Korea's market access security objectives in essential geographic and techno-industrial terms, it has however further altered the ethos and practical means by which they are pursued.

Table 4.3 Geographic breakdown of South Korea's international trade (percentage per trade partner, 1960–1999)

	1960		1970		1980		1990		1997		1998		1999	
	Imports	Exports	Imports	Exports	Imports	Exports	Imports	Exports	Imports	Exports	Imports	Exports	Imports	Exports
Japan	20.2	63.7	40.8	28.0	26.3	17.4	26.6	19.4	19.7	10.6	19.6	10.8	20.2	11.0
China	0.0	0.0	0.0	0.0	0.0	0.0	0.0	0.0	7.2	10.7	7.8	10.9	7.4	9.5
Taiwan	1.9	1.2	1.7	0.8	–	–	2.1	1.9	1.7	3.4	1.8	3.7	2.5	4.4
Hong Kong	0.4	8.1	1.0	3.4	0.4	4.7	0.9	5.8	1.4	7.6	1.3	5.4	0.7	6.3
ASEAN	6.9	2.1	6.3	4.1	6.8	6.6	7.2	6.0	9.6	15.5	9.6	11.1	10.2	12.2
United States	41.2	11.7	29.5	46.7	21.9	26.4	24.3	29.8	19.9	16.4	20.6	21.2	20.8	20.6
Canada	1.9	0.0	1.2	2.3	1.7	2.0	2.1	2.7	1.6	1.3	1.8	2.0	1.5	1.1
Australasia	2.7	0.0	0.8	1.0	3.4	1.5	4.4	1.7	4.5	1.7	4.6	2.2	4.4	1.9
EU15	20.9	12.9	10.5	8.7	7.8	16.7	12.0	13.6	11.2	11.3	11.7	13.5	10.5	14.1
Middle East	0.0	0.0	3.9	0.6	24.6	11.3	7.5	3.1	11.5	3.4	9.4	3.4	12.1	4.1
Africa	0.1	0.0	0.3	1.9	0.5	2.7	0.7	1.5	1.4	1.4	1.0	1.4	2.6	1.9
Latin America[1]	3.2	0.0	0.3	0.5	1.6	2.7	2.5	3.1	2.1	4.7	2.2	5.2	2.4	5.9
Other	0.6	0.3	3.0	2.0	5.0	8.0	9.7	11.4	8.2	12.0	8.6	9.2	4.7	7.0

Note: 1. Includes the Caribbean states.

Source: IMF Direction of Trade Statistics, various editions.

4.4.3 Finance–Credit Security

Unlike Taiwan and Singapore, South Korea maintained a strong reliance on foreign debt for much of the post-war period. This is both a legacy of its structural trade deficit predicament and past government policy preference for more 'arm's length' dealings with foreign capital as opposed to more direct contacts, for example through inward FDI. However, the state retained strong control over the financial reins of the economy until the early 1990s. The subsequent retraction of state capacity and the corresponding liberalization and deregulation in South Korea's financial sector is discussed later in the chapter, with special reference to the 1997/98 crisis. Suffice to say here that the crisis more than anything else dramatically revealed the fragility of South Korea's finance–credit security position.

In the pre-crisis period, the finance–credit security objectives of the South Korean authorities primarily centred on maintaining foreign creditors' confidence in the country's ability to eventually pay off its loans. This was notwithstanding the fact that much of the *chaebols'* foreign loan-funded investments were tied up in long-term strategic projects, most of which with little prospect of yielding any positive return for many years. Generating enough foreign exchange reserves to offset frequent trade deficits was another prime objective. Thus, the decline in semiconductor prices and the rise in oil prices in the global market constituted a significant finance–credit security concern for the country's FEP protagonists. While these objectives remain critical, new objectives and policy approaches have been added since the 1997/98 crisis.

Alleviating South Korea's external liquidity shortage and regaining access to the international capital markets were early international finance policy priorities in the 1997/98 crisis aftermath. To convince international financiers further of the country's credit-worthiness, the Kim Dae-jung Government has pursued further IMF-inspired neo-liberal reforms in its FDI and international finance policy regimes, opening up South Korea's economy and its currency to greater foreign interaction. Links here can be made with the country's new market access security approach. It has seen fit to align this economic security interest and its objectives more closely to systemic security aspects by trusting in financial globalization and the IMF's managerial functions. However, in light of the IMF's apparent deficiencies in heading off the crisis and containing its contagion effects, South Korea has joined a growing chorus of other East Asian states in calling for a revamping of its institutional capacities and methods.

As noted earlier, crisis-prevention has become an underlying principle of South Korea's post-crisis FEP. Consequently, the pursuit of its finance–credit security objectives embraces a much broader and more strongly allied set of technical policy measures. Of these, the country's post-crisis liberalized inward FDI regime has perhaps played the most significant new role by providing alternative sources of foreign capital to that of external loans. Furthermore, the post-crisis surge of inward FDI into South Korea helped integrate the domestic economy more into the circuitry of global capital and finance, hence more effectively attuning its firms to the extant finance–credit threats and opportunities of the global economy. Yet, this neo-liberal embrace of the inherent financial insecurity may backfire. Although the creation of the FSC has improved the state's regulatory and supervisory capacity in the international financial sector, retracting capacity elsewhere could prove counter-productive. For example, the radical liberalization of trade policy may precipitate a trade-deficit crisis that subsequently escalates into a wider financial and economic crisis. Thus, the pursuit of South Korea's finance–credit security objectives requires a more coherent multi-policy management approach.

4.4.4 Techno-Industrial Capability Security

South Korea's semi-periphery dependence on foreign technology remains critical. Even the most powerful *chaebols* still lack fundamental independent capabilities in original core technology design and development (Chong *et al* 2000; Enos and Park 1988; Hobday 1994; Shin 1998; Simon and Soh 1994; Smith 1997, 1999; Woo 1993; Ursacki and Vertinsky 1994). Hence, the country's techno-industrial capability security objectives have been especially entwined with those of supply, market access and alliance security. In addition, the objectives in question have naturally changed with evolving circumstances. For example, in the early post-civil war period South Korea's most crucial issues of techno-industrial capability concerned acquiring defence-enhancing technologies and maintaining the indigenous capacity of defence-related industries given the nebulous threat of military invasion from North Korea. As South Korea's EOI strategy progressed, additional techno-industrial concerns competed for attention as the economy's growing integration into, and stature within the world economy made the sector-wide upgrading of its industries more imperative.

Up to the 1997/98 crisis, South Korean governments maintained a general preference for foreign technology licensing and other more 'arm's-length' methods of inducing technology transfer, for example reverse engineering. This changed after the crisis as part of a more open domestic commercial environment, with high-tech inward FDI now proactively attracted to assist South Korea's techno-industrial restructuring and new technology infusion. It is too early to judge whether this new FEP strategy will prove a viable alternative to past policy methods. Moreover, while the deconstruction of the developmental state has meant that South Korean industrial policy is far less active than before, its techno-industrial capability security concerns remain fundamentally unchanged in that the country is simply switching one mode of technological dependency (e.g. licensing) for another (i.e. inward FDI). However, what is most relevant is which method is best able to safeguard the longer-term techno-industrial capability security of the South Korean economy. In this regard, South Korea's ability to commit foreign multinational enterprises (MNEs) to establish research and development (R&D) facilities in the country quicker than the rate the *chaebols* are relocating theirs overseas will prove a critical test.

4.4.5 Socio-Economic Paradigm Security

Previous discussions in this text have contended that of the NIE-3, South Korea had in the past maintained perhaps the strongest defence of its 'developmental' socio-economic paradigm. Its strong developmental statism and neo-mercantilism were mutually reinforced by an ardent economic nationalism. These constituted worthily defendable socio-economic values in South Korea's economic diplomacy negotiations with counter-paradigm states such as the US, whose powerful neo-liberal advocacy has proven so difficult to resist over recent decades. Despite such pressure, South Korean trade diplomats effectively defended many neo-mercantilist practices for some time, motivated by the fact that the failure to do so could loosen the underpinnings of the domestic political economy.

However, South Korea's socio-economic paradigm has also undergone the most dramatic change of the NIE-3. The deconstruction of the developmental state and the Kim Young-sam and Kim Dae-jung Governments' endeavours to embrace neo-liberal globalism have entailed an often fraught paradigmatic struggle within South Korea's bureaucratic and societal strata. In one sense, the embrace of globalism in particular implies a negation of defending any form of 'South Korean model', especially where compliance to 'international' or 'global' standards is sought: as such, the pursuit of socio-economic paradigm security objectives becomes meaningless. While the aforementioned 'ideological osmosis' has over time softened the hard neo-mercantilist edges of the country's FEP – thus more readily accommodating the demands of external neo-liberal advocacy as demonstrated in OECD accession negotiations and assimilating the IMF 'bailout' programme – we have already acknowledged how persistent economic nationalism has acted as a significant counter-pressure here.

Furthermore, although the foundations of a new post-crisis socio-economic order in South Korea are growing they are by no means complete. What the 1997/98 crisis demonstrated is that the South Korean developmental state is not just comprised of a governmental apparatus but is rather socio-economically and socio-culturally embedded, and it therefore possesses an inherent resilience given the frequent slow pace of socio-cultural change. As certain post-crisis events demonstrated, South Korea still maintains a neo-mercantilist style approach on various culture-sensitive issues (e.g. agriculture, screen quotas, trade-labour linkage) where domestic societal opinion and pressures have significantly shaped FEP objectives in these areas. As noted elsewhere in this chapter, this transitionary phase in South Korea's socio-economic paradigm will create conflicting signals within its FEP, insofar as these paradigmatic struggles come to the fore in technical policy-making and economic diplomacy.

4.4.6 Transborder Community Security

South Korea's transborder community security concerns are strongly focused on North Korea, as North Koreans share the most significant and immediate transborder community association with their southerly neighbours. An increasingly critical objective of South Korean FEP is to gradually engage with the North Korean economy in anticipation of future re-unification (Yang 1998). Building on the success of the inaugural Inter-Korean summit of June 2000 between Kim Dae-jung and North Korea's Kim Jong-il, economic interaction and even partial integration between the two Koreas is likely to progress.[47] However, a gradualistic approach is essential to South Korea's economic security given the fragility of the North Korean economy and potential instability brought on by a hasty integration of the two economies.

In both current and projected future circumstances, an initial phase of reunification would impose considerable resource-demand pressures upon the South Korean economy (Young *et al* 1998). North Korea's GDP per capita of $930 in 1999 was around a tenth of South Korea's, and the former's widespread social and economic structural imbalances would undoubtedly render integration an extremely costly exercise on practically all accounts. Since September 1995, North Korea appealed for the first time to the UN's World Food Programme for emergency food-aid in a bid to head off widespread famine. Whilst substantial multilateral and bilateral food-aid has been granted, the country's famine predicament remains at a critical level. A 1999 study estimated that some 2.5 million North Koreans died of starvation and hunger-related illnesses from 1994 to 1998.[48] Apart from North Korea's hard-line Stalinist regime presiding over a potential humanitarian disaster zone, the country's autarkic economy – starved of imports and foreign technology – is crumbling, with negative growth recorded for nine consecutive years over 1991 to 1999.

Reunification is therefore both a 'holy grail' and 'poisoned chalice', and thus a significant economic security challenge to South Korea through all expected phases of Korean economic integration. Judging whether the structural integrity and prosperity generating capacities of the South's economy are strong enough to withstand reunification-induced pressures is extremely important in the calculus of South Korea's economic security, and hence its future policy towards North Korea. Given the North's food crisis, the lifting of transborder restrictions on labour flows must be carefully managed given the potential for a Northern exodus of refugees to the South. For these and other reasons, seeking greater international assistance to help with both the costs and technical difficulties of Korean economic integration will become a prominent aspect of South Korea's FEP, if reunification does proceed. There is a general acceptance in the South that the long-term economic benefits of Korean integration outweigh the intermediate costs of reunification, but in the meantime the most important questions on the latter concern its sequencing, scale and pace.

Re-building a trans-Korea economic community must begin with fostering mainly microeconomic linkages, such as trade promotion, technical co-operation and assistance, increased South Korean FDI in North Korea, infrastructural projects and other forms of joint venture and economic exchange. Macroeconomic linkages (e.g. on currency matters) must come much later after greater convergence between the two economies becomes apparent. In general terms, the economic content of Seoul's 'Engagement Policy' towards North Korea will increase. Moreover, as reunification proceeds, a gradual shift in emphasis from South Korea's military security concerns to those of its economic security will become increasingly evident for the above reasons.

South Korea's other transborder community security issues primarily relate to developments in Northeast Asian sub-regional integration. Northeast Asia is one of the world's most prominent economic regions and yet regionalist developments remain comparatively limited. At the eve of the 21st century, it contained five of the world's six last economies (South Korea, North Korea, Japan, China, Taiwan and Papua New Guinea) not party to any bilateral or regional free trade agreement. Moreover, the most important regional economic co-operation project yet to emerge in Northeast Asia is the Tumen River Area Development Programme (TRADP) and this is sub-regional in nature, encompassing the North Korea's Rajin-Sonbong Economic and Trade Zone, Eastern Mongolia, China's Yanbian Korean Autonomous Prefecture in the Jilin Province, Russia's Primorsky Territory and South Korea itself, which provides key technical and financial support for the Programme (Marton *et al* 1995). The TRADP's activities have largely focused on large-scale transport and energy infrastructure projects, although its ambitions have far outweighed its achievements (Akaha 1999, Aldrich 1997). Moreover, South Korea's participation in the Programme has waned, owing both to crisis-induced financial weakening and the lack of perceived economic security benefits over time. As we later note, more FEP interest in Seoul is now placed on seeking free trade agreements with its Northeast Asian neighbours rather than on promoting 'low-key' sub-regional co-operation projects.

4.4.7 Systemic Security

Systemic security interests and objectives have become an increasing priority amongst South Korea's FEP protagonists. With the country's growing international stature and deepening engagement in IEOs (e.g. OECD, WTO) has come the expectation of greater systemic responsibility. Being still primarily an export-based economy by the mid-1990s, it had a clear interest in upholding the multilateral trade order and hence in providing systemic support to the WTO and other reinforcing international regimes, such as the IMF. Yet as a semi-periphery power pursuing neo-mercantilist policies, this support formed a relatively minor aspect of South Korea's pre-crisis FEP objectives, although *receiving* systemic support was a much higher priority.

While the IMF 'bailout' programme of financial assistance was by far the most significant single element of systemic support South Korea had ever received, it also corresponded with a marked change of attitude and policy approach amongst the country's FEP protagonists on matters of systemic security. As previously contended, the Kim Dae-jung Government's embrace of neo-liberal globalism ultimately progressed South Korea's previous *Segyehwa* economic policies from a 'one-way' globalization perspective (i.e. primarily exploiting new global commercial opportunities) to an acceptance of a 'two-way' globalization, whereby both economic openness and systemic responsibility are fostered. Consequently, the South Korean state has placed greater faith in the global market and IEOs to ensure its economic security. This is notwithstanding the fact that both the IMF's dealings in the 1997/98 East Asian financial crisis and the WTO's aborted launch of the New 'Millennium' Round at its 1999 Seattle Ministerial Meeting have recently revealed critical fault-lines in IEO systemic governance. Thus, South Korean FEP protagonists have become stronger advocates of fortifying IEO regimes and agendas since the crisis, in the aforementioned case of restructuring the international financial architecture under the IMF, and with respect to strengthening and developing of the WTO's rules more generally.[49] As discussed later, this is reflected in South Korea's recent economic diplomacy endeavours at systemic confidence building.

4.4.8 Alliance Security

There has been much change but also continuity in South Korea's alliance security concerns. The country's most prominent strategic economic partner remains the US, whose guarantor role in both economic and military security terms had engendered South Korea's 'policy of obligation' towards America, as exemplified in past preferential market access deals conferred to American business interests (Dent 1999). This perceived role has arguably been strengthened since the crisis, with the US's economic buoyancy during the latter 1990s – a period when the spectre of global economic recession loomed – both helping absorb South Korean exports and further demonstrating American entrepreneurial and techno-industrial supremacy over Japan and the EU. Nevertheless, over the longer-term South Korea has reduced its 'clientistic' alliance dependency on the US as part of a broader diversification of its international economic relations, as later shown in the economic diplomacy section that follows. It has of necessity maintained an important but uneasy alliance with Japan in its twin functions as key strategic techno-industrial supplier and regional hegemon. Alliance building with other partners, such as China and the EU, emerged as new FEP objectives during the 1990s and part of this diversification, or rather 'globalization' of Korea's economic relations.

The recently initiated rapprochement with North Korea may, of course, provide the basis for an important alliance economic security relationship for South Korea, but not for some considerable time. Ideological differences between Seoul and Pyongyang remain stark with practically no ground for shared 'core values', except in an ethno-cultural sense, which may have very limited foreseeable FEP significance. Moreover, reunification on the Korean peninsula, whilst having potentially very significant external impacts, is more a domestic-alliance focused process rather than an international alliance *per se*.

Arguably the most important post-crisis development in South Korea's pursuit of alliance economic security is its participation in the recent APBFTA trend. Although not as proactive as Singapore (see Chapter 3), South Korea's interest in signing up free trade agreements with a wider range of trading partners has become an intriguing new aspect of its FEP, this being its free trade advocacy. Not only, then, has this expressed itself in South Korea's new systemic security objectives, where more ardent support for the multilateral free trade system is now perpetrated, but also in the country's bilateral economic relations. Like other APBFTA players, South Korea's proclivity for forging these free trade-based alliances is partly risk-averse motivated by acting as some form of market access 'insurance policy' against the event of systemic failure, for example a continually stalled launch of the WTO's 'Millennium' Round. South Korea's FEP protagonists also perceive them as an effective vehicle for realizing various other economic diplomacy objectives, such as diversifying the country's economic relations into emerging market zones (e.g. Chile, Mexico and Latin America) and consolidating those with key strategic trade partners such as Japan.

4.5 TECHNICAL POLICY REALMS

It is the technical aspects of South Korea's FEP that have experienced arguably the most profound change since the 1997/98 crisis. The Kim Dae-jung Government has sought to align various technical FEP regimes to neo-liberal norms, albeit in the face of significant domestic-level constraints. Furthermore, certain technical policies have been conferred much greater priority. Before the crisis, trade policy largely dominated the *core* technical policy realm of South Korea's FEP formation. However, since 1997/98 the country's inward FDI and international finance policies have gained increasing salience. In addition, the growing importance of South Korea's official development assistance and co-operation (ODAC) programme can be expected with the country's progression to higher levels of income and systemic responsibility. Many changes are also evident in the *associative* technical policy realm, although as we argue later South Korea's continued fixation with national competitiveness advancement has maintained the critical importance of this FEP function. Many past developments in the technical policy realm of South Korea's FEP have been previously noted. Therefore, this section will concentrate on more recent developments, especially since the 1997/98 crisis.

4.5.1 Trade Policy

As has already been established, there exists a strong correlation between the decomposition of South Korea's developmental state and the diminishment of its neo-mercantilist trade practices. Traditionally, the government had pursued a protectionist trade policy that was also closely linked with export-enhancing industrial policies. South Korean exports consequently garnered a reputation for attracting various types of foreign protectionist barriers, including anti-dumping duties, subsidy-countervailing duties, and safeguard measures (Kim and Han 1995). However, the 1997/98 crisis significantly accelerated the liberalization of the country's trade policy, which had first begun in the early 1980s[50] and had taken a prior qualitative step forward with South Korea's compliance to the 1994 Uruguay Round of GATT (Chung 1995, WTO 1996).

Central to the Kim Dae-jung Government's new trade policy was the vision to transform South Korea into an 'open trading nation', based on implementing a 'free, fair and market-oriented trade regime'. This would be established within a 'Long-Term Trade Policy' framework, primarily referring to a continuous review process to monitor neo-liberal reforms, although it is interesting to note the long-term strategic thinking still deployed here by the South Korean state. As its 2000 WTO Trade Policy Review observed, South Korea's trade policy had undergone substantial liberalization since the 1997/98 crisis in accordance with commitments undertaken at the multilateral (WTO and IMF), plurilateral (OECD), regional (APEC) and bilateral (e.g. US and EU diplomacy) levels (WTO 2000b). An overview of the main aspects of post-crisis trade policy liberalization can be summarized as follows:

- Reductions in the average tariff rate from 7.9% in 1996 to 7.5% by 2000.
- Only rice and beef subject to quantitative restrictions by the end of 2000, those on the latter being lifted the following year.

- Removal of three of the last four export-related subsidies, with only one remaining on fruit and flower exports by 2001.
- Abolition in June 1999 of the euphemistically entitled Import Diversification Programme (IDP) that since 1978 had imposed restrictions on various Japanese imports. Additional import restrictions on Japanese cultural imports (e.g. cinema, music) were also gradually lifted from 1998.
- Closer alignment of South Korea's sanitary–phytosanitary schemes and technical standards with international norms.
- The easing of various import restrictions on cosmetics and pharmaceuticals.
- Duty-free access conferred on the imports of 80 commodities from 48 less developed countries (LDCs).

As discussed later, this new trade liberalism in South Korea's post-crisis FEP is also strongly evident in the economic diplomacy domain, for example in the bilateral free trade agreement projects being explored with other APEC members. However, while the South Korean Government claimed, amongst other things, that the country's domestic markets were 99.9% open by 2001 in terms of official foreign access (see Table 4.1), in reality a lingering protectionism still characterized many aspects of South Korea's trade policy. For example, many of its trade partners point to the recent enhancement of the country's anti-dumping regime as evidence of South Korea's persisting neo-mercantilism.[51] In November 1999, several European Industry Ministers accused the Government of continuing to subsidize South Korean shipbuilders, suggesting that some IMF 'bailout' funds may even have been deployed to such purposes. Meanwhile, in the culture-sensitive industries of cinema and agriculture, US trade diplomats and firms have accused South Korea of maintaining an excessively protectionist trade policy on screen quotas, thus restricting Hollywood-based export penetration. In 2000, the US also highlighted alleged domestic-level barriers to trade that endured in South Korea's pharmaceutical (complex certification and testing procedures) and government procurement (airport construction contracts) sectors (Yang and Kim 2000).

Furthermore, South Korea only made comparatively marginal average tariff rate concessions in the post-crisis period, from 7.9% to 7.5%, and the current level is still relatively high for an economy of its development and income level. By 2000 it also maintained a median of 50% tariff rate in its highly protected agricultural sector. The WTO further highlighted the highly complex tariff system retained by South Korea with 125 different types of duty,[52] and was critical of the numerous tax incentives introduced by the Kim Dae-jung Government aimed at promoting exports (WTO 2000b). Meanwhile in terms of export promotion, the government announced in early 2001 its intention substantially to extend its export-related financial support system, while in addition tax and tariff benefits were extended to trading companies.[53] In addition, MOCIE announced in April 2001 that the Government would undertake measures to augment and diversify the marketing of South Korean exports, commencing in May that year with a 'Sales Diplomacy' campaign initially to explore new commercial opportunities in the Middle East region. As we later note under economic diplomacy, though, the diminishment in both the range and intensity of South Korea's trade disputes can be largely attributed to the country's post-crisis trade policy liberalization, which has on balance brought important new changes to the country's FEP.

4.5.2 Foreign Direct Investment (FDI) Policy

Inward FDI policy

The development of South Korea's inward FDI policy can be divided into three historical stages. During the early years of the 'institutionalization' phase (1960–1983), newly inaugurated policies under the Foreign Capital Inducement Act (FCIA) of 1960 were intended to underpin the economy's shift from an ISI to EOI strategy, providing selective foreign technology infusions to develop the techno-industrial capacity of South Korea's export industry. Inward FDI was especially directed to the free export zones in Masan and Iri. However, foreign investment remained heavily restricted, for example in ISI protected sectors, and the penchant for more arm's-length engagements with foreign firms and capital (e.g. technology licensing) persisted during this period.[54]

In the 'early liberalization' phase (1984–1997), the Government commenced liberalizing its inward FDI regime in response to new economic imperatives, in particular the need for techno-industrial upgrading from an HCI-based to cleaner, more knowledge-based economy. Consequently, the positive list system was replaced with a negative list system in which all industries not listed were FDI eligible. As part of its OECD accession process, further liberalization ensued with the 1996 Act on FDI and Foreign Capital Inducement amending the FCIA accordingly and bringing South Korea's inward FDI regime more in line with international norms and standards.

More critical changes were to occur in the third and current phase of 'active investment promotion' (1998 to present), making inward FDI policy a far more salient technical policy feature of South Korea's FEP. Many of the motivations behind this radical policy change have already been discussed, yet it is worth citing Kim Dae-jung's own words that South Korea's new FDI policy was intended to 'catch five birds with one stone', bringing not only an injection of new capital but also enhanced transparency of business management, the transfer of advanced management techniques, an expansion of markets and job creation.[55]

The 1998 Foreign Investment Promotion Act (FIPA) essentially reshaped South Korea's inward FDI regime from one of 'investment regulation' to that of 'investment promotion',[56] introducing new legislation designed to create 'an investor-oriented policy environment by streamlining foreign investment procedures, strengthening investment incentives and establishing an institutional framework for investor-relationship management'.[57] By August 2000, 99.6% of all South Korea's business sectors were open to foreign investment. Under FIPA, the number of FDI restricted industries was reduced from 42 (fully 18, partially 24) to 31 (fully 13, partially 18) from a total classified number of 1148 industries. It also made the country's administrative procedures for FDI more simplified and transparent, as well as creating new tax incentives and a new institutional infrastructure for attracting inward FDI. The latter centred on two new agencies, these being the Korea Investment Service Centre[58] (a 'one-stop-shop' for foreign firms) and the Office of Investment Ombudsman (dealing with foreign firm grievances). In addition, FIPA introduced new incentives for factory site lease and a new Foreign Investment Zone initiative, conferring greater policy management and control to local governments in this area. Various capital and financial market policy reforms were designed to underpin the Act, such as the elimination and raising of ceilings on foreign ownership[59] (including land purchases) and the liberalization of foreign borrowing. This permitted much greater scope for acquisitional FDI, including that of a hostile nature, and foreign investment in South Korean real estate.

Other parallel developments in South Korea's post-crisis inward FDI policy are worthy of mention, including: the strengthening of the country's intellectual property rights (IPR) regime as a means to induce more foreign investment; the initiation of new bilateral investment treaty (BIT) negotiations, most importantly with Japan and the US; the dispatch of Foreign Investment Promotion Missions from 1998 onwards, beginning with the US, Europe and Japan in that year and spreading to other destinations thereafter. Future policy developments will emphasize improving the business and living environment for foreign investors, a long-term plan to improve the country's FDI infrastructure and 'after care services', and stronger incentives for inducing technology and SME-related inward FDI.[60]

Post-crisis policy liberalization helped induce a sharp increase in inward FDI into South Korea, rising to annual inflows of $8.9bn in 1998, $15.5bn in 1999 and to $15.7bn in 2000. Over the space of these three years, the country had consequently amassed more inward FDI ($40.1bn) than over the preceding 1962–1997 period. However, this surge of foreign investment into the South Korean economy and embrace of a far more liberal inward FDI regime carried certain economic and political risks. Foreign investor firms were viewed as more likely to shed workers and impose more 'flexible' work practices than their Korean-run counterparts, thus potentially generating labour unrest during a volatile phase of industrial relations. While the foreign acquisition of *chaebol* assets alleviates many of their debt and restructuring problems, a more open FDI regime also significantly challenged the domestic market interests of Korean big business, thus leading to possible confrontations between the *chaebol* and the state as foreign investing firms threaten the dominant oligopolistic–monopolistic positions of the *chaebol* in South Korea's domestic markets and other aspects of the South Korean economy (e.g. distribution). In the long run, this represents the over-riding concern for the strategic-minded *chaebol* who arguably feared a liberalized inward FDI policy more than trade policy liberalization.[61] In this respect, Moon and Ko (1999) contended that the 'penetration by [foreign] multinational corporations and their control of strategic industrial sectors, such as finance and telecommunications, could endanger South Korea's economic security' (p. 181).

The additional constraints of economic nationalism on inward FDI policy liberalization are considered later in the chapter, yet this new access to foreign capital also brought important advantages to the economy in general. Some *chaebols*, such as Samsung, viewed the new FDI policy as a means to collaborate more closely with foreign firms and assist their financial restructuring. For example, Renault bought out Samsung Motors while Volvo acquired its Heavy Industry division for $300m in June 1998. In other high profile examples, Daimler Chrysler also bought a 15% stake in Hyundai Motors and LG Electronics signed a new joint venture deal with Philips in June 1999 in which the latter would invest a 50% stake in a newly established company that was a spin-off of a sub-division of the former. As we also later note, inward FDI policy became a centrepiece in South Korea's post-crisis industrial policy.

Outward FDI policy

Although the overseas investments of South Korean firms were first permitted in 1968, it was only from the 1980s that outward FDI was actively state-supported in a general sense. Under the *Segyehwa* programme of the 1990s, it was encouraged as part of the government's support of the *chaebols*' globalization strategies. Furthermore, economic liberalization at home diminished the relative attractions of the domestic market, providing further exigency for overseas investment, to sustain export growth and reduce factor costs. *Segyehwa's* provisions on outward FDI policy included the easing of the application process for outward overseas investment and completely removing investment restrictions in all but three real estate related areas. As a consequence of this liberalization and deregulation there was a significant expansion of outward FDI applications, as well as an increase in large-scale FDI projects. Fatally flawed 'prudential guidance' measures were also implemented in an attempt to prevent reckless overseas investment and minimize potential adverse effects upon the national economy. Over 1997–2000, South Korea experienced a 30% contraction in outward FDI with the *chaebols* retracting or postponing many key overseas investment projects, such as LG's $2.6bn plant in Wales and Hyundai's $3.7bn plant in Scotland – the biggest foreign inward investments ever planned in the EU during the 1990s (Dent and Randerson 1996). South Korea's outward FDI regime was liberalized further by the Kim Dae-jung Government, largely through changes made to the country's international financial policy.

4.5.3 International Finance Policy

The government's control of the finance sector was once a key aspect of the South Korean developmental state. Domestic firms' interaction with international finance was heavily regulated by the state in accordance with developmental objectives, and mainly concerned the distribution of foreign loan credit and manipulation of the country's multiple exchange rate system[62] (Haggard and Cheng 1987, Lim 1985). However, like other technical policy realms of FEP, neo-liberal reforms commenced in South Korea's international finance policy from the early 1980s. After becoming a signatory to the IMF's Article 8, it was obliged to curtail its foreign exchange controls. The new Kim Young-sam Government accelerated the pace of neo-liberal reform. In June 1993, it unveiled its Financial Liberalization and Market Opening Plan, and this was followed in December 1994 by its Foreign Exchange Reform Plan. Both encouraged greater foreign participation in the country's financial and capital markets, permitting South Korean firms to substantially increase their ratios of foreign borrowing. The country's lending from foreign banks subsequently rose from $52bn in 1994 to $108bn by 1996. Much of this liberalization process was driven by South Korea's required compliance to 'international standards' on finance and capital markets in preparatory accession to the OECD, as we discuss later.

More radical policy liberalization came after the crisis, centring on the 1998 Foreign Exchange Transaction Act (FETA). Preceded by immediate 'emergency' liberalization measures enacted in July 1998 in compliance with IMF programme obligations, FETA involved two stages of implementation. First phase liberalization measures were introduced in April 1999, focusing on capital and current account liberalization, expanding foreign exchange serving banks and exchange bureaux, and opening up South Korea's foreign exchange market. This last measure sought to internationalise the South Korean won further by liberalizing overseas trade in the currency, permitting foreigners to issue won-denominated securities overseas, and relaxing regulations on overseas deposit accounts to facilitate overseas financial trade. Second phase measures were introduced in January 2001, bringing the full liberalization of foreign exchange transactions by domestic individuals by permitting them to invest freely overseas.

Events leading up to and during the 1997/98 crisis also played their part in liberalizing South Korea's exchange rate policy. In March 1990, the Bank of Korea had introduced a 0.4% variation rate policy for the won exchange rate based around a central rate against the dollar. This variation rate gradually rose through the 1990s (n.b. to 2.25% by 1995) with an eventual move to a freely floating system on 16 December 1997 in the wake of South Korea's financial crisis. However, the 1997/98 crisis also demonstrated the importance of exchange rate stability. After a 13% appreciation of the won since its pre-crisis level to September 2000, driven by current account surpluses and inward FDI flows, the Government implemented a package of measures, including foreign exchange market intervention, aimed to alleviate upward pressure on the won (OECD 2000). Thus, market interventionism still suits South Korea's FEP protagonists when conditions require.

In sum, the most important recent changes to South Korea's international finance policy have been foreign exchange liberalization; capital account liberalization; promoting the restructuring of the international financial architecture; and greater engagement with international financial institutions.[63] Under the economic diplomacy section that follows, it is also noted how South Korea is working closely with other 'ASEAN Plus 3' members[64] on international finance policy affairs.

4.5.4 Official Development Assistance and Co-operation (ODAC) Policy

Like Taiwan, South Korea's early post-war economic development owed much to received foreign (and particularly American) bilateral and multilateral aid.[65] Hence, in the scheme of its FEP, the country's situation as an aid *recipient* during this period rather than a *donor* was most relevant. Yet like other semi-periphery states in recent times, South Korea has developed an increasingly substantive Official Development Assistance and Co-operation (ODAC) policy of its own. The origins of this date back to the mid-1960s, when the Government invited technical trainees from LDCs to South Korea to learn their industrialization techniques. From 1967, South Korean experts were dispatched on overseas technical missions, and from 1977 and 1984 respectively, the country commenced providing equipment and materials, and provided development study facilities for developing nations. In 1982, an International Development Exchange Programme was established in which policy-makers were invited to participate in various seminars, workshops and field trips. Further institutionalization and development in South Korea's emerging ODAC policy came in January 1987 when the Economic Development and Co-operation Fund (EDCF) was created, which extends soft loans for industrial development projects[66] and currently represents one of South Korea's two bilateral ODA facilities. The EDCF is managed by the Export–Import Bank of Korea, which itself is under the direction of MOFE.

By 1990, different South Korean government ministries had initiated a variety of minor international co-operation programmes. This policy structure was rationalized with the creation of a unified organization, the Korea International Co-operation Agency (KOICA), in April 1991, and operates under the aegis and policy guidance of MOFAT.[67] In essence, KOICA is a policy implementation agency with twin policy operational areas, namely: (1) *grant aid*, which includes the provision of equipment and project aid; (2) *technical co-operation*, which includes development studies, trainee programmes and the dispatch of experts and volunteers overseas. South Korea's contributions towards multilateral aid are dispensed by: (1) MOFE, in subscriptions to international development institutions, e.g. World Bank; (2) MOFAT, in contributions to international organizations, e.g. the United Nations. In 1999, South Korea's official development assistance (ODA) amounted to $317.5m, the equivalent of 0.08% of its GDP.[68] While this is a comparatively low figure in comparison to other OECD nations (0.24% average for that year), it represented a fivefold increase from its 1991 level (Table 4.4). Furthermore, by 1997 South Korea had extended around $1.1bn in government loans to over 20 countries, with China, Vietnam, Indonesia, the Philippines, Sri Lanka, Romania and Poland receiving special attention (Lee, C.J 2000).

The South Korean Government's own stated rationale for developing a more robust ODAC policy relates primarily to four motivations.[69] First, with regard to political and diplomatic motivations, development co-operation is seen as an effective vehicle to promote the country's contribution to fostering international peace and prosperity. Second, its ODAC policy helps cement South Korea's economic relations with developing countries. This is particularly relevant in its relations with 'emerging market' zones of the world economy, such as the developing Asia–Pacific that receives far more than any other region at 62.9% of the 1999 total budget.[70] Third, with regard to humanitarian matters, this area of South Korea's FEP enables it to demonstrate its global citizenship and responsibility within the international system by contributing to the alleviation of extreme poverty and human suffering. As previously considered, if South Korea is to engage more interactively with the North Korean economy, the humanitarian aspect of this process is likely to be very prominent given the deteriorating socio-economic fabric of the latter. Indeed, North Korea is by far the most significant geo-political factor in South Korea's ODAC policy, with the comparatively large amount of food aid sent to the North not counted in KOICA's budget. Fourth, there is a 'return of goodwill' factor or 'reciprocation' principle that underlies South Korea's ODAC policy, in that this now

Table 4.4 *South Korea's ODA (US$m), 1988–1999*

	1988	1989	1990	1991	1992	1993	1994	1995	1996	1997	1998	1999
Bilateral	2.1	5.1	12.3	31.5	45.2	60.1	60.1	71.5	123.3	111.3	124.7	131.4
– Grant	2.1	3.3	3.3	25.0	31.0	32.7	38.5	50.1	53.4	54.8	37.2	39.0
– Loan (EDCF)	–	1.8	9.0	6.5	14.2	27.4	21.6	21.4	69.9	56.5	87.5	92.4
Multilateral	31.9	28.7	48.9	26.0	31.6	51.4	80.2	44.5	35.8	74.3	58.0	186.1
– Contribution	3.6	3.7	4.7	5.8	8.0	10.2	12.9	14.8	30.1	29.1	33.6	68.0
– Subscription	28.3	16.2	44.2	11.8	21.5	25.7	25.7	22.7	5.8	35.5	28.3	129.2
– Other	–	8.8	–	8.4	2.1	15.5	41.6	7.0	–	9.7	–3.9	–11.1
Total ODA	34.0	33.8	61.2	57.5	76.8	111.5	140.3	116.0	159.1	185.6	182.7	317.5
ODA as % of GDP	0.02	0.02	0.02	0.02	0.03	0.03	0.04	0.03	0.03	0.04	0.06	0.08

Source: KOICA

relatively prosperous nation feels obliged to perform a similar role to those once instrumental in assisting its own early industrial development.

Other developmental aspects of South Korea's ODAC policy are pertinent. For instance, it is broadly based on Japan's own ODAC framework, with KOICA modelled on the Japan International Co-operation Agency and the EDCF based on Japan's Overseas Economic Co-operation Fund. There is also the question of whether the recent paradigmatic struggles within the South Korean political economy have had any effect on the post-crisis developmental experience now shared with, and promulgated to LDCs. According to interviewed ODAC policy officials, such proselytizing by the Kim Dae-jung Government representatives occurs more through diplomatic channels than South Korea's ODAC programme, which focuses more on conferring technical expertise and resources. Moreover, in the words of an interviewed KOICA official, Kim Dae-jung's three socio-economic pillars of market economy, democracy and productive welfare are 'not fully reflected in our ODAC policies, and it could take considerable time before they are'.[71] This is perhaps one technical policy realm of South Korea's FEP that has remained relatively immune to ideological contestation. Instead, recent changes have centred on the growing technology-content of South Korea's ODAC programme, such as the Korean Partnership Programme introduced in 2001 and concerned with 'digital divide' issues. Moreover, although South Korea's ODA levels understandably fell during the crisis, there is a stated commitment to gradually improve South Korea's ODAC resources and capacity over the long-term as the country's own prosperity and development progress. Hence, this emerging technical policy realm of South Korea's FEP reveals a stronger semi-periphery advocacy role in the international system, further consolidating the country's position as systemic support *provider* rather than *receiver*.

4.5.5 The *Associative* Technical Policy Realm

Although the Kim Dae-jung Administration intended generally to diminish the state's activist role in the economy, the *associative* technical policy realm of South Korea's FEP remained comparatively prominent at the start of the 21st century. State-assisted infrastructure investment, human resource development, science and technology activities and industrial development continued to be strongly allied to a common cause, namely national competitive advancement within the international economic system. The policy tools and methods may have changed but the state's prioritization of export competitiveness, albeit more passive, has remained. There persists a general consensus in South Korean society that the new techno-industrial paradigm needs some degree of state organization and orchestration, and for the government's efforts to improve export competitiveness, both in qualitative and cost terms, to be maintained.

The *associative* technical policy realm has always been a salient feature of South Korea's FEP, and industrial policy in particular. Over the developmental era, South Korea has proved the most ardent practitioner of strategic trade theory of the NIE-3, and thus attained the closest trade–industrial policy linkage.[72] According to Sohn *et al* (1998), there have been six distinctive phases of trade and industrial policy in post-war Korea, these being:

- *Import substitution (1948–1961)*: characterizing the policy approach in the pre-developmental state period. Chronic trade deficits financed by US bilateral aid, tight regulatory control of imports, industrial policy subsidies directed at infant industry development within heavily protected domestic markets.
- *Export promotion (1962–1972)*: advent of the Park Chung-hee Government and switch to EOI strategy. Various new industrial policy measures introduced, including preferential export credits, tariff exemptions on imported intermediate goods critical to export production, tax exemptions on export income, linkage between export performance and conferred import permits. The Korean Trade Promotion Agency (KOTRA) created as an export promotion agency.
- *Industrial promotion (1973–1979)*: switch within the EOI strategy from a general to more sector-specific industry policy. Promotion of HCI development, including steel and shipbuilding, with the aim of broadening the strategic industrial base of the economy and thus reducing import dependency on capital goods. New export promotion policy measures provided additional financial and technical support, including subsidies, long-term administered credits, tax incentives, skills programmes, and the creation of new techno-industrial research institutes. Tighter import controls imposed in HCI sectors.
- *Economic liberalization (1980–1993)*: start of reversal process of the 1960s/1970s policy era. Gradual elimination of subsidized loans and retraction of targeted sectoral areas for preferential treatment. The 1985 Industrial Development Act streamlines the new industrial policy approach.
- *Globalization (1994–1997)*: associated with the *Segyehwa* programme. Closer alignment of trade–industrial policy linkage to WTO and OECD regime consistency, involving the phased abolition of South Korea's direct subsidy system for export activities, and the downgrading of its tax exemption policy. The state's investment co-ordination links with the *chaebol* also completely eliminated during this period.
- *Crisis/post-crisis (1997–present)*: in compliance with the IMF's 'bailout' programme, South Korea was obliged to hasten the phased elimination of its four remaining export subsidies. Other policy prescriptions on

inward FDI liberalization place this at the new centre of South Korea's industrial policy.

The reversal of industrial policy in the 1980s can be partly attributed to Gershenkronian predictions concerning the gradual withdrawal of state *dirigisme* as the domestic business sector gains greater independent strength. As Sohn *et al* (1998) note, by the early 1980s the EPB no longer possessed a clear informational advantage over South Korean firms who by this time could interpret and develop their own strategic responses to domestic and global market signals. For example, around this time the *chaebols* decided to enter the semiconductor market despite the reservations of the EPB (Yoon 1992). However, to conclude that South Korea's industrial policy has been all but extinguished, and with it its contribution to competitiveness-enhancement, would be erroneous. As Weiss (1998) observed, there had been a redefinition rather than a fundamental change in industry policy objectives by the 1990s, namely from export promotion and industry creation to the co-ordination of innovation and technology diffusion. As in any dynamic economy, the fast-changing technological environment required new or adapted industrial policy tools for new tasks. Well after the 1997/98 crisis, the Korean Institute for Industrial Economics and Trade (KIET), a key state research agency, continued to target sectors with future export potential.[73] In addition, 103 priority technologies were identified by KIET for future development, and to this end the government enlarged budget spending in this area over 2000–2001, although this was contingent upon substantial increases of knowledge-intensive inward FDI.[74] Other state agencies, such as KOTRA, the Korean Advanced Institute of Science and Technology (KAIST) and the Korea Institute for International Economic Policy (KIEP), maintain South Korea's industrial intelligence-gathering infrastructure that helps facilitate the co-ordination of innovation and technology diffusion and subsequently improves export competitiveness and developing techno-industrial capacity.

In new post-crisis developments in South Korea's industrial policy, the more fervent restructuring of traditional industries (e.g. semiconductors, autos, steel, petrochemicals) became a key priority. The New Industrial Development Committee was established in August 1998, comprised of related organizations and industry experts, academia and research institutions, with the purpose of selecting new promising industry fields and devising development plans, including Action Programmes on deregulation, technology development, and technical manpower cultivation.[75] Moreover, in the perceived state–business division of labour, the government will develop basic technologies whilst industrialization and application is to be pioneered by the private sector. In July 2000, the government also introduced a Three Year Action Plan for the Development of a Knowledge-Based Economy, with state provision of infrastructure innovations and new policy directives related to the International Mobile Telecommunication 2000 programme.[76]

In laying out his vision for improving South Korea's industrial competitiveness, Minister of Commerce, Industry and Energy, Kim Young-ho, proposed to take the country down a middle way between the US economy – 'software-oriented, focusing on the industrialisation of IT' – and the Japanese economy – 'hardware-oriented, focusing on the digitalization of manufacturing industry'.[77] He further highlighted the state's special promotion of biotechnology, optical electronics and environmental equipment activities, and plans to 'establish a national innovation system' by the Government helping to 'build the infrastructure for technology, information and logistics'. This less *dirigiste*, more context-setting approach does not possess the same hard edges of South Korea's past industrial policies, and state-business tensions have impeded progress in the new post-crisis industrial policy paradigm. Nevertheless, there remains a strong consensus in South Korean society for an industrial policy of some kind, and for it to make a continued effective contribution to advancing the country's competitive position in the global economy.

4.6 ECONOMIC DIPLOMACY

In Kim Dae-jung's inaugural Presidential speech, he remarked that: 'diplomacy in the twenty-first century will centre around the economy and culture. We must keep expanding trade investment, tourism and cultural exchanges in order to make our way in the age of boundless competition which will take place against a backdrop of co-operation'.[78] This affirmed the continued pivotal role played by economic diplomacy in the conduct of South Korea's international affairs. In many ways, Kim Dae-jung's words echoed the aforementioned five fundamental principles of South Korea's 'new diplomacy' (globalism, diversification, multi-dimensionalism, regional co-operation, future orientation) first articulated by Foreign Minister Han Sung-joo in May 1993. As South Korea entered the 21st century, the country faced important economic diplomacy challenges on all fronts. Many of these derived from the persisting paradigmatic struggles within the South Korean political economy, mainly centred here on the Kim Dae-jung Administration's increasingly fervent free and open trade advocacy. The 'open trading nation' basis of South Korea's new post-crisis trade policy, for example, implied a stronger and more positive economic diplomacy engagement with multilateral, regional co-operation and bilateral free trade activities. As a consequence, a far more promotive and less defensive approach in the country's economic diplomacy was evident. In the following sections, broad developments in South Korea's economic diplomacy are considered at the bilateral, regional/inter-regional, and plurilateral–multilateral levels.

4.6.1 Bilateral

Since the 1950s, the evolving structure of South Korea's bilateral economic relations has experienced four overlapping phases, these being:

- *Unipolar clientism (1950s–1960s):* based on ultra-dependency on American aid, markets, technology, capital and technocratic policy expertise and guidance. South Korea a client state of the US.
- *Bipolar economic dependency (1970s–1980s):* whereby Japan's role as a strategic economic partner increased, joining the US as a key economic security guarantor. Japan's provision of technology, capital and developmental experience particularly valued by South Korea.
- *Tripolarity (1990s):* in which economic exchange with the EU and developing East Asia (i.e. beyond Japan) expands within a post-Cold War, tripolarized world economy. More proactive economic diplomacy engagement with Europe and other East Asian states that parallel ambitious *chaebol* strategies to consolidate their commercial position within the Triad region (i.e. North America, East Asia, Europe) markets.
- *Multipolarity (late 1990s to present):* the 1997/98 crisis lends additional imperative to diversify more comprehensively South Korea's bilateral economic relations. Wider geographical dispersal of its trade and FDI promotion missions and new types of bilateral economic relations sought.

This phased dispersal of foreign economic relations in many ways corresponded to South Korea's periphery–semiperiphery evolution within the international economic system. After initially attaining a critical development momentum courtesy of a benign dependency relationship with the US, which was later accelerated by Japan's own developmental contributions, South Korea's growing techno-industrial strength and diversity (as exemplified by its *chaebol* firms) led to an increasing penetration of global markets. Moreover, as it has progressed from a comparatively weak semi-periphery economy to a strong one, so accordingly have its links with its bilateral economic diplomacy proliferated. The *chaebols'* export and investment 'globalization' strategies, often promoted by the state, have undoubtedly provided the underlying basis of such linkages. South Korea's growing sense of systemic responsibility and the aforementioned catalytic effects of the 1997/98 crisis have also played their part in the gradual diversification of the country's bilateral economic relations.

Despite the palpable shift from a defensive to promotive bilateral economic diplomacy, South Korea's economic relations with its major partners remain marred by a variety of trade disputes. As the country entered the new millennium, its exporters faced 35 bilateral import restrictions imposed by trade partners[79] (Yang and Kim 2000). These were mainly concentrated in core sectors of South Korean industry, notably steel, automobiles, semiconductors, consumer electronics, shipbuilding and textiles. Ongoing disputes with the US, Japan and the EU have involved other sectors such as pharmaceuticals, alcoholic beverages, agriculture and cinema distribution. This may be understood in terms of the 'embedded neo-mercantilism' still evident within South Korea's trade policy (Moon and Yoo 1997). Even after the 1997/98 crisis, the country's economic diplomats were engaged in various counter-protectionist activities. For example, in July 1998, MOFAT formed a new task force with a mandate to assist South Korean firms cope with anti-dumping duties and other trade barriers imposed on their products, and also to develop diplomatic and legal strategies to reduce the number of anti-dumping duties imposed.

However, this lingering neo-mercantilist approach co-exists with an ascendant free trade advocacy in the conduct of South Korea's economic diplomacy. At the bilateral level, this is most clearly manifest in the Kim Dae-jung Government's penchant for free trade agreements (FTAs). As previously noted, this forms part of a wider recent 'lattice regionalism' trend within the Asia–Pacific but South Korea's participation has gained the special attention of observers given its neo-mercantilist tradition. In the past, South Korea's reaction to any expansion of FTAs has usually been to push the WTO to strengthen or more strictly apply its rules against such developments under Article 24. This, though, proved problematic given that the vast majority of WTO members already participate in some form of bilateral or regional FTA (Cheong 1998). According to MOFAT officials, there are three main motivations behind this new FTA diplomacy. First, the Government maintains that its free trade advocacy at bilateral and multilateral levels is consistent, seeing the twin processes as complementary, and is sometimes referred to as a 'WTO plus' endeavour. Second, it will prevent it from being marginalized or left out of the APBFTA trend, which the Government believes is making an increasingly significant impact on the international political economy of the Asia–Pacific. Third, the new FTA diplomacy helps institutionalize the Government's 'open trading nation' policy and further advance the economic opening of South Korea.[80]

South Korea's first FTA project was initiated at the 1998 APEC Leaders' Meeting, where it agreed with Chile to explore the possibility of creating a bilateral FTA between them. Further proposals to establish bilateral FTAs with Japan, Thailand, Mexico, Australia, New Zealand, Turkey, Israel and South Africa arose over the next two years, with feasibility studies thereafter commissioned by both sides in most cases. Formal negotiations for the Chile FTA began in late 1999, and three rounds of talks were conducted by November

2000. However, Chile's application of an anti-dumping case against certain South Korean producers in the meantime threatened the FTA negotiation process. By the end of 2000, the wider anti-dumping issue had become contentious, with Chile wanting to omit counter-rules on anti-dumping in the FTA pact while South Korea wished to include them. On the one hand, this was indicative of the embedded neo-mercantilism in South Korea's FEP, but on the other it reflected a 'broad band' nature of recent bilateral FTAs in that they also included a range of complementary measures. As Chapter 3 noted, the Japan–Singapore Economic Partnership Agreement incorporated various economic co-operation elements, such as those on investment treatment, technical assistance, and finance. South Korea has adopted a similar approach with its 'New Generation' FTAs.

Like all FTAs, assessing their trade diversion and trade creation effects depends upon the relative complementarity or competitive nature of the partners' industries. Chile's less advanced techno-industrial base and similar competitive strengths in textiles leave little scope for competitively induced trade creation, while seasonal differences between the two countries also mean less tension over agri-product competition. However, some of Chile's trade partners could express trade diversionary concerns over the improved market access gained by South Korean firms that could relatively disadvantage more competitive third country producers who still face Chilean import tariffs and other trade barriers. A Japan–South Korea FTA presents a different case. Here, the highly competitive interaction between South Korean and Japanese industry in autos, consumer electronics and other sectors provide significant scope for trade creation, and thus reactive domestic opposition as discussed later in this section. Furthermore, South Korea's economic diplomats are likely to confront corresponding demands from European and American auto producers to permit them similar market access as enjoyed by their Japanese rivals.

In addition to free trade advocacy, South Korea has adopted a more positive post-crisis stance on bilateral investment treaties (BITs) as part of its new 'promotive' inward FDI regime. This was an agenda issue in summits held with the US and Japan in the latter half of 1998. South Korea began negotiating a BIT with the US in June 1998 but persistent problems over screen quotas and IPRs from the US side, and national treatment concerns from the South Korean side (e.g. over financial services), prolonged these negotiations. Moreover, the possibility of establishing a US–South Korea FTA, as mooted by the American Chamber of Commerce in Seoul and some other stakeholders, would only be practically feasible with a concluded BIT in place.[81] South Korea's own motivation for forming a bilateral FTA with the US, as with that of Japan, has a strong strategic dimension in that it would significantly fortify South Korea's alliance security position and further advance the diplomatic encirclement of North Korea.

Indeed, there has always been a strong strategic dimension to South Korea's economic relations with the US. As noted earlier, South Korea's economic diplomacy of the 1950s and 1960s was primarily oriented by its unipolar clientistic links with America, and whose close politico-military ties have long underpinned the bilateral economic relationship. This explains why it arguably still pursues a 'policy of obligation' towards the US, whereby American commercial interests receive a deference not enjoyed by other foreign economic partners (Dent 1999). While South Korea's stricter application of MFN treatment in its trade relations has somewhat attenuated this policy, its overt deference to the US in matters of economic diplomacy remain. As one US diplomatic interviewee remarked, 'South Korea still expects the US to take a lead in most if not all economic matters'.[82] Certainly, the Kim Dae-jung Government appeared generally compliant with Washington's strong neo-liberal advocacy of South Korea's economic reforms during the late 1990s.

There is, however, a twist to this tale. Some South Korean Government officials were critical of the US's relatively slow response to the 1997/98 crisis in comparison with its reaction to the 1994/95 Mexican peso crisis. Moreover, as Weiss and Hobson (2000) argued, 'far from seeking to buttress the Korean state as it had done in other times of difficulty, the United States was now prepared to stand back and let the crisis rip through the institutional fabric it so wished to tear apart' (p. 67). One could similarly contend that the US used the crisis to its own strategic advantage by adding its considerable weight behind South Korea's domestic neo-liberal advocates calling for substantive market opening as part of a wider economic reform process. This was consistent with past US policy towards South Korea. A few years earlier in July 1995, US Assistant Treasury Secretary, Jeffrey Shafer, had stated that South Korea should 'open itself fully to the world', implicitly threatening with the comment that 'our MFN exemption will permit us to differentiate among countries going forward, depending on how much access they are willing to accord to us'.[83] Although subsequently many trade barriers once confronting American producers have been removed in the post-crisis period, other significant barriers remain, particularly in the auto and pharmaceutical sectors. Preventing potential trade conflicts with the US was also one of the stated top priorities for South Korea's new Trade Minister, Hwang Doo-yun, after entering office in early 2001.[84]

South Korea's economic diplomacy with Japan has perhaps undergone more changes than with any other bilateral partner in the post-crisis period. As previously noted, South Korea has long maintained a dualistic economic relationship with Japan, based on an intense commercial rivalry in core industrial sectors (e.g. autos) as well as a still pronounced technological and capital dependency on Japan (Hyun and Okonogi 1995). However, since the 1997/98 crisis, the South Korean Government has particularly tried to foster a more interdependent relationship with Japan based on a more engaged economic partnership. Japan's own response has been quite positive, and both countries have not only sought to enhance economic and technical co-operation between their respective industries but also to liberalize their bilateral trade. South Korea's abolition of the IDP, lifting of restrictions on Japanese cultural imports, and initiation of its BIT negotiations with Japan in the late 1990s alone constituted radical changes in the calculus of their economic diplomacy. The proposed bilateral FTA, though, was the most radical of all given *both* countries' strong neo-mercantilist traditions.

The Japan–South Korea FTA was formally proposed in 1999, and the governments of both countries commissioned their respective economic think tanks – KIEP and Japan Institute of Developing Economies (JIDE) – to undertake a joint study into the project that was published in June 2000. In addition, the country's peak business associations – South Korea's FKI and Japan's Keidanren – conducted their own joint studies to evaluate the FTA's potential impact on business, with these due to be promulgated in mid-2001 and formal inter-state negotiations commencing soon thereafter. Although the joint KIEP–JIDE study noted the bilateral FTA's positive long-term influence on South Korea's economy growth (e.g. through intensified competition, industrial co-operation and other efficiency-generating factors), there were also significant short-to-medium term economic and political risks for the Kim Dae-jung Government to consider. For example, a significant public backlash could arise from any subsequent flood of Japanese imports into the country. South Korea embarked on this FTA project without an *ex post* evaluation of what impact its contemporaneously lifted long-standing bans on Japanese imports would have upon its bilateral trade balance.[85] Estimates from the KIEP–JIDE study itself conceded that South Korea's trade deficit with Japan would substantially increase over the medium-term on realizing the FTA.[86] Moreover, strong opposition from South Korea's agricultural producers, who supported the continuance of the Government's highly protectionist trade regime in their sector, proved a formidable counter-lobbying force. Japan's own agriculture lobby mirrored this position, and furthermore there existed some apathy amongst its wider business community to the proposed FTA given the relatively small size of the South Korean market, the unforeseen counteracting forces of Korean economic nationalism, and thus the unknown import stimulating effect of South Korean trade liberalization.[87]

While some circumspection towards the bilateral FTA was evident at the societal and business levels in both South Korea and Japan, their respective governments foresaw its important longer-term advantages, and in particular the aforementioned strategic dimension of a Japan–South Korea FTA. The significant strengthening of this bilateral axis in Northeast Asia is partly intended to make North Korea more compliant in international negotiations. In this respect, North Korea's diplomatic encirclement would be complete if China were to enter into a trilateral FTA with Japan and South Korea, an idea already proposed at the 1999 Japan–Korea Business Forum. This may be possible given the broader emerging trend of enhanced promotive economic diplomacy in the Northeast Asian political economy. As part of the 'ASEAN Plus 3' framework discussed later under regional economic diplomacy, the three states have worked closely together in a post-crisis context to improve regional governance mechanisms in finance and monetary affairs. Here, South Korea has generally welcomed Japan's attempts in developing a hegemonic regional role in financial co-operation. China's increasing engagement in these matters is also welcomed by Seoul owing to the geo-economic counter-balance this provides. Moreover, South Korea's economic diplomacy with China has received growing attention since the post-Cold War normalization of relations between the two countries in 1992. The main focus for South Korea's economic diplomats has been the burgeoning commercial opportunities and threats that China's rapidly developing economy poses to South Korean firms. Since 1997/98, China's relative importance as a foreign economic partner has surpassed that of Southeast Asia, which owes as much to persisting crisis-related economic troubles amongst some ASEAN states as its does to China's continued economic ascendancy. Nevertheless, South Korea's bilateral economic relations with the collective ASEAN group remain a key priority. In 1999, Southeast Asia accounted for $29.9bn of South Korea's trade and a $6.5bn cumulative stock of South Korean outward FDI in 1999, making the sub-regional group South Korea's fourth largest important trade partner and third largest destination of overseas investment.

South Korea's bilateral economic diplomacy with the EU also gained increasing priority over the 1990s (Dent 1998b, 1999). As noted earlier, this should be understood in South Korea's phase-shift from *bipolar dependency* to *tripolarity* in the structure of its bilateral economic relations. In a post-Cold War world economy seemingly dominated by the Triad regions, it became imperative for South Korea actively to promote its comparatively underdeveloped economic relations with Europe (Kim 1995). The EU's newly consolidated Single Market and plans for economic and monetary union added greater cause to do so. The 1996 Korea–EU Trade and Co-operation Agreement marked an important turning point in their bilateral economic diplomacy. From the EU's perspective, it represented a formal acknowledgment of the potential importance afforded to South Korea as a pivotal EU economic partner in East Asia. It also provided some basis for fostering a more promotive bilateral economic diplomacy and a symbolic departure from the conflictual trade relations of the past.

In the decade leading up to the 1997/98 crisis, South Korea's trade, investment and financial links with the EU had flourished. During the crisis and its aftermath, South Korea looked to the EU for finance-related assistance and to European financial systems to emulate, while the EU also proved a vital 'safety valve' market for South Korean exporters. Despite the EU's recent ascendance within the hierarchy of South Korea's foreign economic relations, it remains the 'Cinderella' (i.e. poor third relation) of the Triad regions in this respect (Dent 2001). Both the US and Japan, for historic and other reasons previously noted, are still perceived as more critical strategic partners by South Korea's FEP protagonists, as reflected in Seoul's lukewarm reaction to the euro's launch in January 1999. Furthermore, adversarial trade relations persist across various sectors. South Korean firms continue to encounter a panoply of EU anti-dumping duties, whilst EU trade diplomats have recently taken South Korea to task over its lingering neo-mercantilist trade policies, such as alleged state subsidies conferred to South Korean shipbuilders.[88]

Moreover, the current phase-shift in South Korea's bilateral economic relations from *tripolarity* to *multipolarity* infers that the EU and East Asian trade partners must increasingly compete with newer partners for South Korea's diplomatic attentions. In the post-crisis diversification of the country's bilateral economic diplomacy, both MOFAT and MOCIE have dispatched their trade and investment promotion missions to relatively unfamiliar commercial territory for South Korean firms, including Central and Eastern Europe, Latin America and Southern Africa. Furthermore, as part of its mediating semi-periphery role in international economic diplomacy, South Korea has become more proactive in championing the LDCs' more effective integration into the global economy. The Kim Dae-jung Government has introduced various initiatives designed to improve LDC capabilities in internet-related fields and hence close information-knowledge gaps and the 'digital divide' between the developed and developing world. The EDCF is being deployed to these ends as part of South Korea's ODAC policy. It has also substantially increased its contribution to the WTO's technical assistance programme and provided new support for heavily indebted poor countries, for example a $14.5m contribution to the World Bank's Poverty Reduction and Growth Facility.[89] These developments have further broadened the foundations of South Korea's bilateral economic diplomacy and hence the conduct of its FEP.

4.6.2 Regional/Inter-Regional

The regional and inter-regional dimensions of South Korea's economic diplomacy have been progressively salient features of its FEP since the early 1990s (Yoon 1995). More recently, the Kim Dae-jung Government's new 'regional co-operation policy' represented an important post-crisis development in the country's economic diplomacy, whereby South Korea has strived to play a more proactive role in East Asia's post-crisis economic affairs. As such, its promotion of closer Northeast and East Asian relations forms part of a broader crisis-prevention strategy, based on a reinvigoration of South Korea's activities and contribution towards APEC, the Asia-Europe Meetings (ASEM) and the new 'ASEAN Plus 3' process.

In the crisis aftermath, initial developments within the APEC process were not encouraging, with an apparent reversion to defensive economic diplomacy by some East Asian members in reaction mainly to American policy-makers using the crisis to push home its aforementioned commercial and foreign policy objectives. At the November 1998 APEC summit held at Kuala Lumpur, US trade diplomats led APEC's other Anglo-Saxon members (Canada, New Zealand and Australia) in an acrimonious dispute with certain East Asian members of APEC over their import restrictions on forestry and fishery products. South Korea's own highly protectionist agricultural trade regime came under heavy criticism, as did Japan's. The unresolved matter was subsequently transferred to the WTO, and was reflective of the poor progress that had been made on other trade liberalization issues at the 1998 summit. These and other crisis-related troubles risked derailing APEC's 'concerted unilateral liberalization' process, the *modus operandi* of realizing its 2020 free trade and investment zone (Han 1999). Subsequent summits in 1999 and 2000, though far less acrimonious, have achieved little to kick-start APEC-led trade liberalization. Moreover, the emergent APBFTA trend in which South Korea is actively engaged may further expose the institutional weaknesses of APEC and further bypass the same processes. On the other hand, the prospective Japan–South Korea FTA could itself provide much needed momentum to APEC zone trade liberalization, and prove consistent with APEC-driven processes.

Like many other East Asian countries, South Korea has traditionally shown a preference of trade facilitation over trade liberalization within the APEC framework (Han 1999, Ravenhill 2000). While South Korea's new free trade advocacy has altered this somewhat, it retains a strong support for APEC's economic and technical co-operation (or ecotech) initiatives. For example, at the 2000 summit it proposed various ecotech-related schemes, including an APEC Cyber Education Network, APEC Youth Internet Volunteers schemes, and an APEC Social Safety Net as a burden-sharing scheme designed particularly to assist the group's developing country members. As part of Kim Dae-jung's 'Engagement Policy', South Korean delegates even floated the idea of North Korea becoming an associate APEC member, although this found little support.

Since 1996, South Korea has also conducted an inter-regional economic diplomacy within the ASEM dialogue framework, in which nine other East Asian states[90] and the EU15 countries have endeavoured mutually to fortify this weak link in the network of Triadic relationships (Dent 1998a, 2001). The ASEM diplomacy process differs from APEC in three main ways: first, ASEM summits are convened biennially in contrast to APEC's annual summitry, although like APEC it runs various 'track two' activities in between; second, ASEM has economic, political and socio-cultural dimensions as opposed to APEC's singular economic focus; third, ASEM lacks APEC's trade liberalization function, concentrating only on trade facilitation initiatives. Notwithstanding ASEM's less ambitious trade agenda, South Korea has proved a comparatively active East Asian participant, although this may be largely attributed to its role as host at the ASEM 3 summit convened in Seoul in October 2000. Key examples of South Korea's ecotech initiatives proposed within ASEM include the Trans-Eurasia Information Network, aimed at linking up research and information networks between Asia and Europe, the ASEM Fellowship Programme, and the ASEM Vision Group whose function was to generate idea-driven momentum to ASEM's diplomatic development.

Closer to home, South Korea's participation in the new ASEAN Plus 3 framework has been the most significant development in the country's regional economic diplomacy. The framework grew out of early post-crisis consensus amongst East Asian states for strengthened regional economic governance. At the third summit held at Manila in November 1999, the 13 member states of the ASEAN Plus 3 group even contemplated the possibility of establishing a future unified regional market and common currency. However, the structural economic and political profile of East Asia makes these objectives rather utopian, and it is the financial rather than trade aspects of ASEAN Plus 3 policy co-operation that became its main focus. An associated development to the framework has been Japan's New Miyazawa Initiative (NMI), first announced in October 1998 and entailing a $30bn standby fund to extend various levels of financial assistance to future crisis-prone East Asian states (Hughes 2000). Under the NMI arrangement, South Korea is eligible for a financial support facility (loan quota) amounting to $7.5bn. In another development, the Chiang Mai Initiative (CMI) – first proposed in May 2000 and formally launched at the ASEAN Economy Ministers Meeting in October that year – created another regional mechanism for improved financial co-operation. The centrepiece of the CMI was the expanded swap agreement between ASEAN Plus 3 members, whereby local is exchanged for hard currency in a repurchase scheme that would be upholstered in the event of speculative attacks or other currency problems.[91] As part of this process, South Korea and Japan entered into an agreement in which $7bn worth of won could be swapped for yen to assist the former's liquidity problems in another financial crisis.[92] The ASEAN Plus 3 process also entails measures to improve monetary policy monitoring between its members.

At the November 2000 ASEAN Plus 3 summit, Kim Dae-jung proposed the creation of an East Asia Study Group[93] and the launch of an 'East Asian mechanism to nurture East Asia into a single community of co-operation'.[94] He further advocated the formation of a regional business forum, starting with a sectoral approach. Seoul had previously highlighted how the lack of an institutional framework in East Asian co-operation more generally impedes the development of more useful regional economic collaboration. More generally, the South Korean Government hoped that recently initiated 'ASEAN Plus 3' dialogues between foreign, economic and finance ministers would eventually lead to institutionalization, and hence firmer structure of regional economic co-operation and diplomacy.[95] Again, this was indicative of the far more proactive and promotive approach evident in South Korea's post-crisis economic diplomacy.

4.6.3 Plurilateral/Multilateral

As previously discussed, plurilateral and multilateral engagements in South Korea's economic diplomacy have become increasingly prominent (Chun 1995). By acceding to OECD membership in October 1996, Korea's plurilateral economic diplomacy with the AIEs was accordingly enhanced. As an OECD member, South Korea enjoys the provision of technical expertise on complex commercial policy matters, experiences greater familiarity with managing plurilateral–multilateral criticism, and receives peer review of general economic policies.[96] South Korea's multilateral economic diplomacy, especially within the WTO, had also become more salient by this time. Its own implementation of Uruguay Round agreements, signing of new WTO accords (e.g. telecommunications, information technology) and engagement in the new Disputes Settlement Body mechanism, both as a complainant and as the subject of complaint, brought South Korea further into the multilateral fold.

In an endeavour to demonstrate its new trade liberalism and systemic responsibility, the Kim Dae-jung Government submitted twelve position papers (nine on its own, and three jointly with other countries) to the WTO in preparation for the intended launch of the New 'Millennium' Round at the December 1999 WTO Ministerial Meeting convened in Seattle. These papers covered the following areas: services, agriculture, regional trade agreements, the WTO Works Programme, anti-dumping, trade and investment, market access for industrial goods, trade and competition policy, trade facilitation, negotiation on services trade, fishery and forestry products, and government procurement. Many of these reflected long standing trade policy concerns of South Korea, particularly regarding anti-dumping and agri-sectors, while others mirrored some of the country's domestic economic struggles: for example, the trade and competition policy issue was especially resonant with regard to breaking the *chaebol's* oligopolistic dominance back home. Overall, though, this was indicative of a new proactivity in South Korea's multilateral economic diplomacy.

This further extended into international finance, where crisis-related engagements with the IMF had made the South Korean government more attentive to events and developments in this field. It has, for example, actively promoted discussion on the new international financial architecture, in particular on ways to minimize the adverse effects of highly leveraged financial institutions such as hedge funds. In March 2000, Kim Dae-jung even proposed creating a 'Hedge Fund Monitoring Channel' as well as a 'Foreign Exchange Crisis Forecast Model' within APEC to address these issues.[97] The Minister of Finance and Economy, Jin Nyum, had also called for the IMF's quota and representation systems to be adjusted to reflect more accurately East Asia's weight in the world economy.

Returning to the WTO, one of the most interesting recent aspects of South Korea's multilateral economic diplomacy concerns the 'new' trade issues (Sohn 1996, Kim and Choi 1998). Before the 1997/98 crisis, most of South Korea's stakeholding FEP constituencies took a low priority view towards such issues, many citing the country's essentially 'developing' nature with respect to them.[98] Thus, a limited discourse on 'new' trade issues prevailed with the government adopting semi-periphery deference to the AIEs (especially the US and EU) in taking the lead here. To an extent, this persisted after the crisis, although the Kim Dae-jung Government's 'comprehensive approach' to the WTO's New 'Millennium' Round in a similar spirit to developed countries did introduce a more articulated position towards these issues. In addition to these being formally discussed within the newly created Steering Committee for the New 'Millennium' Round, which involved 15 related ministries and other agencies, the Government also more actively sought public opinion on these issues.

Like the other NIE-3 members, the two main 'new' trade issues of concern are environment and labour. Despite the aforementioned post-crisis globalism, the primary focus of South Korea's environmental policy concerns remains almost entirely domestic, for example water and air quality, food waste. Where trade-related environmental issues are tabled for discussion, the country's environmental lobby continue to demonstrate limited interest and capacity in this specific area, as discussed later under 'contesting influences'. The South Korean government's own position remains one of waiting upon the AIEs to lead and establish any trade–environment rules and codes and then respond accordingly. Of the NIE-3, it participates in more trade–environment fora than any other, covering discussions within the OECD's Joint Working Party on Trade and Environment, the UN's Commission on Sustainable Development, and the WTO's Committee on Trade and Environment.[99]

A similar situation is evident concerning trade–labour issues. Up to the 1999 WTO Seattle Ministerial Meeting, the South Korean Government's policy on trade–labour was generally negative owing to its pro-ILO position, this being that technological assistance to developing countries took precedence over trade–labour linkages. However, at Seattle, South Korean representatives supported an EU proposal to establish parallel trade–labour working parties at the WTO and ILO – a compromise on an earlier US proposal for an exclusive WTO working party arrangement. South Korea's semi-peripheral situation largely explained this approach: it remains highly circumspect of protectionist-related motivations behind trade–labour linkage; it is relatively more interested in the ILO's emphasis on technology-transfer. Moreover, South Korea's labour practices are highly culture-sensitive, and consequently there is strong public support for government caution on this issue. Nevertheless, the Kim Dae-jung government's 'comprehensive approach' towards the WTO and new trade agenda in general has engaged the country's FEP increasingly into this area across various plurilateral–multilateral fora.

4.7 CONTESTING 'ACTOR-BASED' INFLUENCES

4.7.1 Domestic

As with Singapore and Taiwan, FEP formation in South Korea has been traditionally state-centric – perhaps more so given that it has practised the most ardent developmental statism of the NIE-3. However, the deconstruction of the South Korean developmental state since the 1980s has permitted non-state, domestic stakeholding FEP constituencies to exert greater contesting influence over the country's foreign economic policy. During the 1990s, this especially applied to the business sector (and *chaebols* in particular) that had enjoyed growing political empowerment since the onset of democratization. Despite the 1997/98 financial crisis accelerating the pace of political and economic reform in South Korea, the country's civil stakeholding FEP constituencies remained marginalized at the turn of the century. Moreover, there persists a low degree of internationalization in Korean civil society and hence a deficient cognitive awareness of many new FEP issues amongst the country's socio-economic interest groups and associations (Kim, Y.R. 1999). In sum, South Korea's FEP retains a high degree of state-centricity (Kim, S.M. 1999). These issues are now discussed in some detail below.

4.7.1.1 Domestic stakeholding FEP constituencies

Although the bureaucratic integrity and coherence of the South Korean state has weakened in recent years, FEP formation remains essentially state-centric in character, as we shall later elaborate. Before we do so, it is worth noting the key changes to the configuration and form of contesting influence exerted by domestic non-state actors, especially since the 1997/98 financial crisis. Generally speaking, contesting influence from non-state stakeholding FEP constituencies within South Korea has strengthened during the post-crisis period, indeed more in relative terms than in Singapore and Taiwan.

As previously discussed, the state–*chaebol* nexus, or *jungkyung yuchak* (political–business connection), has been a defining structural feature of the South Korean developmental state and an orienting determinant in FEP formation. Despite the endeavours of successive Korean governments since the early 1970s to decouple this developmental alliance, the mutual dependency that has evolved between the state and big business has consistently proven difficult to relinquish (Y.T. Kim 1999, Y.H. Lee 1997, McNamara 1999). Taking the example of corporate governance, the *chaebols* have continually proven their resilience to government attempts at reform. As Gills (1999) cites, Kim Young-sam's

> initial anti-*chaebol* measures and attempts to dismantle vested interests and root out corrupt practices made part of the middle classes uneasy, reviving a conservative backlash against reform... More fundamentally, Kim Young-sam concluded he could not conduct his economic policy without the co-operation of the *chaebol*, and thus turned away from the idea of a decisive break in the government–*chaebol* alliance (p. 9).

From an economic perspective, South Korean governments have been reluctant to undermine the *chaebols'* scale production advantages in key export sectors, especially where their expansion into inter-related industrial fields enabled economies of scope to be captured.[100] In addition, South Korea's FEP protagonists were hesitant to liberalize trade and inward FDI regimes too far in case foreign competition compromised the aforementioned *chaebol* strengths, or further weaken the country's traditionally precarious external trade balance through significant rises in import levels. Such a development would pose a significant economic security threat to the country. For this and other reasons, bureaucrats within many government ministries were highly sceptical of Kim Young-sam's plans during the 1990s for rapid liberalization of Korea's external sectors, with bureaucratic inertia ensuing.

With some degree of success, President Kim Dae-jung was able to harness the twin forces of crisis and new government to push through *chaebol*-related reforms from the late 1990s onwards, partly designed to decouple the state–*chaebol* nexus and weaken *chaebol* economic and political power.[101] While the *chaebols* put up a strong and effective resistance to many parts of the reform programme, an important development concerning their contesting influence in FEP matters emerged. As Kim, Y.T. (1999) observed during the late 1990s, 'the hierarchical, dominant relationships between the state and the *chaebol* are being transformed into a new kind of symbiotic and collaborationist partnership between them' (p. 454). In other words, the state–*chaebol* nexus was being transformed into something else rather than experiencing diminishment. By 1995, South Korean business representatives sat on 78 advisory, consultative and decision-making commissions attached to the

Government.[102] These links had been gradually expanded over the 1990s as the South Korean developmental state moved more from an authoritarian to a consensual mode of state–business relations. Moreover, the focus of state–business dialogue had widened to cover both broad structural and specific sectoral aspects of economic policy-making (Kim, Y.T. 1999). Furthermore, crisis-related exigencies required the South Korean state to work more closely with *chaebol* representatives to effectively address new economic policy-related challenges.

All research interviewees from the peak business organizations approached (i.e. FKI, KCCI and KITA – the Korean International Trade Association) share the view that the South Korean business community remains closely connected with the Government. Instances disclosed by them in the specific FEP context include both the FKI and KITA's collaborative work with the Government on WTO Disputes Settlement Body issues, in particular regarding cases of foreign anti-dumping duties applied on South Korean exports. All regularly submit a variety of policy suggestions to the Government, of which a good majority are accepted.[103] A main function of KITA's Trade Support Department is to channel opinions from its *chaebol*-dominant membership concerning trade policy issues through to the Government, and it is also extensively engaged in joint field research with state bureaucrats on trade policy impacts upon South Korean firms.[104] Regarding previously noted tensions arising between the *chaebol* and state over the post-crisis liberalization of inward FDI policy, the FKI has used its various dialogue channels maintained with the Government to mitigate such policy changes. Individual *chaebols* also exerted significant contesting influence over the emerging shape of South Korea's post-crisis FDI policy. For example, Hyundai and Daewoo energetically lobbied the Government to limit the number of new foreign investment projects in the autos sector. Meanwhile, the KCCI participates in various Government-led committees such as those on tariff and industrial policy deliberation, safeguard and anti-dumping issues.

In sum, the contesting influence enjoyed by the *chaebols* over South Korea's FEP formation remains considerable. Moreover, it is likely to strengthen with the further shift from developmental authoritarianism to developmental democratization, but this also depends on whether the *chaebols* continue to dominate the commanding heights of the economy. Apart from the transnational challenge to this position, derived from the still small but growing base of foreign MNEs now operating in South Korea, the much recently state-promoted small and medium-sized enterprise (SME) sector represents the main domestic challenge to the *chaebol* hegemony.[105] However, despite a variety of Government programmes designed to foster small firm growth, South Korea's SME sector remains a relatively weak stakeholding FEP constituency. Moreover, its peak organization, the Korean Federation of Small Businesses, is primarily focused on domestic corporate affairs with no separate division that specifically addresses international trade and other FEP issues.

South Korea's NGO movement has also experienced much change in its contesting influence over the country's FEP formation. This stemmed from the improving legal and financial support it has enjoyed from the Kim Young-sam and Kim Dae-jung governments as part of their respective efforts to strengthen the democratization process (Kim, H.R. 2000a). Kim Dae-jung's Administration has sought much closer relations with domestic NGOs, partly to build a new political power-base founded on civil societal rather than business sector linkages. Civil organizations such as the Citizens' Coalition of Economic Justice (CCEJ), the Korea House for International Solidarity (KHIS) and the People's Solidarity for Participatory Democracy (PSPD) have joined environmental and labour movements in taking an increasing interest in South Korea's FEP affairs. According to an interviewed senior representative, a primary concern for the CCEJ is 'the economic dominance of the US over the world market and the effect of this on the Third World', and it advocates, 'fair trade based on fair competition'. It was further proposed that the 'global standard advocated by the US is unfair', citing US pressure for the 'unconditional opening of South Korea's investment market' as an example, and that 'the economic crisis has awakened the Korean people to an awareness of government policy which stimulates them to participate in the citizens' movement'.[106] Meanwhile, an interviewed KHIS representative noted that South Korean civil society remains weak but its civil organizations are working in a more mutually reinforcing way on FEP-related issues. For example, the KHIS works alongside the KFEM on environmental matters concerning trade and FDI, while the CCEJ and trade unions collaborate on various labour issues under a common 'Action Network'. The KHIS has also lobbied the government to adopt its formulated codes of conduct for both Korean and foreign MNE behaviour,[107] while the PSPD's Overseas Korean Enterprise Watch initiative also monitors *chaebol* activities abroad.

On the whole, the Kim Dae-jung Government has promoted the stakeholding FEP capacity of NGOs and their interest in foreign economic policy matters, even though this attempted shift from a state-centred to society-centred FEP formation exposed it to protectionist pressures from domestic interest groups. Yet as we see later, this 'NGO empowerment' policy has had a limited impact on more purposely internationalizing South Korean civil society, and hence engaging it in many important FEP issues. Let us now, though, consider the various mediating factors of 'actor-based' contestability within South Korea's FEP formation.

4.7.1.2 State bureaucratic power, culture and dynamics

Of the NIE-3, South Korea has experienced the highest degree of executive centralization within the state's economic bureaucracy, largely a consequence of the country's past military regime's more interventionist policy style (Cheng *et al* 1998). Under Park Chung-hee's Government, key policy instruments (e.g. trade, finance and foreign exchange management) were placed under the centralized control of the EPB. Other economic bureaucracies had to obtain EPB approval for any major proposed policy initiative. In this system, the Presidential Office (the Blue House) and Park himself took a very close view of economic developments, co-ordinating the direction of economic policy through the EPB.

The structure and culture of this system more or less persisted until the early 1990s, and it was the EPB's merger with the Ministry of Finance (MOF) to form MOFE in 1994 that heralded the most important change to the state bureaucracy for many decades. As previously noted, the subsuming of the South Korean developmental state's key pilot agency into a wider ministerial body marked both a practicable and symbolic diminishment of state activism in the economy, and to some extent state-centricity in FEP formation. This more 'hands-off' style was indicative of Kim Young-sam's general policy approach, which left most of economic policy management and initiative taking to his aides given his relative lack of aptitude in this area. Furthermore, according to Moon and Rhyu (2000), Kim Young-sam failed to orchestrate and monitor the economic policy process properly, especially towards the end of his presidential tenure. The constant turnover of economic ministers, who serve also as Deputy Prime Ministers, exacerbated the problem of policy inconsistency. In addition, the ideological struggles within the state bureaucracy discussed earlier exacerbated inter-ministerial conflicts, with the Blue House office acting as a broker in the economic policy-making process. For example, when the Bank of Korea (BOK) alerted the President of an impending foreign exchange crisis as early as July 1997, both MOFE – by then a major force of neo-liberal advocacy – the President's economic secretary downplayed the warning signs, instead stressing healthy macroeconomic foundations. Both the MOFE and BOK were embroiled in a turf war over finance policy competence just before the crisis, and just as then the Blue House sided with MOFE on this occasion.

During the 1990s, there were two major reorganizations within South Korea's FEP ministerial machinery. In addition to the EPB's merging with the MOF to form MOFE in December 1994, the Ministry of Trade and Industry was renamed the Ministry of Trade, Industry and Energy (MOTIE). In February 1998, the new Kim Dae-jung Administration conferred both MOFE's and MOTIE's main trade policy functions to the newly created MOFAT (ex-Ministry of Foreign Affairs), whilst MOTIE was renamed MOCIE accordingly. It was these three ministries that dominated the state-centred network of South

Korea's FEP formation by 2000. In this division of labour, MOFAT has most widespread FEP competence especially in terms of trade and ODAC policies, and regarding all levels of trade diplomacy. Its newly expanded trade-related functions were defined in terms of the formulation, implementation, integration and co-ordination of foreign policies related to foreign trade, trade negotiation and international economic activities. As such, it is South Korea's external representation in most cases of economic diplomacy. The implementation of trade policy within MOFAT involves 15 different divisions, as well as co-ordination with an increasing number of other ministries. This includes MOCIE, which retains competence for various sectoral trade issues, trade and outward FDI promotion, and perhaps most importantly the principal responsibility for promoting inward FDI.

Although MOFE has seen its FEP competence officially diminish in recent years, many outside observers and even some MOFAT officials concede that MOFE still exercises considerable influence over South Korea's FEP formation. Its Chief Minister performs a role as arbitrator between FEP-related ministries where necessary in the regular Economic Ministers Meetings.[108] Furthermore, the Customs Office – a key trade policy agency – is under MOFE's aegis, and MOFAT trade diplomats often require the technical assistance of their MOFE counterparts. By the end of 2000, MOFE was also manoeuvring to regain their previously held FEP competences, engaging in a turf war with MOFAT in particular. This included the External Economy Policy Committee, originally transferred from MOFE to the Blue House in 1998 but which had remained effectively inert ever since.

It was noted earlier how, as part of a political strategy to push through the post-crisis economic reforms, President Kim Dae-jung centralized even greater state bureaucratic power within the Blue House. However, in practice, the key state-centred loci of FEP formation remain within MOFAT, MOFE and MOCIE. The Presidential Office has no separate office to deal specifically with FEP issues, although it has an economic section headed by the President's Chief Economic Advisor.[109] Most recently, this section has been mainly preoccupied with domestic matters, and most Presidential decrees on foreign economic policy matters have originated in the three key FEP ministries. Nevertheless, Kim Dae-jung's proactive summit diplomacy has proved an important vehicle for new FEP initiatives, such as South Korea's recent interest in signing bilateral free trade agreements. On his visit to Tokyo in October 1998, Kim set in motion the more co-operative path of Japan–South Korea economic relations evident from the late 1990s onwards, announcing his government's intentions to lift long-standing import embargoes on Japanese cultural products.[110]

As with Taiwan and Singapore, the ministerial management of South Korea's FEP has become more complex as other ministries and government agencies are increasingly engaged in decision-making processes. Both the Ministry of

Environment (MOE) and Ministry of Labour (MOL) are particularly involved in dealing with 'new' trade issues, although their preoccupation with their respective domestic affairs and their bureaucratic deference to MOFAT, MOFE and MOCIE means their contesting influence is effectively marginal.[111] In the context of South Korea's post-crisis developmental reform and transition, a major problem of this emerging managerial complexity is the persisting ideological tensions between FEP-related ministries. For example, the ardently neo-liberal MOFAT has experienced several clashes with the Government's primary industry and culture-related Ministries, most specifically the Ministry of Agriculture and Forestry (MOAF), the Ministry of Maritime Affairs and Fisheries, the Ministry of Health and Welfare, and the Ministry of Culture and Tourism (MOCAT). These have proved the most resistant to neo-liberal policy reform and the most protectionist on trade policy matters. For example, during the late 1990s MOFAT and MOCAT feuded over South Korea's 'screen quota' system – designed to insulate the domestic film industry from foreign competition – where officials from the latter strongly opposed calls to scrap the system.[112] A similar conflict arose between MOFAT and MOAF over the former's plans to partially liberalize the country's agricultural trade regime in accordance with MOFAT's free trade agreement strategy. Furthermore, MOCIE often exhibits protectionist impulses, for instance in developing South Korea's anti-dumping policy that it oversees into a higher profile trade policy function. Generally speaking, MOFE's bureaucratic culture is moderately neo-liberal, with many personnel concerned over aspects of neo-liberal reform but ultimately acknowledging the difficulties of ignoring external neo-liberal pressures to conform.[113]

Despite the 1998 ministerial rationalization of duties, various overlaps of policy competence persist between the main FEP ministries, as are apparent from their respective organizational structures.[114] Each maintains similar policy units covering similar aspects of trade, FDI and economic co-operation policy. According to one research interviewee, the permitting of such inter-ministerial 'policy competition' by the Blue House is part of 'Kim Dae-jung's strategy to neutralise the bureaucracy by setting one ministry against the other'.[115] In the early post-crisis period, MOFE and MOCIE in particular were engaged in a struggle for control over FDI promotion. Indeed, there remains a Commission of FDI Policy, chaired by MOFE, which in the words of one participating government official, 'mobilises and formulates FDI policy'. In addition, there exists a Steering Committee on FDI Policy, chaired by MOCIE, which according to the same source 'is in charge of FDI policy direction'. The same official conceded that their 'main roles are the same'.[116] A similar contestation over international finance policy competence between MOFE and the BOK also persists. In April 2001, MOFE was opposed to the Bank's intention unilaterally to mobilize foreign exchange reserves to help stabilize a volatile won exchange rate.[117] This was motivated by BOK officials' anxiety over imported inflation. The Ministry, however, is supposedly in overall charge of foreign exchange policy, informing the BOK whether to intervene in the market or not after appropriate consultation, which on this occasion did not transpire.

More generally, an interviewed MOFAT official conceded that the ministerial coherency of FEP formation was 'not working as well as it should', and that MOFAT had experienced 'considerable difficulty in obtaining co-operation from other ministries', partly owing to its strong neo-liberal position. Moreover, there was a 'lack of clarity and consensus over FEP priorities within South Korea's state bureaucracy', and the Blue House was partly responsible, as its 'priorities are not set clearly or strongly enough'.[118] Furthermore, Lee, D.H. (1999) comments in relation to the South Korean state's FEP management that 'it is not clearly defined which ministry has the ultimate authority of co-ordination, which raises concern that there will be confusion between ministries and that, as a result, inefficiency might emerge again in economic and trade diplomacy' (p. 125).

To some extent, then, the South Korean state's FEP management is characterized by a notable degree of inter-ministerial conflict, confused policy competences and overlaps, dysfunctional bureaucratic dynamics, and weakened bureaucratic purpose and coherence. At the same time, state bureaucratic reform – and with it the gradual dissipation of both bureaucratic inertia and resistance to implementing a more neo-liberal FEP paradigm – has emerged within the South Korean polity. Kim Dae-jung's policy of replacing around a third of the Government's top bureaucrats with experts from other social sectors – including firms, trade unions and general technicians – is being implemented. As one interviewed MOCIE official commented in November 2000, the 'behaviour, framework and personnel of the Government is changing fast'. Finally, while the executive branch of South Korea's government remains the pre-eminent force in shaping FEP, the country's legislative branch (the National Assembly) has seen an improvement in its contesting influence with deepening democratization, although this influence is still relatively insignificant (Kim, S.M. 1999).

4.7.1.3 Level of democratisation

We have previously discussed how deepening democratization from the late 1980s onwards has increasingly empowered the country's business and civil society groups within the South Korean polity. Although the contesting influence of the business sector (and especially the *chaebols* and their peak organizations) over FEP formation is significant, that of South Korea's civil groups remains weak. This can be partly attributed to the continued preoccupation of the country's NGOs with the fallout of the 1997/98 crisis and other domestic matters at the expense of concern about international economic issues *per se*. As Koo (2000) generally observed regarding South Korea's labour movement, 'given the more pressing problems they face in work places and their low level of influence on local unions, national unions have been barely able to develop and promote a creative societal agenda for social transformation' (p. 249). He further argues, though, that this role was being taken up by the country's civil society organizations, such as the CCEJ. Koo additionally proposed that the 1997/98 crisis, by exposing the managerial failures of both the state and big business, relatively strengthened the political standing of South Korean civil society. This also arose from the Kim Dae-jung Government's 'NGO empowerment' policy, which was partly an attempt to broaden his Administration's social base of support to overcome strong resistance to economic and social reforms.

Despite this empowered contesting influence enjoyed by many of South Korea's civil stakeholding FEP constituencies, they have rarely exercised it. Indeed, the state has invariably been the proactive party in discussions on FEP-related issues with civil society groups. For example, in preparation for the ill-fated 1999 launch of the New 'Millennium' Round of WTO trade negotiations, the Government convened various public meetings to gauge South Korean society's views on the matter. This was partly because the country's NGOs had been relatively inert in lobbying the Government on this matter in the first place, with the exception of the KoPA movement (the Korean People's Action against Investment Treaties and the WTO New Round) noted later. While this situation has changed somewhat, many domestic stakeholding FEP constituents seem ill prepared to engage effectively in the 'two-level' game process. Thus, despite the deepening democratization evident in South Korea, it will take some time before the country's civil stakeholding constituencies learn to utilize their new mediatory power effectively in FEP-related matters. This may be more widely indicative of the gradualized nature of the shift from developmental authoritarianism to developmental democratization. Furthermore, as one research interviewee contended, deepening democratization has given rise to a new stakeholding counter-liberal opposition to market opening in South Korea, as seen from post-crisis societal reactions from the agriculture, environmental and certain manufacturing communities, for example steel and autos. However, over the longer-term, when the country's new embrace of globalism is more complete, we can anticipate greater attention paid by South Korean civil society to FEP-related issues, as discussed in more detail below.

4.7.1.4 Internationalization of civil society

There are close connections between South Korea's level of democratization and the internationalization of its civil society. As hinted above, a principal reason why the country's democratically empowered civil groups have under-utilized their contesting influence in FEP affairs is due to a persisting lack of interest. Although according to an interviewed CCEJ representative, 'South Koreans have become far more aware of international economic issues as a consequence of the crisis', this 'especially applied to the work of international economic institutions such as the IMF and World Bank'.[119] There remains a shortage of experts on international issues within the country's NGO community, reflecting a persistent preoccupation with mainly domestic concerns (Hwang 2000). Furthermore, while there may be growing public support in post-crisis South Korea for a stronger ODAC policy, only 10% of people surveyed in 2000 had actually heard of KOICA. Kim Dae-jung has more strongly promoted the humanitarian aspect of South Korea's FEP – as exemplified by the relatively generous assistance package granted to Turkey in 1998 to help earthquake victims, and aid granted to East Timor in the late 1990s – yet this has scored few political points amongst the South Korean public.

South Korea's civil society engagement in the 'new' trade issues provides further illustration. In September 2000, the Presidential Commission on Sustainable Development was created with strong civil society representation, and the country's two main environmental NGOs – the Korean Federation of Environmental Movements (KFEM) and Green Korea United (GKU) – played an active role here. In addition, the MOE established the Private Environmental Organizations Policy Consultation Council as another channel for garnering civil societal opinion in the policy-making process. Yet both the KFEM and GKU have shown relatively little interest in trade–environment issues.[120] Although South Korea's environmental groups enjoy growing influence over economic-related policy formation, their energies have been almost entirely directed to domestic rather than international issues. Similarly, the country's two peak labour organizations – the Federation of Korean Trade Unions (FKTU) and the Korean Confederation of Trade Unions (KCTU) – have, like their environmental counterparts, taken only a limited interest in trade–labour issues.[121] The FKTU has less of a developed position on trade–labour linkage but takes a comparatively more positive view than the KCTU, which has adopted a more overt 'anti-globalization' approach towards such issues, especially since Seattle. Indeed, the latter opposed the Government's FDI promotion policies fearing the negative impact upon domestic labour markets. Consequently, the KCTU's more adversarial relations with the MOL here, combined with respective vague positions from the Government and FKTU, have not made for a constructive state–societal dialogue on this matter.

Notwithstanding these deficiencies, South Korea's labour movement has become one of the country's most internationalized civil sector groups. The KCTU has stressed the need for developing nations being able to adopt their own domestic models of development. On the trade–labour issue, it supports in principle the incorporation of labour clauses in trade, but this must cover basic standards such as the prohibition of forced labour and child labour, noting that when deploying 'the social clause as a trade barrier, it must have reasonable, objective procedures' and that 'at least participation of trade unions must be guaranteed'.[122] With the post-crisis promotion of inward FDI, the country's trade unions have become increasingly wary of foreign 'vulture capital', namely the asset stripping of indigenous Korean firms by foreign MNEs. Furthermore, according to an interviewed FKTU representative, 'South Korea's foreign economic policy is increasingly important to Korea's labour movement as it is making an ever bigger impact on domestic working conditions'.[123] Like the KCTU, the FKTU is monitoring the development of the WTO agenda and changes in the Government's inward FDI policies with increasing scrutiny, and takes a similar stance to KCTU on labour clauses in trade.

In addition, there is a growing trend for NGO networking and collaboration on FEP-related issues in South Korea. For instance, the Korea NGO Council for Overseas Co-operation (KCOC) provides a permanent organizational basis for this, while the Korean People's Action against Investment Treaties and the WTO New Round (KoPA) is a looser yet broad association of disparate civil society groups focused on specific foreign economic policy issues. Launched in September 1999, KoPA is composed of more than 25 organizations, including the KCTU, KFEM, KHIS, PSPD and GKU. In its own words, it has primarily 'campaigned against neo-liberalism and especially against the IMF, Investment Treaties, and the WTO'.[124] Such deepening internationalization evident in certain quarters of South Korea's civil society is beginning to exert some degree of contesting influence over the country's FEP formation.

4.7.1.5 Economic nationalism

The critical significance of economic nationalism as a mediating factor of contestability in South Korea's FEP formation has been previously acknowledged. Events surrounding the 1997/98 financial crisis exposed the underlying strength of the country's economic nationalism, whereby various manifestations of societal resistance to South Korea's embrace of globalization, the IMF 'bailout' programme and other perceived 'foreign threats' to the country's socio-economic paradigm security were evident.[125] As alluded to earlier, the original roots of South Korea's economic nationalism derived from the country's anti-colonial, independence struggles against the Japanese during the early 20th Century. It was later propagated by developmental statism to help realize the state's transformative economic objectives, but with a negative consequence for more recent governments who have encountered considerable socio-cultural resistance to external sector liberalization.

Various instances of South Korean economic nationalism can be cited. For example, Korean consumer associations have frequently conducted 'frugality campaigns' in which social pressure is brought to bear to resist the purchase of luxury (i.e. imported) products: the procurement of such goods was generally considered disloyal to the national economic cause. When the Jinro Group, a mid-sized *chaebol*, experienced serious financial problems during the crisis, many South Korean consumers responded by switching from drinking imported spirits to Jinro's soju liquor. In December 1997, when the South Korean won was in free fall on the currency markets, households responded by donating US dollars and gold to the Government, assisted by many of the country's NGOs (Joo 2000). In another instance, 40 civic and consumer groups banded together to form the United Council of the Popular Movements to Save Kia Group[126] to apply pressure upon the Government to save the *chaebol* from falling into foreign ownership. Elsewhere in the country reports abounded of how foreign-made cars were frequently being refused service at gas stations, while foreign fast food chains were compelled to advertise that their produce was 100% home-grown to avoid consumer boycotts.[127] Fila Korea also adopted a similar strategy in 1999 by placing new advertisements showing the high percentage of Korean content in their own products.[128] More recently, a February 2001 survey revealed that attitudes toward imported cars had actually worsened since 1999.[129]

While the crisis had made the public more appreciative of the benefits of inward FDI (for example as a new source of employment), there remains a significant discrepancy between the Government's willingness to embrace foreign investment and the persistent view of South Korean society that equates foreign ownership with colonialism.[130] As one interviewed MOFAT official commented, 'selling Daewoo to Ford, GM or any other foreign company to many Koreans equates to selling your country'.[131] Thus, the potential for a significant adverse reaction to any large-scale influx of foreign firms and their products remains.[132] With particular respect to inward FDI, there was considerable public concern expressed over the perceived 'fire sale' prices at which South Korean assets were being frequently acquired by foreign investors.[133] Given the choice, South Koreans have also traditionally preferred to work for indigenous companies rather than foreign inward investor firms for reasons of 'national loyalty' (Park 1997). This trend persisted even during the high unemployment conditions of the early post-crisis period. From the foreign firms' perspective, the general South Korean public hostility towards inward investors continued to be a major concern in the post-crisis period[134] (Kang 1999, Kim J.D. 1999, Yun M. 1999). There was also evidence that the *chaebols* were stirring up Korean economic nationalism in an endeavour to modulate inward FDI,[135] a practice previously deployed by the *chaebols* to counter foreign pressure on South Korea to reform its corporate governance system.

Socio-cultural values are slow to change, and South Korea's economic nationalism should be anticipated to prevail as a significant contesting influence over FEP formation, certainly for much longer than most neo-liberal reformers would concede. However, this influence relates more to societal feedback effects rather than the actual initiation of new FEP measures. In other words, FEP protagonists themselves are attempting to shift the policy agenda from economic nationalism to globalism but strong counter-pressures from various separate and aligned domestic interest groups mitigate this. Moreover, economic nationalism has tended to determine how effective the impact of new FEP measures has been, for example in the liberalization of inward FDI policy.[136]

South Korea's economic nationalism is not just manifest at societal level but also within the state bureaucratic cadres. While most top-level politicians and bureaucrats are confessing neo-liberal advocates, many lower level FEP bureaucrats remain recalcitrant national developmentalists. We previously discussed how MOFAT had locked horns with both MOAF and MOCAT, both of which maintained a strong protectionist position regarding market opening to foreign economic partners in the agriculture and cinema sectors. In the latter case, the desire of Hollywood firms to expand on their monopolistic 70% share of the South Korean cinema market only hardened both public and MOCAT resolve to resist pressure to liberalize. In a broader sense, we should expect a particularly intense economic nationalist reaction on matters of cultural sensitivity, as evident in South Korea's agriculture and cinema industries. However, the broad industrial culture of South Korea – as demonstrated by societal pride taken in the country's production achievements in the automobile, semiconductor, shipbuilding and other industries – makes it a more special case.

In recognition of the above, Kim Dae-jung has personally addressed South Korea's economic nationalism issue. At televised national town hall meetings during the late 1990s, he urged consumers to choose best quality goods at best available prices, regardless of national origin. In addition, high-level government officials published articles in major newspapers warning against nationalist attitudes towards imports and new foreign investors.[137] Trade Minister Han Duck-soo even bought a Saab car to set a public example, even though at the time it still took on average one month for Korean garages to mend foreign cars as opposed to a few hours for domestic produced equivalents. The Government also officially reversed any implicit policy of specifically targeting owners of foreign cars for tax audits, however as one research interviewee observed, this practice still lingers owing to '40 years of entrenched economic nationalism'.[138] Indeed, the withering of South Korean economic nationalism may be a question of demographics, as the younger 'globally-minded' citizens of the country displace their older 'nationalist-thinking' counterparts in both societal and state bureaucratic strata.

4.7.2 International and Transnational

As discussed earlier, contesting influences at the international level had become increasingly significant by the mid-1990s via new economic diplomacy channels and international regime rules and norms to which South Korea now adhered. The impingement of US relational and structural power upon South Korea remains strong, while emerging economic partners (for example the EU) have seen their international contesting influence over the country's FEP formation grow. Indeed, these aspects of international contesting influence have already been analysed in our evaluation of South Korea's bilateral economic diplomacy. Suffice to reiterate here that the US still enjoys the most significant singular influence on this specific account.

According to an FKI interviewee, 'South Korea's trade policy is still passive rather than proactive in that it relies on foreign pressure to transact most changes'.[139] Although many would contest this view, counter-arguing that the Kim Dae-jung Administration's economic policy reform programme exhibits a more proactive approach in comparison to its predecessors, South Korea's FEP formation lies increasingly exposed to international contesting pressures. This can be perhaps best demonstrated by the country's engagements with two key IEOs during the 1990s – the OECD and IMF.

To prepare for OECD membership in 1996, the South Korean Government was compelled to liberalize the country's capital and financial markets in general alignment with international norms. In addition, South Korea was obliged to meet other OECD membership criteria that included measures relating to taxation, export credits, competition policy, biotechnology, investment, labour market, maritime regulations, and agriculture. One Seoul-based American research interviewee commented, 'most European countries initially did not support the South Korea's application for membership, seeing them as a difficult trading partner. This gave the US more influence over dictating the terms of its accession'.[140] Consequently, relatively strong neo-liberal entry criteria in the above areas were set for South Korea, leading another research interviewee to contend that this constituted 'an IMF-style programme in advance of the crisis'.[141]

Certainly, OECD membership placed the formation of South Korea's FEP more firmly into a neo-liberal culture and environment, and more generally in the words of an interviewed MOFE official, 'accelerated the transition in South Korea's economic policy-making approach'.[142] However, according to Lee, D.H. (1999), 'Korea hurriedly and prematurely applied for membership, without solid economic fundamentals to withstand the shock that would occur upon obtaining OECD membership, thus accelerating the advent of foreign exchange and financial crises' (p. 119). Indeed at the time that South Korea acceded to the OECD, the country's foreign debts had ballooned to over $100bn as a consequence of diminished developmental state capacity to regulate the commercial borrowings and other financial operations of South Korean firms (Lee C.J. 2000). The OECD has subsequently proved to be a significant channel of neo-liberal advocacy. In its 2000 Economic Survey of South Korea, the OECD proposed the need for 'limiting government intervention in the economy' and expanding a 'reliance on market forces' (OECD 2000).

From earlier readings of this chapter, we should be aware that the IMF's own international contesting influence over South Korea's FEP has been even stronger. Lee, D.H. (1999) and Moon (1998) have even gone so far as to separately argue that the IMF's dealings with South Korea during the 1997/98 crisis and its aftermath significantly constrained the country's economic sovereignty. Moreover, although most South Koreans were grateful for the systemic support conferred by the IMF to their country, many perceived it as partially representing the international systemic causes that lay behind the crisis. As such, it was seen as a negative contesting influence over South Korea's FEP in certain quarters of the public, with many South Koreans talking in terms of the 'IMF-crisis' rather than the 'IMF-solution'. There was nevertheless a general consensus that the country's compliance with the IMF's 'bailout' programme was essential, if not only to secure future systemic support if required.

As a tactical move, the Government was expected further to prioritize its relations with the US as a means of appeasing the IMF, the logic being that American structural power wielded over the Washington-based organization could help make the IMF more conciliatory towards South Korea in implementing the 'bailout' programme. In another example demonstrating the impact of US structural and relational power, the arrangements for South Korean bank debt roll-over took place in New York, despite the fact that both European and Japanese bank exposure to South Korean defaults were higher than that of American banks. This event, together with the manifest American influence over the IMF, only heightened South Korea's hegemonic expectations of the US in international economic affairs.[143]

The South Korean Government's response to IMF advice was extremely compliant, especially in the early post-crisis period. In the words of a KDI interviewee, 'the Government accepted every word of the IMF's advice as though it were from God'. However, he further commented that many Government officials soon became more sceptical and critical of this advice, 'not assuming that IMF "truths" were based on empiricism',[144] hence more closely following Japan's approach in dealing with the 'Washington consensus' institutions, that is, the IMF and World Bank (Wade 1996). Nevertheless, MOFAT officials remained particularly supportive of the IMF's foreign economic policy prescriptions, proving once again a bridgehead for external neo-liberal advocacy. According to a senior MOFAT interviewee, there persisted a view within the Ministry that 'the IMF programme was a good compass for how South Korea should have been before the crisis'.[145] In June 2000, the IMF's Managing Director, Horst Koehler, was himself proud to announce that the 'market-driven approach has become the core approach in Korea',[146] not least achieved by the IMF's wide-ranging policy prescriptions discussed earlier.

Turning more specifically to transnational contesting influences, it should first be noted that these have been traditionally weak in the calculus of South Korea's FEP formation. Various factors may be attributed to this but the main reasons include the low level of foreign investment (and hence operating foreign firms) in South Korea, the primarily domestic focus of its civil society, and the limited penetration made by transnational NGOs (e.g. Greenpeace) and civil movements in the country. Even powerful American MNEs have remained only indirectly involved in the US–South Korea economic diplomacy process, unless very significant problems have arisen. However, this narrow base of contesting influence is likely to broaden quite considerably. South Korea's state bureaucratic cadres are engaged in an expanding set of trans-governmental alliances and policy-networks, as can be seen in South Korea's more proactive economic diplomacy since the 1997/98 crisis, for example in APBFTA projects, APEC and ASEM processes, and the Chiang Mai Initiative. Through this channel of contesting influence will flow a greater stream of new policy ideas and an increase in trans-governmental collaborations on FEP issues.

The substantial post-crisis influx of foreign MNEs may also significantly alter the country's political economy and socio-economic fabric, bringing greater transnational influences to bear on South Korea's FEP interests, stake-holding constituencies and decision-making processes. Finally, South Korean society's firmer embrace of globalism will further expose itself to transnational influences through various informal and formalized channels, and accordingly affect society-centred interests regarding the country's FEP. For example, growing public pressure may be expected for the environmental and humanitarian aspects of South Korea's foreign economic policy to be strengthened as a consequence. This too would be constituent to the broader shift to a developmental democratization within the South Korean political economy. More generally, South Korea's more open engagement in the international economic system after the 1997/98 crisis makes the *system-centred* approach to its FEP formation arguably more relevant insofar as it has become more compliant with IEO regime rules and norms, as particularly discussed under trade policy and plurilateral–multilateral economic diplomacy earlier in this chapter.

4.8 CONCLUSION

This chapter has charted the development of South Korea's FEP, with particular reference to the impact of, and reactions to the 1997/98 financial crisis. It was shown how critical changes have occurred in the development context of the country's FEP, where the Kim Dae-jung Government has sought to convert South Korea into a more market-based economy and 'open trading nation'. This transformation had, of course, begun well before the crisis, yet it served to amplify pre-existing pressures to change, and therefore proved both as accelerator and catalyst. Moreover, neo-liberals would contend that South Korea's developmental statist and neo-mercantilist practices are incommensurate with the norms and imperatives of contemporary global capitalism. While this is contestable (see Chapter 2), this chapter has shown how certain structural economic, institutional and socio-cultural factors continue to underpin key aspects of South Korean developmental statism and neo-mercantilism. Yet it was also acknowledged that these 'organic' forms are evolving into something new, with according implications for the current and future development of the country's FEP. Furthermore, the crisis exposed the semi-periphery fragility of the South Korean economy, and the persisting critical factor of dependence in its FEP formation.

Regarding cognitive–ideological approaches, it was shown how the ideological osmosis that has become increasingly evident within South Korea's economic bureaucracy, combined with a general rising tide of neo-liberal advocacy, brought more market-conforming ideas into the country's FEP formation. However, the respective shifts from neo-mercantilism to neo-liberalism, and from economic nationalism to globalism are far from complete within the South Korean political economy, despite the fervent efforts of the Kim Dae-jung Administration over recent years. The long-term socialization of mercantilist ideas and practices referred to by Moon and Ko (1999) and others will take years to dissipate for both socio-cultural and demographic reasons.

In matters of economic security, we discussed how South Korea faced a number of old and new challenges in the post-crisis period. Its continued semi-periphery dependence on the AIEs for techno-industrial resources remains a critical factor in FEP objective-setting, as does the country's access to critical export markets. Its lack of natural resources infers that crucial attention is still afforded to matters of supply security. The 1997/98 crisis has further increased priority to South Korea's finance–credit security interests. It was also noted how the opening up of the economy has arguably exposed South Korea to greater economic security threats. However, neo-liberals would contend this very same exposure that may improve the country's longer term economic security capacity, for instance by disciplining domestic economic agents to the intensified rigours of international competition. Furthermore, South Korea has placed greater faith in IEOs such as the WTO and IMF to uphold its economic security interests in the international system. Finally, South Korea's highly developed security complex – still dominated by the issue of North Korea – was recognized. It was argued that South Korea's FEP protagonists conduct a strong implicit pursuit of economic security, even though security thinking amongst the country's policy-elites is still somewhat narrowly focused on traditional politico-military security issues. However, this may change as and when economic co-operation and integration with North Korea gradually progresses, and more overt matters of economic security become more apparent in inter-Korea relations.

Concerning the technical policy realms of South Korea's FEP, it was shown how liberalization and deregulation have made much progress, especially since the 1997/98 financial crisis. The Kim Dae-jung Administration, on its own volition and in accordance with IMF 'bailout' programme prescriptions, has accelerated the pace of neo-liberal policy reform in areas of trade, FDI and international finance. Despite these substantive changes, a persisting neo-mercantilism still lingers in both formal and informal aspects of South Korea's trade policy. Nevertheless, technical policy moves towards converting the country into an 'open trading nation' have had a profound effect in matters of economic diplomacy. At least in rhetorical terms, the South Korean Government has positioned itself as a free trade advocate, lending vocal support to WTO-led trade liberalization and seeking to partner free trade agreements with other Asia–Pacific countries. In addition, the more proactive and promotive approach evident in South Korea's post-crisis economic diplomacy has further intensified its engagements at the regional, plurilateral and multilateral levels, with it demonstrating the country's willingness to take on greater systemic responsibility in keeping with a maturing semi-periphery economy.

On the issue of domestic contesting 'actor-based' influences, it was contended that South Korea's FEP formation remains primarily *state-centric*. This was notwithstanding the growing political power and influence of the *chaebol* and the country's civil society groups over recent years. Post-crisis developments in South Korea's democracy culture have provided the country's peak business organizations with the opportunity to participate in a more two-way dialogue with the state on FEP matters. To some, this constituted a shift from developmental statism to developmental capitalism whereby the state still wielded considerable power but in a more collusive arrangement with a more politically empowered business community (Kang 2000). However, the state–*chaebol* nexus, while still strong, has exhibited signs of critical tension in the post-crisis fallout between politics and corporate interests. Meanwhile, Kim Dae-jung's 'NGO empowerment' policy may have conferred greater contesting influence to South Korean civil society, but this is being exploited far more effectively in matters of domestic rather than foreign economic policy. This can be largely attributed to the still stunted level of civil society 'internationalization' in South Korea. Indeed, where South Korean society does connect with international economic issues, an economic nationalist response remains a strong societal expression of opinion and behaviour.

Furthermore, South Korea's entrenched economic nationalism has proved a notable impediment to the Kim Dae-jung Government's endeavours at constructing a more neo-liberal FEP. As argued in this chapter, it has more generally augmented certain aspects of South Korea's neo-mercantilism by conferring domestic public support for strategic trade policies designed to increase the country's power and economic security within the international system. Meanwhile, international contesting influences have become stronger in recent times through the mediation of the US and IEOs, especially via the OECD and IMF which have engendered deeper systemic conditioning of South Korea's FEP protagonists, thus making the *system-centred* approach increasingly relevant. Transnational contesting influences remain weak but can be anticipated to grow in future strength with the post-crisis influx of foreign firms, expanding trans-governmental policy-networks, and deeper societal embrace of globalism.

In final conclusion, this chapter has recognized critical post-crisis changes to South Korea's FEP but also continuity factors of considerable importance. At many levels, the country is undergoing a transformation into an 'open trading nation' that is additionally far more open to inward foreign investment and willing to advocate free trade on the international stage. The deconstruction of the South Korean developmental state and the associated retraction of its neo-mercantilist practices were undoubtedly advanced by the events and developments surrounding the 1997/98 crisis. However, the inter-locking structural relationships and modes of socio-economic behaviour spawned by developmental statism identified in this chapter, that have proved a resistant force to neo-liberal change, should not be too readily discounted. As noted in the introduction, this particularly relates to aspects of societal and state bureaucratic economic nationalism, the state–*chaebol* nexus, South Korea's 'export-orientation' culture, and matters of national economic security, that point to the embedded nature of the country's broadly conceived neo-mercantilism. South Korea's FEP will as always adapt to changing domestic and international circumstances, but a wholesale paradigmatic transformation should not be expected too soon, despite the notable catalytic effects of the 1997/98 crisis.

NOTES

1. Officially known as the Democratic People's Republic of Korea and the Republic of Korea respectively, the latter being created in 1948.
2. *Juche* ideology is essentially one of self-reliance, first formally proclaimed by President Kim Il Sung in December 1955. It subsequently permeated all aspects of North Korea's economic and political society, and by 1972 had replaced Marxism–Leninism in the party programme. This 'self-reliance' ideology largely explains the persisting autarkic basis of North Korea's crumbling economy and the country's general resistance to engage in the international system.
3. Around half of Korea's industrial base was destroyed in the civil war.
4. The principal objective of the First FYP (1962–1966) was the expansion of the country's infrastructure, while the Second FYP (1967–1971) was primarily focused on developing labour-intensive manufacturing capabilities. In its Third FYP (1972–1976), the South Korean

Government initiated Korea's heavy and chemical industry (HCI) that provided the economy with a broader industrial foundation on which higher value-added sectors could be developed and economies of scope captured. Both export promotion and industrial policy had been broadly sector-neutral up until the HCI drive but thereafter became more sector-specific, as well as firm-specific in character. For example, in the 1970s Hyundai was virtually compelled to venture into the production of large-scale shipbuilding by the Park Government from a practically non-existent skill base. The Fourth FYP (1977–1981) heralded a further shift in techno-industrial priorities, this time towards the development of more technology-intensive activities, e.g. electronics and automobiles.

5. In 1975, the *chaebol* company groups were to further emulate Japan's corporate model when the state helped establish a framework for general trading companies (GTCs) to form, based on the Japanese *sogo shosha*.
6. Over the 1960s to 1990s, Korea scored frequent double-digit annual economic growth rates. In the 1960s, its average annual growth rate was 8.6%, rising to 9.5% in the 1970s, 9.7% in the 1980s, but falling to 7.3% over the 1990–96 period.
7. The EPB was established in 1961 and headed by the Deputy Prime Minister.
8. For example, under a credit control system introduced in 1974, the state was able to direct and control the *chaebol's* expansion in selected industrial sectors.
9. For example, Kim Jae-ik became senior Presidential advisor, whilst Kang Kyong-shik, Kim Ki-hwan and Kim Man-jae – all with PhDs from US universities – were appointed to key positions in the EPB.
10. According to one research interviewee, the KDI's own view on the causes of South Korea's 1997/98 crisis was revealing, laying the blame mainly on state over-regulation, state–*chaebol* ties, mis-managed finance and moral hazard (i.e. crony capitalism).
11. A related example is provided by Haggard and Mo (2000), who contend that the Government finally allowed Samsung to enter car production in December 1994 after the *chaebol* company agreed to locate the factory in Pusan, the home city of President Kim Young-sam.
12. This comprised new measures to further liberalize South Korea's finance sector, open up selected home markets, fortify competition policy, introduce greater transparency into trade policy, make domestic regulations more consistent with international standards and lift various restrictions on foreign investment (both inward and outward) as well as import licensing.
13. However, this still included measures for cheap credit and the early implementation of state projects.
14. See Ungson *et al* (1997).
15. For example, see Borensztein and Lee (1998), Chang (1998), Chang *et al* (1998), Choi (1998), Demetriades and Fattouh (1999), Haggard and Mo (2000), Kim K.H. (1998), Kim Y.S. (1998), Kim and Koo (1999), Mathews (1998); Ra and Gong (1998), Yoon (1999), and Yun J.K. (1999).
16. Marked by a record trade deficit of $20.6bn in 1996.
17. The average debt–equity ratio of the top 30 *chaebols* was 387% in 1997.
18. As Haggard and Mo (2000) observed, South Korea experienced an investment boom just prior to the crisis over 1994–1996. During this period, investment in manufacturing capital rose 38.5% per annum. Much of this was financed by short-term foreign capital, raising the country's dependence on foreign currency borrowings to a relatively high 20.4% in comparison to the previous investment booms of 1972–97 (12.9%) and 1983–91 (12.1%).
19. The Bank of Korea spent $6.7bn of valuable foreign exchange reserves over 11–21 November 1997 defending the won.
20. An examination of South Korea's finances over the mid-1990s reveals how critical the country's financial position had become at the onset of crisis. Taking December 1993 to December 1997 as the examining period, South Korea's foreign debts had risen from $43.9bn to $153.0bn, foreign reserves fell from $20.2bn to $12.4bn, exchange rate depreciated from 1US$:W808 to 1US$:W1,696, stock exchange index dropped from 860 to 370, and level of non-performing loans expanded from W2.4 trillion to estimates of up to W32 trillion.
21. See Sohn and Yang (1998) for a detailed analysis of this.

22. Examples of such measures to follow included the liquidation of some banks, the Government-promoted auction of others to foreign bidders, the implementation of stricter bank capital adequacy ratios, selected bank mergers, the separation of the Bank of Korea from MOFE, and the establishment of the Financial Supervisory Commission, Korea Asset Management Corporation and other supervisory bodies.
23. In the words of one research interviewee, this represented 'the usual attempt by recent new Governments to disassociate politics from economics'.
24. Daewoo's bankruptcy was largely attributable to an over-extended globalization strategy based on a corporate empire expansion that fatally included the acquisition of dilapidated auto and home appliance plants in Central and Eastern Europe and less developed countries (LDCs), resulting in a burgeoning debt increase from $19bn in 1995 to $50bn in 1998.
25. According to a research interviewee, the FKI – the principal peak organization of the *chaebol* – lobbied the Government to adopt a gradualist approach to IMF prescribed reforms. By end of 1998, the Government had negotiated with the IMF for greater policy latitude in many areas of prescribed reform.
26. There was even significant public support for the *chaebols* buying up Korean banks ahead of foreign investors (*Korea Herald* 7 July 1999).
27. *Asian Wall Street Journal*, 6 March 2001.
28. Many of Kim's ideas on such principles were previously articulated in his text entitled '*Mass Participatory Economy*' (Kim, D.J. 1996).
29. Han Duck-soo, speech: 'A New Paradigm of Development in the Age of Globalisation: Korea's Perspective', 15 February 2000. In this speech, he commented that 'the old model of growth created institutional mechanisms that became increasingly incompatible with the globalising economy', a direct critique of past South Korean developmental statist practices.
30. *MOFAT press release*, 26 September 2000.
31. Han Duck-soo, speech: 'A New Paradigm of Development in the Age of Globalisation: Korea's Perspective', 15 February 2000.
32. A point conceded in most research interviews with Government officials.
33. Speech delivered to the Korea Council on Foreign Relations, 12 May 1994.
34. Many research interviewees identified Trade Minister Han Duck-soo as the prime example of such a neo-liberal FEP protagonist. In 1998, he spoke of utilizing foreign pressure to South Korea's advantage, in that it would help push through those neo-liberal economic reforms he ardently supported.
35. *Korea Times*, 15 August, 1998
36. This was even conceded by a neo-liberal advocate interviewed at KIEP, November 2000.
37. There is also growing evidence in post-crisis South Korea of a broader civil society backlash against global neo-liberalism. As a Citizens Coalition for Economic Justice (CCEJ) research interviewee commented in late 1999, 'among citizens and a certain group of academics, there is a growing trend of opposing neo-liberalism in South Korea'. Moreover, according to one foreign ambassadorial official interviewed in October 1999, the view that 'imports are bad, exports are good' still continues in post-crisis South Korea. He further commented that 'South Korea is still perceived as essentially and fundamentally a mercantile state' by the foreign ambassadorial community in Seoul.
38. *Korea Times*, 8 April, 1999.
39. *Korea Times*, 13 January, 1999.
40. Interview with officials from the Institute of Foreign Affairs and National Security, November 2000.
41. A long-resident foreigner in Seoul active in FEP-related issues.
42. Interviews with MOFE and MOFAT officials respectively, October 1999 and November 2000.
43. Interview, November 2000.
44. *MOCIE press release*, 3 February, 2001.
45. *Korea Herald*, 25 April, 2001.
46. As a KCCI interviewee commented, South Korea's domestic business community 'are generally behind the Government's "open trading nation" policy [see 'trade policy' section later in the chapter] as alternative means to secure wide market access', November 2000.

47. For example, the two sides signed four economic agreements in December 2000 covering mutual guarantees on each other's corporate investments, double taxation avoidance, direct financial transactions, and the creation of an organization to resolve potential trade disputes. *Korea Herald*, 17 May, 2001.
48. 'The Politics of Famine in North Korea', United States Institute for Peace Special Report, August 2, 1999, p. 8.
49. Han Duck-soo, speech: 'The New Round: Korea's Perspective', 20 March, 2000.
50. At the beginning of the 1980s, South Korea maintained an average tariff rate of 24.9% and virtual embargoes on 31.4% of imported items. By the decade's end, these rates had fallen to 11.4% and 3.7% respectively.
51. Over the 1997–1998 period, South Korea initiated 18 anti-dumping cases, the ninth highest number for any country and the highest in East Asia. However, this rate of application decreased slightly over 1999–2000.
52. Comprising 96 *ad valorem* rates, 11 specific taxes and 18 alternate rates.
53. *MOFAT press release*, 11 January, 2001.
54. For example, EPB approval was required on all FDI proposals and technology transfer agreements.
55. Kim Dae-jung, speech: 'Opening Address of the APEC Forum on Shared Prosperity and Harmony', 31 March, 2000.
56. MOFAT Report, 'Korea's New Economy: Recovery, Reform, Liberalisation, and the Road Ahead', 3 June, 2000.
57. 'Recent Trends and Policy Directions in Foreign Investment Policy: 12 October 2000', MOCIE, p. 5.
58. Created in April 1998 and staffed by experts from various agencies, including representatives from MOFE, MOCIE, Korea Customs Service, and local governments.
59. Earlier, under the conditions of the IMF 'bailout' programme, the limit on foreign ownership was raised from 26% to 50% by the end of 1997. FIPA further raised this to 55% by the end of 1998.
60. As revealed by an interviewed senior FDI policy-maker, November 2000.
61. A view maintained by numerous research interviewees. Furthermore, *chaebol* recalcitrance over reform had further undermined foreign confidence in Korea's inward FDI regime reform process (*Economist Intelligence Unit*, 9 June, 1999; *Korea Herald*, 30 November, 1998).
62. South Korea switched from a fixed to a multiple-basket pegged exchange rate system in February 1980, which in turn was replaced in March 1990 by the more liberalized Market Average Exchange Rate System.
63. According to an interviewed senior MOFE official working in this area.
64. Includes the ten states of the Association of Southeast Asian Nations (ASEAN) plus South Korea, Japan and China.
65. The United States Agency for International Development and Japan's own Overseas Economic Co-operation Fund being the most important bilateral sources here, while the International Development Associations, the United Nations Development Programmes, the World Bank and Asian Development Bank represented the most important multilateral donor sources.
66. These are either loans to foreign governments, government agencies or other development organizations, or loans to South Korean firms and overseas investment projects.
67. More specifically, KOICA is attached to the Development Co-operation Division of MOFAT's International Economic Bureau.
68. Around two-fifths of this was bilateral aid and the rest multilateral.
69. See www.koica.or.kr.
70. As KOICA itself concedes, this is attributable to factors of 'geographic proximity, growth potential, and [East Asia's] overall historic, political, social, and cultural relationships with Korea' (p. 1). KOICA Annual Report 1998. This has not, though, deflected criticism from MOFAT for using ODA for overtly diplomatic purposes, for instance the initiation of large aid-based projects in China and Vietnam unashamedly used to augment normalizing ties with South Korea in the mid-1990s.
71. Interview, November 2000.

72. In the words of a KIET interviewee, South Korea's trade policy has always been broadly conceived, embracing FDI and industrial policies, etc.
73. Including auto-electronics, environmental technology, telecommunications, digital electronics, micro-electronics, laser disk technology, design, internet, optical fibres and instruments.
74. Interview with KIET official, October 1999.
75. 'Directions of New Industrial Policy for Economic Revival in Korea', MOCIE, 27 October, 1998.
76. *MOFE press release*, 26 July, 2000.
77. Kim Young-ho, speech: 'Building a New Foundation for Industrial Competitiveness', 27 April, 2000.
78. Full text in *Korea Herald*, 26 February, 1998.
79. This compared to an annual average of 78 during the period of 1985–1992 (Kim and Han 1995).
80. Interview with MOFAT officials managing this aspect of economic diplomacy, November 2000.
81. Acknowledged by both American and MOFAT representatives interviewed.
82. Interview, April 1998.
83. Remarks made to the US-Korea Business Council, 24 July, 1995.
84. *Korea Herald*, 24 February, 2001.
85. Subsequent sharp increases in Japanese imports were especially anticipated in key product lines, such as autos, audio-visual electronic products, computer disk drives and cellular phones, *MOFE Economic Update*, 20 April, 2000.
86. *Korea Times*, 21 August, 2000. South Korea's trade deficit with Japan had already increased sharply over 1998 to 2000, from \$4.6bn to \$11.4bn, with many suggesting this to be a direct consequence of the IDP's abolition (*Korea Herald*, 25 April, 2001).
87. Interview with official at the Japanese Embassy, Seoul, November 2000.
88. The European Commission had initiated one of its Trade Barrier Regulation investigations into this issue in December 2000. *MOFAT press release*, 21 January, 2001.
89. *MOFAT press release*, 31 March, 2000.
90. Comprising Japan, China, Brunei, Indonesia, Malaysia, the Philippines, Singapore, Thailand and Vietnam.
91. This extended the preceding ASEAN Swap Agreement established after the crisis between Indonesia, Singapore, Malaysia, the Philippines and Thailand.
92. *Korea Herald*, 16 May, 2001.
93. This was formally launched in March 2001 with the remit of drafting ASEAN Plus 3 policy proposals based on the recommendations of the East Asia Vision Group, another of Kim Dae-jung's initiatives, as were the Industry-specific Business Fora meetings.
94. *Korea Herald*, 23 November, 2000.
95. Han Duck-soo, speech: 'East Asia Economic Co-operation', 17 April, 2000.
96. South Korea is especially active in trade, competition, e-commerce, labour and employment issues on OECD committees.
97. Kim Dae-jung, speech: 'Opening Address of the APEC Forum on Shared Prosperity and Harmony', 31 March, 2000. In an earlier speech, MOFAT Minister Lee Hun-jai proposed the possible introduction of safeguards against short-term capital movements initiated by hedge funds, 'Reform Beyond Crisis Resolution', 3 June, 1999.
98. Research interviews conducted with various stakeholding groups on this issue.
99. Singapore also participates in the latter two, and Taiwan will in the very last once it has joined the WTO.
100. Samsung's foray into automobile production in the mid-1990s presents an instance of this where its electronics and heavy engineering expertise could be transferred into this line of production. However, as Weiss (1998) argues, the investment co-ordination capacity of the South Korean developmental state, and hence its ability to steer the *chaebols* away from ensuing over-investment and overcapacity, was diminished by the partial liberalization of the country's financial sector in the early 1990s. This effectively cut many of the cords of

chaebol financial dependence on the state, and hence the latter's co-ordination of sectoral development in the economy.

101. See earlier discussion on Kim Dae-jung's reforms concerning *chaebol* cross guarantees, restrictions on *chaebols* entering new business sectors, and new regulations on debt–equity ratios.
102. Ministry of General Administration, various reports, 1995.
103. The FKI are particularly successful, with around a 80–90% acceptance rate (from October 1999 research interview).
104. KITA particularly works closely with MOCIE in these areas.
105. Since the democratization began in the late 1980s, new governments have sought to promote SME development and empowerment, largely driven by the public's strong anti-*chaebol* sentiment (Haggard and Mo 2000).
106. Interview with CCEJ officials, October 1999.
107. This was linked to its 'Monitor MNEs Project' introduced in the late 1990s, involving: the monitoring of workers' rights for those employed by MNEs, the realization of MNE social responsibilities; observing international speculative finance. The KHIS also undertook a 'law-suit campaign' against the IMF 'bailout' programme's impact on Korean workers and its 'flexible' labour market clauses.
108. As Kim, H.R. (2000a) comments on MOFE, 'its centrality in hierarchical inter-ministerial co-ordination as well as in control over the budget and monetary policy has allowed the EPB and now MOFE to exert tremendous power over economic decision-making' (p. 107).
109. In early 2001 this was Lee Ki-hoo.
110. *Korea Herald*, 10 October, 1998.
111. Conceded by both MOE and MOL representatives interviewed, November 2000.
112. *Korea Times*, 18 August, 1998.
113. These views have been distilled from various research interviews with government and other officials.
114. See MOFAT, MOCIE and MOFE websites.
115. Interview with MOFE official, October 1999.
116. Interview with MOCIE official, November 2000.
117. *Korea Herald*, 7 April, 2001.
118. Interview with MOFAT official, November 2000.
119. Interview with CCEJ officials, October 1999.
120. This was even conceded by an interviewed KFEM representative, although the organization was taking a growing interest in the environmental impact of inward FDI projects and had established a Citizen's Committee for WTO Agriculture Product Law in 1999.
121. The FKTU is the more established and larger of the two with a reputation for moderation and mainstream unionism. The KCTU was formed in November 1995 with a broad social agenda and an inherently more antagonistic stance adopted towards the Government (Gills and Gills 2000).
122. From www.ktcu.org.kr.
123. Interview with FKTU official, October 1999.
124. See http://picis.jinbo.net/index_e.html.
125. A research interviewee from the CCEJ even contended that: 'Economic nationalism has become stronger since the crisis. For example, South Korea held the Taegu Round, an international meeting that strongly criticized the IMF and World Bank, and called for controls on international speculative capital'.
126. This even included the CCEJ, a prominent anti-*chaebol* NGO.
127. *Canberra Times*, 4 June, 1998.
128. *Far Eastern Economic Review*, 26 March, 1999.
129. *Korea Herald*, 18 April, 2001.
130. Korea has been invaded around 900 times in its 5000 year history. In a psychological-based analysis of inward FDI in Korea by Lee Si-hyung of the Korea Institute of Social Psychiatry it was argued that this association could be partly attributed to the Koreans' 'collective unconscious' that divides friends and foes (*Korea Times*, 24 May, 1998).
131. Interview, November 2000.

132. Although there was a huge surge of inward FDI over the 1998–1999 period (from $8.9bn to $15.5bn), this may only reflect an investor's rush to acquire cheap Korean assets and may not be indicative of a longer term trend. Furthermore, this sharp rise in Korea's inward FDI figures was also partly inflated by the *chaebols'* practice of bringing back foreign money to Korea under different named sources. In addition, inward FDI as share of Korea's GDP in 1998 was only 2.6%, a low figure in most international comparisons.
133. *Euromoney*, September 1998; *International Herald Tribune*, 21 August, 1998. South Korea's opposition parties revived this criticism in a high profile conflict with the Government in April 2000.
134. Indeed, there was a near fourfold increase in the number of strikes in foreign firms over 2000 in comparison to 1999.
135. *The Economist*, 14 November, 1998.
136. As an interviewed MOFE official involved at the heart of the neo-liberal reform process conceded in November 2000, 'economic nationalism remains a significant constraint on policy implementation and effectiveness'.
137. *MOFAT press release*, 26 September, 2000.
138. Interview with Foreign Embassy representative, November 2000.
139. Interview, October 1999.
140. Interview at US Embassy, April 1998.
141. Interview at French Embassy, April 1998.
142. Interview, October 1998.
143. The US's part in scuppering Japan's initiative to create an Asian Monetary Fund (AMF), a potential rival to the IMF in financial crisis management, further compounded this.
144. Interview, October 1998.
145. Interview, October 1999.
146. *MOFAT press release*, 3 June, 2000.

5. Taiwan: the FEP of a contested state

5.1 INTRODUCTION

Taiwan's 'contested statehood' predicament is arguably the most important defining feature of its foreign economic policy (FEP). Its ambiguous position in the international community derives from the People's Republic of China's (PRC) insistence that Taiwan is a Chinese province and not a sovereign nation-state, a view formally accepted by the large majority of national governments. Despite the extensive internationalization of Taiwan's economy, its FEP protagonists are nevertheless confronted by significant external constraints that primarily derive from this predicament. It has thus had comparatively limited 'diplomatic space' in which to manage its foreign economic relations, although changes in the nature of the international political economy – particularly the growing salience of non-state units and actors – have created new diplomatic possibilities for Taiwan. Moreover, Taiwan has been forced more down the FEP 'low politics' route due to many conventional 'high politics' foreign policy routes being closed off. A corollary of this is that few other FEP powers have exercised their foreign economic policy to such dedicated service of realizing 'high' political objectives, and more specifically to fortify Taiwan's claim for internationally recognized statehood. Taiwan's accession to the WTO provides the most important recent example of this, the accession process of which has been a key feature of its FEP. However, this chapter will show how the pursuit of economic security is frequently overridden by Taiwan's 'higher' politico-military security interests.

Taiwan's contested statehood has also meant that the 'mainland China' variable looms large in every interactive function of Taiwan's FEP, with the PRC's considerable economic and political gravitational forces shaping many aspects of its economic diplomacy and technical policy realms. In addition, the proliferation of Cross-Strait trade and investment has forged stronger economic inter-linkages between Taiwan and mainland China. Consequently, Taiwan's FEP protagonists are compelled to manage the opportunities and threats posed by this expanding economic relationship.

There are other important thematic issues addressed by this chapter. We discuss to what extent the recent transition of political power, from the long incumbent Kuomintang (KMT) government to the new Democratic People's

Table 5.1 Key economic indicators of the Taiwanese economy (1952–2000)

Year	GNP[1] (US$)	Per Capita GNP[1] (US$)	Exports (US$m)	Imports (US$m)	Trade Balance (US$m)	Exchange Rate (NT$/US$)	Foreign Exchange Reserves (US$m)
1952	1,674	196	116	187	–71	10.28	–
1955	1,928	203	123	201	–78	15.60	–
1960	1,717	154	164	297	–133	36.23	–
1965	2,811	217	450	556	–106	40.05	245
1969	4,915	345	1,049	1,213	–164	40.05	361
1970	5,660	389	1,481	1,524	–43	40.05	540
1971	6,589	443	2,060	1,844	216	40.05	617
1972	7,906	522	2,988	2,514	475	40.05	952
1973	10,727	695	4,483	3,792	691	38.00	1,026
1974	14,458	920	5,639	6,966	–1,327	38.00	1,092
1975	15,429	964	5,309	5,952	–643	38.00	1,074
1976	18,492	1,132	8,166	7,599	567	38.00	1,516
1977	21,681	1,301	9,361	8,511	850	38.00	1,345
1978	26,773	1,577	12,687	11,027	1,660	36.00	1,406
1979	33,229	1,920	16,103	14,774	1,329	36.03	1,467
1980	41,360	2,344	19,811	19,733	78	36.01	2,205
1981	47,955	2,669	22,611	21,200	1,412	37.84	7,235
1982	48,550	2,653	22,204	18,888	3,316	39.91	8,532
1983	52,503	2,823	25,123	20,287	4,836	40.27	11,859
1984	59,780	3,167	30,456	21,959	8,497	39.47	15,664
1985	63,097	3,297	30,726	20,102	10,624	39.85	22,556
1986	77,299	3,993	39,862	24,181	15,680	35.50	46,310
1987	103,641	5,298	53,679	34,983	18,695	28.55	76,748
1988	126,233	6,379	60,667	49,673	10,995	28.17	73,897
1989	152,565	7,626	66,304	52,265	14,039	26.16	73,224
1990	164,076	8,111	67,214	54,716	12,498	27.11	72,441
1991	183,736	8,932	76,178	62,861	13,318	25.75	82,405
1992	216,254	10,470	81,470	72,007	9,463	25.40	82,306
1993	226,243	10,852	85,091	77,061	8,030	26.63	83,573
1994	243,934	11,597	93,049	85,349	7,700	26.24	92,454
1995	262,978	12,686	111,659	103,550	8,109	27.27	90,310
1996	274,568	13,362	115,942	102,370	13,572	27.49	88,038
1997	285,299	13,592	122,081	114,425	7,656	32.64	83,502
1998	269,227	12,361	110,674	104,746	5,928	32.22	92,810
1999	290,517	12,325	121,591	110,690	10,901	31.40	106,235
2000	314,439	14,216	148,356	140,014	8,342	31.01	106,712

Note: 1. Current price figures.

Source: CEPD statistical database, Department of Budget, Accounting and Statistics.

Party (DPP) government, will bring changes to Taiwan's foreign economic policy. At the time of writing – just one year after the DPP's electoral victory in March 2000 – this remains highly speculative, although early indications suggest continuity in approach. We also examine how Taiwan's evolving developmental statism remains a prime foundation to its FEP formation. Not only does strong state-centricity persist but also the government's 'liberalization plus' approach of neo-liberal reform in technical policy realm (e.g. trade and industry policy) is combined with substantive forms of compensatory state capacity. Furthermore, Taiwan may well be the fourth largest economy in East Asia and the world's seventeenth largest – with a GDP of $314.4bn in 2000 (Table 5.1) – as well as the world's twelfth largest trader and seventh largest foreign investor, yet its continued semi-peripheralization in the international economic system forms another prime basis underlying its foreign economic policy.

5.2 TAIWAN'S DEVELOPMENT CONTEXT

5.2.1 Taiwan's History of Economic Development: Shaped by Contestation?

The prevailing contestation between the Beijing and Taipei governments over Taiwan's sovereignty forms part of a historic series of international struggles for control of the island territory. To some significant extent, the determinants of Taiwan's economic development in the modern historic period are closely linked to the outcomes of these struggles, and the subsequent economic policies implemented by the incumbent power to consolidate their position of governance. Taiwan had long been peopled by both its aboriginal contingent and settlers mostly from southern China before the first European explorers arrived in the form of Portuguese navigators in 1590. The new visitors referred to it as 'Ilha Formosa', meaning 'beautiful island', and established a settlement to the north. In 1622, the Dutch East India Company spearheaded a more assertive colonization of Taiwan. Despite ongoing military conflicts with the Chinese, the Dutch managed to establish a thriving trading centre at Anping on the island's southwestern coast, and in doing so integrated Taiwan for the first time into the world trade system. The consolidation of the Dutch commercial position here was intended to help resist counter-imperial pressures from rival Spanish colonists, who themselves had established two forts and some commercial activity in northern Taiwan by the late 1620s. However, it was the Dutch who prevailed and exercised effective control over the island from 1642 to 1662. During this period, Taiwan's primary economic function was as a transhipment centre for trade between Holland, Batavia (the main centre of Dutch power in Asia at the time), Japan and China. Taiwan's agricultural development also gathered pace, and its general economic development was assisted by the growing number of mainland Chinese immigrants attracted to the island by its comparative peace and stability (McBeath 1998).

Taiwan reverted to Chinese-led rule after the eventual success of local revolts against the Dutch colonists in 1662. Agricultural development continued to progress, as did sugar refining and salt production under the revolt-leading Cheng family rule that ended in 1683. Thereafter, Taiwan was absorbed into Ch'ing Dynasty governance as part of the Fujian province. Successful rice cultivation over forthcoming decades made the island a net exporter of the commodity by the early 19th Century. However, more generally Taiwan's economic development suffered at the hands of neglectful Ch'ing administrators, although this changed significantly with the advent of the Opium Wars. Renewed foreign commercial interest in Taiwan spurred the Chinese authorities to improve the island's economic and military infrastructure, lift its ban on mainland immigration, initiate new construction projects and economic resource development policies, and reform the administrative procedures and laws governing the economy (Davidson 1988). Yet after China's defeat in a military skirmish against Franco-British armed forces, it conceded access to two ports on Taiwan's eastern coast to the two victorious powers under the conditions of the 1858 Treaty of Tientsin. A further spur to Taiwan's economic development came in the late 1880s, when the first governor of the newly created Taiwan province introduced fresh policies to educate the local populace, reform its tax system and modernize the island's military defences.

However, these changes did nothing to stop Taiwan's reversion to colonized rule under the terms of the 1895 Treaty of Shimonoseki, whereby the island was ceded to Japan who governed until 1945. Like the Dutch before them, the Japanese integrated Taiwan's economy into its own imperial division of labour. The island's primary economic functions this time were to supply Japan's expanding population with food and provide a colonial market for industrial products. It also experienced its most profound economic transformation up to then through capitalist industrialization, agricultural modernization, infrastructural investment, the raising of education standards and the development of its finance and trade sectors. The foundation of Taiwan's heavy industry development was laid during the last decade of Japanese colonial rule, with the island making an increasingly important economic contribution to Japan's war effort. This growing strategic role performed by Taiwan also largely explains why Japan sought to invest progressively more in the island's economic development. Yet these developmental benefits also incurred substantial social costs to Taiwan's population, similar to those endured by Korea under its own Japanese colonial rule (see Chapter 4). Although Taiwan suffered relatively little war damage, the economy fell victim to lawlessness, corruption, hyperinflationary conditions and general inefficiencies under the management of the local Nationalist Party, or Kuomintang (KMT) administration during the immediate post-war years (Gold 1986, 1988). However, this soon changed after the arrival of KMT leader Chiang Kai-shek's retreating forces from mainland China in 1949, making Taiwan the last enclave of the incumbent Republic of China (ROC) regime after its mainland defeat against Mao Tsetung's Communists.

As before, this next historic phase of Taiwan's economic development initiated by Chiang Kai-shek's Administration can be understood in the context of domestic and international struggle. With generous American financial assistance and technical support, the Taiwan-based ROC regime began to implement developmentalist policies designed primarily to strengthen the island's total defence against potential invasion, as well as other forms of sovereign contestation, from Mao's communist People's Republic of China (PRC). A land reform programme implemented over 1949 to 1953 diversified the island's industrial base with incentives given to rural landlords to invest in manufacturing enterprises. In addition, US financial aid, at an average annual \$100m between 1951 and 1964, made a major contribution to upgrading Taiwan's industrial capital and improving economic efficiency. However, the emergence of the developmental state paradigm during the 1950s was arguably the single most important determining factor in Taiwan's modern economic development. In the various analyses that follow, it will be shown how Taiwan's developmental statism and its associated foreign economic policy have been broadly oriented by the predicament of contested statehood.

5.2.2 The Evolution of Taiwan's Developmental State

As with its NIE-3 counterparts, the link between Taiwan's economic development and national security has remained strong over recent decades, and Taiwan's developmental statism has evolved within this shared context (Amsden 1985, So and Chui 1995, Wade 1990, Weiss 1998, White 1988). The KMT, which held power continuously in Taiwan from 1945 to 2000, pursued proactive economic policies that centred on facilitating capitalist activity whilst simultaneously guiding the strategic decision-making of Taiwanese companies through setting national economic development objectives within 'plan' frameworks. Hence, White (1988) and Wade (1990) have referred to this development paradigm as a 'guided capitalist market' and a 'governed market' respectively. The government has, for example, prioritized key sectors for investment, directly promoted the development of new industrial capabilities, selected companies for promotion in international markets and in the past imposed state control over many of the economy's 'commanding heights'. Furthermore, state power has been traditionally buttressed by a relatively large state-owned enterprise (SOE) sector, the tight regulation of finance, and the state-corporatist organization of business associations (Chu 1994).

According to Cheng *et al* (1998), Taiwan's early developmental state apparatus comprised three main *economic bureaucracy constituents*. The first of these was the economic planning agencies, such as the Council of Planning and Development (CEPD) and the Industrial Development Bureau (IDB). The CEPD's original precursor was the Council for International Economic Co-operation and Development, which was known from 1973 as the Economic Planning Council, and then the CEPD in 1978. As noted in Chapter 2, the CEPD was the Taiwanese developmental state's key 'pilot agency' with a similar encompassing character and level of technocratic insulation enjoyed by South Korea's Economic Planning Board. However, its importance as a centre of economic decision-making has varied over time (Weiss 1998). In more recent times, the CEPD's planning functions are based more on projected visions of Taiwan's economic development embodied with 'white paper' proposals rather than the more *dirigiste* methods deployed in the past. Kim H.R. (2000a) even suggests that it plays mostly an advisory role now in economic policy process. However, in the words of a senior CEPD official, it remains 'primarily responsible for the overall planning and supervision of national economic development, and co-ordinates key aspects of economic policy and activities between related ministries and agencies'. [1]

The second bureaucratic constituent was *foreign exchange and trade*, with the establishment of the Foreign Exchange and Trade Review Commission in 1955. Its partial co-ordinative powers over the administration of US aid bestowed the Commission with power but with this gone by the end of the 1960s, the agency weakened and then finally dissolved with its trade functions being reverted to the Ministry of Economic Affairs (MOEA), and its foreign exchange function transferred to the Central Bank of China (CBC). The third bureaucratic constituent of the early developmental state apparatus was the *institutional complex of agencies administering US aid*, the key agencies here being the Economic Stabilization Board, the Council for US Aid and the Council for International Economic Co-operation and Development, the aforementioned CEPD precursor.

In the financial domain, the Ministry of Finance (MOF) and the state-owned banks were relatively autonomous from other economic bureaucracies, but as US aid ended, so Taiwan depended more on domestic savings and therefore its domestic bank capital. Previously, the state-owned banks' independence from the economic planning agencies limited the scope for selective sectoral policies until the Bank of Communication was reconstituted into a development bank in 1979, providing the financial mechanisms for industry policy development. In general, fiscal incentives have been used as the main device for export industry promotion. The CBC itself is independent of the Cabinet and exercises absolute control over Taiwan's domestic banking system. It has generally supported the KMT's prudent macroeconomic policies and enjoys substantial influence over stability-oriented fiscal and monetary policies via the MOF. This has made for a less *dirigiste* policy style than South Korea, though a range of effective co-ordination mechanisms are still deployed. Moreover, as discussed later, the CBC retains significant controls over Taiwan's foreign exchange transactions.

While the Taiwanese developmental state has fostered close government–business relations, these have been less intimate than those developed in either Japan or South Korea. Comparisons with the Singapore state's framework of consultative relations with its hosted foreign business sector may, though, be drawn. In addition, both the Taiwanese and Singapore states have pursued a similar SOE development strategy. Yet the fundamental small and medium-sized enterprise (SME) based nature of Taiwan economy is more important to understanding how Taiwan's developmental state and its economic policies have evolved. For example, the application of strategic trade policies to Taiwan's SME economy structure is problematic as the scope for extracting the oligopoly–monopoly rents from the promotion of 'national champion' firms has been generally limited to the SOE sector. Hence, there has been more emphasis on arm's-length policy instruments rather than selective measures that benefit particular firms. The horizontal nature of Taiwan's economic policy tradition is, moreover, based on fostering external economies of scale, as seen in the state's various research and development (R&D) and infrastructure initiatives that have formed the backbone of its plan framework, from which derive the state's export competitiveness and promotion policies. This was epitomized by the Taiwanese Government's Six Year Plan for National Economic Development (1991–1996), which incorporated a $229bn infrastructure development initiative and plans to prioritize the development of ten strategic high-tech industries.

These and other industrial policies are discussed in more detail later on when we examine the 'associative' technical policy realm of Taiwan's FEP. To set some initial development context to these discussions, the government continues to offer generous tax breaks for investments made in R&D, automation, pollution control and energy saving techniques. These latter policies are consistent with the Taiwanese state's move towards the new developmental objectives first discussed in Chapter 2, such as creating a more environmentally sustainable development paradigm. In an amendment to Taiwan's Constitution in May 1992, it was stated that economic development and environmental protection should be mutually supportive. Following this, the Executive Yuan established the National Committee of Sustainable Development (NCSD) in August 1997. In the FEP context, this implies that Taiwan's trade and foreign investment objectives should strive for environmental compatibility, and indeed Trade and Environment comprises one of the NCSD's eleven working groups, and is chaired by the MOEA.[2] The state's transformative capacity also remains salient in traditional areas of co-ordinating sectoral investment, correcting information asymmetries and publicly funded R&D in informatics industries such as computers, telecoms and semiconductors.

Like its NIE-3 counterparts, Taiwan's relatively early switch from an import substitution industrialization (ISI) strategy to one based on export-led industrialization (EOI) was a key feature of post-war developmental experience. The export imperative was heightened, however, by the island's lack of natural resources and relatively small domestic market. As with the NIE-3 in general, it was export-led growth that drove Taiwan's techno-industrial transformation. Taiwan's trade–GDP ratio of 45.9% in 2000 was higher than South Korea's but lower than Singapore's. Consistent and substantial trade surpluses have also provided Taiwan with the world's third highest accumulation of foreign exchange reserves, this representing a critical asset to its foreign economic policy as we later discuss.

Taiwanese producers retain a considerable import dependency upon American and Japanese firms (Table 5.2). Moreover, Taiwan's SMEs often serve as subcontractors for large US firms and medium-sized Japanese firms. Inward flows of foreign direct investment (FDI) have also played a comparatively important role in Taiwan's economic development. American firms were early investors, riding on the back of the US aid programme of the 1950s and early 1960s. Taiwan's pioneering export processing zones (EPZs), established first at Kaohsiung in 1966 and then at Nantze and Taichung in 1969, also did much to stimulate multinational investment in the economy by offering a mix of attractive location-specific advantages.[3] Levels of inward FDI peaked in 1989 when it accounted for around 25% of the economy's gross capital formation. However, inward FDI is now only a significant determinant of development within a few sectors of the economy, such as electronics.

Outward flows of Taiwanese FDI have risen dramatically since the mid-1980s as Taiwan's firms strived to maintain a competitive cost advantage in more labour-intensive activities by shifting production offshore, principally to mainland China and Southeast Asia. The pattern of Taiwan's overseas investments is generally consistent with the factor endowment theory of international production: more labour-intensive investments being made in developing East Asia, and more capital-intensive FDI concentrated in North America and West Europe. Most overseas investments have been low-risk and small-scale in nature, and original equipment manufacture (OEM) arrangements remain an important vehicle of internationalization (Guiheux 1998). This is the case even for large firms such as ACER and Tatung, Giant and First International Computer owing to their relative lack of access to overseas distribution outlets.

Table 5.2 *Geographic breakdown of Taiwan's international trade (percentage per trade partner, 1960–1999)*

	1960		1970		1985		1990		1997		1998		1999	
	Imports	Exports	Imports	Exports	Imports	Exports	Imports	Exports	Imports	Exports	Imports	Exports	Imports	Exports
Japan	35.4	37.5	42.7	15.1	25.2	9.5	28.8	12.3	24.1	9.2	26.9	8.0	27.6	9.2
China	0.0	0.0	0.0	0.0	0.3	0.5	0.6	3.3	3.0	12.2	4.1	13.1	3.7	14.1
South Korea	0.1	3.6	1.0	1.9	0.8	0.9	2.3	2.1	4.0	1.8	5.4	1.3	6.0	2.1
Hong Kong	1.6	12.5	1.8	9.5	3.6	7.5	6.4	10.8	4.1	11.9	4.6	10.5	4.0	9.4
ASEAN	3.4	13.2	7.3	11.8	6.9	5.5	7.4	11.8	15.7	10.4	14.1	10.3	16.3	11.0
United States	38.2	11.5	23.8	39.7	23.4	49.4	21.5	34.6	17.8	24.9	19.1	26.9	17.9	26.3
Canada	0.7	0.7	1.1	3.6	1.5	2.6	1.3	2.6	1.0	1.8	0.8	2.1	0.7	2.2
Australasia	1.3	0.2	3.4	1.5	3.9	2.5	2.8	2.3	2.9	1.7	3.1	1.7	2.8	1.6
EU15	10.0	5.6	10.6	11.3	14.1	6.5	21.4	11.6	15.0	13.2	13.9	16.9	12.0	16.0
Middle East	6.7	10.9	4.1	1.4	5.9	8.0	2.5	4.6	2.2	3.1	2.7	1.7	3.6	1.6
Africa	0.7	2.2	0.7	3.0	2.2	1.3	0.9	0.3	1.1	1.8	1.6	1.0	1.9	0.8
Latin America[1]	0.1	0.1	3.4	1.0	3.0	1.5	2.4	1.9	3.0	1.9	1.6	3.1	1.2	2.4
Other	0.1	0.1	3.4	1.0	2.7	1.0	2.4	1.9	3.0	1.9	2.1	3.4	2.3	3.3

Note: 1. Includes the Caribbean states.

Source: IMF Direction of Trade Statistics, various editions.

In a similar way to South Korea, much of Taiwan's outward FDI to the US and Europe concentrated heavily in electronics manufacture sectors.

The above trends in Taiwan's trade and FDI can be placed in the context of the NIE-3's dynamic semi-peripheral development. Taiwan's SME-based economy retains a substantial degree of dependency on the 'core' group of advanced industrial economies (AIEs) through the extensive circuitry of its sub-contracting links within global production chains. Yet like its NIE-3 counterparts, Taiwan has made a success of this semi-peripheral dependency in terms of progressively moving to higher value-added levels of export production, and generating substantial foreign exchange reserves as a consequence. To some extent, the growing shift from OEM to original design manufacture (ODM) and often to original design logistics/global logistics (ODL/GL) in Taiwanese SME subcontracted network production denotes an improvement in the economy's technological self-reliance. However, as Gereffi (1998) contends, Taiwan's economy is essentially locked into 'buyer-driven' global commodity chains as opposed to their 'producer-driven' variants, whereby in the former case the determining power lies in procuring contractor firms. Furthermore, Taiwan's SMEs maintain a prime dependence on OEM/ODM for access to key foreign technologies and markets.

As discussed at various points in this chapter, the recycling of Taiwan's foreign exchange reserves has coupled with the imperative to shift its own lower-tech industrial activities increasingly to its neighbouring periphery, and in particular mainland China and Southeast Asia, where the vast majority of Taiwan's outward FDI is concentrated. In the meantime, Taiwan still requires large doses of technology-intensive inward FDI so as to continue serving the 'sub-contractual' needs of AIE-originating multinationals, thus maintaining a critical dependence on foreign technology capital. Thus, despite certain periphery economies becoming increasingly dependent themselves on Taiwan's capital and technology, its persisting fundamental dependence on the AIE core still firmly roots it in the semi-periphery strata.

While developmental statism remains strongly evident in Taiwan's political economy, it has nevertheless succumbed to partially eroding forces of neo-liberalism. The systematic liberalization and deregulation of the economy began in the early 1980s, the pace of which being driven by domestic and external sources of neo-liberal advocacy. With the onset of democratization came growing domestic political pressure to move more towards a market democracy. Considerable US bilateral pressure upon Taiwan to adopt more neo-liberal, less state-active policies was reinforced by parallel pressures via Taiwan's WTO accession negotiations during the 1990s. However, as argued in Chapter 2, neo-liberal reform *per se* does not necessarily lead to the deconstruction of the developmental state. Rather, specific questions pertaining to the manner in which economic liberalization is implemented is more important, with particular respect to what other re-regulatory measures accompany neo-liberal reform. We note later how Taiwan's international financial policy regime provides a good example of this synchronous 'liberalization with re-regulation' approach, and hence the adaptive nature of the Taiwanese developmental state. Taiwan's trade–industry policy nexus further demonstrates the state's retention of transformative economic objectives, and the evolution rather than retraction of policy mechanisms designed to serve such ends. In other words, the Taiwanese developmental state has been re-engineered to meet the challenges of globalization (Chu 1999a, 2000).

Aspects of Taiwan's evolving developmental state are evident elsewhere. Developmentalist planning, albeit less *dirigiste* in tone and content, remains a key element of Taiwan's economic policy formation. In the CEPD's 'Plan for National Development into the Next Century' introduced during the late 1990s, 'enhancing competitiveness' was one of three overarching goals, along with 'raising quality of life' and 'sustaining development'. This embodies Taiwan's transition to the new developmentalism, with new environment and welfare-focused developmental objectives co-existing with those of national economic advancement. Hence the state, though less interventionist, still provides the developmental vision and blueprint for other economic agents. More generally, Taiwan's evolving developmental statism is closely linked to the change in government's role from essentially regulatory and restrictive in nature to that of being more facilitative and constructive, whereby the state has become more of a customer-oriented service provider rather than the guiding orchestrator of the past (Schive 1999). As we have seen in previous chapters, this forms a common NIE-3 theme.

5.2.3 Regional Crisis, Domestic Politics and WTO Accession

Taiwan proved the most crisis-resistant economy in its region during the turbulent events of 1997 and 1998,[4] and this can be at least partly attributed to its adaptive developmental statism (Chu 1999b, Schive 1999, Weiss 2000). This particularly relates to the aforementioned synchronous 'liberalization with re-regulation' approach. For example, whilst the government opened up Taiwan's capital markets to foreign competition and relinquished many controls on foreign borrowing by domestic firms, the CBC retained its strong supervisory and monitoring capacities – unlike many liberalizing Southeast Asian states and South Korea – and also simultaneously applied stipulations on foreign exchange trading and foreign borrowing, as we later examine in detail. Consequently, Taiwan's banks and firms were left comparatively unexposed to crisis risk.

Taiwan's SME-based economy also provided the microeconomic flexibility to respond effectively to the crisis conditions. For example, Taiwan's extensive subcontracting chains allowed for greater mediation between internal and external pressures caused by the crisis. Indeed, the crisis highlighted the contrast between Taiwan's vertically disintegrated production networks in the post-Fordist vein with the Fordist vertically integrated production and rigid command-structures of South Korea's *chaebol* conglomerates. In addition, the comparatively prudent loan practices of Taiwan's banks and the economy's sound financial position, with around $85bn of foreign exchange reserves at the time, helped sustain investor confidence through the crisis (Table 5.1). Taiwan was nevertheless affected by the crisis in indirect ways. For example, Southeast Asian and South Korean currency depreciations undermined the competitiveness of Taiwanese companies in both their domestic and export markets, while a crisis-induced slowdown in the East Asian economy reduced the demand for Taiwanese products.

Like Singapore, the post-crisis context of Taiwan's FEP is nowhere as strong as that for South Korea's foreign economic policy. However, two other recent developments provide additional key contextual factors for consideration. The first of these concerns the end of 55 continuous years of KMT governance in Taiwan and the rise of the DPP to political power after its election victory in March 2000. In DPP leader Chen Shui-bian's inaugural presidential speech on 20 May 2000, he stated that 'the age of "large and capable" governments has now passed, replaced by one of "small and effective" governments, which have established partnership relations with the people', and that 'we should... actively expand the role of public participation'. This suggests an intended shift from a *state-centred* to a more *society-centred* approach to policy-making. Chen's comments also connect to the 'strong state, strong society' principles of Weiss' governed interdependence concept, whereby democratizing developmental states work best when societal groups are able to respond effectively to the state's ongoing transformative objectives. As noted in Chapter 2, a stronger engagement of societal groups in the policy-making process bestows upon the state new ideas on how to meet new developmental challenges. Chen Shui-bian was later that year to outline his vision of making Taiwan a 'Green Silicon Island', thus exemplifying a proposed transition to a new developmentalist model.[5] Furthermore, in August 2000 Taiwan's new government launched its 'Plan to Develop a Knowledge-Based Economy', mirroring similar developmental policy frameworks introduced in Singapore and South Korea around the same time. These issues are discussed later in more specific relation to the possible impact on Taiwan's FEP formation.

In Chen Shui-bian's inaugural presidential speech, he further commented 'the responsibility of a modern government is to raise administrative efficiency, improve the domestic investment environment, and maintain financial order and stock market stability, so as to allow the economy to move toward full liberalization and globalization through fair competition. Based on these principles, the vitality of the public will naturally bloom and create a new phase in Taiwan's economic miracle'. The commitment to press on toward embracing 'full liberalization and globalization' is consistent with the rhetoric found in the speeches of Chen's KMT predecessors, Chiang Ching-Kuo and Lee Teng-hui.[6] It furthermore remained unclear a year into Chen's presidency as to how far his administration intended to force the pace of neo-liberal reforms. Early economic troubles experienced during 2000–2001 seemed to narrow both the scope and confidence of Chen's experimentation with new economic policies. Taiwan's stock market fell by almost 40% in the first nine months of the new DPP government's rule. In response to this and other economic warning signs, the new government organized a two-day national economic conference in January 2001 between high profile business leaders, professional economists and politicians. Eighteen major resolutions originating from the conference were chosen by the government to stimulate Taiwan's economy in accordance with three main objectives, namely improving the investment climate, boosting domestic demand and the liberalization of Cross-Strait economic exchange.[7]

However, as we later discuss, the DPP government subsequently reversed its position on this latter objective by continuing with the previous government's cautious 'no haste, be patient' policy on Cross-Strait trade and investment – a key technical aspect to Taiwan's foreign economic policy. Indeed, the vast majority of research interviewees anticipated no substantial change to Taiwan's domestic and foreign economic policies under the new DPP government.[8] The third and last recent contextual development is Taiwan's accession to the WTO, a process that has bared much influence over Taiwan's FEP formation since the early 1990s. Debate on Taiwan's WTO accession forms a continuous seam through the analysis that follows.

5.3 COGNITIVE–IDEOLOGICAL APPROACHES

Taiwan's FEP protagonists openly acknowledge its neo-mercantilist past and the persistence of this legacy in trade and other technical policy realms.[9] More importantly, their embrace of neo-liberalism has occurred within a strong institutional and developmentalist context. This 'liberalization plus' approach, as I refer to it, takes many forms and provides one of the two prime cognitive–ideological foundations to Taiwan's recent FEP formation. The second such foundation relates to the 'contested statehood' predicament, and how the 'mainland China factor' has shaped the ideas and the practical ideology that orientate Taiwan's foreign economic policy. Moreover, there exists a significant linkage between these cognitive–ideological approaches, and both essentially derive from the persistent state-centricity in Taiwan's FEP formation.

In general, Taiwan has adopted a controlled and gradual approach to economic liberalization with strong state mediation. Consequently, neo-liberal reform in the technical policy realms of Taiwan's FEP has been accommodated within a firm institutional framework, with due attention to gradualistic sequencing that often entails the implementation of compensatory measures. This is demonstrated in Taiwan's trade policy, where the Government has removed trade barriers while simultaneously augmenting its trade competitiveness-enhancing programmes. Such an approach has its roots in the Government's twin 'liberalization' and 'internationalization' policies that were formally introduced by Premier Yu Kuo-hua in 1984, and have contained the principal coterminous ideas orienting Taiwan's FEP ever since. Similarities can be drawn between the cognitive–ideological basis of this Taiwanese 'liberalization plus' approach with that underpinning the *Segyehwa* (globalization) policy pursued by South Korea's FEP protagonists during the 1990s (see Chapter 4). Just as *Segyehwa* constituted a policy means to advance South Korea's ultimately mercantilist commercial interests, especially in its first phase, Taiwan's economic liberalization programme has represented a vehicle to achieve comparable goals. Generally speaking, Taiwan's FEP protagonists have been willing to embrace neo-liberal ideas insofar as they help integrate Taiwanese firms and the economy with more commercial success into the international system.

Moreover, liberalization has been viewed not only as a vehicle to exploit the new commercial opportunities presented by globalization but also for internationalizing both Taiwan's economy and its diplomatic interests, and it is thus closely associated with the contested statehood predicament. By more firmly embracing liberalization and neo-liberal economic norms, Taiwan has been able to develop its informal diplomatic links with its main foreign economic partners more extensively. This is evident across various diplomatic linkages that Taiwan's economic liberalization has helped foster, such as from induced inward investments from large foreign MNEs, the proliferation of foreign commercial offices in Taipei, and perhaps most importantly Taiwan's accession to the WTO. In this latter case, the pay-off of Taiwan's required liberalization of its trade-related policies to meet WTO entry criteria is the significant expansion of its diplomatic space within the international system.

As hinted earlier, internationalization also has a flip side. Whilst liberalization has opened up the economy more to foreign competition, the Taiwanese Government has pursued simultaneous measures to fortify the techno-industrial basis of its export economy, thus strengthening Taiwan's own international competitive position. Recent developments in trade and industrial policy discussed later clearly indicate this approach, whereby both liberalization and evolving forms of state activism combine to underlie the technical policy realms of Taiwan's FEP. This is consistent with the general evolution of the Taiwanese developmental state, in that it is adapting to the new economic challenges of the globalization era by combining economic openness with compensatory policies designed to enhance national competitiveness.

Another aspect of Taiwan's 'liberalization plus' approach is apparent in recent developments in its international financial policy. Here, liberalization has been accompanied by a tighter supervisory mechanism and the re-regulation of Taiwan's capital and currency markets. According to Chu (2000), this is primarily attributable to the ideological commitment of Taiwan's leadership to monetary discipline and financial stability in resistance to foreign pressure for unbridled financial liberalization. As is later examined, the CBC's policy management during the events leading up to and during the 1997/98 East Asian financial crisis exemplified this approach.

The proclivity of the Taiwanese state to liberalize within a strong institutional and regulatory framework is strongly connected to broader economic and other security imperatives. A prime reason for the state's extensive mediation in the liberalization process derives from various anxieties over potential developments in Cross-Strait economic relations, and this pervades every stratum of Taiwan's FEP bureaucratic cadres. These more specifically relate to how the opening up of the Taiwan economy makes it ultimately susceptible to Beijing's attempts to undermine the ROC regime, through either direct or indirect means. For example, full economic liberalization would permit the PRC to undertake the following: invest in Taiwan's strategically sensitive industries; foster Taiwan's dependency over time on key imports from mainland China; make substantial transactions in Taiwan's currency market, hold large reserves of the NT dollar, and hence be in a position to threaten its financial stability. Thus, the Taiwanese Government maintains a comparatively strict regulatory approach on Cross-Strait economic relations. Trade and investment barriers have been removed but various restrictions on economic exchange still remain. We note later how any future moves by the PRC to bring pressure to bear upon Taiwan within the WTO framework – once the two parties have joined – to remove its Cross-Strait trade and investment barriers will be undoubtedly resisted by Taipei. In the context of our broader discussion Taiwan's contested statehood predicament, Weiss (1999) argued that:

> In spite of the growing importance of liberal economic ideas in Taiwan's public discourse it is likely that the continuing geopolitical threat (the China question) together with Taiwan's peculiar diplomatic isolation, served as important countervailing pressures that tempered and moderated the domestic push to embrace economic liberalism. As a result, state actions in Taiwan by and large continued to

view the state both as an important goal setter for the national economy and as an indispensable means of sustaining an internationally competitive industry (p. 324).

Finally, some comment is required on what difference the transition from KMT to DPP power will make to the above. During its long reign in power, the KMT elite consistently demonstrated their belief in maintaining strong state capacity in economic affairs, as alluded to above. In a research fieldtrip conducted in April 2000 for this book – just one month before the DPP would assume government power – the vast majority of research interviewees anticipated that the cognitive–ideological approach to Taiwan's FEP under the new Chen Shui-bian Administration would not differ significantly from that of the preceding KMT government. This was generally attributed to the fact that the same geo-political and geo-economic imperatives remained. In other words, Taiwan's relations with mainland China continue to set the main ideological and cognitive parameters in Taiwan's foreign economic policy. In addition, the DPP is at least rhetorically just as pro-business as the KMT, though many expect a deepening democratization in Taiwan and a gradual empowerment of societal stakeholding constituency influence over FEP formation. Hence, as in South Korea, the shift from a state-centric to a more society-centric approach is a stated policy objective of the government. However, this depends on the longevity and policy effectiveness of the DPP in political office. We note later in the chapter how early indications of manifest change were not positive.

5.4 GENERIC 'ECONOMIC SECURITY' OBJECTIVES

In keeping with the NIE-3 norm, Taiwan presides over a deep and extensive security consciousness that primarily derives from mainland China's threat environment (Roy 1996). Accordingly, relations with the PRC largely orient the economic security objectives of Taiwan's FEP protagonists. As publicly stated by the BOFT, 'Cross-Strait economic and trade exchanges are built on the premise of the preservation of Taiwan's security and economic competitiveness', and 'imports from mainland China… are permitted providing they are not counter to national security interests and will not have any adverse effects on related industries'.[10] Hence, economic security and traditional politico-military security objectives are often not easily reconcilable in Taiwan's Cross-Strait relations, and it is invariably the former that defer to the latter. This in itself reflects the overt *neo-realist* approach of Taiwan's security policy elite in keeping with the NIE-3 norm.

Notwithstanding the frequent opposing nature of Taiwan's economic and politico-military objectives, there is some considerable overlap between them. This mainly centres on a growing economic dependence on mainland China, which makes Taiwan commercially vulnerable by relying increasingly on a singular and unpredictable source as well as providing channels of infiltration by which the PRC could potentially compromise the ROC regime. Taipei maintains a constant alert to identify such threats. In December 1999, allegations arose from Taiwan's National Security Bureau chief, Ting Yu-chou, that the PRC was exploring ways to conduct 'economic warfare' against Taiwan from a special fund located in the US. Although the details of these warfare measures were not disclosed, they were generally thought to target Taiwanese investments on mainland China.[11] There have also been numerous examples of Taiwanese companies on the mainland experiencing adverse discriminatory treatment by PRC authorities. A recent incident occurred just after the DPP's electoral victory in March 2000, in which Beijing specifically targeted Taiwanese firms with tax inspections, audits and other forms of harassment.

The PRC's own growing reliance on Taiwanese capital and technology undoubtedly mitigates this threat potential to some significant degree via the negative feedback effects of threat behaviour. Nevertheless, Taiwan's economic dependence on the PRC will most likely deepen: in the context of Taiwan's advancing semi-peripheralization, mainland China presents a natural 'economic' partner both to assist its techno-industrial restructuring and to absorb its higher value-added exports. This turns dependency theory on its head insofar as Taiwan's FEP protagonists are more expressly concerned with its dependence on a non-core power rather than its more extensive economic dependence on AIEs, as we later comment. But as McBeath (1998) succinctly phrased it, 'Taiwan's international vulnerability makes the state sensitive to increased dependence on anyone, particularly its closest and most powerful rival, the PRC' (p. 241).

Despite the strong realist tradition in Taiwan's security thinking, recent policy proposals and developments indicate that a more 'comprehensive security' approach is emerging, as well as more distinct attention to issues of economic security. Just before the March 2000 election, the Lee Teng-hui Administration were working to establish a 'national security network', embracing a wide co-ordination of agencies such as the CBC, MOEA, MOF and Mainland Affairs Council (MAC) that would monitor the flow of capital, trade and personnel from mainland China, as well as constantly analyse Cross-Strait interactions in general.[12] Around the same time, Chen Shui-bian's policy team set out a proposal for an 'economic security development strategy' to be based on both 'constructive' and 'defensive' measures. The former were designed to encourage economic development in order to strengthen economic stamina, encourage a high standard of living, foster national cohesion, ensure political stability and improve Taiwan's international position in the world economy – thus being commensurate with the working definition of 'economic security' developed by this book. The latter elements included measures to maintain the order and stability of raw material supplies, exports, finance and securities markets. Moreover, the overarching principle of this strategy was to use 'development to alleviate risk and consolidate security'.[13] However, as this strategy had yet to transpire into actual economic policy-practice a year into Chen's administration, its attempt to partly reconcile Taiwan's economic and national security interests cannot be evaluated.

In June 2000, and a month after the DPP's installation to office, academic economist and Deputy-Governor elect of the CBC, Chen Shih-meng, proposed the introduction of a 'national security tax' on Taiwanese firms' investments on mainland China. This was intended to replace existing 'command and control' restrictions on such activities with a more economic or market-based instrument.[14] Professor Chen suggested an initial tax rate of between 0.5–1.0% that would raise an estimated $15m a year in revenue, but this idea found little support. Later on that year, he advocated the promotion of Cross-Strait economic interdependence. This would meet Taiwan's security objectives by fostering the PRC's growing reliance on Taiwanese capital and commerce, and hence raises its stake in Taiwan's economic stability and continued prosperity, thereby underpinning Taiwan's security.[15] However, this assumed a subservience of economic objectives to those of high politics, and correspondingly received a lukewarm response from Taiwan's political leadership. There were, though, indications in late 2000 that Taiwan's National Security Council (NSC) would consider discussing economic issues for the first time, these being mainly focused on Cross-Strait economic relations.[16] The extent to which economic security issues will permeate into the future thought processes of Taiwan's security policy elites remains unclear. Let us now more specifically consider Taiwan's generic economic security objectives in the FEP context.

5.4.1 Supply Security

Taiwan's economic supply security interests and objectives are similar to South Korea's. Its relative lack of natural resources gives rise to concern over supplies of strategic industrial materials, such as oil. This also explains why, as in South Korea, the government conferred particular priority to early outward FDI projects in mining and other raw material-based sectors. During the 1950s and 1960s, Taiwan's foreign investment in these industries accounted for between 60 to 70% of its total outward FDI. Furthermore, Taiwanese firms remain significantly techno-dependent upon Western and Japanese companies. This extends to safeguarding key foreign sources of strategic industrial products such as intermediate componentry and high-tech capital goods. By the late 1990s, high-technology imports constituted around 50% of Taiwan's total imports[17] (CEPD 2000).

For Taipei, a crucial economic security interest remains mitigating Taiwan's supply dependency on the PRC. While mainland China presents a natural offshore partner for an economy such as Taiwan experiencing dynamic techno-industrial transformation, developing a reliance on it for industrial supply lines carries both distinct economic and political risks. In pure economic terms, becoming highly dependent on any singular partner is unwise as Taiwan's own economic fortunes are held hostage to that partner. This also helps explain why its FEP protagonists began purposely to diversify Taiwan's economic ties away from just Japan and the US during the 1980s. Moreover, Taipei has wished to avoid the hazards of providing Beijing with any politico-military or commercial leverage that supply dependency bestows. Up to now, Taiwan's FEP protagonists have taken great care in moderating such dependency by maintaining several regulatory and control mechanisms in trade, FDI and international finance policy. Subsequently, Taiwan imports only one product from mainland China for every seven products it exports there, and much of this import trade is of an intra-firm nature between mainland-investing Taiwanese companies. Enterprises from the PRC are also not permitted to invest in Taiwan, thus negating any potential supply dependency on PRC capital and technology. On a similar theme, since the 1980s Taiwan has purposely amassed huge supplies of foreign oil and food reserves – reportedly enough to sustain the population for a year – as a contingency against a potential blockade made by the PRC (Chu 2000).

5.4.2 Market Access Security

Like its NIE-3 counterparts, Taiwan is a relatively small, export-oriented economy and export production remains a main engine of economic growth and development. Securing international market access thus persists as a critical FEP objective for Taiwan. This is pursued under difficult diplomatic circumstances by its FEP protagonists given Taiwan's contested statehood – an issue considered further in some detail under economic diplomacy. A core purpose of the government's 'internationalization' policy, initiated in the early 1980s, was progressively to diversify Taiwan's trade and hence market access interests. At this time, Taiwan's export dependency on American markets was acute, ranging around half of its total exports (Table 5.2). The contemporaneous down turn in the US economy and its negative impact on Taiwanese exports highlighted the inherent risks of this dependency. Europe, Southeast Asia and eventually mainland China were especially targeted by BOFT trade missions later that decade as the emerging markets with most potential for export development.

From a more global perspective, WTO accession would mark Taiwan's most significant achievement in terms of its market access security. Taiwan's lack of formal diplomatic ties with its major trade partners had meant that the vast majority of its trade was not protected either by international treaties or by other forms of formal international agreements. Acquiring WTO membership would therefore considerably improve Taiwan's market access security: not only would it provide a legal and judiciary basis to resolve many problems of market access for Taiwanese firms, but it also offered a multilateral context for negotiation thus diminishing vulnerability to excessive exercises of political leverage (i.e. relational power pressure) in bilateral relations. Moreover, WTO accession would assist the diversification of Taiwan's export interests generally by improving channels of contact with its trade partners, as well as creating a firmer environment in which its foreign trade agreements *per se* could be sustained. Perhaps most importantly concerning the latter, it will improve Taiwan's options for participating in the recent Asia–Pacific bilateral free trade area (APBFTA) trend discussed in previous chapters. Taiwan's FEP protagonists should ideally develop some form of strategy here, especially as an insurance policy against APEC institutional failure to push forward more open market access in the Asia–Pacific.

Taiwan's market access security interests pursued in relation to the PRC present somewhat of an FEP conundrum. On the one hand, mainland China has become a crucial export market for Taiwan, without which it would actually be in overall trade deficit. The PRC market is a particularly important export outlet for lower-tech manufactures: for example, approximately a third of Taiwan's textile exports are currently despatched to the PRC. By 2000, around 15% of Taiwan's total exports were destined for the PRC, generating just under a $20bn annual surplus trade flow. It is Taiwan's substantive trade surplus with mainland China that provides a significant source of foreign exchange reserves, thus providing a linkage between Taiwan's market access security and finance–credit security objectives. On the other hand, the government's continued export restrictions imposed on Taiwanese companies trading with mainland China is a clear instance of Taiwan's politico-military security interests overriding its economic security interests. However, its 'Go South' policy of promoting stronger trade and other commercial links with Southeast Asia is designed to compensate for such a compromise to these latter interests.

5.4.3 Finance–credit Security

The pursuit of finance–credit security objectives is a key priority of Taiwan's FEP protagonists, as maintaining financial and monetary stability in the international system has long been perceived by the state as an important security interest. Indicative of this is the CBC's unique status it occupies within Taiwan's FEP bureaucracy, being part of both the economic policy and national security apparatus (Chu 2000). Taiwan is fortunate insofar as it possesses the same trinity of financial virtues as Singapore: proportionately large and consistent trade surpluses, abundant foreign exchange reserves and a strong net capital inflow position. These strengths undoubtedly assisted Taiwan during the turbulence of the 1997/98 East Asian financial crisis. Although this is not to imply that it remains immune to the vagaries of financial globalization, interviewed foreign bankers in Taipei were of the opinion that currency speculators had general confidence in Taiwan's sound finances, and the CBC's supervisory competence and monetary rectitude.[18]

Taiwan's comparatively high level of foreign exchange reserves, that it has maintained for the last two decades or so, are perceived as a critical asset within its FEP framework. By April 2001, these stood at $111.7bn – the third highest in the world behind Japan and China. This level far exceeds Taiwan's annual requirements to pay for imports, and the CBC and MOF invest most of these reserves in bonds issued by AIE governments. The rest is used to aid Taiwanese firms in their overseas investments and other foreign corporate activities, develop a foreign currency call-loan market in Taiwan, and offer financial aid to other states, especially amongst the 29 small developing countries (Diplomatic 29 group) that formally recognize Taiwan's statehood. Taiwan's financial virtuosity further extends to the extremely low foreign debt serviced by the Taiwan Government, which stood at only $500m in 2000.

Maintaining this finance–credit security position constitutes a major orienting factor in Taiwan's foreign economic policy, and can be examined from various perspectives. First, its foreign exchange surplus provides a crucial degree of financial self-reliance, as Taiwan cannot draw upon the International Monetary Fund (IMF) for assistance, even in time of regional crisis. Thus, accumulating foreign exchange reserves and minimizing serviced levels of foreign debt has offered significant latitude in Taiwan's international finance policy. Second, other technical policy realms are closely linked, or even made subservient to upholding this position. These have for instance included measures designed to boost Taiwan's trade surplus (e.g. of a competitiveness-enhancing nature, liberalizing Taiwan's Cross-Strait export trade), and hence foreign exchange earnings.

Third, the Taiwanese state's attention to finance–credit security lies at the centre of its 'liberalization plus' approach, and the due circumspection towards neo-liberal globalization. This has been expressed by recent governors of the CBC, who have commonly viewed the foreign opening of Taiwan's finance markets with considerable caution. As one interviewed foreign banker in Taipei commented, 'one of the Taiwanese Government's most important foreign economic policies concerns the NT dollar. They don't like people speculating with the currency, which explains why they maintain strong regulations between the NT dollar and foreign currencies, and also on foreign currency loans'.[19] Other aspects of Taiwan's cautious approach in its international financial policy are examined later. A fourth and more general perspective concerns the PRC. A fundamental reason for Taiwan's tight controls maintained on its currency is to deny the PRC's influence over international trading of the NT dollar. During the 1980s and 1990s, the CBC deliberately fortified Taiwan's shock-absorbing capacity to withstand international shocks to the economy, or perpetrated actions by the PRC intended to compromise Taiwan's position (Chu 2000). The accumulation of foreign exchange reserves are still deliberately amassed to this end, and hence partly to mitigate the potential threat of economic warfare from mainland China.

5.4.4 Techno-industrial Capability Security

As with its NIE-3 counterparts, Taiwan retains a notable semi-periphery dependency on the core AIE powers for its techno-industrial capacity. For example, it continues to procure large volumes of high standard components and industrial equipment from Japan, and also from the US and EU. Table 5.2 shows how Japan still accounts for around a quarter of Taiwan's imports, and of these half consist of industrial machinery and electrical equipment.[20] More generally, both Taiwan's capital-intensive and technology-intensive imports were still outstripping its labour-intensive imports by the late 1990s. However, as with its economic relations with South Korea, Japan has proved particularly reluctant to transfer higher-grade technologies to Taiwan for fear of competitive feedback, that is the assimilation of these technologies by Taiwanese firms could subsequently compromise the competitive position of their Japanese rivals.

Developing a more self-sufficient techno-industrial capability but simultaneously maintaining critical technology linkages with foreign economic partners are key objectives in Taiwan's associative technical policy realm and economic diplomacy respectively. As discussed later under the theme of industry policy, the Taiwanese developmental state remains active in upgrading the technology-intensiveness of export production. This is partly achieved through fostering network links between Taiwanese firms themselves, and also by encouraging strategic technology alliances with foreign MNEs. Of course, Taiwan's SMEs have extensively engaged in the international subcontracting networks of high technology industries without state assistance. However, Taiwan is susceptible to 'specialization risk' in that its techno-industrial capability is becoming increasingly concentrated in a comparatively narrow sectoral range, with IT and electronics accounting for between 30 to 35% of its exports by the late 1990s. One risk-averse option that FEP protagonists have pursued is promoting Taiwan as a 'High-Tech Silicon Island' in order to attract technology-intensive inward FDI with the aim of developing new export capabilities in other high-tech sectors.

Finally, there exists a close connection between Taiwan's economic and politico-military security interests here, with the state affording great priority to upgrading military technology and defence-related industry capacities. In December 1999, the then Foreign Minister Chen Chien-jen commented that economic globalization and internet-related technologies were rendering obsolete many traditional national security protection methods,[21] and that Taiwan looked to develop technology-based security strategies based on existing strengths in semiconductor production and informational warfare. This forms a major aspect of Taiwan's 'dependent' economic diplomacy with the US, whereby many of its FEP protagonists constantly work to secure defence procurement contracts with American firms. Conversely, the Taiwanese Government imposes various trade and FDI restrictions designed to limit the transmission of Taiwan's own techno-industrial capabilities to mainland China.

5.4.5 Socio-economic Paradigm Security

In one sense, Taiwan's pursuit of socio-economic paradigm security can be reduced to a singular FEP objective: to resist the advances of the PRC's counter-paradigm. Although Beijing's policy on Taiwan is based on the principle and objective of national reunification, the view from Taipei is somewhat different. This is because Taiwan's subsuming back into China implies the ultimate loss in political, social and economic self-determination for the island populace. To most Taiwanese, not even Beijing's stated intention of applying the 'one country, two systems' model to Taiwan's case, as it already does to Hong Kong, is acceptable. Whilst the PRC would be happy for Taiwan's capitalist enclave and associated socio-economic paradigm to fit alongside other such enclaves in China's coastal provinces, Taipei's long stand-off with Beijing over contested statehood has bred ingrained distrust between the two sides. Consequently, Taiwan's leaders are fundamentally suspicious of any proposal from Beijing that promises socio-economic or politico-economic paradigm continuity over a long period, for example 50 years in Hong Kong's own case.

Moreover, the deepening democratization heralded by the DPP's electoral victory in March 2000 has meant to many that Taiwan has, at least in principle, further political achievements to 'defend' against the PRC's irredentist intentions. While the pro-independent stance of the DPP has toned down in recent years, a more virulent defence of Taiwan's self-determination in the international system is likely to be reflected in its foreign economic policy. As we later examine, Chen Shui-bian's new diplomacy policy is strongly based on both encouraging greater democratic participation in the policy-process and on using Taiwan's recent democratic achievements as diplomacy leverage, especially in its relations with liberal democratic powers (e.g. the US) and the international institutions they underwrite (e.g. the WTO). Yet although Taiwan's

FEP protagonists continue to play the socio-economic paradigm security card to legitimize certain actions and strategies, they also understand the limitations of this ploy given the enduring importance of nation-states in the international system. This helps explain the various limitations still imposed on Taiwan in both setting and realizing certain FEP objectives, as is discussed throughout this chapter.

5.4.6 Transborder Community Security

Whilst the pursuit of socio-economic paradigm security involves Taiwan's FEP protagonists in asserting Taiwanese 'national' distinctiveness and distinct interests in the international system, the recent development of a 'Cross-Strait economy' simultaneously requires them to manage various transborder community security issues. Political integration between Taiwan and the PRC may be some way off but *de facto* economic integration has made considerable advances since the Taiwanese Government's lifting of restrictions on Cross-Strait trade and investment – the former officially occurring in 1989 and the latter in 1990.[22] Although this economic exchange is largely uni-directional (that is deriving from Taiwan) its FEP protagonists are faced with the challenge of co-managing an increasingly coherent transborder economic space. The Hong Kong economy is also engaged here, functioning as the key intermediary for Cross-Strait trade and investment given the absence of major direct transport or communication links between Taiwan and the PRC. This explains why the greatest concentration of Taiwanese FDI in mainland China is situated in Guangdong province and not the more proximate Fujian province (LaCroix *et al* 1995, Lin 1998). By 2000, around 40 000 Taiwanese firms were operating in mainland China and had invested a cumulative sum of approximately $60bn,[23] representing around 30% of Taiwan's total outward FDI (see Table 5.3). In addition, Cross-Strait trade was approaching $30bn annually.

If nothing else, this transborder economic space represents an extension of the Taiwan economy, insofar as the main Cross-Strait linkages are between PRC-based Taiwanese firms and their networked connections to Taiwan-based business operations back home. Nevertheless, the former's own network connections with local mainland Chinese enterprises makes it difficult for either Taipei or Beijing to separate respective ROC or PRC commercial interests within this space, thus posing complications to FEP protagonists from both sides. Leng (1996, 1998) argues that this is more to Taiwan's advantage as it undermines the effectiveness of any punitive measures used by Beijing on Taiwanese firms. From a broader perspective, this enlarging spatialized Sino-Taiwanese economic community has necessitated the development of institutionalized mechanisms to manage the relevant transborder issues arising. As later discussed, both Taiwan's Straits Exchange Foundation (SEF) and the

PRC's Association for Relations Across the Taiwan Strait (ARATS) are charged with such responsibility. However, the SEF-ARATS arrangement's handling of pertinent transborder community security issues has been generally disappointing. As Cross-Straits economic interactions intensify, so will transborder issues become increasingly prominent in Taiwan's FEP calculus. For example, its National Security Bureau estimated in 1999 that the non-official number of illegal immigrants from mainland China residing in Taiwan may be 150 000 to 200 000, a considerable rise over recent years.[24]

Taiwan's business community have long lobbied for direct transport links across the Straits, and for a more generally supportive policy from the government regarding Taiwanese commercial interests in mainland China. However, primarily because the government wishes to contain the development of Taiwan's transborder community security interests, it has maintained a gradualistic and somewhat passive approach to improving Cross-Strait economic linkages. This was reflected in the new DPP government's virtual continuation of its KMT predecessor's 'no haste, be patient' policy, first introduced in 1996.[25] However, in a policy move more symbolic than substantive, the Chen Shui-bian Administration did open up the so-called 'three mini links' in early 2001, whereby direct trade, transport and communication linkages between Taiwan's small outlying islands of Kinmen and Matsu, and selected cities on mainland China's southeast coast became operationalized. In sum, we see again the underlying deference of Taiwan's economic security interests to their politico-military security equivalent.

5.4.7 Systemic Security

Taiwan has long professed its willingness for active systemic responsibility, having both the economic and technocratic resources to make a valuable contribution in this respect. Moreover, it provides Taiwan the means by which it can establish its legitimate participation in the international system *per se*. Taiwan's contested statehood predicament has naturally limited its ability either to perform in a systemic *provider* role, or enjoy the benefits and security of being a systemic *receiver*, at least in a formal or institutional sense: as noted under finance–credit security, it could not rely on IMF assistance during the 1997/98 East Asian financial crisis. At the recent centre of Taiwan's demonstration as potential systemic *provider* has been its WTO accession process. Here, Taiwan's FEP protagonists have had to convince incumbent members of their intent to uphold the multilateral trading system, the stability of which Taiwan's largely export-based economy so depends on. Moreover, as the then WTO Director-General, Renato Ruggiero, declared in March 1998:

> Joining the WTO is not like joining a political forum or an organisation which can provide loans or grants; its means hard negotiation with existing members and very often major changes in national policies in order to be able to sign on to binding commitments across the whole trade spectrum. But countries which join the WTO *gain security and predictability* in their trade relations, and gain the assurance of equal access to the disputes settlement system.

Hence, Taiwan's attention to systemic security objectives will be considerably enhanced on entering the WTO, as will be reflected in its multilateral economic diplomacy. In addition, both Taiwan and the PRC's accession to the WTO should bring greater stability and progress in the development of the world trade system, thus meeting their own systemic security objectives as well as those of other members. Moreover, as two major exporters, both will benefit in terms of improving market access security in particular. Taiwan's approach to bilateral and regional economic diplomacy may also be anticipated to change somewhat after securing WTO accession. For example, its FEP protagonists will be better able to explore the systemic linkages between APEC and the WTO, especially on matters of trade liberalization where the former regime is supposed to underpin the latter. As considered earlier, Taiwan may engage in the APBFTA trend after accession but must, like its fellow Asia–Pacific trade partners, simultaneously weigh up the positive and negative impacts of such bilateral trade agreements upon the multilateral trade system.

5.4.8 Alliance Security

Much has already been said on Taiwan's economic alliance security interests, and how vital these have been given its contested statehood predicament. We also analyse later in this chapter how Taiwan's economic diplomacy remains a surrogate for more traditional diplomatic channels for securing alliances. Various means have been deployed within Taiwan's FEP in the pursuit of alliance security. These include developing trade linkages, promoting the international strategic alliances of Taiwanese firms, the generous dispersal of official development assistance (ODA), and the establishment of foreign industrial parks.[26] Beijing often pejoratively refers to this approach as Taiwan's 'dollar diplomacy', especially with regard to the lavish financial aid conferred to the Diplomatic 29 group. Taiwan's alliance security objectives also extend more specifically to mitigating the economy's dependence on mainland China. Hence, the KMT government's 'Go South' policy, continued by the new DPP administration, represents the promotion of alternative, less risky economic alliance security linkages.

However, Taiwan's contested sovereignty has generally limited its ability to build substantive alliance security relationships with its major foreign economic partners. In the past, Taiwan relied significantly on the US as a security guarantor both in political and economic terms, and Washington's switch of official diplomatic recognition from the ROC to the PRC in 1978 dealt a serious blow to Taiwan's whole alliance security structure. Nevertheless, this bilateral alliance relationship is still seen as critical for similar reasons, and as an interviewed American representative in Taipei commented, 'the US exercises a purposeful ambiguity in guaranteeing Taiwan's economic and other security interests'.[27] Taiwan's WTO accession has also been critical to its alliance security objectives, by both providing a firmer legal and judiciary basis for conducting trade relations and by progressively rebuilding its alliance security structure more generally. Its securing of APEC membership made a significant contribution to this latter foreign economic policy objective a decade earlier. Finally, to cement its economic alliance ties still further, Taiwan's FEP protagonists may join the APBFTA trend once WTO membership has been formally achieved.

5.5 TECHNICAL POLICY REALMS

Recent developments in the technical policy realms of Taiwan's FEP have occurred in a relatively gradualistic manner, and broadly derive from an evolving developmental statist process. There is hence a similarity with Singapore's own experience, although Taiwan has, like South Korea, either ditched or reworked the neo-mercantilist principles on which many technical policy aspects are based. Yet whereas South Korea's most profound liberalization of its technical policy realms was primarily catalysed by the 1997/98 financial crisis, Taiwan's own is closely linked to its WTO accession process. Due attention to the simultaneous drives for economic liberalization and internationalization more generally underlie these developments, as do its advanced stage of semi-peripheralization and contested statehood. These two latter aspects largely explain Taiwan's unusually prominent ODAC policy (the most salient of the NIE-3 group) within its FEP framework, whereby surplus economic resources have been deployed to secure and expand Taiwan's diplomatic space. In addition, Taiwan's continued priority afforded to industrial policy, and its close linkage to trade and FDI policies provides a strong *associative* technical policy realm to FEP formation.

5.5.1 Trade Policy

As noted in Chapter 2, Taiwan shares a neo-mercantilist tradition with South Korea. While Taiwan never practised the same level of trade protectionism as its NIE-3 counterpart, it carried high tariff rates and an extensive system of export subsidies into the 1990s (Haggard 1990). This came after a period of sustained trade policy liberalization that commenced, like in many other East Asian NIEs, in the early-to-mid 1980s. Although the emerging global shift to the neo-liberal paradigm at this time largely explains this, in Taiwan's specific case it was national macroeconomic conditions that also drove its trade liberalization process. In 1986, Taiwan experienced a startling 'twin financial surplus' year in which both its internal and external balances historically peaked at 19.8% of GDP.[28] The latter had been achieved by successful neo-mercantilist policies of export trade promotion and domestic industry protection yielding consistent and sizable trade surpluses. This helped Taiwan amass a substantial accumulation of foreign exchange reserves but also applied significant upward pressure on the NT$ in the currency markets (see Table 5.1), whilst high domestic liquidity and low interest rates risked creating an asset price 'bubble' within the economy at large.

Thus trade policy liberalization, and its objective of inducing greater demand for imports, formed part of a wider strategy to head off a potential economic crisis by restoring macroeconomic balance: induced import demand would, for example, in theory exert downward pressure on the NT$ and thus assist the longer-term export competitiveness of Taiwanese exports. Tariff levels were significantly reduced, import and export procedures simplified, and trade licensing regulations relaxed in the process. By 1988, a total of 3467 items covering 45% of Taiwan's trade item nomenclature saw tariff rate reductions up to 41.3%, and in 1989 a further 4700 items had their tariff rates lowered to a 20.2% average. In the same year, Taiwan's average nominal tariff rate was reduced to 9.7%, down from the 1984 figure of 30.8%. By 1995, this had fallen marginally to 8.6%, thus putting the significance of the late 1980s tariff-rate liberalization in perspective. The year before, Taiwan had also introduced a 'negative list' system for import licensing, and with it reduced the number of product lines requiring import permits. By 2001, around 98% of Taiwan's domestic markets were open to trade in terms of official foreign access, whilst its average nominal tariff rate had fallen slightly further to 8.2%.

Central to recent developments in Taiwan's trade policy has been the issue of Cross-Strait economic exchange. From the KMT regime's retreat in 1949 until 1988, the government had banned any form of Taiwanese trade with the mainland. However, these restrictions were gradually lifted from August 1988 onwards, albeit mostly through the intermediary trading hub of Hong Kong. The liberalization of Taiwan's trade policy *vi-à-vis* mainland China precipitated a burgeoning flow of trade across the Straits during the 1990s, providing a key export market and import source of raw materials and semi-finished products for the Taiwanese economy. However, various restrictions on Cross-Strait trade remain in place. For example, the text of Taiwan's Foreign Trade Act of 1993, subsequently amended in 1997 and 1999, embodies the security-related sensitivities from which these restrictions derive, with particular attention to the export of 'strategic hi-tech goods'. Nevertheless, the gradual momentum of Cross-Strait trade liberalization has been maintained. In July 1996, Taiwan introduced a 'negative list' of non-permissible imports from mainland China, replacing the more restrictive 'positive list' of permissible import items, and by April 2000 a total of 5678 product lines (55.4% of the total nomenclature) could be imported by Taiwanese firms across the Straits.

Taiwan's Foreign Trade Act also carries extensive provisions on IPR protection, injurious foreign competition, anti-dumping, export trade promotion and other trade aspects. In many ways, it embodies the 'liberalization plus' cognitive–ideological approach to Taiwan's FEP formation by stressing the need for economic openness in the global era but also robust state activism in promoting techno-industrial competitiveness. This is discussed in more detail under Taiwan's *associative* technical policy realm. Suffice to say here that state activism remains very evident in Taiwan's export trade promotion.[29] For example, the BOFT still works to assist local companies in increasing their international competitiveness through measures such as the Product Image Improvement Plan, various trade training schemes for company personnel, a large export promotion service unit, promoting Taiwan as a Worldwide Purchasing Centre, generous SMEs export credit, export insurance and export financing schemes.[30]

The export trade promotion aspect of Taiwan's evolving neo-mercantilism thus remains strongly evident, and to some extent so does its protective aspect. Taiwan's average nominal tariff rate of 8.2% in 2001 was higher than South Korea's and much higher than Singapore's.[31] Many agri-sector products retain comparatively high tariff rates, such as fruit, frozen foods and meat, while other restrictions on agri-products (for example rice and sugar) remain considerable. Tariffs were also relatively high on automobiles (average at around 44%) and auto component (average at around 17%) imports on the eve of Taiwan's WTO accession. Furthermore, several hundred products were still subject to import licensing requirements by 2001, and in cases ranging from pharmaceuticals to maritime products they represented 'significant barriers to imports' according to the BOFT itself. Many of Taiwan's trade partners continued to complain of arbitrarily enforced standards on certain products (for example air conditioners) and also regarding its import system for alcohol and tobacco products. Like many other NIEs, Taiwan also developed its own anti-dumping policy during the 1990s, hence creating a firmer linkage between its trade and emerging competition policy.

Meanwhile, the BOFT estimated in 2000 that the tariff equivalent of Taiwan's various NTBs over recent years came to an approximate average of 20%. This figure compares favourably against a 1996 estimate of 30.7% for South Korea and a 1994 estimate of 173% for Japan.[32] However, as Chapter 4 discusses, South Korea has removed many of its identifiable NTBs since the mid-1990s, and especially since the 1997/98 financial crisis, and the Japanese Government has sought to achieve the same under its 'deregulation programme'. Moreover, a 20% rate represented an unacceptable level of protectionism to both its government and its main trade partners, who targeted many NTBs in their bilateral WTO accession negotiations with Taiwan.

Indeed, Taiwan's WTO accession process represented by far the most significant external source of neo-liberal advocacy in catalysing trade policy liberalization during the 1990s. In accordance with its accession obligations, Taiwan must implement various liberalization measures over a 2-to 9-year period.[33] These mainly relate to:

- an overall fall in the average tariff rate for agricultural products from a pre-accession level of 15.5% to 12.9% after full implementation, and from 6.2% to 4.3% for industrial products;
- the above tariff concessions will affect 1021 agricultural products and 3470 industrial products;
- average tariffs on automobiles to fall to 16% after phase-in and on auto components to just over 10%, while for textiles these will fall from 12% to 10%, for consumer electronics from low double-digit percentages to single figures;
- reduction in Taiwan's NTB tariff equivalent rate from an estimated 20% to 10%;
- the reduction in import licences;
- negotiation of accession to the Agreement on Government Procurement, with a view to entering into accession to the Civil Aircraft Agreement.

By 2001, Taiwan had implemented most of the WTO accession's legal requirements in the Legislative Yuan. While the deepening of Taiwan's WTO membership will undoubtedly add further impetus to Taiwan's trade policy liberalization, state activism in trade promotion remains salient. Consequently, the trade–industry policy nexus continues to be a strong integral part of the Taiwanese Government's internationalization strategy, whereby the state's extensive involvement in improving trade competitiveness persists.

5.5.2 Foreign Direct Investment (FDI) Policy

In comparative terms, Taiwan's FDI policy has traditionally lain between Singapore's open, proactive approach and South Korea's past closed, reactive approach to foreign investment. Attracting inward FDI, under the policy management of the Investment Commission, became an increasingly important objective with the passing of Taiwan's ISI strategy and US bilateral aid. Huang (1989) has argued that the Taiwanese Government initially adopted a moderate-to-conservative style to regulating inward FDI, preventing the domination of foreign MNEs in most manufacturing sectors. Various restrictions on inward foreign investment were imposed, comprising measures on entry control, ownership regulation, the monitoring of business operations, exchange controls,[34] local content and export performance requirements, and import controls.

On FDI promotion, the 1960 Statute for the Encouragement of Investment – applied to domestic and foreign investment alike – first defined Taiwan's investment incentive and promotion system. This initially had a strong sectoral focus, with information technology, industrial machinery and other strategic industries receiving special attention by and during the 1980s. In addition, Taiwan's pioneering EPZ policy initiated during the mid-1960s played a vital role in inducing inward FDI, emphasis here being placed on integrating complementary and not competing foreign capital with respect to Taiwan's domestic capital interests.[35] The hosted MNEs located in the EPZs were obligated to export all their output, while wide ranging local content requirements once compelled them to source their supply inputs locally to a considerable degree.

The liberalization of Taiwan's outward FDI regime from after 1986 was a means to alleviate the aforementioned macroeconomic instabilities born from Taiwan's twin-surplus predicament of the mid-1980s, providing a 'safety valve' outlet for inflationary capital demand pressures building up within the domestic economy, as well as an outlet to recycle its mass accumulation of foreign exchange reserves. This consequently provided a spur to the internationalization of Taiwanese firms, with an early orientation towards Southeast Asia and later China as certain restrictions on Cross-Strait economic exchange were lifted. Indeed, from 1990 the CBC actively supported this internationalization process by lending US dollars to Taiwanese enterprises via the Bank of Communications, the Export–Import Bank, the International Commercial Bank of China, and the China Development Corporation to cover up to 80% of individual investment project costs.

Unlike South Korea, there have been no radical changes to Taiwan's FDI policy in recent years. Policy liberalization has continued – partly spurred by the WTO accession process – whilst more incentives to attract high-tech inward FDI (e.g. extended tax holidays) have been provided by the government. After 1988, the Investment Commission curtailed its 'case-by-case' approval system of inward FDI projects, replacing it with a 'negative list' system. Many key restricted sectors (for example telecoms, power supply, finance, banking and insurance) on this list have been removed as part of the WTO accession process. Furthermore, the Taiwanese Government's parallel compliance with OECD standards (e.g. in technical areas covering health and safety, environmental, and national treatment regulations) brought its FDI regime more in line with international 'neo-liberal' norms. In addition, Taiwan's local content rules were erased in 2001, although some measures on performance requirements, relating to export and technology transfer quotients, have been retained.

In keeping with the 'liberalization plus' approach to Taiwan's FEP, state activism remains a co-existing key element with economic openness in Taiwan's inward FDI policy, primarily in the form of extensive investment incentives offered to foreign multinationals. More specifically, this currently stems from the ten-year extension of preferential tax measures conferred to foreign investors under the 1990 Statute for Upgrading Industries[36] granted in January 2000. The main relevant measures include: tax credits for investment in R&D, personnel training, environmental technology-based industries, environment-friendly industrial practice; five-year tax exemptions of shareholder credits for companies investing in the ten key emerging industries targeted for development by the Statute.[37] This is further analysed in the *associative* technical policy realm.

A further recent example of state proactivity in attracting inward FDI is the government's Asia–Pacific Regional Operations Centre (APROC) initiative introduced in the early 1990s. The APROC plan sought to promote Taipei in particular as a regional hub for finance, communications and commerce in especial relation to its axis of international trade and investment with mainland China.[38] Taiwan's FDI regime has been allied to other technical policy areas towards this end, comprising trade and FDI policy liberalization, reducing restrictions of foreign labour and capital mobility, and improving IPR protection and the general environment for information management. However, facing strong incumbent competition from Singapore, Hong Kong and Shanghai, APROC had achieved limited success by the end of the decade. By this time, promoting Taiwan as a 'High-Tech Silicon Island' had become a more prioritized marketing device of the government,[39] that particularly aimed to attract foreign investment in the targeted technology-intensive sectors outlined in the Statute for Upgrading Industries.

Finally, the state's regulatory capacity within its FDI policy remains notably manifest. Even after the WTO accession process, Taiwan retained an extensive negative list for inward foreign investments, with restrictions divided into prohibited and restricted sections. Those falling in the former category include agriculture, weapons and certain chemicals, while examples of the latter category are mining, power generation, transportation services, insurance and broadcasting. In addition, the non-PRC foreign investment projects of Taiwanese companies in excess of $50m require both Investment Commission and CBC approval. More significantly, and for reasons of economic security discussed earlier, Taiwan maintains various restrictions on investments made by its firms to mainland China. This particularly relates to strategic high-tech sectors (e.g. semiconductors), infrastructure projects or other products that could potentially enhance the PRC's military capabilities. There is also a $50m ceiling on any investment project to the mainland, and all investments must be authorized by the Investment Commission. In addition, no mainland Chinese investment is permitted in Taiwan for broad security-related reasons.

5.5.3 International Finance Policy

As in the other *core* technical policy realms already discussed, a gradualistic trend of liberalization has been evident in Taiwan's international finance policy for many decades. However, the Taiwanese state's high prioritization of the finance–credit security objectives considered earlier has perpetuated its strong managerial and control capacities in this FEP field. As we note later, the CBC maintains a robust regulatory and supervisory framework for managing Taiwan's international financial position, as was demonstrated during the 1997/98 East Asian financial crisis.

The Taiwanese Government had liberalized its international financial policy in an *ad hoc* and rather piecemeal manner from the 1950s to 1970s. For example, it liberalized certain foreign exchange controls as part of the 1960 Statute for the Encouragement of Investment. It was not until the late 1970s and early 1980s, though, that more substantive liberalization was implemented, in accordance with the general trend in economic policy formation at this time (Kuo and Liu 1998). In February 1979, Taiwan moved from a fixed exchange rate system to a floating rate one, and established the Taipei foreign exchange market. Nevertheless, the CBC frequently intervened in the currency markets up to and during the latter 1980s. This was not least because it wished to mediate the shock-adjustment effects on importers and exporters stemming from Taiwan's 'twin surplus' predicament at the time, especially after its huge trade surplus of 1986 had precipitated a significant inflow of speculative capital, hence applying further upward pressure upon the NT dollar (Table 5.1). The CBC also established open current account transactions in July 1987, and afterwards further liberalized Taiwan's capital account that in turn spurred both FDI inflows and outflows. However, by the late 1980s, the CBC had adopted a less interventionist approach, and significant interventions only occurred in 1991 and 1994 up until the 1997/98 financial crisis.[40]

Yet it was not until the WTO accession process was well underway that other aspects of Taiwan's international finance policy were significantly liberalized. For example, foreign banks faced restricted access to establishing their operations in Taiwan until the 1990s. Moreover, the Statute for Foreign Exchange Regulation embodied the Taiwanese state's retained strong managerial and control capacities within its foreign exchange policy, and still serves as the basis for Taiwan's foreign exchange regulation. Events and developments during the 1997/98 East Asian financial crisis present a good illustration of how these aspects of Taiwan's state capacity were purposely deployed to resist the crisis contagion.

Unlike the South Korean and most Southeast Asian governments, the Taiwanese state had liberalized its financial markets but whilst developing stronger supervisory and monitoring mechanisms, hence fortifying the regulatory powers of both the CBC and MOF (Wang 2000). As a result, Taiwan's financial institutions were compelled to exercise prudence in the extension of their loans secured by stocks (3.7% of their total loans), and consequently non-performing loans constituted a relatively very low 3.8% of the total during the crisis (Kuo and Liu 1999). Similarly, the CBC closely monitored the level of foreign debts incurred by Taiwanese companies, and furthermore stipulated that firms raising foreign currency loans for domestic use had to invest in new plant facilities and not stocks and real estate, thus avoiding the speculative asset bubbles that had beset many Southeast Asian countries. The Bank also prohibited domestic banks from offering local currency accounts for their customers abroad and restricted outbound movements of the NT dollar, thus mitigating the currency's internationalization, that is the growth of its offshore market trading. This allowed the CBC to remain the sole market maker of Taiwan's currency.

Furthermore, after a period of sustained currency market intervention during the late summer months of 1997 to counteract speculative attacks on the NT dollar,[41] the CBC closed a loop-hole in the non-deliverable forward market that effectively constrained the flow of speculative capital flows. In line with the CBC's long-standing policy of restraining the internationalization of the NT dollar, it imposed new stipulations in October 1997 upon banks to decrease bad foreign loan ratios. In May 1998, the Bank reintroduced an old monitoring measure, whereby foreign exchange traders had to report any transactions exceeding $0.5m for individuals and $1m for corporations immediately, requiring the submission of relevant documentation. Two months earlier, the CBC also presided over a $1.36bn relief finance package for Taiwanese investors in Southeast Asia and a NT$10bn extension of export insurance cover to domestic firms exporting to the region via the China Export–Import Bank.

Taiwan's comparative resistance to the region's financial crisis has largely attributed to the retained developmental statist capacities discussed above (Chu 2000, Weiss 2000). Moreover, post-crisis developments in its international financial policy demonstrate a consistency of approach. In January 2000, a $26bn National Stabilization Fund and associated regulations were introduced to protect Taiwan from potential short-term volatility in the international currency markets following WTO entry. This related to the anticipated influx of foreign funds entering Taiwan after the full WTO-induced liberalization of its capital markets, which for instance would permit foreign investors to hold 100% of local company stocks. A month later in February 2000, the CBC restated its intention to intervene in circumstances of severe speculative pressure upon Taiwan's currency. As one interviewed foreign banker observed, 'the Taiwanese Government has consistently pursued a cautious policy on liberalising its foreign exchange markets'. He thereafter told a story of how after his company had tried to sell large amounts of foreign exchange on Taipei's currency markets in early 2000, he received a call within five minutes from the CBC asking why he had done so.[42] This was consistent with the post-crisis tightening of the Bank's monitoring mechanisms noted earlier. Another interviewed foreign stakeholder revealed that foreign banks that earn excessive profits from foreign exchange trading are liable for some form of punitive measures from the CBC. He further commented 'there is still a very protective policy towards Taiwan's strategic assets, including its capital markets and currency'.[43]

There has nevertheless been progressive liberalization in certain aspects of Taiwan's capital markets, mostly driven by the WTO accession process. For example, there are currently no controls in Taiwan's foreign exchange revenues and expenses derived from the trading of commodities, services and government-approved investments, as well as capital revenues and expenses derived from international trade. In addition, resident individuals and companies may freely apply for annual foreign exchange settlements of up to \$5m and \$50m respectively per year that cover management expenses. Non-residents may also freely make remittances, provided they do not exceed \$0.1m. However, the CBC still closely monitors foreign capital entering Taiwan, and many interviewed foreign economic representatives in Taipei contend that it remains difficult for foreign firms to invest in certain Taiwanese funds. In sum, developments in Taiwan's international financial policy are indicative of a 'liberalization plus' approach. As an interviewed CBC official revealingly commented, 'the reason why the Bank has adopted a very gradual pace of liberalisation over time is to ensure as best we can that Taiwan's finance-credit security is not compromised by global market disturbances'.[44] This continues to set the tone for Taiwan's 'liberalization with re-regulation' management of its international financial policy.

5.5.4 Official Development Assistance and Co-operation (ODAC)

Taiwan shares a similar experience with South Korea in their respective transitions from once heavily dependent US aid recipients to gradually developing their own ODAC programmes with the onset of industrial maturity. As with all the NIE-3 group, the evolution of their ODAC donorship mirrors a similar progression from the periphery to the higher semi-periphery strata. Before we examine the development of Taiwan's own ODAC programme, it is worth considering its critical relationship with American aid during the early post-war period. As suggested at the beginning of this chapter, Taiwan owes much of its industrial modernization to a generous and extensive US aid programme. Over its period of duration from 1949 to 1967, this amounted to $1769m, or $187 per capita and represented 40.7% of gross domestic capital formation over the 1952–1960 period and 12.0% over the 1961–1967 period. It also represented the fifth highest donorship of US financial aid of the time. Furthermore, an additional estimated $2384m worth of military assistance aid was bestowed over the same period. It is generally thought that no other East Asian NIE owed as much to US financial aid in its post-war economic development than Taiwan.

The origins of Taiwan's ODAC programme date back to 1961, and mainly comprised the despatching of a few agriculture technical missions to Africa under 'Operation Vanguard'. In 1962, these missions were placed under the institutional banner of the ROC–Africa Technical Co-operation Committee, which was later subsumed into MOFA's Committee of International Technical Co-operation (CITC) in 1972. As with its NIE-3 counterparts, the early emphasis on Taiwan's ODAC policy was more technical than financial in composition. However, this began to change after Taiwan's gradual accumulation of foreign exchange reserves enabled financial aid to play an increasingly important role, and from which originated Taiwan's so-called 'dollar diplomacy'.

In October 1989, the International Economic Co-operation Development Fund (IECDF) was created under the MOEA's aegis, and with initial capital resources of $1.25bn to be allocated over five years. This facilitated a significant expansion of Taiwan's ODAC policy that by then was increasingly providing assistance to developing countries with friendly ties with Taipei. Further institutional changes came in the mid-1990s, starting in July 1996 when the International Co-operation Development Fund (ICDF) replaced the IECDF. A year later, the CITC merged with the ICDF,[45] which consequently made it Taiwan's principal agency for overseeing foreign aid. The ICDF's technical assistance operations comprise the extension of expert consultation services, donations of equipment, training programmes, and general technician services. Placed under the supervision of MOFA, the ICDF has a stated purpose to 'strengthen international co-operation and enhance foreign relations through promoting economic development, social progress and the welfare of the people in partner nations around the world'.[46] It presides over comparatively generous grant and loan facilities, a prime function of which being to help developing states set up their own EPZs and industrial parks.[47] In 2000, Taiwan's total ODA was $380m, representing 0.12% of its GDP.[48] While this was only half the OECD average of 0.24%, Taiwan's ODA ratio has been consistently higher than either South Korea's or Singapore's, or indeed than that for any semi-periphery economy. Moreover, we note later MOFA's proposed substantial rise in the foreign aid budget for 2001.

Taiwan's ODAC policy has been progressively fortified and extended under the ICDF. This can be attributed more to the key diplomatic function performed by this policy rather than the recycling of foreign exchange reserves. A vast proportion of Taiwan's ODA is directed to the Diplomatic 29 group, as well as states targeted as potential diplomatic partners. Regarding the latter, many Central and East European states were selected for this treatment in the early post-Cold War period. For example, Taiwan provided Poland with $20m of soft loans in 1993, and another $20m was donated to the European Bank of Reconstruction and Development in an attempt to cultivate diplomatic favour with other fledgling democratic states of the region. In 1995, Taiwanese capital was also directed towards establishing industrial parks in Lodz, Poland and Plzen in the Czech Republic (Dent 1999). Later on in 2000, the ICDF helped organize the Taiwan-financed Bundardzik Free Economic Zone in Macedonia in which $200m of levered-in Taiwanese company investment was promised to this new diplomatic partner. The year before, Taiwan had also put together a $300m aid package for Kosovo refugees, although ensuing political pressures meant that only a fraction of this was actually disbursed. Such 'dollar diplomacy' has been criticized by the PRC in particular, insofar as developed countries have been allegedly bribed into conferring Taiwan with diplomatic recognition. Yet as Chan (1997) comments, this approach to ODAC policy is logical given Taiwan is financially rich but diplomatically poor. However, in the context of Taiwan's economic alliance security, it has had limited success at expanding the diplomatic space of the contested state. For example, the securing of Macedonia's diplomatic recognition has been the only real achievement of its Central and East European strategy.

Like South Korea, the rising prominence of Taiwan's ODAC policy within its wider FEP framework may be to some extent genuinely attributable to the 'reciprocation' principle, in that having been once a significant recipient itself it now wishes to return the favour to the current generation of developing countries. Furthermore, as with its NIE-3 counterparts, Taiwan's increasingly salient ODAC policy forms part of a stronger semi-periphery advocacy role in the international system. As we discuss later under economic diplomacy, Taiwan has most recently extended various offers of financial assistance to crisis-stricken East Asian states as well as proffering financial support to new developments in regional financial governance.

Over the longer-term, the new DPP government could bring some significant changes in Taiwan's ODAP policy. In opposition, the DPP were critical of the KMT government's 'dollar diplomacy' approach, and may therefore diversify the allocation of ODA further beyond the Diplomatic 29 group. In October 2000, the new DPP Foreign Minister, Tien Hung-mao, outlined the future foreign aid priorities in the following order: formal diplomatic allies, friendly developing nations that have the potential for establishing diplomatic relations, and friendly developing nations that have potential for development.[49] This would, though, imply a degree of continuity in the short term. In the same month, Tien proposed a substantial increase in the ICDF's aid budget, expanding it from $380m in 2000 to $940m for 2001. Such an increase would raise Taiwan's ODA as a percentage of GDP to approximately 0.3%, well above the aforementioned OECD average. Moreover, the new DPP Government's proposed International Co-operation and Development Act – presented to the Cabinet for evaluation in March 2001 – sought to augment Taiwan's foreign aid policy by making it more professional, systematic and transparent.[50] These developments suggest that ODAC policy would become an even more important feature of Taiwan's FEP framework under the DPP's leadership.

5.5.5 The Associative Technical Policy Realm

A key aspect of Taiwan's 'internationalization' strategy has been the state's fixation with improving techno-industrial and export competitiveness. We noted earlier how 'enhancing competitiveness' was one of the three overarching goals outlined in the CEPD's recent 'Plan for National Development into the Next Century'. Just as in Singapore and South Korea, various state economic policies on human resource development, infrastructural investment, science and technology, and general industrial development are to a significant degree subservient to this end. As contended earlier, a strong alignment between industrial policy and its trade and FDI counterparts persists, and it embraces many different elements of the *associative* technical policy realm of Taiwan's FEP. In charting the development of Taiwan's industrial policy below, we show how its apparatus remains broad and highly trade and investment-focused. Moreover, it reflects Taiwan's evolving developmental statism in terms of adapting policy tools and objectives to suit changing international circumstances. For example, the increasing attention paid to environmentally friendly industrial development, both in domestic and export production, is indicative of Taiwan's pursuit of new developmentalist objectives.

Sharing close similarity with its NIE-3 counterparts, and South Korea in particular, Taiwan's industrial policy during the 1950s and early 1960s was inward focused, and shaped to some considerable degree by the US aid policy elite working alongside Taiwan's state bureaucracy. Various ISI policies were deployed in which Taiwan's nascent light industries received heavily insulated protection from foreign competition and financial aid-funded state support in the form of subsidies, soft loans and other *dirigiste* measures. The 1960 Statute for the Encouragement of Investment helped further develop Taiwan's techno-industrial development, and from such a burgeoning export capacity. The introduction of Taiwan's EPZ policy in the mid-1960s formed part of a fuller shift to an EOI strategy that had commenced a few years earlier. This policy has remained integral to the *associative* technical policy realm of Taiwan's FEP, and has furthermore been extended into new areas of enhancing export capacity. In 1979, the Hsinchu Science Park was established primarily to develop Taiwan's IT production capacity, with another science-based industrial park later developed at Tainan during the late 1990s. These two sites have helped increase Taiwan's world shares across key IT product lines, including 64% of scanners, 59% of monitors and 38% of network interface cards by the late 1990s (Kuo and Liu 1998). By 2001, Taiwan had created 88 industrial parks with another 23 in construction – one of the world's highest industrial park ratios. It is at these parks that a close interaction between inward FDI, trade promotion and industrial policy is observed, whereby they act as the foundation for a large proportion of foreign MNE export production in Taiwan.

Developments in Taiwan's industrial policy during the 1970s in many ways mirrored those occurring in South Korea. In 1973, the Taiwanese Government launched its Ten Major Construction Projects that were intended to provide the foundation for the next stage of industrialization into more capital-intensive sectors, with sequels of 12 extra projects in 1978 and 14 more in 1985. Just as in South Korea, this formed part of a heavy and chemicals industry drive that aimed to reduce Taiwan's import dependency on capital goods, and hence advance its position in the semi-periphery strata (Chen and Ku 1999). Part of this second-stage ISI strategy also entailed the nurturing of domestic firms, and particularly SOEs, as bearers of national industrial power and prestige. Simon (1992) contended that without such firms, 'Taiwan's objective to advance its position in the international division of labour will be untenable' (p. 119). This was also consistent with strategic trade theory in which the state-orchestration of scale and scope economies in the industrial sector is intended to secure oligopoly–monopoly rents from the more effective penetration of international markets.

Amsden (1992) argued that Taiwan's industrial policy actually became more active in the 1980s, as the state sought to develop a more technology-intensive economy. The government's direct promotion of high-tech sector development and general techno-industrial upgrading was evident across various fields. In 1982, the Executive Committee to Develop Strategic Industries established under the IDB, was soon joined in 1984 by the Development of New Industrial Products programme. These were constituent to developing Taiwan's national innovation system and improving the technological competitiveness of its export production (Hou and Gee 1993, Howe 1998, Simon 1998). The Taiwanese state was also active in managing external technology relationships at this time, for instance through the promotion and partial management of Taiwan's firms' strategic alliances struck with American and European firms, the prime intention here being to mitigate Taiwan's technological dependency on Japanese firms

(Simon 1998). In 1986, the government also introduced its Ten Year Science and Technology Development Plan that marked a yet clearer shift to the science and technology basis of Taiwan's industry policy.[51] As Amsden (1992) observed, state support here was rendered on a reciprocity basis via required performance standards, such as on meeting export targets.

State activism in industrial policy, and its coupling with trade and FDI policy, continued in a strong vein into the 1990s. The 1990 Statute for Upgrading Industries offered provisions for tax benefits, the establishment and utilization of development funds, technical assistance, industrial district development, and venture capital towards the 'furtherance of industrial upgrading and betterment of economic development' (Article 1). This was allied to the government's Six Year National Plan for National Economic Development (1991–1996) that targeted Top Ten Emerging Industries for development, comprising aerospace, speciality chemicals and pharmaceuticals, information technologies, consumer electronics, pollution control technology and equipment, semiconductors, communications, precision instruments and automatic machinery, new materials and medical equipment. In addition, it selected 25 specific high-tech products for development, with state measures on tax credits, development loans, preferential access to innovation and R&D projects to realize these ends. As previously noted, the 1990 Statute was further amended in January 2000 with a ten-year extension, subsequently continuing to lay out a developmentalist vision for Taiwan and foster international competitiveness into the 21st century.

In 1994, various key industrial technologies for localized development were also targeted by the Taiwanese Government for development,[52] with technology transfers from Japanese firms encouraged to assist this development and thus reversing the previous 'managed dependency' policy concerning Japan noted earlier. In the same year, the government started to promote Taiwan as an 'International Sourcing Centre', the intention being for foreign-investing MNEs to exploit the economy's fortified techno-industrial capacity in hi-tech global production chains. It was also hoped that the government's $229bn infrastructure development programme within its Six Year National Plan for National Economic Development would, *inter alia*, improve the attractiveness of Taiwan's techno-industrial base and enhance economy-wide competitiveness. By the late 1990s, the government had also extended and upgraded Taiwan's R&D capacity via its expanding Industrial Technology Research Institute (ITRI), an incubator centre designed to foster technological entrepreneurship and business growth,[53] and which had made a significant contribution to boosting the technology-intensive exports of Taiwanese SMEs (Chu 2000).

Today, Taiwan's trade-related ministries and their agencies – such as the MOEA, BOFT and IDB – still preside over broad EOI objectives and a 'strengthened export promotion plan' in alignment with a strategic trade agenda.[54] Whilst Taiwan's main industrial policy agency, the IDB, acknowledges the need for Taiwanese firms to embrace a more liberalized industrial environment,[55] it continues to place generally greater stress on EOI promotional strategies and measures. Interviewed IDB officials state that the agency's main function is 'to improve Taiwan's technological upgrading so as to enhance competitiveness'.[56] In recent years, the IDB has even afforded more priority to improve the competitiveness of Taiwan's traditional industries, such as bicycle manufacture and textiles.[57] However, overall the sector-specific emphasis in Taiwan's industrial policy has gradually diminished in favour of horizontal measures, where economy-wide R&D incentives and tax credits on industrial investment are made available. Yet the IDB still maintains five offices for specific sector development, these being information industry, aerospace, biotechnology and pharmaceuticals, precision machinery, and digital video.

While the IDB has moved from a directive to a more facilitative approach, a medium-to-long term planning framework remains evident in many sectoral or generic aspects of Taiwan's industrial policy. Examples include its Five-Year Plans for Upgrading Product Design Capabilities (which began its third five-year phase in 2000), Training of Technical Personnel, National Quality Promotion Programme, and Promotion of Alliances and Competitiveness of Manufacturing Industry. The IDB also continues to set long-term development targets, for instance relating to R&D expenditure and skilled personnel development in key export industries. Furthermore, the IDB is directly active in promoting international industrial co-operation. By February 2000, it had entered into Industrial Co-operation Agreements with 28 foreign contractors under government procurement projects worth around $5.3bn.[58] It is also involved in the management of Taiwan's economic relations with mainland China, targeting of 12 lower-tech, labour-intensive industries for establishing a Cross-Strait division of labour. Yet economic liberalization has diminished the salience of Taiwan's industrial policy in certain areas. For example, its remaining export subsidies were eliminated in January 2000 as part of Taiwan's WTO accession process.

5.6 ECONOMIC DIPLOMACY

5.6.1 The 'Contested State' Predicament in Perspective

It is in the conduct of Taiwan's economic diplomacy that the 'contested statehood' predicament is most clearly seen (Hickey 1992, Kemenade 1998, Kim 1994). Like other recently contested states (e.g. Kosovo, Chechnya, East Timor), Taiwan has sought to define its own politico-territorial boundary and assert its sovereignty in confrontation against an assertive contiguous hegemony, this being the PRC in its case. Before analysing the different levels of Taiwan's economic diplomacy, we shall first consider the evolution of Taiwan's diplomatic status.

From the early 1950s to early 1970s, Taipei was recognized by the Western capitalist community of states as the legitimate seat of government for all China, with Taiwan conferred a UN seat and extensive membership of other international organizations. This changed, though, after the normalization of Sino-American relations in the 1970s, with Taiwan increasingly pushed to the diplomatic margins thereafter. For its part, Beijing has adhered to the 'Hallstein doctrine' on the Taiwan issue, whereby in the 1950s and 1960s West Germany insisted that any nation wishing to maintain diplomatic relations with itself could not simultaneously maintain those with East Germany.[59] The PRC offers a similar 'one China, two systems' arrangement as extended to Hong Kong, thus allowing Taipei to retain a virtual autonomy over economic management for many decades.

However, Beijing has threatened the military invasion of Taiwan if it ever formally declares its independence. The seriousness of the threat was demonstrated in the Cross-Strait crisis of March 1996, when the PRC conducted various military exercises, including missile tests and naval approaches in the Straits themselves, in the run up to Taiwan's Presidential election (Jian 1996, Li 1996, Ross 1996). As it transpired, the incumbent KMT government beat the then pro-independent DPP. As noted earlier this chapter, the new DPP government refrained from proclaiming independence after its subsequent electoral victory in March 2000. While the PRC did not repeat the same sabre-rattling antics on that occasion, Beijing continues to resist any move by Taipei that perceivably threatens China's national coherence.

In the 1990s, Taiwan changed strategy over its mainland China policy, shifting from its 'one China' position, whereby the KMT claimed legitimate rule over all China, to a 'dual recognition' position in which the PRC and Taiwan would co-exist in the international community of states. In May 1991, President Lee Teng-hui formally announced that the civil war was over and called for all concerned to 'accept the reality that, within overall Chinese boundaries, there exists two political entities which exercise jurisdiction over two separate parts of China'.[60] Moreover, as Yahuda (1998b) commented, 'as a democratic polity, Taiwan could no longer claim to represent the whole of China, as its government drew its authority from the electorate alone' (p. 276).

Yahuda further argued that this exercise of democracy was a form of self-determination that serves as a new basis on which Taiwan could fortify its claim for international recognition. In contrast, the PRC derives its sovereignty claims through the triumph in a revolutionary civil war rather than the exercise in self-determination. Moreover, in the post-Cold War period, Taiwan hoped to elicit greater support from liberal democracies. Yet as Deans (1998) contended, increased domestic legitimacy (that is democratization processes at home) does not necessarily lead to increased international legitimacy. By way of illustration, he introduced the concepts of negative sovereignty (right of self-determination) and positive sovereignty (capacity for effective and civil government) to Taiwan's international status, whereby it possesses the latter but not the former. Furthermore, Deans noted that the central principle of public international law and main focus of international jurisprudence are based on negative sovereignty. Taiwan has nevertheless exploited the fact that the international legal order is finding new ways to accommodate non-state entities in the contemporary global economic order (Henckaerts 1996, Yahuda 1998). Taiwan's accession to both APEC and the WTO provide examples of this.

While Taiwan has proved increasingly resourceful in attempts to enlarge its 'diplomatic space', it is still denied diplomatic recognition by its most important foreign economic partners. It is this sense of diplomatic claustrophobia that provides the defining context in Taiwan's management of its foreign economic relations. The lack of formal diplomatic channels has meant that Taiwan has particularly relied on 'track two' diplomacy, utilizing cultural and business representations and low profile government officials to manage these relations. Moreover, the classification of Taiwan's different endeavours to optimize its informal diplomatic channels and options has concerned the following:

- *holiday diplomacy*: whereby high-ranking Taiwanese officials are sent on 'unofficial' visits to foreign countries, President Lee and Premier Chan's 'holiday' trip to Southeast Asia over the cusp months of 1993 and 1994 being a prime example.
- *dollar diplomacy*: the deployment of Taiwan's considerable financial resources to secure and retain diplomatic recognition amongst obliging developing countries and foster closer informal relations with others, as best exemplified in its ODAC policy.
- *total diplomacy*: Chiang Ching-kuo's strategy based on Taiwan's 'one China' objective, and which called for the mobilization of all available resources including political, economic, scientific, technological, cultural and sporting to develop substantial links with states that had transferred diplomatic recognition to Beijing.
- *flexible diplomacy*: introduced by President Lee with his inauguration in 1988, its principles were omni-directional and pragmatic, as opposed to the politico-ideological approach of 'total diplomacy' that had largely failed (Kim 1994). Its objectives were threefold: consolidating and strengthening existing diplomatic links; developing functional ties with other states; seeking membership and participation in international organizations and activities.

The new DPP government introduced further changes to Taiwan's general diplomacy policy. New Foreign Minister Tien Hung-mao, in a speech given in June 2000 at the Legislative Yuan, outlined the new regime's approach to *comprehensive pragmatic diplomacy*, based on 'using democracy and our economic achievements as an axis', thus in some way connecting to the more democratic political transition in Taiwan after the DPP's electoral victory in March 2000,[61] as well as to the prescribed approach of Yahuda (1998) discussed earlier. More specifically, this new diplomacy was to be founded on three overlapping principles, namely:

- *Democracy-based diplomacy*: by promoting democracy and human rights within international society;
- *Civilian-based diplomacy*: actively encouraging the participation of civil society groups in foreign policy-making processes;
- *Public opinion-based diplomacy*: seeking the views of the public on various issues of foreign affairs.

This constituted another attempt to expand Taiwan's diplomatic space, this time by appealing to the shared democratic sensibilities of its major economic partners in North America, Europe and East Asia, that is the 'Triad' regions.[62] However, as Jie (2000) contended, 'for both the DPP and the KMT, Taiwan's economic and trade prowess, not its democracy, is what matters most to other governments' (p. 32). In addition, we discuss below how Taiwan continues to face considerable hurdles in developing its economic diplomacy portfolio at most levels.

5.6.2 Bilateral

Taiwan maintains trade relations with over 160 countries but only conducts formal diplomacy relations with 29 of them,[63] and this group accounts for only 4% of Taiwan's total trade volume.[64] Moreover, Taiwan's disputed sovereignty severely restricts its ability to enter into any legally binding, FEP-related treaties with major foreign economic partners. Consequently, it has signed no bilateral investment treaties (BITs) other than with the Diplomatic 29 group. However, it can sign non-legally binding bilateral agreements that aim to facilitate trade, investment and other forms of economic exchange, but these can be easily reneged by Taiwan's partners as there is invariably no contractual obligation by international law for them to comply. Moreover, as one research interviewee commented, 'Taiwan's major trade partners often play the "China card" to gain advantage in commercial negotiations with Taipei, that is by threatening to defer relative beneficial treatment to Beijing'.[65] On securing WTO membership, Taiwan's fellow members are, though, legally obliged to grant her 'most favoured nation' treatment in their trade relations. The impact of WTO accession is an underlying theme of this section, but let us first consider the development of Taiwan's economic diplomacy with its major trade partners.

It makes sense to begin with PRC economic relations, as this axis orientates much of Taiwan's economic diplomacy generally. As previously discussed, Cross-Strait economic relations are still dictated by overriding politico-security objectives. For four decades after the KMT's retreat to Taiwan in 1949 there had been no official political dialogue between ROC and PRC representations. However, economic imperatives compelled Taipei to reconsider its 'closed' diplomacy with mainland China. A sharply appreciating NT dollar and intensified rivalry from Southeast Asian producers in Taiwan's more labour-intensive industries (e.g. textiles) severely squeezed its competitive position in these sectors. Permitting Taiwanese firms to relocate lower-tech production to mainland China also assisted techno-industrial transformation in the domestic economy, as envisioned by the IDB, CEPD and other economic planning agencies. In November 1987, Taipei lifted its travel ban on trips to the PRC. A year later, the PRC's State Council passed 22 regulations that permitted Taiwanese investment on the mainland.[66] This was followed up by the Taiwan Compatriot Investment Promotion Act of March 1994 that conferred the principle of national (i.e. equal) treatment upon Taiwanese business people and firms operating in the PRC.

In response to the transborder economic space emerging in the Straits zone, Taiwan established the Straits Exchange Foundation (SEF) in November 1990 as its principal unofficial Cross-Strait representative body. Dr. Chen-fu Koo of Taiwan Cement has chaired the SEF since its inception, and nine of the organization's 27 directors are also Taiwanese business leaders. Further institutional capacity to manage Cross-Strait relations was added by the Mainland Affairs Council (MAC), a new Taiwanese Government agency set up in January 1991. In its own response to these developments, the PRC established the Association for Relations Across the Taiwan Strait (ARATS) in December 1991 as a mirror organization to the SEF. Subsequent SEF–ARATS meetings, the first being held at Singapore in April 1993, represented the most significant step forward in Taiwan's economic diplomacy with mainland China.

However, the extent to which SEF–ARATS dialogue has helped manage Taiwan's economic relations with the PRC is questionable. Early meetings were largely preoccupied with peripheral 'transborder' issues (for example hijacking, smuggling, illegal immigrants) and achieved little to allay Taiwan's anxieties over more primary interests, such as the legal safeguarding of its firms' investments on the mainland (Moeller 1994). Furthermore, in June 1995, Beijing broke off its Cross-Strait dialogue with Taiwan. This resumed in April 1998 after the SEF and ARATS re-established contacts, but Beijing once more retracted in July 1999 after Lee Teng-hui's announcement of his 'special state-to-state' model to define PRC–Taiwan relations. Even when dialogue occurred in this short period, little progress was made on substantive issues of Cross-Strait economic exchange. Most recently, the new DPP government's decision to perpetuate the KMT's 'no haste, be patient' policy, thus retaining restrictions on Cross-Strait economic exchange for reasons of military and economic security, places a further break on Taiwan's economic diplomacy with the PRC. Moreover, the largely symbolic decision to permit the 'mini-three-links' in direct trade, transport and communications between Taiwan's offshore islands and mainland China will only have a limited commercial impact.

Whilst Taiwanese Governments may continue to practise extreme caution in developing economic relations with mainland China, it is likely that external sources of neo-liberal advocacy will bring increasing pressure to bear to force the pace of change. For example, future WTO obligations may compel Taiwan to remove many of its existing trade restrictions on Cross-Strait economic exchange, particularly relating to the unilateral blocking of many direct imports from mainland China. After formal accession, the PRC can also take Taiwan to the WTO's dispute mechanism to lodge complaints regarding these restrictions. However, WTO derogations permit members to restrict trade on the grounds of legitimized national security interests, and also WTO rules do not make specific stipulations about investment and shipping.

There are similarities between Taiwan and South Korea in their respective economic diplomacies conducted with Japan. Like their South Korean counterparts, Taiwan's FEP protagonists were initially cautious in developing economic dependence on Japan owing to unsavoury memories of Japanese colonial control. Nevertheless, both strategic necessity and the post-colonial legacy required Taiwan to foster a close economic relationship with Japan. As time progressed, Japan offered some counterbalance to both US and PRC contesting influence. Taiwan also drew upon Japan's developmental lessons, sending its managerial elite to its universities and economic bureaucracies to learn and train in the arts of developmental statism. Furthermore, it was with Japan that Taiwan first pioneered the use of 'non-official' ties, whereby an exchange of unofficial offices occurred, under the guise of trade and cultural offices and staffed by diplomats whose official status was temporarily suspended. Today, Taiwanese and Japanese business representatives conduct annual meetings via the East Asia Business Congress, switching between Taipei and Tokyo where they discuss pertinent issues to Taiwan–Japan economic exchange.

Japanese firms were key foreign investors in Taiwan's EPZs from the beginning, using them as low cost offshore sites. Another important aspect of this technological relationship is the strategic alliances between Japanese and Taiwanese firms, the most crucial being Toshiba and Tatung, Fujitsu and Taiwan Semiconductor Manufacturing Company (TSMC), and Hitachi and

United Microelectronics Corporation (UMC). Japanese technology transfer remains a key aspect of Taiwan's economic relations with the region's leading economy. Its attempts to move beyond OEM subservience to Japanese MNEs – in which they remain Taiwan's most important foreign technology partner in terms of subcontracting links – can be understood in the still strong semi-periphery context of these relations. This extends into the general field of trade, where Taiwan's chronic trade deficit with Japan ($16.3bn in 1999) largely derives from a persisting dependence on Japanese capital good and high-tech componentry imports. Although Taiwan is nowhere near as reliant on Japanese finance, Japan's banks – including Tokai, Sanwa, Fuji and Daiichi Kangyo – were amongst the first foreign banks established in Taiwan.

The strong semi-periphery context of Taiwan's bilateral economic diplomacy with the major powers clearly extends to the US. Taiwan was essentially a 'client state' of the US during the 1950s and early 1960s when it was significantly dependent on American financial aid (Tucker 1994). As its rapid industrialization proceeded, Taiwan's dependency on the US progressed to higher-grade technologies, inward FDI, strategic imports and export markets (Table 5.2). As with South Korea, the US was willing to absorb Taiwan's exports as part of a wider Cold War strategy to consolidate East Asia's capitalist bulwark against the advance of communism in the region. However, Taiwan's extent of developed dependency on American markets, and the associated burgeoning trade surplus with the US, eventually became a key concern of its FEP protagonists. To ease economic diplomacy tensions, Taiwan introduced 'buy American' purchasing missions and conferred preferential market access deals to US firms (Robinson 1998). This formed part of Taiwan's wider 'policy of obligation' pursued by its FEP protagonists towards the US, whereby American commercial interests enjoyed deference over their foreign counterparts owing to close developed economic and military security linkages (Dent 1999). For example, American firms secured all seven insurance licences issued by Taiwan to foreign firms when the sector was first liberalized in 1988, with European firms able to enter only through their US subsidiaries.[67] In a further instance, British whisky attracted higher liquor taxes than American bourbon throughout the 1980s.

Although Taiwan's 'policy of obligation' has diminished in recent years, the US maintains an advantage in the political dimension of trade relations over the EU, Japan and other AIE powers. The US's security function in Taiwan's international affairs may have considerably weakened since the Sino-American *rapprochement*, yet Taipei still depends on Washington for both moral and political support in its relations with Beijing. Moreover, under the 1979 Taiwan Relations Act (TRA), the US continued selling military hardware to Taiwan, and there was also an implicit commitment of American counteraction to any military infringements from mainland China. In 1994, the Clinton Administration enhanced the framework of US diplomacy towards Taiwan, instigating the Taiwan–US Sub-Cabinet Economic Dialogue meetings in June 1995. It later passed the Taiwan Security Enhancement Act (TSEA) in February 2000, fortifying American commitments encoded within the TRA. The US's continued political support for Taiwan is recompensed in the economic domain, where its FEP protagonists are comparatively compliant with American neo-liberal advocacy, as most recently demonstrated in the WTO accession process. The interplay between politics and economics in Taiwan–US economic diplomacy was further illustrated in February 2001, when new US Trade Representative, Robert Zoellick, stated America's strong support for Taiwan's entry into the WTO as a distinct economic entity from China, rebuffing Beijing and Hong Kong's attempts to delay Taiwan's accession proceedings.[68]

Despite Taiwan's progress on trade and FDI liberalization, US economic diplomats continue to highlight key areas of contention. According to interviewed American representatives, the two most important issues concern Taiwan's pricing system in pharmaceuticals and medical equipment sales (which make no distinction between patented and unpatented products, leading to lower profit and innovation motives for US firms), and lax IPR regulations (especially on microchip production, CD stamping, and counterfeiting).[69] Taiwan's main concerns with US trade policy have recently centred on its anti-dumping policy. Up to the 1980s, as Chan (1987) observed, Taiwan achieved some notable success at 'lessening or evading the full impact of US protectionist pressures by resorting to such tactics as problem redefinition, leverage control, exploiting loopholes, linkage politics, and cultivating transnational interest ties' (p. 265). A continuation of this strategy proved successful into the 2000s. Like South Korea, Taiwan maintains a series of lobby-active offices near vital power centres in the US. Taiwan's business representatives are also used to assist MOFA's political goals, for instance by channelling foreign investment to politically conducive areas of US constituencies that may advocate Taiwan's interests.[70] Furthermore, the Taiwanese Government extensively lobbies multiple sections of US political society, including policy elites, business, academics, state governments and municipalities (Robinson 1998).

While Taiwan has weaned itself off overall dependence on the US, its SMEs are extensively engaged in OEM/ODM subcontracting links with American firms, especially in the IT sector. Furthermore, around 40% of firms in Hsinchu Science Park were established by Sino-Americans, mostly by Taiwanese entrepreneurs returning from the US. The Taiwanese economy also continues to assist the techno-industrial restructuring of the US economy but hosting relocated lower-tech production from America's industrial districts (McBeath 1998). However, as an MOFA official commented, 'in the wider scheme of things, Taiwan is more concerned with its growing economic dependence on mainland China than with the global diversification of its export markets, away from traditional markets such as the US'.[71]

Mitigating Taiwan's economic dependence on the PRC provides an important context for its economic diplomacy with the ASEAN group, as Southeast Asia has been promoted as an alternative developing country region to mainland China for Taiwan to develop closer economic linkages (Chan 1996, Chen 1993). In this general sense, Taiwan's economic diplomacy with ASEAN can be understood in the framework of semi-periphery–periphery relations, where Southeast Asia's advancing development has assisted the Taiwanese economy's own techno-industrial restructuring through the mediation of outward FDI. Moreover, this has entailed far less political risk than Taiwan's Cross-Strait FDI relationship. The government's 'Go South' (i.e. to Southeast Asia) policy implemented in 1994 became a major element in Taiwan's FEP. However, this policy was more reactive to events than a catalyst of them as it was generally perceived to follow behind the substantive overseas investments Taiwanese firms had made in Southeast Asia by the late 1980s. The policy framework extended supporting measures to these firms' operations in the region, including tax incentives and special credit lines. According to one research interviewee, this constituted a function of developmental statism, where the government took active FEP involvement in working alongside Taiwanese business in a transformative economic context.[72]

The precursor to the 'Go South' policy's launch were the aforementioned 'holiday diplomacy' trips made by President Lee and Premier Chan to Southeast Asia over the cusp months of 1993 and 1994. Soon after their return, the Executive Yuan passed the 'Guidelines for Strengthening Economic and Trading Relations with Southeast Asia', its intentions being to promote and manage the growing economic interdependence between Taiwan and the region. This framework was extended in 1997 to incorporate Australia and New Zealand into Taiwan's 'deeper Southern policy'. In January 1998, Vice-President Lien Chan visited Singapore and Malaysia, while the BOFT also dispatched high profile trade missions to Indonesia, Malaysia, the Philippines and Thailand. The APROC initiative was also aimed at linking Cross-Strait exchanges with Taiwan's economic interactions in Southeast Asia, thus broadening the transnationalized production and distribution networks of Taiwanese businesses through *guanxi* connections across the Chinese Diaspora.

The ASEAN group's free trade area (AFTA) project, initiated since 1992, provided additional strategic imperative for Taiwan to develop its economic partnership with the region. Taiwan's FEP protagonists were particularly concerned about the exclusivity measures of AFTA, in particular the negative effects of AFTA-induced trade diversion on Taiwanese exporters to Southeast Asia. However, there are currently 40 000 Taiwanese investor firms operating within ASEAN, thus conferring significant insider advantages once AFTA becomes operational. Indeed, since the introduction of the 'Go South' policy, Taiwan's bilateral economic exchange with Southeast Asia has expanded considerably. By 1999, Taiwan's direct investment in the region had risen to $40bn, thus not too far behind its outward FDI in mainland China (Table 5.3). In the same year, bilateral trade between Taiwan and ASEAN was $26.6bn. Southeast Asia is also a large recipient of Taiwan's ODA, with Vietnam, Indonesia and the Philippines particularly benefiting (Lin 1995).

Table 5.3 Taiwan's inward FDI by geographic source (approved projects, percentage shares of cumulative totals, 1952–1999)

	1952–1988		1952–1999	
	Inward	Outward	Inward	Outward
US	34.4	31.5	32.9	18.3
Japan	25.5	27.1	27.0	16.5
Hong Kong	10.8	11.1	9.2	6.4
PRC	–	–	–	28.2
Other East Asia	9.6	8.9	10.5	17.6
Europe	12.2	11.7	11.2	8.1
Africa	0.5	1.1	2.4	1.7
Oceania	4.4	1.5	4.8	1.9
Other	2.6	7.1	2.0	1.3

Sources: Investment Commission, UNCTAD database.

As discussed earlier, for Taiwan's FEP protagonists promoting closer ties with Southeast Asia remains a critical economic security objective, remaining strongly posited in the calculus of mitigating its trade and investment dependency on mainland China. However, in the words of one research interviewee, 'the government cannot make Taiwanese firms invest in Southeast Asia or alter entrepreneurial realities, and moreover the novelty effect of the 'Go South' policy is fast wearing off'.[73] In attempts to further reinforce economic relations with the ASEAN group, Taiwan has signed many bilateral agreements with Southeast Asian countries, through their respective 'representative offices', designed to facilitate trade and investment.[74] The content of these bilateral relationships consists of working-level or ministerial-level consultations, mutual visits up to relatively high ranking bureaucratic and political officials, technological assistance (e.g. agri-tech missions to Thailand and Indonesia, agricultural training programmes offered to Vietnam, the young entrepreneur programme operating in Indonesia), financial assistance (e.g. soft loans to the Philippines, Indonesia and Vietnam), humanitarian aid and other forms of contact and exchange.[75] However, like other informal agreements Taiwan has signed, these lack legal binding, and have often been reneged by some Southeast Asian states, the Philippines change of heart over an air freight traffic agreement with Taiwan in August 1999 being a prime example.[76]

The EU is Taiwan's fourth most important trade and investment partner, but enjoys much less intimate ties with Taipei in comparison with either the US or Japan. There are many reasons for this: the relative lack of political and socio-cultural connections, low European firm penetration of Taiwan's economy (partly hindered by the Americanization of industrial standards in Taiwan), geographic distance, low priority afforded by FEP protagonists on both sides to foster closer ties generally (Dent and Johnson 2000). As one senior BOFT official pointed out, 'the EU's lack of a US-style TRA places it at a disadvantage, as the TRA empowers and authorises the American Institute in Taiwan (AIT) to negotiate certain legal agreements, while the EU does not possess this framework or facility'.[77] The EU's 'Cinderella' position in the hierarchy of Taiwan's economic relations with the Triad powers (i.e. US, Japan, EU) was strongly acknowledged by all interviewed European stakeholding FEP constituencies in Taipei. Yet during the 1990s Taiwan's FEP protagonists endeavoured more to develop closer economic relations with the EU as part of a risk averse approach to spread its dependency away from the US and Japan. However, according to a French commercial official, 'Taiwan's diversification strategy towards Europe has not worked', and he primarily attributed this to a developed 'path dependence on the US'.[78] Taiwanese firms' subcontracting links with American and Japanese firms are far more extensive in comparison with European companies.

Nevertheless, Taiwan's semi-peripheral position in the world economy continues to make Europe important in the globalization and technology transfer strategies of Taiwanese firms, especially as most acknowledge that the EU holds much untapped commercial potential for them. Many European, and especially French firms such as Dassault and Matra, have experienced some success at securing key defence and civil procurement contracts from the Taiwanese Government. The WTO accession process also required Taiwan and the EU to address many critical bilateral trade and investment issues more vigorously, as well as to intensify their economic diplomacy interaction. Taiwan has 26 representative offices across the EU, while 11 European states had set up semi-official offices in Taiwan to act as *de facto* embassies by the 1990s. In addition, the European Commission has indicated it may set up a representative office in Taipei after Taiwan formally enters into WTO membership, which would confer greater recognition of the ROC's political and economic status.

Finally, Taiwan's contested statehood and associated diplomatic constraints have sidelined it from the recent Asia–Pacific bilateral free trade agreement

(APBFTA) trend, in which both South Korea and Singapore have actively engaged. This may be of great significance given the potential of this trend to reinforce Taiwan's diplomatic and even economic marginalization further within the Asia–Pacific community. It presents a relative loss of opportunity to foster closer bilateral economic ties with most of Taiwan's key economic partners in the transregion, for example the US, Japan, South Korea. Furthermore, this emerging 'lattice regionalism' within the Asia–Pacific, based on a growing network of APBFTAs, could undermine APEC itself and hence the value of one of Taiwan's most prized international organization memberships. As we discuss later, Taiwan has also been denied participation in the recently launched ASEAN Plus 3 process. To compensate in some way for this marginalization, Taiwan has proposed the idea of establishing bilateral FTAs, or even wider free trade zones, between itself and the Diplomatic 29 group once it formally accedes to WTO membership.[79] However, this received a lukewarm reception from many countries, as well as from Taiwan's business community owing to the limited commercial benefits such arrangements would create.

5.6.3 Regional/Inter-regional

Although Taiwan's contested statehood has limited its scope to engage in regional and inter-regional economic diplomacy, it has nevertheless achieved progressive success in this area from the 1960s to the 1990s. In 1966, Taiwan became a member of the Asia–Pacific Council along with eight other countries, the group seeking to promote regional co-operation and trade. This formed part of an early regional alliance-building at a time when the rudimentary basis for a Pacific economic community was emerging, largely centred on the intellectual and technocratic initiatives of Japan and Australia. In a similar vein, Taiwan joined the Pacific Trade and Development (PAFTAD) conference framework in 1969, which provided a forum for academic debate on regional economic co-operation. It was at the PAFTAD conferences that much of the early technical discussions on Pacific economic integration in the region took place. In 1983, Taiwan secured membership of the Pacific Basin Economic Council (PBEC), first established in 1968 and an extension of an original Australia–Japan private sector forum which came to include the US, New Zealand and Canada, whose aim was to enhance commercial co-operation across the Asia–Pacific. A few years later in 1986, Taiwan became part of the Pacific Economic Co-operation Conferences (PECC) framework that was later to evolve into the inter-governmental Asia–Pacific Economic Co-operation (APEC) forum.

Taiwan's accession to APEC in 1991 represented its most successful achievement in terms of institutional economic diplomacy. It was a major diplomatic victory for Taipei as it deferred recognition to Taiwan as an equal partner in the

Asia–Pacific economic community (Klintworth 1994). In 1990, the twelve incumbent APEC members unanimously informed Beijing that all three Chinese economies (that is the PRC, Taiwan and Hong Kong) would have to join together or not at all. Beijing generally accepted this, largely because it believed that APEC would not amount to anything substantive. Furthermore, Taiwan's accession to APEC also helped circumscribe diplomatic pressure from Beijing to some degree by drawing upon the moral support of the group's liberal democratic members, not just on APEC matters but also regarding the WTO accession process. Over time, APEC membership also assisted Taiwan's 'Go South' policy by strengthening policy co-operation and elite networking with the Southeast Asian states. However, while APEC constitutes an important mechanism for managing Taiwan's economic relations with the PRC and other key trade partners, it has had to accept certain political constraints within this economic organization. For example, Taiwanese Government officials are not permitted to attend summit or ministerial meetings, having to utilize the services of quasi-diplomat business leaders such as Chen-fu Koo. At Beijing's insistence, Taiwan has also had to accept the designation of 'Chinese Taipei' within APEC.

Despite these limitations, Taiwan has played an active role in APEC matters. Its past responsibilities include: convenor of the Group on Services under the Committee on Trade and Investment; convenor of the Steering Group of Development Co-operation under the Telecommunications Working Group; lead shepherd of the Maritime Resources Conservation Working Group, the Trade Promotion Working Group, and the Experts Group on Agricultural Technical Co-operation; and international co-ordinator of the Education Network under the Human Resources Development Working Group. At APEC's 2000 summit held in Brunei, Taiwan's delegation proposed a similar 'digital development' initiative to that of South Korea (see Chapter 4). However, APEC's recently demonstrated shortcomings have been a cause of some concern in Taipei given the diplomatic importance attached to its active membership. In the late 1990s, the failure of APEC's Early Voluntary Sectoral Liberalization initiative – intended to hasten trade liberalization on a sectoral basis – further significantly undermined confidence in the regional organization. The additional failure of APEC's Brunei Summit of 2000 to draw a consensus on launching the WTO's New 'Millennium' Round of global trade talks was another considerable disappointment for Taiwan's FEP protagonists. Taipei's concern here was largely twofold: it more sharply highlighted APEC's institutional shortcomings in fostering cohesion within the Asia–Pacific economic community – the membership of which it valued so highly – while also impeding the WTO's own institutional progress, the new economic organization it would soon accede to, and which promised to confer even greater diplomatic value.

Taipei's recent frustrations in regional and inter-regional economic diplomacy extend to other areas. While the purely economic basis of APEC permitted

Taiwan to accede to membership, the political dimension of the Asia–Europe Meetings (ASEM) framework does not allow the same. Hence, East Asia's fourth largest economy is sidelined in this emerging inter-regional arrangement for fostering closer economic, political and socio-cultural ties with the EU. More importantly, though, Taiwan is being marginalized in fast changing post-crisis developments in the East Asian international political economy. During the crisis, Taiwan extended its 'dollar diplomacy' to the more crisis-afflicted economies of East Asia. It was allowed to provide multilateralized financial assistance through contributions to the Asian Development Bank (ADB),[80] with Thailand and the Philippines being the main beneficiaries.[81] Taipei also lent firm support to Japan's ill-fated Asian Monetary Fund (AMF), further exploiting FEP opportunities created by the 1997/98 financial crisis to alliance-build in the region and demonstrate its responsibilities as an obliging neighbourly state. Taiwan also, of course, had significant trade and investment interests in Southeast Asia that it sought to protect.

However, more substantive exercises of 'dollar diplomacy' were effectively blocked by Beijing, both through bilateral and APEC channels.[82] In the APEC case, this consisted of a proposed collaboration between Taiwan, Singapore, Brunei and Japan in which they offered a $3bn bond issue as a loan guarantee facility to hard-hit Southeast Asian countries, with Malaysia particularly in mind after it refused IMF assistance. Most critically, Taiwan remains outside the ASEAN Plus 3 framework and process discussed in previous chapters, and hence outside any consequent developments in an East Asian economic group coagulating from it. Finally, Taiwan's contested statehood left it outside the aforementioned 'lattice regionalism' trend of APBFTAs, and hence marginalized in another crucial post-crisis development in the regional political economy.

5.6.4 Plurilateral/Multilateral

Taiwan's participating membership of international organizations often determines the extent of its 'diplomatic space' and of its engagement in plurilateral and multilateral diplomacy. In 1992, Taiwan was granted official member status in 12 international inter-governmental organizations (IIGOs) and 695 international NGOs. By 2000, these figures had risen to 16 and 970 respectively. However, of these 16 IIGOs only two were economic in orientation, namely APEC and the ADB. Hence, Taiwan's comparative scope to conduct plurilateral and multilateral economic diplomacy was severely limited. It was forced to leave the IMF and World Bank in 1978 as a consequence of the Sino-American *rapprochement*. Some years before in 1971, the ROC regime lost its observer status in the General Agreement on Tariffs and Trade (GATT), the WTO's precursor. Subsequent attempts by Taipei to regain membership of these key international economic organizations (IEOs) have proven extremely problematic, and only possible where statehood is not an entry criterion, as is the case for the WTO. Even then, as one interviewed MOFA official commented, 'Taiwan has to explain *why* it wants to join these organisations while other countries do not'.[83]

Table 5.4 charts Taiwan's relationship with GATT and the WTO, and the progress of events concerning its re-accession to the multilateral trade order that commenced in 1990. Taipei was compelled to pursue this under the formal rubric of the 'separate customs authority of Taiwan, Penghu, Kinmen and Matsu' but had re-secured observer status of GATT under the designation of 'Chinese Taipei' in September 1992, a position continued under the WTO from January 1995 onwards. Taiwan's accession process was coupled with the PRC's own on Beijing's insistence, meaning that it could not join the WTO until the PRC had. According to interviewed FEP protagonists, Taiwan had been tracking developments in WTO rules and accords and unilaterally implementing many of them to pre-empt pressures from incumbent members in their bilateral accession negotiations with Taipei.[84] In total, Taiwan conducted over 200 rounds of consultation with the 26 WTO members that had requested bilateral negotiations.[85] By 2000, Taiwan had also held ten Working Party meetings in Geneva regarding its accession. In alleged attempts to sabotage this process, the so-called 'Gang of Five' allies of Beijing – namely Bangladesh, Cuba, Pakistan, Sri Lanka and Uruguay – tried to obstruct Taiwan's WTO application at the Working Party Report stage, the findings of which thereafter were sent to the General WTO Committee. While this exercise failed owing to counter international pressures, Taiwan's bilateral negotiations with Hong Kong remained still outstanding by early 2001, again allegedly deriving from Beijing's political leverage.

In assessing the economic benefits of WTO membership, a CEPD survey estimated that the 5–10 year effects of accession would bring a 0.7 to 4.7% spur to Taiwan's annual economic growth rate. Another study conducted by the Chung-Hwa Institute of Economic Research predicted that if Taiwan had accepted the 1994 Uruguay Round's agreed tariff rates, and had been a WTO member itself, it would have boosted Taiwan's exports by $1.7bn (or 16.7%) and imports by $0.7bn (or 12.1%).[86] The wider impacts of WTO accession for Taiwan are significant. In terms of economic diplomacy modes and exercises of power, it will reinforce Taiwan's shift from defensive to promotive economic diplomacy but also make it increasingly susceptible to exertions of structural power through the WTO regime conduit. Taiwanese exporters are expected to benefit considerably from the ensuing removal of trade barriers. Conversely, once textile trade quotas are eradicated in 2005 as part of the WTO's Agreement on Textiles and Clothing, Taiwan can expect to face more anti-dumping suits from its trade partners after the consequent expansion of Taiwanese textile trade. Hence, the new export opportunities of WTO membership will most likely be accompanied by protectionist tension in bilateral economic relations.[87]

Table 5.4 Timeline of Taiwan's WTO membership bid

30 October 1947	Republic of China (ROC) signs the Final Act of Geneva to create the General Agreement on Tariffs and Trade (GATT)
21 May 1948	ROC becomes a founding member of GATT
Spring 1950	ROC (Taiwan) withdraws from GATT
16 March 1965	Taiwan begins to attend GATT meetings as an observer
19 November 1971	Taiwan loses observer status in GATT
1990	Taiwan begins its endeavour to rejoin GATT
September 1992	Working Group to consider Taiwan's application appointed; granted observer status in GATT under the designation 'Chinese Taipei'
January 1995	Taiwan awarded WTO observer status; application transferred to WTO following its establishment
March 2001	All bilateral negotiations completed with incumbent members except Hong Kong. Formal accession to WTO expected later in the year.

Source: BOFT

Once becoming a WTO member, Taiwan is also expected to face mounting pressure from the PRC to remove its restrictions on Cross-Strait trade. However, as previously mentioned, WTO members may refuse deferring MFN treatment to another on the grounds of compromised national security. Moreover, Beijing has announced that it would utilize Article 35's 'non-application' clause towards Taiwan, thus denying it formal acknowledgement of WTO membership, although Taipei is not expected to reciprocate.[88] What these issues imply for APEC's parallel process of establishing transpacific free trade by 2020, in which both China and Taiwan are supposed to participate, is another matter.

Another important dimension of Taiwan's WTO membership is that it provides for the first real time an international legal framework in which Taiwan may conduct its economic diplomacy, offering greater certainty in trade agreements signed with foreign economic partners. In addition, the MOFA's Department of International Organizations is currently exploring how WTO membership may expand further Taiwan's scope for plurilateral–multilateral economic diplomacy. The WTO is at the centre of growing inter-IEO connections being created by globalization-induced linkages and overlaps between trade, investment, development, finance and other internationalizing activities.

In the future, new opportunities could arise for Taiwan to participate laterally in the IMF, OECD and other key economic organizations.[89] In the words of an interviewed Department official, 'the WTO could be a bridge to other international economic organisations in this respect'.[90] However, Beijing is aware of this strategy and will undoubtedly seek to limit Taiwan's room for such manoeuvre within the WTO, just as it does within APEC. The degree to which other WTO members will permit China to question Taiwan's full WTO membership rights remains unknown.

Managing the so-called 'new' trade issues presents another critical issue for Taiwan's FEP protagonists. As the BOFT's own literature comments, 'Taiwan, though not yet a member of the WTO, has come under increasing pressure to implement "WTO-plus" liberalisation measures', thus it has had to jump on board a running vehicle, being 'required to grasp both traditional and emerging WTO issues and to ease the implementation of such issues for which rules exist in our economy'.[91] Taiwan is indeed joining the WTO at a critical juncture of the organization's development, where it has had to reconcile powerful state and business-driven forces to push forward the trade liberalization agenda, via the proposed New 'Millennium' Round, against growing counter-forces from an emerging global civil society movement that has demanded both greater societal accountability of IEOs in general and a more circumspect approach to neoliberal globalization.

By 2001, the official positions taken by Taiwan's government and societal groups on the 'new' trade issues were very similar to that of their NIE-3 counterparts, this being a semi-periphery deference to the core AIE group in taking a lead, and from hence they would make a reactive decision as to how far to follow this. This was the stated view of interviewed officials from BOFT's multilateral division and the Environmental Protection Administration (EPA) on trade–environment issues arising through the WTO's Committee on Trade and Environment (CTE). Moreover, as we shall later examine, the limited capacity of the Taiwan Environmental Protection Union (TEPU) on international economic issues largely explains its lack of any real formulated or coherent position on CTE matters.[92] The BOFT's multilateral division and the Council for Labour Affairs (CLA) adopt a similar position on trade–labour issues, essentially waiting on an AIE consensus to emerge before proposing the formal view of the Taiwanese Government. However, Taiwan's premier labour movement, the Chinese Federation of Labour (CFL) has proved more assertive than the TEPU on its associated 'new' trade issue, voicing the representative concerns at the WTO's 1999 Seattle Ministerial Meeting. Finally, both the Taiwan government and business sector share a growing interest in trade–competition policy issues, stemming from a common interest with their South Korean counterparts in addressing the frequent imposition of antidumping duties on their respective imports. However, both stakeholding constituencies are playing a 'wait and see' game on this emerging multilateral trade issue as well.

Regarding Taiwan's engagement with other key IEOs, Taiwan became a dialogue partner of the Organization for Economic Co-operation and Development (OECD) in 1989, but as recognized country status is required for membership this is as far as Taiwan has been able to participate. Taiwan's representatives have attended various OECD seminars and sit in on its Trade Committee and Competition Policy Committee meetings as this does not require sovereignty status. With many incumbent OECD members having a lower GDP per capita level and a less developed techno-industrial base, Taiwan would normally be a prime candidate for membership. Furthermore, in 1999 most OECD member states were reportedly amenable to Taiwan's application for observer status, but the government withheld, as full support from all member states must be assured to make submitting an application worthwhile.[93] Taiwan is even less involved at the margins of the IMF. Given the 1997/98 East Asian financial crisis, securing IMF membership is a significantly higher priority for Taiwan's FEP protagonists, yet this will remain out of grasp whilst contested statehood is at issue.

5.7 CONTESTING 'ACTOR-BASED' INFLUENCES

5.7.1 Domestic

A strong state-centric approach remains evident when examining the contesting influences over Taiwan's FEP formation, thus following the NIE-3 norm. Yet like Singapore and particularly South Korea, a more society-centred approach became increasingly apparent in Taiwan's economic policy-making processes during the 1990s. This is expected to deepen as a consequence of the DPP's electoral victory in March 2000, and its implications for advancing democratization in Taiwan. However, there is some uncertainty over how far and how fast its non-state domestic stakeholding constituencies in Taiwan can exert their new potential influence over FEP formation. As with the NIE-3's civil society groups in general, their current under-developed interest and awareness in FEP issues hampers their influence capacity. Moreover, the persisting strength of the development state paradigm in Taiwan's political economy presents a case for expecting a fundamental state-centric approach to continue for some time yet. Let us now examine these issues in more detail.

5.7.1.1 Domestic stakeholding FEP constituencies

An important feature of Taiwan's political economy was the KMT's policy of deliberately constraining the growth of private oligopoly–monopoly capital so as to prevent the emergence of contesting power centres from within Taiwan's native economic society. This largely explains the state's proclivity for SOEs rather than fostering the large conglomerate business groups that dominate the South Korean economy (i.e. the *chaebols*).[94] Moreover, for some time the mainlander-dominated KMT kept the business elite on the margins of the KMT power structure, thus further maintaining a quasi-ethnic division of power (Aberbach *et al* 1994, Chu 1994, Fields 1995). Where Taiwan's business leaders were recruited to government and KMT organizations, their influence was invariably restricted to issues of low politics and policy-making. An additional separating factor between the Taiwanese state and the business community was SME predominance in the economy, in which a widely dispersed business representation made it naturally more difficult for the economic bureaucracies to assert influence. Therefore, to foster more effective state–business relations and to fortify its 'infrastructural power' more generally, the Taiwanese developmental state organized the business community into a number of 'peak' associations, such as the Chinese National Federation of Industries (CNFI) and the Importers and Exporters Association of Taiwan (IEAT). This enabled more robust policy-networks and state–business dialogues to develop over time, although these originally served the main purpose of transmitting state policies to the business community (Gold 1986, Kuo 1998, Wade 1990, Weiss 1998).

However, a more bottom-up mode of corporatism emerged from the mid-1980s onwards, driven partly by the state seeking closer relations with the private sector in its strategy to improve the economy's techno-industrial capacity. Consequently, Taiwan's domestic business sector enjoyed greater representation in the economic policy-making process, although Chu (1994) argued that this was more politically motivated. With the onset of democratization after 1987 came the need for the KMT to draw upon the financial support of the local business community, resulting in the Taiwanese business community finding new levels of contesting influence over economic policy. This was also generated via the legislative process, where democratization had opened up new effective channels for business interest-group lobbying. Through such channels of influence, the business sector generally adopted a dualistic strategy of pressing for liberalization from government regulation but also greater state activism in upgrading Taiwan's techno-industrial capacity.[95] From this time a greater institutionalization of state–business policy-networks was also evident with the formation of joint industry task forces, regularized policy consultations and other organizational arrangements (McBeath 1998).

Taiwan's main peak business organization, the CNFI, works closely with the government to enhance Taiwan's competitiveness, and to identity and strategize against trade barriers confronting Taiwanese business. In an example of the latter, it operates alongside the IDB in the government's Committee for Trade Relief, which has recently been strengthened to address anti-dumping and injurious foreign competition issues. Furthermore, during the 1997/98 financial crisis, the CNFI co-ordinated with the BOFT in managing the $400m worth of extended export credits and investment insurance cover from the Executive Yuan's Development Fund to compensate Taiwan's exporters, especially those operating in Southeast Asian markets. The IEAT's own close relationship with the government derives from the channelling of views from most of Taiwan's 150 000 trading businesses. It has also been an important domestic source of neo-liberal advocacy, pushing for import tariff liberalization on behalf of both import traders and exporters with high import content in manufacture. Like the CNFI, it has a cross-sectoral membership profile, and therefore promotes the general interests of Taiwan's trading business sector on FEP-related issues. Furthermore, the IEAT has strong affiliated connections with the CNFI, as well as with the government. For example, 16 trade-related ministerial agencies have set up 'one-stop shop' offices within the IEAT's Joint Service Centre, an important interface between Taiwan's trading businesses and the government.

The Taiwanese state has in the past depended on business associations for directly managing certain aspects of foreign economic policy. For example, the Taiwan Textile Federation (TTF) was given authority by the government to negotiate with foreign trade partners on textile quotas and other aspects of this sectoral trade diplomacy. The TTF remains the main textile quota manager for Taiwan, and acted as an intermediary between the BOFT and WTO members on accession negotiations.[96] More generally, business representatives continue to perform a crucial quasi-diplomatic role in Taiwan's FEP formation, and there are around six main 'ambassadors at large' as these representatives are often referred to. We have already mentioned Chen-fu Koo of Taiwan Cement in relation to his work as SEF Chairman. He has also performed quasi-diplomatic duties in promoting ties with Japan, and as Taiwan's representative at PECC, PBEC, and most recently APEC. His nephew, Jeffrey Koo of the China Trust Corporation, is currently Taiwan's most prominent quasi-diplomat, promoting Taiwan's interests globally and is particularly active in the US, Europe and Southeast Asia. Y.C. Wang of Formosa Plastics is an important Taiwan representative in Cross-Strait economic diplomacy, while Y.F. Chang of Evergreen Corporation is another key protagonist in Taiwan's economic relations with mainland China, and plays an important economic diplomacy role in relations with Europe. Douglas Hsu of Far Eastern Group is also prominently involved in Taiwan–EU economic diplomacy.

While the quasi-diplomatic function performed by Taiwan's business leaders would seem to confer some considerable contesting influence, the strong technocratic insulation maintained by the state's FEP bureaucracy has meant that implementation rather than determination of policy is most relevant with respect to the business sector's role here. Moreover, with Taiwan engaging in higher and higher-level political representations (e.g. ministerial level), its 'ambassadors at large' have become gradually less important in economic diplomacy conduct. The prevalence of state-centricity is further evident when examining the general contesting influence exerted by Taiwan's civil society, which remains comparatively weak. However, we discuss later the implications of the DPP's electoral victory in terms of empowering civil society, and its consequences for the societal set of mediating factors of contestability in Taiwan's FEP formation. Before we do so, let us examine the role of the state in closer detail.

5.7.1.2 State bureaucratic power, culture and dynamics

More harmonious inter-ministry relations are generally evident in the Taiwanese state's management of FEP issues in comparison with the more adversarial bureaucratic relations that often characterize the inner workings of the South Korean state on such matters. In further similarity with Singapore, a more rational and specialized functionality has long been established between the Taiwanese state's different FEP bureaucratic agencies and units, thus avoiding the policy competence overlaps still manifest in South Korea's FEP bureaucracy. In further comparison, the significant cognitive–ideological differences that persist between South Korea's FEP protagonists are not apparent amongst their Taiwanese counterparts, with a general consensus evident around the 'liberalization plus' approach to FEP formation. Notwithstanding these points, Taiwan's embrace of the 'new' trade issues has introduced greater complexity into the state's FEP bureaucratic management.

Between 1949 and 1954, Taiwan's trade policy was primarily managed through two agencies: the Business and Finance Group of the Taiwan Provincial Production Management Commission, and the Taiwan Provincial Foreign Exchange and Trade Review Group. In 1955, trade administration was moved to central government, with the Foreign Exchange and Trade Review Commission (or Foreign Trade Commission, FTC) set up under the Executive Yuan. In another government reorganization, the FTC evolved into the Board of Foreign Trade (BOFT) in 1969. As a MOEA agency, the BOFT still remains largely responsible for managing Taiwan's trade policy and diplomacy. As such, it has primarily managed Taiwan's WTO accession process. The BOFT also regularly consults with private sector representations and convenes cross-authority meetings with other government agencies on trade-related issues. For instance, it is the state bureaucratic locus of vertical and horizontal inter-agency co-ordination on initiatives designed to improve Taiwan's international competitiveness ranking.[97]

Other MOEA agencies are central to the technical policy realm management of Taiwan's FEP. The Investment Commission has primary policy competence for inward and outward FDI policy, although it does co-ordinate closely with the CBC on related financial regulations. The Commission also works alongside another MOEA agency, the Industrial Development and Investment Centre (IDIC), in promoting Taiwan as an attractive location for inward investment. However, the IDIC is essentially a service-centre agency for foreign MNEs in Taiwan, thus lacking the Investment Commission's policy and regulatory influence. In recent years, the Investment Commission has entered into higher levels of inter-agency co-ordination over FDI policy (for example with the IDB and BOFT) owing to its growing interface with trade and industrial policies. The IDB itself – another MOEA agency – works closely with: the BOFT on trade-related industry policy issues; the MOF on tax incentives and credits, and tariff reductions, where the IDB evaluate the impact of tariff reductions on Taiwanese firms; the IDIC on foreign commercial missions; and with the MOFA regarding the provision of industrial assistance to Taiwan's diplomatic partner countries. In addition, the IDB works with all major business associations, such as the CNFI, for instance in examining the impact of tariff reductions stemming from the WTO accession process.

The CBC enjoys primary competence for Taiwan's international financial policy. As previously discussed, it regulates transactions in the currency market and oversees the regulation of capital inflows and outflows. Moreover, the MOF general defers to the CBC on financial matters – for example, the CBC can overrule the MOF on matters of financial deregulation and internationalization. The most important co-ordinative contact between the CBC and other FEP bureaucratic agencies occurs within the cabinet, where it enjoys comparable contesting influence to the MOEA and MOFA in Taiwan's FEP formation (Chu 2000). While the MOF's own contesting influence is minimal, it does work with the BOFT, IDB and CEPD on the government's Tariff Committee, and was involved in WTO accession matters on tariffs and finance sector liberalization.

The MOFA's own involvement in the Taiwanese state's FEP management mainly centres on matters of economic diplomacy. Clearly defined parameters of policy competence have long existed between the MOFA, the MOEA and the CBC, thus avoiding the frequent inter-ministerial conflicts arising in the South Korean state's FEP bureaucracy. Moreover, there exists a generally effective co-ordination between the MOFA and other FEP ministerial agencies, mediated through its Department of Economic Affairs (DETA). For example, DETA worked with their CEPD and ICDF counterparts in setting up power-generating plants in selected developing countries, and in generally promoting the 'Taiwan experience' to other LDCs. It also works with the business sector, for instance in networking the recently privatized China Steel Corporation with Taiwanese SMEs overseas.[98] Taiwan's ODAC policy is another FEP responsibility of MOFA, setting the budget and policy parameters of the ICDF. In the past, tension has been evident between the MOFA and MOEA over the use of

Taiwan's financial aid, with the latter wishing to utilize this to reinforce trade and investment ties in East Asia and Asia Pacific rather than to deploy the aid to secure new diplomatic partners – the principal aim of MOFA. For its part, the CEPD's co-ordinative capacity in the state's overall management of FEP-related issues remains quite strong. This is particularly evident in trade and industrial policy linkages, for example where it takes managerial interest in higher-tech export industry development and general competitiveness issues. It further extends its contesting influence over Taiwan's FEP formation in its policy think-tank function performed for the Presidential Office.[99]

As with other FEP powers, the management of 'new' trade issues has brought greater complexity to Taiwan's FEP formation. However, the introduction in the early 1980s of new, more flexible mechanisms to enhance intra-ministerial co-ordination provided an established means by which this complexity could be more easily accommodated. Essentially, these reforms enfranchised once marginal ministries into the economic policy loop, thus fostering a more democratic state bureaucracy culture and a broad stakeholder consensus approach to policy decision-making. On trade–environment issues, the EPA currently works in co-ordination with MOEA agencies at the sub-committee level as part of the government's Task Force for Participation in International Economic and Trade Organizations. In addition, the EPA works alongside Investment Commission officials in conducting environmental impact assessments on foreign investments in Taiwan, and also with the Council of Agriculture on trade in wildlife and some agricultural trade issues. However, its actual contesting influence on Taiwan's emerging trade–environment policy is small, deferring to the BOFT on all principal issues. Yet this is universally evident amongst FEP powers in general, where the state's established trade policy agency remains the ultimate broker of policy formation.

The same situation applies to other 'new' trade issues. For example, the CLA has become nominally active in the Taiwanese Government's trade–labour policy, participating in 31 different government working parties on FEP issues, including services trade, trade policy review, national competitiveness, and e-commerce. Its representatives have also engaged in economic diplomacy, such as attending the OECD's Informal Symposium on Trade, Employment and Labour Standards in 1996. However, it wields only limited contesting influence over shaping the technical policy realms of Taiwan's FEP. Furthermore, like its civil society counterparts, the CLA remains mainly preoccupied with domestic issues, and ultimately follows the BOFT's lead in developing Taiwan's position on trade–labour issues. Nevertheless, the two agencies have exchanged somewhat conflicting views in inter-ministerial meetings over the trade–labour linkage, with BOFT taking a more negative view owing to the perceived adverse impact on Taiwan's competitiveness.

5.7.1.3 Level of democratization

Just as in South Korea, deepening democratiszation in Taiwan since the late 1980s has helped enfranchise a wider range of domestic stakeholding FEP constituencies, although it is the business rather than civil society sector that has seen its contesting influence grow most significantly as a consequence. From a general perspective, deepening democratization and the associated ascendancy of legislatures in the Taiwanese political economy have generally weakened state autonomy. This is particularly the case with regard to the business sector. As Hsu (2000) comments, 'the processes of legislation affecting the vital interests of business groups have often turned into an arena of undisguised trading of power, prerogatives, money, and political loyalty and support among the party leadership, lawmakers, economic bureaucracy, and business groups' (p. 189). Certainly, neither the KMT elite nor the executive branch was able to impose its will upon the Legislative Yuan during the 1990s in comparison to the authoritarian era. Yet Hsu further notes that on issues of vital economic security interests (e.g. financial-credit) it is the state's will that prevails where it diverges with the objectives of Taiwan's major business groups.

To a large degree, this is attributable to the corporate sector's willingness to maintain Taiwan's developmental alliance between state and business, not least because it perpetuates the state's support for business development in the wider scheme of things. In addition, Taiwan now presides over an increasingly complex post-industrial society where new developmental objectives (e.g. environment-related) are gradually displacing those of a 'growth first' nature. This new developmentalism, as discussed elsewhere in this book, has also permitted new civil society interests in Taiwan to come to the fore. However, the extent to which these are reflected in Taiwan's FEP formation remains limited owing to a persistently dominant state-centricity, young democratic culture, and yet-to-flourish pluralist society.

The DPP electoral victory of March 2000 – the first time a change of government in Taiwan has resulted from the democratic process – could, though, mark a key turning point in the move towards a more society-centred approach to FEP formation. As previously discussed, the new Chen Shui-bian Administration's 'comprehensive pragmatic diplomacy' approach foresees a stronger role for civil society, and for Taiwan's promotion of democratic ideals through diplomatic channels. Yet a year after Chen's inaugural Presidential speech, when he stated, 'we should… actively expand the role of public participation' in policy-making, it was unclear how this was to be effectively achieved. Moreover, changes in Taiwan's political culture cannot be achieved overnight, and the vestiges of developmental authoritarianism take time to erode. Thus, the new principles of civilian-based diplomacy (i.e. actively encouraging the participation of civil society groups in foreign policy-making processes) and public opinion-based diplomacy (i.e. seeking the views of the public on various issues of foreign affairs) as first outlined by DPP Foreign Minister Tien Hung-mao in June 2000 will take time to establish in an institutional and cultural sense. Most of Taiwan's civil society groups are also comparatively young. For example, official trade unions have only been permitted to exist since martial law was lifted in 1987. Furthermore, as we next examine, the current contesting influence of Taiwan's domestic civil society is hindered by its continued low priority afforded to international affairs.

5.7.1.4 Internationalization of civil society

The persistent low degree of either demonstrated awareness of, or developed interest in FEP-related matters amongst Taiwan's civil society groups is representatively illustrated by its environmental and labour movements. For example, by an interviewed representative's own admission, foreign economic issues barely register within the TEPU.[100] Both within the organization itself and with other stakeholding FEP constituencies, it maintains no real discourse on these issues. As stated previously, this may be attributed to the almost exclusive focus of the TEPU and Taiwan's other environmental movements on domestic issues. Consequently, they do not exert any significant contesting influence on Taiwan's FEP formation. Indeed, an interviewed EPA official commented that the government has experienced 'difficulty finding civil groups with the capacity to participate in environment-related FEP issues'.[101] This may explain why none of Taiwan's environmental NGOs participate in the government's National Committee of Sustainable Development's (NCSD) Working Group on Trade and Environment. However, according to the same aforementioned TEPU interviewee, the organization would like to see environmental clauses attached to trade policy if it pressurizes the government to improve Taiwan's environmental management. Moreover, Taiwan's Green Party has most recently developed an anti-globalization policy position against the WTO in the post-Seattle context. Yet, despite these developments, they have not manifested themselves in any effective contesting influence actions regarding Taiwan's FEP formation.

However, Taiwan's main labour movement, the CFL, has proven relatively more proactive on FEP-related issues. This applies to multilateral trade–labour issues, where CFL representatives have been involved at the margins in WTO and International Labour Organization (ILO) discourses. For example, a CFL delegation was sent to the WTO's 1999 Seattle Ministerial Meeting as a separate representation to Taiwanese Government officials. The CFL also participates in the Asia–Pacific Labour Network (APLN), a recent initiative from the International Confederation of Free Trade Unions (ICFTU) designed to push forward labour-related issues in the region's policy agenda.[102] Notwithstanding this emergent proactivity, the CFL's organizational and resource capacities in managing international economic affairs remain generally weak, thus sharing the general predicament of its NIE-3 civil society counterparts. Like the CFL, the Taiwan Labour Front (TLF) maintains a somewhat vague official position on trade–labour standards.[103] Taiwan's labour movements have nevertheless had increasingly to confront the challenges of globalization and the growing domestic–international interface, the WTO accession process being of particular relevance here, for example on the net employment effect of WTO entry.

5.7.1.5 Economic nationalism

Unlike South Korea but like Singapore, a comparatively low degree of economic nationalism is evident in Taiwan. From socio-cultural and ethnic perspectives, most Taiwanese citizens see themselves as part of a broader Chinese Diaspora both regionally and worldwide. There is also limited attachment to 'national' products, although *michu* (a locally produced liquor) has enjoyed relatively strong state and societal support.[104] However, most Taiwan nationals relate strongly to the notion of 'economic survival', an issue comprehensively discussed earlier under the pursuit of economic security. This is closely associated with the long established state–society consensus in Taiwan on how advancing economic development provides the means (e.g. military hardware and technology) to deter invasion across the Straits. Events in Tiananmen Square in June 1989 strengthened this consensus, and created a new wave of Taiwanese nationalism through every strata of society (Chao and Myers 2000). More generally, though, the most discernible sense of economic nationalism derives from maintaining Taiwan's distinctiveness from mainland China as a separate definable identity.

Yet manifest actions stemming from this do not take the form of chauvinistic consumer behaviour or state bureaucratic preference in treating domestic and foreign firms, as in South Korea. Rather it concerns the proclivity of the Taiwanese state, firms and other economic agents to resist attempts by the PRC to undermine Taiwan's economic, social and political achievements, or subsume the island economy further into its own. Hence, many Taiwanese are circumspect of developing strong economic ties with mainland China insofar as they pull Taiwan into a transnationalized, Cross-Strait economic space, thus undermining the aforementioned 'quasi-national' distinctiveness. There is thus a strong connection here to the upholding of Taiwan's socio-economic paradigm security objectives discussed earlier.

However, many other domestic stakeholding constituencies in Taiwan, especially in the business sector, hold a counter-position owing to the commercial benefits that investing in, and exporting to the PRC has conferred on them. Thus, as with many other aspects of Taiwan's FEP, mainland China is a primary orienting force in determining most manifestations of Taiwanese economic nationalism. According to an interviewed senior CEPD official, other examples include the nationalist sentiment aroused against US pressure during the mid-1980s on Taiwan to liberalize its economy and revalue the NT dollar, and subsequent minor bouts of this behaviour during the WTO accession process.[105] It is to such issues of international (and transnational) contesting influence over Taiwan's FEP formation that we now turn.

5.7.2 International and Transnational

On the one hand, Taiwan's FEP protagonists have proved generally compliant to exertions of foreign contesting influence. As Dreyer (1994) more generally argued, Taiwan has frequently seen fit to adjust its policies on sensitive international and transnational issues as part of substantiating its position as a responsible and willing actor in international affairs. This hence explains, for example, Taiwan's relatively close alignment on WTO rules (e.g. on IPR and market access) outside the accession process. In 1999, the government also introduced a new public procurement law proximate in detail to the WTO's own Government Procurement Act.[106] On the other hand, foreign contesting influence over Taiwan's FEP formation has been carefully mediated by the state, in accordance with its controlled, gradualistic approach in accommodating neo-liberal reform. As an interviewed MOF official commented, 'liberalisation has been driven more by an autonomous domestic process in Taiwan rather than by international pressure'.[107] This, in turn, is indicative of the substantial developmental statist capacity that continues to underpin Taiwan's FEP management.

Moreover, *system-centric* influence over Taiwan's FEP formation has tended to be informalized owing to its lack of IEO membership. It is therefore not surprising that international contesting influence over its foreign economic policy has been principally bilateral. This was even the case within the framework of the WTO accession process as this source of external neo-liberal advocacy derived almost exclusively from the series of bilateral negotiations conducted with incumbent members, each with their separate agendas, albeit these often closely overlapped. The expectations of these foreign economic diplomats were heightened owing mainly to Taiwan's significant integration into international structures of trade, finance, technology and production, thus demonstrating that it was already well conditioned to the rigours of global competition.

The US has been Taiwan's most influential 'contesting' foreign economic partner ever since the 'donor–client' relationship was first established in the 1950s. Moreover, the Taiwanese Government publicly acknowledges America's significant and long-serving role as liberalization 'advocate'.[108] By the 1980s, the US faced a burgeoning trade deficit with Taiwan, and was instrumental in persuading Taipei to revalue the NT dollar (Chou 1992). Although Taiwan's semi-periphery dependency on the US made it highly susceptible to American contesting influence, Chan (1987) argued that the Taiwanese Government were generally effective in moderating this bilateral pressure, largely attributing this to 'sound policy capacity [that] can enable a weak country to obtain relatively favourable outcomes in dealing with a strong country' (p. 286). Yet as previously mentioned, Taiwan nevertheless conferred preferential market access deals to the US in areas such as IPR, banking and insurance. American relational power has been augmented by key organizations and groups, such as the American Chamber of Commerce (AmCham) in Taipei and the USA–ROC Business Council. AmCham is the biggest foreign business representative agency in Taiwan and plays a significant advocacy role in Taiwan–US economic relations. It uses the US Trade Representative office and other Washington-based agencies of leverage to assist the exertion of American commercial interests in Taiwan. AmCham also produces a regular and influential White Paper that outlines the US's market access issues. American multinationals normally, though, approach the Taiwanese Government direct on FEP-related issues, only using AmCham and AIT channels on rare occasions. They have also been known to use key senators on the USA–ROC Business Council, such as Jay Rockerfeller (West Virginia) and Frank Murkowski (Alaska), as their advocates.[109]

As discussed earlier, the WTO accession process has been a crucial vehicle for the US and other incumbent members to shape Taiwan's trade and trade-related policies. For example, in compliance with sustained US pressure, Taiwan opened up it stock market to foreign institutional investors in 1991. While the CBC compelled the MOF to impose strict investment caps on foreign investments (up to $50m initially) these were gradually ratcheted up in concessions made mainly to the US in WTO accession negotiations. The pace of liberalization would have been much quicker if not for the effective insistence of Taiwan's FEP protagonists that this should be progressively implemented. By 1997, the individual investor cap had been raised to $600m. Taiwan's compliance with APEC-driven liberalization provides another instance of the state's moderation. As part of its APEC commitments, it was obliged to remove all restrictions on portfolio investment by 2001. However, in keeping with the 'liberalization plus' approach, the government simultaneously planned to introduce new measures to control stock market volatility induced by hot money flows. This was in addition to the aforementioned $26bn National Stabilization Fund set up in February 2000.

Turning more specifically to transnational contesting 'actor-based' influences, the growing Cross-Strait business community has seen its bearing on Taiwan's FEP formation increase over recent years. It was previously noted how the Taiwanese Government has deferred Cross-Strait economic diplomacy competence to its business stakeholders in the SEF. Furthermore, Taiwan's mainly SME-based investor associations of firms, with extended operations on the mainland, have allied with their host provincial authorities in forging common interest groups, which as Mengin (1998) noted even managed effectively to postpone Beijing's implementation of a new labour law. These associations have created a transnational socialization network of Cross-Strait SMEs that convene regularized meetings with representatives from core FEP ministries (e.g. MOEA), MAC, the SEF and Legislative Yuan. In the process, they have become a key transnational stakeholding constituency in Taiwan's FEP, with particular influence over Taipei's 'mainland' policies in general. During early 2001, for example, these business associations expressed their disappointment over the DPP leadership's decision to renege on its election manifesto pledge to end the KMT's 'no haste, be patient' policy on Cross-Strait economic exchange.[110] The government did not fully succumb to such lobbying, yet the future contesting influence of the Cross-Strait business community should be anticipated to grow as the transnational Cross-Strait economic space itself grows. In the wider transnational perspective, it is also the business societal contesting influence that has proved more substantive rather than the civil societal. The latter remains generally weak for reasons discussed earlier, with transnational NGOs having very limited interface with Taiwan's FEP formation.

5.8 CONCLUSION

As this chapter has shown, understanding Taiwan's foreign economic policy very much centres on its 'contested statehood' predicament. Its ambiguous position in the international system has narrowed the conventional diplomatic latitude of Taiwan's FEP protagonists, subsequently preventing them from advancing various economic security interests. Taiwan's considerable financial resources, adaptive developmental statism and strengthening semi-periphery development have nevertheless kept many FEP options open. Furthermore, Taiwan's situation forms part of a wider global trend, discussed partly in Chapter 1, where an increasing number of sub-national economic territorial powers are emerging in the context of 'region states' (Ohmae 1995). On gaining membership to the WTO, Taiwan will also have secured a major diplomatic achievement by conferring acknowledgement of its legitimate position in the international trade community.

Together with 'contested statehood', it was argued that the 'liberalization plus' approach of Taiwan's FEP protagonists is a key prime foundation in the cognitive–ideological dimension. This takes various forms. For example, in the twin 'liberalization' and 'internationalization' policies first initiated in the early 1980s, the government has opened up the economy to foreign competition but also undertakes simultaneous measures to fortify export competitiveness. In its international financial policy, the state has gradually implemented neo-liberal reforms in certain aspects of Taiwan's capital and financial markets, yet has also re-regulated other aspects. Such retained levels of state capacity are perhaps most clearly seen in the CBC management of Taiwan's currency market. With particular reference to the contested statehood predicament, the 'mainland China factor' still significantly shapes the ideas and the practical ideology that orientate Taiwan's foreign economic policy. We also noted the significant linkage between these two prime cognitive–ideological foundations in that both essentially derive from the persistent state-centricity in Taiwan's FEP formation, and that this may be anticipated to continue under the new DPP government.

Regarding the generic economic security objectives of Taiwan's foreign economic policy, the considerable gravitational forces exerted by the PRC are again strongly evident. Taiwan's FEP protagonists are particularly anxious about developing dependencies on mainland China for economic resources, logistics and markets. There are also recent signs of more explicit economic security thinking amongst Taiwan's security policy elite, although new policy plans based on this are yet to be practically implemented. Moreover, 'higher' politico-military security interests often override the strong implicit pursuit of economic security objectives, as best demonstrated in Cross-Strait economic relations.

In matters of supply security, Taiwan's dependency on the PRC is more of an expressed concern than its more extensive supply dependency maintained on the AIE core. In market access security, WTO accession is the key current issue as it not only helps diversify Taiwan's still concentrated market dependencies but also provides a stronger legal and judiciary basis for conducting and sustaining market access agreements. Taiwan's finance–credit security objectives have meanwhile primarily focused on the maintenance of its comparatively strong financial position, which remains critical given that it cannot rely on systemic support from the IMF. As hinted above, Taiwan's techno-industrial capability security still broadly centres on its semi-periphery dependency on the AIE core, and especially on Japan and the US. Mitigating the transmission of Taiwan's own techno-industrial capabilities to the PRC is another concern here, as suggested by various Cross-Strait trade and investment restrictions retained by the government. The pursuit of socio-economic paradigm security objectives is largely reducible to Taiwan's FEP actions to resist the PRC counter-paradigm. However, this must be reconciled with the growing transborder economic community linkages being forged by intensified Cross-Strait economic relations. Taiwan's systemic security objectives are closely associated with its WTO accession process, and the opportunities this creates to advance its economic diplomacy to a new level, as well as to provide a more secure trading environment for its firms. The above forms the general context for Taiwan's pursuit of economic alliance security objectives.

The 'liberalization plus' approach in Taiwan's FEP is highly relevant to its technical policy realms. Trade, foreign investment and international finance policies all reflect the combination of greater economic openness with parallel state-activism in terms of competitiveness-enhancing and re-regulatory measures. More specifically, the trade–industrial policy nexus remains salient in that the government still gives much priority to promoting the development and export of 'strategic' industrial products. Thus, while the WTO accession process has ended various forms of state intervention and protectionism, Taiwan's 'internationalization' policies continue to keep its evolving developmental state active in finding new ways to advance the economy's position in the global system. Thus, the promotive aspect of neo-mercantilism remains an orienting factor within the wider 'liberalisation plus' approach. In addition, Taiwan has applied its financial muscle to resource a comparatively generous ODAC policy, although its success in realizing economic alliance security objectives has met with limited success.

This chapter has also shown that Taiwan's economic diplomacy has been largely oriented by its contested statehood and the aforementioned concentrated dependency on the US, Japan and increasingly mainland China. Its chronic lack of diplomatic recognition also generally confined this diplomacy to bilateral levels. However, as the 1990s progressed, Taiwan FEP protagonists developed certain solutions to these dilemmas, albeit to varying degrees of effectiveness. Its diversification of bilateral economic linkages towards Southeast Asia, Europe and other regions has achieved some success. The securing of APEC membership in 1991, and the likely accession to WTO membership by late 2001, significantly expand Taiwan's latitude for regional and multilateral economy diplomacy. Nevertheless, being denied formal diplomatic recognition by all its important foreign economic partners remains a significant constraint for Taiwan's FEP protagonists. Recent developments in the Asia–Pacific international political economy, such as the APBFTA trend and the emerging ASEAN Plus 3 regional framework, currently underscore the inherent problems of Taiwan's diplomatic marginalization.

Finally, in examining the contesting 'actor-based' influences over Taiwan's FEP formation, it was contended that while the recent empowerment of societal influences are evident, it is state-centric forces of influence that strongly prevail. As in South Korea, deepening democratization in Taiwan since the late 1980s provided the business community in particular with greater opportunity to affect the various executive and legislative paths of FEP formation. However, this was actively sought by the state anyway, as shown by the corresponding extension of institutionalized channels of dialogue between itself and the business sector. The new DPP government has more recently stated its intention to develop similar state–society linkages with Taiwan's still emerging civil society. However, as the research findings of this comparative study of NIE-3 foreign economic policy have generally shown, Taiwan's still weak civil society mostly lacks both the capacity and the interest to engage purposely on foreign economic policy issues. In the international and transnational domains of contesting influence, Taiwan's WTO membership will make it increasingly susceptible to exertions of structural power, and most likely to stronger applications of external neo-liberal advocacy. More generally, Taiwan's new level of systemic engagement that WTO membership brings will no doubt herald a new phase in its foreign economic policy development, although fundamental challenges – especially in relation to the PRC – look set to persist well into the 21st century.

NOTES

1. Interview with senior CEPD official, April 1999.
2. The stated 'issue area' for this Working Group concerns 'environmental protection and trade issues addressed by international economic and trade organization'. *Environmental Policy Monthly*, July 1999, p. 6.
3. Including infrastructural provision, preferential tax rates, low land rents, and low interest financing.
4. It registered the highest economic growth rate (6%) in East Asia in 1998.
5. This represented a modification of the previous government's maxim of transforming Taiwan into a 'High-Tech Silicon Island'.
6. Chiang Kai-shek was the ROC regime's political leader from 1949 to 1975. He was succeeded by his son, Chiang Ching-Kuo, who ruled until 1988, the year before the KMT lifted martial law in Taiwan. Lee Teng-hui then ruled from 1988 to 2000.
7. *China Post*, 10 January, 2001.
8. As one research interviewee at the Board of Foreign Trade commented in April 2000, 'Taiwan faces the same challenges of WTO accession and of further strengthening our export-based economy, and these will remain key policy objectives for both the KMT and DPP alike. Moreover, they prescribe similar methods to reach these ends'.
9. *'Making Trade Policy Under the Force of Globalisation'*, BOFT website.
10. *'Trade Policies and Measures'*, BOFT website.
11. *Taipei Times*, 26 December, 1999.
12. *Taiwan Economic News*, 17 January, 2000.
13. Chen Shui-bian quoted in the *United Daily News*, 8 November, 1999.
14. *Economic Daily News*, 9 June, 2000.
15. *Liberty Times*, 2 August, 2000.
16. *Taipei Times*, 8 September, 2000.
17. In the early 1980s, this figure was around 60%. Meanwhile, around 40% of Taiwan's exports fell into the high-technology category by the late 1990s.
18. Interviews, April 2000.
19. Interview at DKB, April 2000.
20. Taiwan Statistical Data, CEPD.
21. *Central News Agency*, 14 December, 1999.
22. Some flow of Cross-Strait trade nevertheless occurred before 1989. Previously in 1987, restrictions were eased on civilians travelling to mainland China for family visits.
23. *China Post*, 8 September, 2000.
24. *Taipei Times*, 24 December, 1999.
25. This was after Chen Shui-bian had initially proclaimed his intention to reverse this policy.
26. One of the highest profile parks being at Subic Bay in the Philippines.

27. Interview at the AIT, April 2000.
28. The internal balance equation: savings 37.3%, investment 17.5%. The external balance equation: exports 58.1%, imports 38.3%.
29. Acknowledged by the vast majority of interviewed FEP ministerial officials.
30. *'Trade Policies and Measures'*, BOFT website.
31. This figure was derived from a pre-accession average rate of 15.5% for agricultural products and 6.2% for industrial products.
32. *'Taiwan's WTO Accession Package'*, BOFT website.
33. Phased-in liberalization periods for individual sectors are: fruits and vegetables (2–5 years); meat products (4 years); automobiles (2–9 years); auto components (4 years); semiconductors (2 years); textiles and apparel (2–3 years).
34. Imposed on repatriated profits and foreign exchange trading, and involving CBC administration.
35. Between 1966 and 1970, the Kaohsiung EPZ attracted 22.9% of Taiwan's total inward FDI that in turn accounted for 70% of the zone's total capital (Schive 1999).
36. This replaced the 1960 Statute for Encouragement of Investment, which was extended for two more ten-year periods in 1970 and 1980 with several revisions being made in the meantime.
37. *'Investment Incentives'*, Investment Commission website.
38. However, since 1997 the APROC initiative has been downscaled somewhat.
39. According to interviewed IDB officials, April 2000.
40. According to an interviewed official, the CBC has adopted no particular rule on targeted exchange rate movements since 1989 (April 2000).
41. From early July to mid October, the CBC used around US$7bn dollars' worth of foreign exchange reserves to buy NT dollars in support of the currency. According to an interviewed foreign banker, the CBC implicitly tried to maintain the NT$'s level of 27.5 against the US$ through currency market transactions and interest rate rises in the money market from 5% to around 10%. On 17 October, it stopped its interventions and in subsequent months intervened only occasionally. By the end of 1997, the NT dollar had depreciated 14.8% against the US dollar, although this was a relatively low figure for a developing East Asian country during this crisis period.
42. Interview, anonymous source, April 2000.
43. Interview with Taipei-based European official, April 2000.
44. Interview at the CBC, April 2000.
45. This effectively merged the financial and technical dimensions of Taiwan's ODAC policy into one agency framework.
46. *ICDF Annual Report 1999*, Taipei.
47. The MOEA's International Co-operation Department (ICD) also plays a relatively minor role in technical assistance aspects of Taiwan's ODAC policy. Its activities include running the Entrepreneur Training Programme, which since 1995 has been a mechanism for sharing Taiwan's SME entrepreneurial skills, training and experience with mainly Southeast Asian countries. In addition, the ICD organizes high-level conferences (ministerial and above), overseas missions and protocols for FEP-related visits to Taiwan, as well as working on technical co-operation issues with international organizations such as the International Cotton Organization and Asian Productivity Organization.
48. In the same year, the ICDF had over 300 staff in the field working in 39 missions in 34 countries. These were the Diplomatic 29 group plus the Philippines, Thailand, Vietnam, Papua New Guinea and Saudi Arabia.
49. *Liberty Times*, 23 October, 2000
50. *Liberty Times*, 28 March, 2001.
51. Furthermore, the government significantly increased its R&D expenditure during the 1980s, with public R&D reaching 60% of the total by the end of the decade.
52. These comprised auto components, LCD devices, integrated circuits, high-resolution colour TV tubes and the chemical and p-xylene.
53. By 1998, ITRI was Taiwan's largest R&D organization with 6000 employees and an annual revenue of NT$15.5 billion.

54. As stated in research interviews with relevant government officials, April 1999 and April 2000.
55. Even here, the IDB emphasize the need to maintain a robust anti-dumping policy against 'unfair' foreign competition. See IDB website.
56. Interviews at IDB, April 2000.
57. Textiles remain an important export sector, in 1999 accounting for $1.4bn of Taiwan's exports and $1.1bn of earned foreign exchange.
58. Foreign firms included Matra, Boeing, Mitsubishi and General Electric.
59. For example, when Latvia opened a consular office in Taipei in 1992, Beijing suspended its diplomatic relations with the Baltic state until it capitulated.
60. *Free China Journal*, 2 May, 1991, p. 1.
61. Tien Hung-mao, *'The Current State of ROC Diplomacy'*, speech given at the Legislative Yuan, 5 June, 2000.
62. As further expounded by Tien Hung-mao in his speech before the World Affairs Council at Los Angeles, 28 November, 2000.
63. These comprise five in Asia, two in Europe, eight in Africa and 14 in Latin America.
64. The nadir of Taiwan's diplomatic recognition was 1978–1980 when only 22 states obliged. This compared to 67 in 1969. However, the situation improved over the 1980s, rising to 27 by 1990.
65. Interview, April 1999. A long-standing member of the foreign business community in Taipei also commented in another interview that 'Taiwan is often treated like a prostitute by her foreign economic partners, in that she is enjoyed by others but they are careful not to be seen to do so', April 2000.
66. New by-laws introduced by Beijing in December 1999 further strengthening the rights of Taiwanese investors operating on the mainland. *Economic Daily News*, 12 December, 1999.
67. Interview with European business representative, April 1999.
68. *Taipei Times*, 1 February, 2001.
69. Interviews at AmCham and the AIT, April 1999 and April 2000 respectively.
70. Interview at MOFA's Department of North American Affairs, April 2000.
71. Interview at MOFA, April 2000.
72. Interview with Taiwan Institute of Economic Research analyst, April 2000.
73. Interview with IDIC official, April 1999.
74. An example being the *'Agreement between the Taipei Economic and Cultural Office in Hanoi and the Vietnam Economic and Cultural Office in Taipei on the Promotion and Protection of Investments'*.
75. Interview with MOFA official, April 2000.
76. As highlighted by an interviewed MOFA official, April 2000.
77. Interview at BOFT, April 1999. The same interviewee used the example of a mutual recognition agreement that both sides wished to sign but could not for this reason.
78. Interview at the French Institute in Taipei, April 2000.
79. *Taipei Times*, 30 November, 1999.
80. Taiwan had secured ADB membership in 1988.
81. This amounted to an undisclosed figure of less than $1bn. Interview with MOFA official, April 2000.
82. In the APEC case, this consisted of a proposed collaboration between Taiwan, Singapore Brunei and Japan in which they offered a $3bn bond issue as a loan guarantee facility to hard-hit Southeast Asian countries, with Malaysia particularly in mind after it refused IMF assistance.
83. Interview at MOFA, April 2000.
84. For example, Taiwan shadowed the GATS accord of the 1994 Uruguay Round Agreement by taking unilateral measures to liberalize its capital market, banking and insurance sectors.
85. These comprised South Africa, Czech Republic, Slovak Republic, El Salvador, Turkey, Columbia, Uruguay, Chile, South Korea, Australia, New Zealand, Japan, Iceland, Norway, Malaysia, Philippines, Thailand, Hungary, Mexico, Argentina, Singapore, US, Switzerland, EU, Canada and Hong Kong.
86. *'Making Trade Policy Under the Force of Globalisation'*, BOFT website.

87. Many of Taiwan's FEP protagonists I interviewed stated an anticipation of such pressure.
88. From an interview at BOFT, April 2000.
89. According to a foreign Taipei-based official, the Taiwanese Government has paid huge sums on employing foreign consultants to help develop this strategy.
90. Interview at MOFA, April 2000.
91. *'Making Trade Policy Under the Force of Globalisation'*, BOFT website.
92. Conceded in interview with TEPU official, April 2000.
93. *Central Daily News*, 28 December, 1999.
94. However, the Taiwanese state has also provided considerable financial assistance to many large domestic business groups (*guanxiqiye*) and promoted the development of large trading companies.
95. Parallel developments in the rise of business association power could also be witnessed in South Korea from the late 1980s onwards under similar democratizing circumstances.
96. Interview at the TTF, April 2000. Other sectoral business associations have also practised 'quota management' in the past.
97. Interview with senior BOFT official, April 1999.
98. Interview with DETA officials, April 1999 and April 2000.
99. As contended by various government interviewees, April 1999 and April 2000.
100. Interview at TEPU, April 2000.
101. Interview at EPA, April 2000.
102. The APLN held its inaugural meeting at Wellington in August 1999.
103. Interviews with CFL and TLF officials, April 2000.
104. It was only with 'strong reluctance', for example, that the government bowed to international pressure to tax *michu* at the same rate as vodka, its foreign equivalent product. Moreover, just before this tax differential was to be eliminated, the government had to ration the sale of *michu* after Taiwanese households rushed to buy up pre-tax hike stocks.
105. Interview, April 1999.
106. As one long-standing European official in Taipei contended, 'Taiwan's determination to enter the WTO has been very serious, and with it a commitment to comply with the regime's demands'. Interview at the German Trade Office, April 2000.
107. Interview, April 2000.
108. BOFT website.
109. Interview at AmCham, April 1999.
110. *Taipei Times*, 29 January, 2001.

6. Conclusion: a comparative summary

6.1 INTRODUCTION

This book has made a comparative study of Singapore, South Korea and Taiwan's foreign economic policies. In this final chapter, we highlight its most important research findings and draw further direct comparisons between the FEP experiences of these three newly industrialized economies (the NIE-3). The macro-analytical framework developed in Chapter 1 forms the basis for this comparative summary.

6.2 COGNITIVE–IDEOLOGICAL APPROACHES

While this study has illustrated the NIE-3's respective idiosyncrasies of the cognitive–ideological approach to FEP formation, significant commonalities are also evident. For example, South Korea and Taiwan share a neo-mercantilist tradition derived primarily from an emulation of the Japanese developmental model. In its own late industrialization context, Japan had demonstrated the critical contribution made by a neo-mercantilist FEP in the path of rapid techno-industrial advancement. Yet as Gerschenkron (1962) predicted, neo-mercantilism normally serves a transitional developmental purpose, and moreover has become increasingly untenable in a global political economy characterized by a strengthening momentum for multilateral free trade and ascendant neo-liberalism (see Chapter 2). Certainly, the foreign economic policies of the NIE-3 have made relative concessions to the neo-liberal approach, especially South Korea since the 1997/98 financial crisis. Nevertheless, remnants of the neo-mercantilist approach to FEP formation are manifest in both South Korea and Taiwan. This may be explained by the enduring nature of structural relationships fostered by the developmental state (e.g. between state and business), attention afforded to critical economic security objectives (e.g. pertaining to techno-industrial capability) and underpinning socio-cultural factors (e.g. economic nationalism).

In another comparison, both Singapore and Taiwan's embrace of neo-liberalism has occurred within a strong institutional and developmentalist context. Singapore's 'guided' liberalization approach aimed to develop new productive and financial capacities in the city-state, opening up its interaction with the global economy but down particular developmental pathways. In Taiwan's 'liberalization plus' approach, a controlled and gradual approach to economic liberalization has prevailed with strong state mediation. Thus, while the Taiwanese government has removed trade barriers it has simultaneously and significantly augmented trade competitiveness-enhancing programmes. This dualistic approach of Taiwan's is also evident in Singapore, and more generally signifies the prevalence of state capacity in their respective FEP formations. In post-crisis South Korea, the Government is still finding its way to cultivate globalism and market liberalism within the domestic political economy. As part of this process, it is more specifically attempting to make South Korea into an 'open trading nation' in the same mould as Singapore. However, the embedded mercantilism deeply ingrained within South Korea's socio-cultural fabric could eventually lead to a similar dualistic approach to neo-liberalism as practised in Singapore and Taiwan. This depends to a large extent upon the future reinvigoration or diminishment of state capacity in South Korea.

In further comment on the socio-cultural dimension, the shared Confucian value-system tradition has, to some probable extent, shaped the NIE-3 approaches to both developmentalism and foreign economic policy itself. While not wishing to exclude the relevance of socio-cultural determinants in FEP analysis, the extent to which such connections can be established is nevertheless problematic as hinted in preceding chapters. Insofar as developmental statism constitutes the basis of a shared 'value-system' between the NIE-3, this presents a more empirically testable alternative. Moreover, the accommodation of a 'transformative' or 'developmental' economic culture in the NIE-3's cognitive–ideological approach to FEP formation should continue, at least in some form, whilst they remain in the semi-periphery strata. Thus, the 'late industrialization' context to FEP-making amongst the NIE-3 will continue to be highly relevant for some time yet.

6.3 ECONOMIC SECURITY

For the NIE-3, the pursuit of economic security has probably been more critical than for most other FEP powers. Each were confronted with their own national survival predicament: Taiwan's contested sovereignty by mainland China, Singapore's precarious position between Malaysia and Indonesia, and South Korea's potentially volatile frontier shared with North Korea. In many ways, this galvanized both state and society with developmental purpose, providing urgency to the techno-industrial transformation of the NIE-3. As Woo-Cumings (1996) comments, 'the genius of the state in South Korea and Taiwan was in harnessing very real fear of war and instability into a developmental energy'

(p. 339).[1] Rapid economic development was hence seen as a forward defence against those intent on territorial infringement. As such, the general economics–security nexus has been a very salient feature of NIE-3 foreign economic policy, even though previous chapters testify to how this has not been explicitly institutionalized: while all three possess national security councils, matters of 'economic security' are rarely specifically discussed there. We can, however, make a number of generalized observations regarding NIE-3 economic security objectives.

6.3.1 Supply Security

Securing access to key materials and intermediate products has been critical to maintaining the developmental path of the economy within the NIE-3 group. Their mutual lack of indigenous natural resources makes the securing of the supply of essential industrial inputs such as oil a special FEP priority. Singapore's dependences on Malaysian freshwater and Indonesian gas supplies remain defining features of its economic diplomacy with its two neighbouring states. Meanwhile, both South Korea and Taiwan's persisting dependency on technology-intensive imports from Japan receives similar critical attention in this channel of bilateral economic diplomacy.

6.3.2 Market Access Security

Outlets for exported products are critical for trade-oriented developmental states such as the NIE-3. Their progress beyond semi-peripheralization is based largely on securing and developing footholds in key overseas markets. Singapore is especially trade dependent given its entrepot trade and MNE export production platform functionalities. Yet given the essential export-orientation of their economies, the pursuit of market access security remains of equal, vital importance to all the NIE-3, as revealed by the fact that their trade promotion agencies have all dispatched missions to relatively uncharted commercial territory (e.g. Central Asia) in recent years. Taiwan's accession to the World Trade Organization (WTO) will mark its most significant achievement in terms of its market access security. In a common attempt to improve bilateral market access, both South Korea and Singapore have embarked on various bilateral free trade agreement (FTA) projects with other Asia–Pacific economies.

6.3.3 Finance–Credit Security

Retaining control over finance is a traditional capacity function of developmental states, but this has succumbed to financial globalization as most clearly demonstrated in South Korea's 1997/98 crisis experience. As discussed in Chapter 2, many semi-peripheral economies remain dependent on, or at least vulnerable to foreign 'core' banks, other financial institutions and short-term financial flows (Onis and Aysan 2000). However, the successful trade strategies of developmental states can yield accumulated foreign exchange reserves generated by trade surpluses, as consistently exemplified by both Taiwan and Singapore.[2] Moreover, we saw in Chapters 3 and 5 how the respective strong state capacities retained in these two economies in the finance–credit domain proved a key factor in resisting the regional crisis contagion.

6.3.4 Techno-Industrial Capacity Security

This is a crucial economic security objective of the NIE-3 given the 'transformative' goal-setting of developmental states. Close attention is paid to this by semi-periphery states in their endeavours to move towards 'core' status. Examples from our study of the NIE-3 include South Korea's 'G7 Project', Singapore's 'Industry 21' strategy, and Taiwan's promotion of itself as a 'High-Tech Silicon Island'. As hinted earlier, this continues to provide a still firm basis for the *associative* technical policy realm within their respective FEP frameworks, and moreover an important impetus behind closing the developmental gap between themselves and the advanced industrial economies (AIEs).

6.3.5 Socio-economic Paradigm Security

This generally concerns the meta-economic and socio-cultural determinants of the developmental state. Thus in the case of South Korea's economic nationalism, the resistance to foreign neo-liberal advocacy owes much to its perceived eroding effects on the country's socio-economic paradigm. We noted in Chapter 3 how Singapore's prospective 'defence' of its socio-economic paradigm relates mostly to any externalized threats to the state's developmentalism, however unlikely such foreign intimidation may arise given the city-state's economic openness. In Chapter 5 it was contended that Taiwan's pursuit of socio-economic paradigm security might be reduced to a singular foreign economic policy objective: to resist the advances of the PRC's counter-paradigm. This has heightened meaning given Taiwan's new phase of democratic development marked by the Democratic People's Party election victory of March 2000.

6.3.6 Transborder Community Security

Given the specificities of their own geographic situation, each of the NIE-3 has very particular issues at stake here, as previous chapters showed. For Singapore, these largely centre on the Indonesia–Malaysia–Singapore Growth Triangle

(IMSGT) project it initiated in the late 1980s, playing an important part in safeguarding the city-state's economic security by, for example, the fostering of a more prosperous development at Singapore's borders. Meanwhile, Chapter 4 examined how South Korea's transborder community security concerns are strongly focused on North Korea, as North Koreans share the most significant and immediate transborder community association with their southerly neighbours. In a similar context of kinship-linked ties, Taiwan's own transborder community security interests are becoming more pronounced with the development of a Cross Straits economy that increasingly binds it in a commercial sense to mainland China. In all cases, the NIE-3 foreign economic policies have needed to confer greater priority to emerging transborder economic developments, both actual and prospective.

6.3.7 Systemic Security

This is particularly relevant to the semi-periphery economies' dependence on a stable international trade and finance system. Furthermore, with their growing techno-industrial development comes the greater shift in balance from systemic support *receivers* to *providers* (see Chapter 1). In other words, they are increasingly able to contribute towards the public goods produced by a stable international economic system rather than simply consuming them, and the NIE-3's more positive engagements in international economic organizations (IEOs) is illustration of this.[3] Singapore's long-standing free trade advocacy has made it a comparatively established, ardent and widely acknowledged supporter of the multilateral trade system. Accompanying South Korea's new aspirations to become an 'open trading nation' has been a new commitment to raise its levels of systemic responsibility. Moreover, the country has placed more faith in the systemic security as it becomes more economically open. Although still denied access to many forms of systemic assistance (for example IMF loans), Taiwan's entry into WTO membership confers improved security and predictability in its trade relations within the international economic system. Thus, in trade at least, the systemic security interests of the NIE-3 are converging.

6.3.8 Alliance Security

The NIE-3 have relied on key foreign economic partners for their development. As previously noted, this especially relates to the US and Japan which have played critical roles in the supply, market access, finance–credit and techno-industrial capacity security aspects of the NIE-3's foreign economic policies. Reference here can be made to the NIE-3's semi-periphery economic relations with the AIE 'core'. For small, outward-oriented economies like Singapore, especial priority is afforded to nurturing foreign economic relations, and its FEP protagonists have proved effective alliance initiators and catalysts in this respect, as seen in its bilateral FTA strategy and perpetration of inter-regional economic relations. While South Korea and Taiwan still depend significantly on their economic alliances with the US and Japan, both have attempted to diversify the foreign economic relations as part of a risk-averse strategy. Given Taiwan's contested sovereignty predicament, it has had to draw upon its diplomatic resourcefulness to cultivate economic alliances where and how it can.

6.4 TECHNICAL POLICY REALMS

In our study of the NIE-3, we posited the central role played by trade strategies in the developmental state's transformative project. These commenced with an initial phase of import-substitution industrialization (ISI) before progressing to export-oriented industrialization (EOI). In ISI strategies, the substitution of imports by domestic production is achieved by a combination of trade protectionism and policies aimed at developing infant industries, the idea being to allow them to reach scale production within closed or insulated domestic markets. The intellectual underpinning for ISI strategies draws much upon dependency theory and its axioms of self-sufficiency. Unlike Latin American NIEs such as Mexico and Brazil, which adhered to these policies for some considerable time, their East Asian counterparts made an early switch to EOI strategies owing to the perceived developmental advantages this conferred: it conditioned domestic producers to the disciplines of global competition, hence spurring resource efficiency; the targeting of large international markets permitted the more effective exploitation of scale and scope economies; to maintain their international competitive edge, exporters were compelled to innovate constantly and invest in new technology. For the NIE-3, this policy switch occurred during the first half of the 1960s. As Beeson and Robison (2000) comment, EOI was 'designed to force the pace of industrialisation and promote national economic development' (p. 11), and the NIE-3's highly successful EOI policies inspired other semi-periphery states to emulate them, becoming the 'new development orthodoxy' (Haggard 1986). Preceding chapters also illustrate how this became an early defining feature of their foreign economic policies.

We further noted how the neo-mercantilist principles on which at least South Korea and Taiwan's EOI strategies were founded have become increasingly untenable in the global, neo-liberal era. This had two key implications in the context of our FEP analysis. First, in the *core* technical policy realm, the continued liberalization of trade, FDI and international finance regimes is a common foreign economic policy feature of the NIE-3. Especially in Singapore and Taiwan's case, as previously noted, this liberalization process took place within a retained strong institutional and developmentalist context. We also argued in Chapter 4 that even in South Korea, where the Kim Dae-jung Administration has sought to scale back government intervention, elements of state capacity have required strengthening to oversee certain aspects of FEP-related liberalization. Second, and as Chapter 1 argued, the incorporation of the *associative* technical policy realm into Singapore, South Korea and Taiwan's FEPs has somewhat weakened. This especially relates to industrial policy, which has now become less unified with trade policy formation. Yet as our study has revealed, this and other associative policy links nevertheless remain notably salient within the NIE-3's foreign economic policy formation. The persisting developmental mindset of FEP protagonists and the semi-periphery predicament still compel attention to this technical policy realm.

Returning to aspects of the core technical policy realm, the EOI approach to trade policy will, at least in general terms, remain central to NIE-3 economic development strategy. Their economies can still be defined, both in structure and essence, as 'trading states', with exports remaining crucial to maintenance of their economic security (Rosecrance 1986). This increasingly co-exists, however, with the 'transnational restructuring' strategies of their firms – both indigenous and hosted foreign – whereby industrial development is determined by configurations of inward and outward FDI. Our study has further shown that the NIE-3 developmental experience with FDI is quite mixed, yet comparisons and commonalities can still be drawn. For example, South Korea has traditionally resisted inward FDI in accordance with the state's desire to maintain its powers of control and co-ordination capacity over the domestic economy. This also stems from both an historic mistrust of foreign capital incursions into the country – particularly during the Japanese colonial period – and a fervent economic nationalism. Chapter 4 showed, however, how inward FDI has been actively promoted as part of the economy's post-crisis reform and restructuring process. In contrast, Taiwan has traditionally used inward FDI to complement rather than compete against domestic capital, as demonstrated by its pioneering export-processing zones since the mid-1960s. This required the state to pursue a sectoral selective approach, opening the doors to foreign investment in some industries whilst closing or modulating the inward investment flow in others. While Taiwan has been more open to inward FDI than South Korea, there are few places in the world that court foreign capital so effectively as Singapore, which promotes itself as a high-tech production platform and services hub for foreign MNE activities in Southeast and East Asia. This remains integral to the city-state's developmental strategy and orientates many aspects of its foreign economic policy. The Singapore developmental state pursues an even more sectorally selective inward FDI regime than its Taiwanese counterpart, inducing those investment projects most likely to develop knowledge-based economy capacities. In further comparison, the NIE-3 have at some time actively promoted outward FDI – a rare policy stance by international comparison – as a vehicle for techno-industrial restructuring at home and promoting their economic relations abroad. This is evidenced in Singapore's foreign industrial park policy, South Korea's *Segyehwa* (globalization) policy and Taiwan's 'Go South' (i.e. to Southeast Asia) policies of the 1990s, with all reflecting a developmental statist approach to their respective FEPs.

Finally, as semi-periphery economies, the NIE-3 have only recently introduced substantive official development assistance and co-operation (ODAC) programmes into their foreign economic policy frameworks. Their growing importance should be anticipated for various reasons. These are primarily linked to previously made assumptions of the NIE-3 moving gradually towards 'core' levels of income and economic development, and thus the expectation for them to develop a stronger sense of international responsibility. An increasing prioritization of ODAC programmes also confers diplomacy advantages to the NIE-3, a fact well appreciated by Taiwan in particular given its contested statehood predicament. More generally, a substantive ODAC programme marks a rite of passage for semi-periphery states, demonstrating their progression from 'developing' recipient to the 'developed' donor status.

6.5 ECONOMIC DIPLOMACY

In terms of economic diplomacy *levels of engagement*, some correlation can be established between the advancing economic development of the NIE-3 and their growing engagement in plurilateral and multilateral economic diplomacy. While periphery states make up a large proportion of IEO membership, as found in the WTO and IMF, their lack of development and associated resources (e.g. technocratic) limits their participative capacity. In contrast, advanced semi-periphery economies such as Singapore, South Korea and Taiwan are able to become more proactive, for example by demonstrating their developed country-like capabilities to implement plurilateral accords signed within the GATT/WTO, in addition to acceding to plurilateral IEOs (for example the OECD in South Korea's case) and regimes. In Chapter 3, it was contended that for such a small state Singapore maintains a highly active economic diplomacy at multiple levels, and has been especially advocative of the multilateral economic diplomacy. Post-crisis South Korea, as noted earlier, is following in Singapore's footsteps, while Taiwan's entry into WTO membership will bring a significant expansion in its economic diplomacy options.

Our study has further shown how there exists a strong regional development dimension to the NIE-3's economic diplomacy. Singapore, South Korea and

Taiwan have been key constituents of the regional economic interdependence to emerge in contemporary East Asia. All three are APEC members, and thus form part of a wider Pacific economic community attempting to forge closer commercial, infrastructural and policy linkages across the transregion. At a sub-regional level, each of the NIE-3 are more or less expected to pursue an increasingly proactive economic diplomacy amongst their neighbours, be it Singapore in its 'hub services' role within its local 'growth triangle' and Southeast Asia, or South Korea in the Tumen River Area Development Programme, or Taiwan in providing capital investment and technology in southeast coastal China. The economic diplomacy expectations upon East Asia's principal semi-periphery economies amongst its less developed regional neighbours are rising, as previously suggested.

Following on from our discussion on the softening of neo-mercantilist practices, the NIE-3 have generally moved more from *defensive* to *promotive* economic diplomacy modes. The once-infant industries no longer require the protected insulation from foreign competition with their own improved competitive standing in the global marketplace. Moreover, the globalization–liberalization nexus makes protectionism increasingly difficult to legitimize. In addition, the relative shift in position from systemic support *receivers* to *providers* associated with a more proactive engagement in plurilateral and multilateral processes has brought a *de facto* strengthening of the NIE-3's promotive economic diplomacy. Yet the significant competitive threat these semi-periphery economies particularly pose to the AIEs in key industry sectors makes *defensive* economic diplomacy still highly relevant. This especially applies to South Korea and Taiwan where foreign access to markets and capital in some sectors remains problematic.

In terms of *exercises of power* in economic diplomacy, the relational power of strengthening semi-periphery states may be expected to increase, commensurate with their growing economic weight on the international stage. The NIE-3 have undoubtedly enjoyed greater bargaining leverage in matters of economic diplomacy as a consequence. However, as the case of Japan has revealed, the conversion of geo-economic weight into its geo-political equivalent is by no means assured. With regard to structural power analysis, the more proactive engagement of semi-periphery states in plurilateral–multilateral economic diplomacy may have two main effects. First, they can find themselves more susceptible to foreign structural power influence through a firmer compliance with multilateral norms and rules, as Taiwan may experience within the WTO over forthcoming years. Second and conversely, their ability to mitigate this influence can strengthen them, especially if combined with others that seek a similar objective. For example, the NIE-3 and other semi-periphery constituents may form a coalition with developing countries to resist the demands from core FEP powers to incorporate 'new' trade issues more firmly into the WTO agenda. However, as earlier contended, semi-periphery states such as the NIE-3 are in theory potential mediators between the core and periphery in matters of economic diplomacy owing to their intermediate position in the international system.

6.6 CONTESTING 'ACTOR-BASED' INFLUENCES

In Chapter 2, we made a number of inferences that concern how the changing development context of the NIE-3 will affect the contesting 'actor-based' influences upon their respective foreign economies' policies. In the traditional developmental state paradigm, state economic bureaucrats dominate the policy-formation process. Although institutionalized state–business co-operation permitted business representatives some input into this process, it was the state bureaucracy that determined both policy objectives and the parameters within which policy was formulated. This broadly complies with the *state-centred* approach to FEP formation, where developmental authoritarianism generally modulated the contesting influence of societal stakeholding constituencies. However, the shift to developmental democratization, especially in South Korea and Taiwan, has brought significant changes. In these economies, the independent contesting influence of the business community has considerably strengthened. Democratization has also gradually enfranchised and empowered a wide range of previously marginalized stakeholding FEP constituencies in South Korea and Taiwan. This particularly relates to civil society NGOs (e.g. trade unions, environmental groups) that have a growing interest in FEP issues. Whilst they remain relatively weak in their domestic context, they form part of global social movements that are contesting the governance of multilateral economic institutions and their agendas (McMichael 2000, O'Brien *et al* 2000). Events at and since the 1999 Seattle WTO Ministerial Meeting revealed the potential power that mobilized civil society can exercise over institutionalized processes, inspiring the development and activism of domestic civil society in the NIE-3. In addition, as a consequence of the 1997/98 financial crisis there is growing pressure across East Asia upon governments to introduce greater transparency and more democratic forms of governance into economic policy-making processes. In the comparatively undemocratized Singapore, though, an ardent state-centric approach to FEP formation remains just as strong.

Yet as discussed throughout this study, democratization does not necessarily signal the demise of the developmental state but rather its further evolution. The foreign economic policies of the NIE-3 still reflect the transformative goal-setting of the developmental statism but are now also increasingly penetrated by domestic societal interests and preferences (Bernard 1996). Hence, a shift towards a more *society-centred* approach to FEP formation is evident though this should be understood in the context of 'strong state, strong society', the underlying principle of Weiss' (1995, 1998) 'governed interdependence' thesis. Indeed, preceding chapters demonstrated how environment, labour and other welfare-related issues are gradually emerging within the FEP framework of the NIE-3 as part of the new developmentalism. Generally speaking, though, the internationalization of NIE-3 civil society remains broadly underdeveloped, with many of its civil groups still primarily focused on domestic rather than international issues of concern. This further continues to limit the scope of contesting influence from transnational civil movements over the NIE-3's foreign economic policies. In addition, the weakened *control* capacity and infrastructural power of the NIE-3 developmental states may have loosened the bureaucratic grip on FEP formation, but the *managerial* capacity and technocratic insulation of FEP bureaucrats remains largely intact. Thus, while the state has undoubtedly conceded contesting influence to domestic stakeholders, FEP formation in the NIE-3 is still very much *state-centred*.

The many changes in international and transnational contesting influences over the foreign economic policies of the NIE-3 have also been examined by this study. In sum, globalization has strengthened the power of these influences over FEP formation generally, and more specifically has undermined the developmental state's capacity for national economic management. Foreign transnational firms already play a big part in Singapore's FEP formation albeit in strict state-defined parameters. After the post-crisis liberalization of South Korea's inward FDI regime and ensuing influx of foreign transnational firms, the country's FEP may be expected to reflect their interests increasingly in a more open policy environment. Similarly, the growing transnationalization evident in Taiwan's economic development makes its FEP also more susceptible to these sources of contesting influence. The 1997/98 East Asian financial crisis furthermore strengthened the hand of external neo-liberal advocates in affecting the liberalization of the NIE-3's economic policies via economic diplomacy and other channels. This was perhaps most clearly witnessed in the IMF's 'bailout' programme prescribed to South Korea.

In addition, the increasing engagement of the NIE-3 in plurilateral–multilateral economic diplomacy has brought about a stronger FEP congruity to international regime rules, behavioural norms and expectations, hence conferring greater relevance to the *system-centred* approach. Singapore, South Korea and Taiwan's trade policies should be anticipated to become more closely aligned with WTO rules and norms: with advancing development comes the expectation of greater multilateral responsibility. Similarly, the growing participation of South Korea, Singapore and Taiwan's FEP protagonists in trans-governmental alliances and policy networks is ever more evident, as recent developments in APEC and other international regimes or institutional processes show. This openness to international and transnational contesting FEP influence is likely to increase as the NIE-3 seek progression beyond the semi-periphery.

6.7 A FINAL COMMENT

This study has analysed the foreign economic policies of Singapore, South Korea and Taiwan from multiple perspectives. It has charted how their rapid economic development within the world economy has shaped the formation of these respective policies, and their impact upon the international economic system. This study also developed a macro-framework for FEP analysis that was deployed in analysing the NIE-3 but which also has a general application purpose. Moreover, it was contended that developmental statism and semi-peripheralization form the common development context for examining the NIE-3's foreign economic policies, and that this seems likely to prevail for some time yet.

NOTES

1. In a later work, Woo-Cumings (1999) commented that 'the pursuit of power and plenty, in the context of either the security state or of catching up with the rest of the world (more often both), is vastly more effective in generating developmental energy than a general appeal to increase welfare, *à la* Latin American "populism"' (p. 23).
2. Both these economies have been amongst the world's top six foreign exchange reserve holders for many years. More recently, South Korea has moved into this virtuous position. By April 2001, Taiwan was the world's third largest foreign exchange holder (after Japan and China) with \$111.7bn, South Korea the fifth largest with \$94.4bn (after Hong Kong) and Singapore the sixth largest with \$76.8bn.
3. To this extent, the NIE-3 exemplify the 'pro-systemic' approach of the semi-periphery as proposed by Wallerstein (1979), in contrast to Chase-Dunn's (1989) stress on the 'anti-systemic' behaviour of semi-periphery states.

References

Aberbach, J.D., Dollar, D. and Sokoloff, K.L. (eds) (1994), *The Role of the State in Taiwan's Development: Taiwan in the Modern World*, M.E. Sharpe, Armonk.

Adams, J. (1984) 'Foreign Economic Policy: Challenges of the 1980s', *Journal of Economic Issues*, **18**(1), pp. 275–94.

Adler-Karlsson, G. (1968), *Western Economic Warfare, 1947–67: A Case Study in Foreign Economic Policy*, Almqvist and Wiksell, Stockholm.

Akaha, T. (ed.) (1999), *Politics and Economics in Northeast Asia: Nationalism and Regionalism in Contention*, MacMillan, London.

Akamatsu, K. (1962) 'A Historical Pattern of Economic Growth in Developing Countries', *The Developing Economies*, No. 1 (March–September), pp. 3–25.

Akao, N. (ed.) (1983), *Japan's Economic Security*, St. Martin's Press, New York.

Aldrich, D. (1997), 'If You Build It, They Will Come: A Cautionary Tale About the Tumen River Projects', *Journal of East Asian Affairs*, **11**(1), pp. 299–326.

Alting von Geusau, F. and Pelkmans, J. (1982), *National Economic Security: Perceptions, Threats and Policies*, John F. Kennedy Institute, Tilburg.

Amerongen, O.W. (1980), 'Commentary: Economic Sanctions as a Foreign Policy Tool', *International Security*, **5** (Autumn), pp. 159–67.

Amsden, A. (1985), 'The State and Taiwan's Economic Development', in P.B. Evans, D. Rueschmeyer and T. Skocpol (eds) *Bringing the State Back In*, Cambridge University Press, Cambridge.

Amsden, A. (1989), *Asia's Next Giant: South Korea and Late Industrialisation,* Oxford University Press, Oxford.

Amsden, A. (1992), 'Taiwan in International Perspective', in N.T. Wang (ed.) *Taiwan's Enterprises in Global Perspective*, M.E. Sharpe, New York.

Amsden, A. and Hikino, T. (2000), 'The Bark is Worse than the Bite: New WTO Law and Late Industrialisation', *Annals of American Political and Social Science*, **570**(July), pp. 104–14.

Anderson, P. (1974), *Lineages of the Absolutist State*, New Left Books, New York.

Appelbaum, R.P. and Henderson, J. (eds) (1992), *States and Development in the Asian Pacific Rim*, Sage, London.

Arrighi, G. (1990), 'The Developmentalist Illusion: A Reconceptualisation of the Semi-Periphery', in W.G. Martin (ed.) *Semi-Periphery States in the World Economy*, Greenwood Press, New York.

Asher, M.G. (1994), 'Some Aspects Of Role Of State In Singapore', *Economic And Political Weekly*, **29**(14), pp. 795–804.

Atkinson, M.M. and Coleman, W.D. (1992), 'Policy Networks, Policy Communities and the Problems of Governance', *Governance*, **5**(2), pp. 154–80.

Baldwin, D. (1986), *Economic Statescraft*, Princeton University Press, Princeton.

Barber, J. (1979), 'Economic Sanctions as a Policy Instrument', *International Affairs*, **55** (July), pp. 367–84.

Baughn, C.G. and Yaprak, A. (1996), 'Economic Nationalism: Conceptual and Empirical Development', *Political Psychology*, **17**(4), pp. 759–78.

Belo, W. (1998), 'East Asia: On the Eve of the Great Transformation?', *Review of International Political Economy*, **5**(3), pp. 424–44.

Beeson, M. and Robison, R. (2000), 'Introduction: Interpreting the Crisis', in R. Robison, M. Beeson, K. Jayasuriya and H.R. Kim (eds) *Politics and Markets in the Wake of the Asian Crisis*, Routledge, London.

Bergsten, C.F. (1992), 'The Primacy of Economics', *Foreign Policy*, No. 87, Summer.

Bernard, M. (1996), 'States, Social Forces, and Regions in Historical Time: Toward a Critical Political Economy of Eastern Asia, *Third World Quarterly*, **17**(4), pp. 649–65.

Bhagwati, J. (1998), 'Yes to Free Trade and Maybe to Capital Control', *Wall Street Journal*, 16 November, p. A38.

Blank, S. (1978), 'Britain: The Politics of Foreign Economic Policy, the Domestic Economy, and the Problem of Pluralistic Stagnation', in P.J. Katzenstein (ed.) *Between Power and Plenty: Foreign Economic Policies of Advanced Industrial States*, University of Wisconsin Press, Madison.

Blomqvist, H.C. (1996), 'The "Flying Geese" Model of Regional Development: A Constructive Interpretation', *Journal of the Asia Pacific Economy*, **1**(2), pp. 215–31.

Bobrow, D.B. (1985), 'Japan's Economic Security', *Pacific Affairs*, **58**(1), pp. 138–41.

Bonvicini, G., Falautano, I. and Farella, R. (1998), 'Italian Foreign Economic Policy: Challenges Ahead', *International Spectator*, **33**(1), pp. 121–38.

Borensztein, E. and Lee, J. (1998), 'Financial Distortions and Crisis in Korea', paper presented at the *Korean Economic Association Meetings*, August.

Brander, J.A. and Spencer, B.J. (1985), 'Export Subsidies and International Market Share Rivalry', *Journal of International Economics*, **16**, pp. 83–100.

Bridges, B. (1993), *Japan and Korea in the 1990s: From Antagonism to Adjustment*, Edward Elgar, Aldershot.

Brown, S. (1995), *New Forces, Old Forces, and the Future of World Politics*, Harper Collins, New York.

Buzan, B. (1991), *People, States and Fear*, Harvester Wheatsheaf, London.

Buzan, B., Waever, O. and de Wilde, J. (1998), *Security: A New Framework of Analysis*, Lynne Rienner, Boulder.

Cable, V. (1995), 'What is International Economic Security?', *International Affairs*, **71**(2), pp. 305–24.

Cable, V. (1996), 'The New Trade Agenda: Universal Rules Amid Cultural Diversity', *International Affairs*, **72**(2), pp. 227–46.

Calder, K.E. (1988), 'Japan's Foreign Economic Policy Formation: Explaining the Reactive State', *World Politics*, **40**(July), pp. 517–40.

Calder, K.E. (1991), 'Domestic Constraints and Japan's Foreign Economic Policy of the 1990s', *International Journal*, **46**(4), pp. 607–22.

Castells, M. (1988), 'The Developmental City State in an Open World Economy: The Singapore Experience', *University of California (Berkeley) Working Paper*, No. 31.

Castells, M. (1992), 'Four Asian Tigers with a Dragon Head: A Comparative Analysis of the State, Economy and Society in the Asian Pacific Rim', R. Appelbaum and J. Henderson (eds) *States and Development in the Asian Pacific Rim*, Sage, Newbury Park.

CEPD (2000), *Taiwan Statistical Data Book 1999*, CEPD, Taipei.

Cerny, P. (1995), 'Globalisation and the Changing Logic of Collective Action', *International Organisation*, **49**(4), pp. 595–625.

Chakravarthi, R. (2000), 'After Seattle, World Trade System Faces Uncertain Future', *Review of International Political Economy*, **7**(3), 495–504.

Chan, G. (1996), 'Sudpolitik: The Political Economy of Taiwan's Trade with Southeast Asia', *Pacific Review*, **9**(1), pp. 96–113.

Chan, G. (1997), 'Taiwan as an Emerging Foreign Aid Donor: Developments, Problems and Prospects', *Pacific Affairs*, **70**(1), pp. 37–56.

Chan, H.C. and Obaid, H. (eds) (1987), *S. Rajaratnam: The Prophetic and the Political*, St. Martin's Press, New York.

Chan, S. (1987), 'The Mouse that Roared: Taiwan's Management of Trade Relations with the United States', *Comparative Political Studies*, **20**(3), pp. 251–92.

Chan, S., Clark, C. and Lam, D. (eds) (1998), *Beyond the Developmental State: East Asia's Political Economies Reconsidered*, MacMillan, London.

Chang, H.J. (1998), 'Korea: The Misunderstood Crisis', *World Development*, **26**(8), pp. 1555–61.

Chang, H.J. (1999), 'The Economic Theory of the Developmental State', in M. Woo-Cumings (ed.) *The Developmental State*, Cornell University Press, Ithaca.

Chang, H.J., Park, H.J. and Yoo, C.G. (1998), 'Interpreting the Korean Crisis: Financial Liberalisation, Industrial Policy and Corporate Governance', *Cambridge Journal of Economics*, **22**, pp. 735–46.

Chao, L. and Myers, R.H. (2000), 'The Divided China Problem: Conflict Avoidance and Resolution', *Essays in Public Policy*, No. 101, Hoover Institution, Stanford University.

Chapman, J., Drifte, R. and Gow, I. (eds) (1983), *Japan's Quest for Comprehensive Security: Defense-Diplomacy-Dependence*, St. Martin's Press, New York.

Chase-Dunn, C. (1989), *Global Formation: Structures of the World Economy*, Blackwell, Oxford.

Chen, J. (1993), 'The Taiwan Problem in Peking ASEAN Policy', *Issues and Studies*, **29**(4), pp. 95–124.

Chen, P.S.J. (1983), *Singapore Development Policies and Trends*, Oxford University Press, Singapore.

Chen, T.J. and Ku, Y.H. (1999), 'Second Stage Import Substitution: The Taiwan Experience', in G. Ranis, S.C. Hu and Y.P. Chu (eds) *The Political Economy of Taiwan's Development into the 21st Century*, Edward Elgar, Cheltenham.

Cheng, T.J., Haggard, S. and Kang, S. (1998), 'Institutions and Growth in Korea and Taiwan: The Bureaucracy', *Journal of Development Studies*, **34**(6), pp. 87–111.

Cheong, I.K. (1998), *The Evolution of US Policy Toward Free Trade Agreements and Implications for Korea*, Korea Institute for International Economic Policy, Seoul.

Chia, S.Y. (1986), 'Direct Foreign Investment and Industrialisation Process in Singapore', in C.Y. Lim and P. Lloyd (eds) *Singapore: Resource and Growth*, Oxford University Press, Oxford.

Chin, K.W. (1998), 'Singapore: Towards Developed Country Status – The Security Dimension', in L. Low (ed.) *Singapore: Towards a Developed Country Status*, Oxford University Press, Singapore.

Cho, Y.J and Kim, J.K (1995), 'Credit Policies and Industrialisation of Korea, *World Bank Discussion Paper No. 286*, Washington DC.

Choi, Y.B. (1998), 'On Financial Crisis in Korea', *Korea Observer*, **29**(3), pp. 485–510.

Chong, A. (2001), 'Singapore Incorporated and the Fine City: Gains and Sacrifices in the Image Building in Singapore's Foreign Policy of Economic Survival', in A. Chong and J. Valencic (eds) *The Image, the State and International Relations*, European Foreign Policy Unit Working Paper No. 2001/2, London School of Economics.

Chong, J.Y., Hwang, H.R., Choi, J.H. and Rim, M.H. (2000), 'Transition of Latecomer Firms from Technology Generators: Korean Semiconductor Firms', *World Development*, **28**(5), pp. 969–82.

Chou, Y.J. (1992), 'Economic Dependence and Changes in Taiwan Trade-Policy, 1984–89', *Issues and Studies*, **28**(1), pp. 96–118.
Chu, Y.H. (1994), 'The Realignment of Business–Government Relations and Regime Transition in Taiwan', in A. MacIntyre (ed.) *Business and Government in Industrialising Asia*, Cornell University Press, Ithaca.
Chu, Y.H. (1999a), 'The Institutional Foundation of Taiwan's Industrialisation: Exploring the State-Society Nexus', in G. Ranis, S.C. Hu and Y.P. Chu (eds) *The Political Economy of Taiwan's Development into the 21st Century*, Edward Elgar, Cheltenham.
Chu, Y.H. (1999b), 'Surviving the East Asian Financial Storm: The Political Foundation of Taiwan's Economic Resilience', in T. Pempel (ed.) *The Politics of the Asian Economic Crisis*, Cornell University Press, Ithaca.
Chu, Y.H. (2000), 'Re-engineering the Developmental State in the Age of Globalisation: Taiwan in Defiance of Neo-liberalism', paper presented at *Taiwan as a Development Model for the 21st Century*, SOAS, University of London, 21–22 September 2000.
Chua, B.H. (2000), 'The Relative Autonomies of State and Civil Society in Singapore', in G. Koh and G.L. Ooi (eds) *State–Society Relations in Singapore*, Oxford University Press, Singapore.
Chun, S.K. (1995), 'Enhancing Korea's Multilateral Trade Diplomacy', in Sejong Institute (ed.) *Korea's Economic Diplomacy*, Sejong Institute, Seoul.
Chung, J.Y. (1995), 'The Uruguay Round Negotiation: Process, Result and Beyond', in Sejong Institute (ed.) *Korea's Economic Diplomacy: Survival as a Trading Nation*, Sejong Institute, Seoul.
Clark, C. and Chan, S. (1994), 'The Developmental Roles of the State: Moving Beyond the Developmental State in Conceptualising Asian Political Economies', *Governance*, **7**(4), pp. 332–59.
Cohen, B.J. (ed.) (1968), *American Foreign Economic Policy: Essays and Comments*, Harper and Row, New York.
Cohen, B.J. (1977), *The Making of United States International Economic Policy: Principles, Problems and Proposals for Reform*, Praeger, New York.
Condliffe, J.B. (1944), 'Economic Power as an Instrument of National Policy', *American Economic Review*, **34**(March), pp. 305–14.
Cooper, A.F. (1986), 'Subnational Activity and Foreign Economic Policy Making in Canada and the United States: Perspectives on Agriculture', *International Journal*, **41**(3), pp. 655–73.
Cotton, J. (2000), 'The Asian Crisis and the Perils of Enterprise Association: Explaining the Different Outcomes in Singapore, Taiwan and Korea', in R. Robison, M. Beeson, K. Jayasuriya and H.R. Kim (eds) *Politics and Markets in the Wake of the Asian Crisis*, Routledge, London.
Cowhey, P.F. (1990), '"States" and "Politics" in American Foreign Economic Policy', in J.S. Odell and T.D. Willett (eds) *International Trade Policies:*

Gains From Exchange Between Economics and Political Science, University of Michigan Press, Michigan.

Crane, G.T. (1998), 'Economic Nationalism: Bringing the State Back In', *Millennium*, **27**(1), pp. 55–75.

Cumings, B. (1984), 'The Origins and Development of the Northeast Asian Political Economy: Industrial Sectors, Product Cycles, and Political Consequences', *International Organisation*, **38**(1), pp. 1–40.

Cutright, P. (1963), 'National Political Development Measurement and Analysis', *American Sociological Review*, **28**, pp. 253–64.

Davidson, J.W. (1988), *The Island of Formosa: Past and Present*, Oxford University Press, New York.

Deans, P. (1998), 'Contested Sovereignty: The Impact of Taiwan's Political Changes on the China Policy of Asia–Pacific Region's Major Countries', paper given at *The Development of Contemporary Taiwan and its Implications For Cross-Strait Relations, the Asia–Pacific Region and Europe* Conference, Institute of National Policy Research, Taipei, 16–17 December.

Demetriades, P.O. and Fattouh, B.A. (1999), 'The South Korean Financial Crisis: Competing Explanations and Policy Lessons for Financial Liberalisation', *International Affairs*, **75**(4), 779–92.

Dent, C.M. (1997), *The European Economy: The Global Context*, Routledge, London.

Dent, C.M. (1998a), 'The ASEM: Managing the New Framework of the EU's Economic Relations with East Asia', *Pacific Affairs*, **70**(4), pp. 495–516.

Dent, C.M. (1998b), 'New Interdependencies in Korea–EU Trade Relations', *Journal of Contemporary Asia*, **28**(3), pp. 366–89.

Dent, C.M. (1999), *The European Union and East Asia: An Economic Relationship Examined*, Routledge, London.

Dent, C.M. (2000), 'What Difference a Crisis?: Continuity and Change in South Korea's Foreign Economic Policy', *Journal of the Asia Pacific Economy*, **5**(3), pp. 275–302.

Dent, C.M. (2001), 'ASEM and the Cinderella Complex of EU–East Asia Economic Relations', *Pacific Affairs*, **74**(1), pp. 25–52.

Dent, C.M. and Johnson, D. (2000), 'Taiwan–EU Economic Relations: A European Perspective', *EurAmerica*, **30**(1), pp. 109–57.

Dent, C.M. and Randerson, C. (1996) 'Korean Foreign Direct Investment in Europe: the Determining Forces', *The Pacific Review*, **7**(4), pp. 531–52.

Destler, I.M. (1980), *'Making Foreign Economic Policy'*, Brookings Institute, Washington D.C.

Deutsch, K. (1961), 'Social Mobilisation and Political Development', *American Political Science Review*, **60**, pp. 493–514.

Deyo, F. (ed.) (1987a), *The Political Economy of the New Asian Industrialism*, University of California Press, Berkeley.

Deyo, F. (1987b), 'Coalitions, Institutions, and Linkage Sequencing: Towards a Strategic Capacity Model of East Asian Development', in F. Deyo (ed.) *The Political Economy of the New Asian Industrialism*, University of California Press, Berkeley.

Dieter, H. (1997), 'APEC and WTO: Collision or Co-operation?', *Pacific Review*, **10**(1), pp. 19–38.

Doxey, M.P. (1980), *Economic Sanctions and International Enforcement*, Oxford University Press, New York.

Dreyer, J.T. (1994), 'Taiwan's Position Regarding Transnational Issues', in R.G. Sutter and W.R. Johnson (eds) *Taiwan in World Affairs*, Westview, Boulder.

Drezner, D. (1997), 'Allies, Adversaries, and Economic Coercion: Russian Foreign Economic Policy Since 1991', *Security Studies*, **6**(3), pp. 65–111.

Enos, J.L. and Park, W.H. (1988), *The Adoption and Diffusion of Imported Technology: The Case of Korea*, Croom Helm, London.

Ermisch, J.F. and Huff, W.G. (1999), 'Hypergrowth In An East Asian NIC: Public Policy And Capital Accumulation In Singapore', *World Development*, **27**(1), pp. 21–38.

Evans, P. (1979), *Dependent Development*, Princeton University Press, Princeton.

Evans, P. (1987), 'Class, State, and Dependence in East Asia: Lessons for Latin Americanists', in F. Deyo (ed.) *The Political Economy of the New Asian Industrialism*, Cornell University Press, Ithaca.

Evans, P. (1995), *Embedded Autonomy: States and Industrial Transformation*, Princeton University Press, Princeton.

Evans, P. (1996), 'Government Action, Social Capital and Development: Reviewing the Evidence on Synergy', *World Development*, **24**(6), pp. 1119–32.

Evans, P. (1997), 'The Eclipse of the State? Reflections on Stateness in an Era of Globalisation', *World Politics*, **50** (October), pp. 62–87.

Feldstein, M. (1998), 'Refocusing the IMF', *Foreign Affairs*, **77**(2), pp. 20–33.

Fields, K.J. (1995), *Enterprise and the State in Korea and Taiwan*, Cornell University Press, Ithaca.

Fine, B. (1999), 'The Developmental State Is Dead: Long Live Social Capital?', *Development And Change*, **30**(1), pp. 1–19.

Friedberg, A.L. (1991), 'The Changing Relationship Between Economics and National Security', *Political Science Quarterly*, **106**(2), pp. 265–76.

Friedman, D. (1988), *The Misunderstood Miracle*, MIT Press, Cambridge MA.

Fukuyama, F. (1992), *The End of History and the Last Man*, Free Press, New York.

Garrett, G. and Lange, P. (1995), 'Internationalisation, Institutions, and Political Change', *International Organisation*, **49**(4), pp. 627–55.

Gereffi, G. (1998), 'More than the Market, More than the State: Global Commodity Chains and Industrial Upgrading in East Asia', in S. Chan, C. Clark, and D. Lam (eds) *Beyond the Developmental State: East Asia's Political Economies Reconsidered*, MacMillan, London.

Gerlach, M.L. (1992), *Alliance Capitalism: The Social Organisation of Japanese Business*, University of California Press, Berkeley.

Gerschenkron, A. (1962), *Economic Backwardness in Historical Perspective*, Harvard University Press, Cambridge, MA.

Geske, M.B. (1996), 'Sovereignty and Citizenship in Contemporary US Foreign Economic Policy', *Alternatives*, **21**(2), pp. 191–210.

Gills, B.K. (1996), 'Economic Liberalisation and Reform in South Korea in the 1990s: A Coming of Age or a Case of Graduation Blues?', *Third World Quarterly*, **17**(4), pp. 667–88.

Gills, B.K. (1999), 'Globalisation, Crisis and Labour in South Korea', paper given at the International Political Economy Group workshop, University of Hull, 13 March.

Gills, B.K. and Gills, D.S. (2000), 'Globalisation and Strategic Choice in South Korea: Economic Reform and Labour', in S.S. Kim (ed.) *Korea's Globalisation*, Cambridge University Press, Cambridge.

Glaziev, S.Y. (1993), 'Russian Foreign Economic Policy and Defense Conversion', in M.P. Claudon and K. Wittneben (eds) *After the Cold War: Russian-American Defense Conversion For Economic Renewal*, New York Universities Press, New York.

Gold, T.B. (1986), *State and Society in the Taiwan Miracle*, M.E. Sharpe, Armonk.

Gold, T.B. (1988), 'Colonial Origins of Taiwanese Capitalism', in E. Winckler and S. Greenhalgh (eds) *Contending Approaches to the Political Economy of Taiwan*, M.E. Sharpe, London.

Goldstein, J. (1988), 'Ideas, Institutions and American Trade Policy', *International Organisation*, **42**(1), pp. 179–218.

Goldstein, J. (1989), 'The Impact of Ideas on Trade Policy: The Origins of US Agricultural and Manufacturing Policies', *International Organisation*, **43**(1), pp. 31–72.

Gore, C. (2000), 'The Rise and Fall of the Washington Consensus as a Paradigm for Developing Countries', *World Development*, **28**(5), pp. 789–804.

Gowa, J. (1994), *Allies, Adversaries, and International Trade*, Princeton University Press, Princeton.

Grabowski, R. (1994), 'The Successful Developmental State: Where Does it Come From?', *World Development*, **22**(5), pp. 413–22.

Grossman, G.M. and Helpman, E. (1995), 'Trade Wars and Trade Talks', *Journal of Political Economy*, **103**(4), pp. 675–708.

Guerrieri, P. and Padoan, P.C. (1986), 'Neomercantilism and International Economic Stability', *International Organization*, **40**(1), pp. 29–42.

Guiheux, G. (1998), 'The Internationalisation of Taiwanese Firms', paper given at *The Development of Contemporary Taiwan and its Implications For Cross-Strait Relations, the Asia–Pacific Region and Europe* Conference, Institute of National Policy Research, Taipei, 16–17 December.

Ha, Y.S. (1999), 'The Historical Development of Korean Globalisation', in C.I. Moon and J. Mo (eds) *Democratisation and Globalisation in Korea: Assessments and Prospects*, Yonsei University Press, Seoul.

Haas, P. (1990), *Saving the Mediterranean*, Columbia University Press, New York.

Haggard, S. (1986), 'The Newly Industrialising Countries in the International System', *World Politics*, **38**(2), pp. 343–70.

Haggard, S. (1990), *Pathways from the Periphery: The Politics of Growth in the Newly Industrialising Countries*, Cornell University Press, Ithaca.

Haggard, S. and Cheng, T.J. (1987), 'State and Foreign Capital in the East Asian NICs', in F. Deyo (ed.) *The Political Economy of the New Asian Industrialism*, University of California Press, Berkeley.

Haggard, S. and Mo, J. (2000), 'The Political Economy of the Korean Financial Crisis', *Review of International Political Economy*, **7**(2), pp. 197–218.

Haggard, S. and Moravcsik, A. (1993), 'The Political Economy of Financial Assistance to Eastern Europe, 1989–1991', in R.O Keohane, J. S. Nye and S. Hoffmann (eds) *After the Cold War*, Harvard University Press, Cambridge MA.

Han, H. (1999), 'Korea's Role in APEC Co-operation', *Korea's Economy: 1999*, Korea Economic Institute of America, Washington D.C.

Hanrieder, W.F. (1982), 'Germany as Number Two? The Foreign and Economic Policy of the Federal Republic', *International Studies Quarterly*, **26**(1), pp. 57–86.

Hawley, J.P. (1983), 'Interests, State Foreign Economic Policy, and the World-System: The Case of the US Capital Control Programs, 1961–1974', *Sage International Yearbook Of Foreign Policy Studies*, **8**, pp. 223–54.

Heckscher, E.F. (1955), *Mercantilism*, MacMillan, New York.

Heginbotham, E. and Samuels, R.J. (1998), 'Mercantile Realism and Japanese Foreign Policy', *International Security*, **22**(4), pp. 171–203.

Henckaerts, J.M. (ed.) (1996), *The International Status of Taiwan in the New World Order*, Graham and Trotman, London.

Hermann, C.F. (1982), 'Instruments of Foreign Policy', in P. Callahan. L.P. Brady and M.G. Hermann (eds) *Describing Foreign Policy Behaviour*, Sage, Beverly Hills.

Hickey, D.V.V. (1992), 'US Policy and Taiwan's Reintegration into the Global Community', *Journal of Northeast Asian studies*, **11**(1), pp. 18–32.

Higgott, R. (1998), 'The Asian Economic Crisis: A Study in the Politics of Resentment', *New Political Economy*, **3**(3), pp. 333–56.

Higgott, R. (2000), 'The International Relations of the Asian Economic Crisis: A Case Study in the Politics of Resentment', in R. Robison, M. Beeson, K. Jayasuriya and H.R. Kim (eds) *Politics and Markets in the Wake of the Asian Crisis*, Routledge, London.

Hobday, M. (1994), 'Export-Led Technology Development', *Development and Change*, **25**(2), pp. 333–61.

Hocking, B. (1993), *Localising Foreign Policy: Non-central Governments and Multilayered Diplomacy*, MacMillan, London.

Hocking, B. and Smith, M. (1997), *Beyond Foreign Economic Policy: The United States, the Single European Market and the Changing World Order*, Pinter, London.

Hofhansel, C. (1990), 'Explaining Foreign Economic Policy: A Comparison of US and West German Export Controls', *Journal of Public Policy*, **10**(3), pp. 299–330.

Hon, P.M.L. (1999), 'Singapore', in D. Glover and T. Jessup (eds) *Indonesia's Fires and Hazes: The Cost of Catastrophe*, Institute of Southeast Asian Studies, Singapore.

Hou, C. and Gee, S. (1993), 'National Systems Supporting Technical Advance in Industry: The Case of Taiwan', in R. Nelson (ed.) *National Innovation Systems: A Comparative Analysis*, Oxford University Press, Oxford.

Howe, C. (1998), 'The Taiwan Economy: The Transition to Maturity and the Political Economy of its Changing International Status', in D. Shambaugh (ed.) *Contemporary Taiwan*, Clarendon, Oxford.

Hsu, S.P. (2000), 'Rethinking State Policy Choice and State Autonomy in an Era of Financial Internationalisation: Comparing Taiwan and Indonesia During the Asian Financial Crisis', *Issues and Studies*, **36**(2), pp. 155–94.

Huang, C. (1989), 'The State and Foreign Investment: The Cases of Taiwan and Singapore', *Comparative Political Studies*, **22**(1), pp. 93–121.

Huff, W.G. (1987), 'Patterns in the Economic Development of Singapore', *Journal of Developing Areas*, **21**(April), pp. 305–26.

Huff, W.G. (1994), *The Economic Growth Of Singapore: Trade And Development In The Twentieth Century*, Cambridge University Press, Cambridge.

Huff, W.G. (1995a), 'The Developmental State, Government, And Singapore Economic Development Since 1960', *World Development*, **23**(8), pp. 1421–38.

Huff, W.G. (1995b), 'What is the Singapore Model of Economic Development?', *Cambridge Journal Of Economics*, **19**(6), pp. 735–59.

Huff, W.G. (1999), 'Turning the Corner in Singapore's Developmental State?', *Asian Survey*, **39**(4), pp. 214–42.

Hughes, C.W. (2000), 'Japanese Policy and the East Asian Currency Crisis: Abject Defeat or Quiet Victory?', *Review of International Political Economy*, **7**(2), pp. 219–53.

Huntington, S. (1993), 'Why International Primacy Matters', *International Security*, **17**(4), pp. 68–83.

Hwang, C.S. (2000), 'New Environments for the Development of Korean NGOs', paper presented at *Northeast Asian Civil Society: Current Status and Challenging Roles of NGOs in Korea, Japan and China*, Yonsei University, Seoul, 11 November.

Hyun, I.T. and Okonogi (eds) (1995), *Korea and Japan: Searching for Harmony and Co-operation in a Changing Era*, Sejong Institute, Seoul.

Ikenberry, G.J. (1988), 'Conclusion: An Institutional Approach to American Foreign Economic Policy', *International Organisation*, **42**(1), pp. 219–43.

Ikenberry, G.J., Lake, D.A. and Mastanduno, M. (eds) (1988), *The State and American Foreign Economic Policy*, Cornell University Press, Ithaca.

Jayasuriya, K. (2000), 'Authoritarian Liberalism, Governance and the Emergence of the Regulatory State in Post-Crisis East Asia', in R. Robison, M. Beeson, K. Jayasuriya and H.R. Kim (eds) *Politics and Markets in the Wake of the Asian Crisis*, Routledge, London.

Jian, C. (1996), 'Understanding the Logic of Beijing's Taiwan Policy', *Security Dialogue*, **27**(4), pp. 459–62.

Jie, C. (2000), 'The Influences of Democracy on Taiwan's Foreign Policy', *Issues and Studies*, **36**(4), pp. 1–32.

Johnson, C. (1982), *MITI and the Japanese Miracle*, Stanford University Press, Stanford.

Johnson, C. (1987), 'Political Institutions and Economic Performance: The Government–Business Relationship in Japan, South Korea and Taiwan', in F.C. Deyo (ed.) *The Political Economy of the New Asian Industrialisation*, Cornell University Press, Ithaca.

Jomo, K.S. (2000), 'Comment: Crisis and the Developmental State in East Asia', in R. Robison, M. Beeson, K. Jayasuriya and H.R. Kim (eds) *Politics and Markets in the Wake of the Asian Crisis*, Routledge, London.

Jones, J. (1999), 'A Foreign Perspective on the Business Environment', *Korea's Economy: 1999*, Korea Economic Institute of America, Washington D.C.

Joo, S.S. (2000), 'Understanding the NGO Revolution in Korea', paper presented at the *Northeast Asian Civil Society: Current Status and Challenging Roles of NGOs in Korea, Japan and China* conference, Yonsei University, Seoul, 11 November.

Kaempfer, W.H. and Lowenberg (1988), 'The Theory of International Economic Sanctions: A Public Choice Approach', *American Economic Review*, **78**(September), pp. 786–93.

Kahler, M. (1980), 'America's Foreign Economic Policy: Is the Old-Time Religion Good Enough?', *International Affairs*, **56**(3), pp. 458–73.

Kang, I.S. (1999), 'Foreign Direct Investment in Korea: Trends and Prospects', *Korea's Economy: 1999*, Korea Economic Institute of America, Washington D.C.

Kang, C.S.E. (2000), 'Segyehwa Reform and the South Korean Developmental State', in S.S. Kim (ed.) *Korea's Globalisation*, Cambridge University Press, Cambridge.

Katzenstein, P.J. (1976), 'International Relations and Domestic Structures: Foreign Economic Policies of Advanced Industrial States', *International Organisation*, **30** (1), pp. 1–45.

Katzenstein, P.J. (ed.) (1978), *Between Power and Plenty: Foreign Economic Policies of Advanced Industrial States*, University of Wisconsin Press, Madison.

Kaufman, B.I. (1982), *Trade And Aid: Eisenhower's Foreign Economic Policy, 1953–1961*, Johns Hopkins University Press, Baltimore.

Kenis, P. and Schneider, V. (1987), 'The EC as an International Corporate Actor: Two Case Studies in Economic Diplomacy', *European Journal of Political Research*, **15**(4), pp. 437–57.

Keohane, R. and Milner, H. (1996), *Internationalisation and Domestic Politics*, Cambridge University Press, Cambridge.

Kim, C.O. (1995), 'Korea in the Tripolar World Economic System', in Sejong Institute (ed.) *Korea's Economic Diplomacy: Survival as a Trading Nation*, Sejong Institute, Seoul.

Kim, D.J. (1996), *Mass Participatory Economy: Korea's Road to World Economic Power*, University Press of America, Lanham.

Kim, H.R. (2000a), 'The Viability and Vulnerability of Korean Economic Governance', *Journal of Contemporary Asia*, **30**(2), pp. 199–220.

Kim, H.R. (2000b), 'The State and Civil Society in Transition: The Role of Non-Governmental Organisations in South Korea', *Pacific Review*, **13**(4), pp. 595–613.

Kim, J.D. (1999), 'Policy Environment for Foreign Direct Investment', *Korea's Economy: 1999*, Korea Economic Institute of America, Washington D.C.

Kim, K.H. (1998), 'Korean Economic Crisis', *Korea Observer*, **29**(3), pp. 467–84.

Kim, K.S. (1997), 'From Neo-mercantilism to Globalism: The Changing Role of the State and South Korea's Economic Prowess', in M.T. Berger and D.A. Borer (eds) *The Rise of East Asia: Critical Visions of the Pacific Century*, Routledge, London.

Kim, S.M. (1999), *The Politics of the Two-Level Game: US–Korea Agricultural Trade Negotiations*, Yonsei University Press, Seoul.

Kim, S.S. (1994), 'Taiwan and the International System: The Challenge of Legitimation', in R.G. Sutter, and W.R. Johnson (eds) *Taiwan in World Affairs*, Westview, Boulder.

Kim, S.S. (ed.) (2000a), *Korea's Globalisation*, Cambridge University Press, Cambridge.

Kim, S.S. (2000b), 'Korea and Globalisation (*Segyehwa*): A Framework for Analysis', in S.S. Kim (ed.) *Korea's Globalisation*, Cambridge University Press, Cambridge.

Kim, Y.R. (1999), 'Emerging Civil Society and the Development of Interest Group Politics in Korea, *Korea Observer*, **30**(2), pp. 247–68.

Kim, Y.S. (1998), 'The Financial and Industrial Crisis: Cause and Implications', *Korea Observer*, **29**(3), pp. 511–34.

Kim, Y.S. and Koo, H.K. (1999), 'The Korean Crisis: A Year After', *Korea Observer*, **30**(3), pp. 397–410.

Kim, Y.T. (1998), 'The Origins of the Developmental State in South Korea, 1910–1979', *Asian Profile*, **26**(6), pp. 463–75.

Kim, Y.T. (1999), 'Neo-liberalism and the Decline of the Developmental State', *Journal of Contemporary Asia*, **29**(4), pp. 441–61.

Kim, W.S. and Choi, N.G. (1998), *The Global Trading System, Challenges Ahead: A Korean Perspective*, Institute for Global Economics, Seoul.

Kim, W.S. and Han, B.Y. (1995), 'Trade Pressures in Korea's Foreign Economic Frictions', in Sejong Institute (ed.) *Korea's Economic Diplomacy*, Sejong Institute, Seoul.

Kindleberger, C.P. (1977), 'US Foreign Economic Policy, 1776–1976', *Foreign Affairs*, **55** (January), pp. 395–417.

Klintworth, G. (1994), 'Taiwan's Asia–Pacific Policy and Community', *Pacific Review*, **7**(4), pp. 447–56.

Kokubun, R. (1986), 'The Politics of Foreign Economic Policy-Making in China: The Case of Plant Cancellations with Japan', *China Quarterly*, **105**, pp. 19–44.

Koo, B.H. (1992), *Socio-Cultural Factors in the Industrialisation of Korea*, Occasional Paper No. 32, International Centre for Economic Growth, San Francisco.

Koo, H. (2000), 'The Dilemmas of Empowered Labour in Korea: Korean Workers in the Face of Global Capitalism', *Asian Survey*, **40**(2), pp. 227–50.

Koopmann, G. (1998), 'German Foreign Economic Policy in the Age of Globalisation', *International Spectator*, **33**(1), pp. 38–60.

Knorr, K and Trager, F.N. (eds) (1977), *Economic Issues and National Security*, Regents Press, Lawrence.

Krasner, S. (ed.) (1983), *International Regimes*, Cornell University Press, Ithaca.

Kreinin, M.E. (1980), 'US Foreign Economic Policy: An Overview', *Journal of Economic Issues*, **14**(3), pp. 703–34.

Krueger, A.O. (1990), 'Free Trade is the Best Policy', in R.Z. Lawrence and C.L. Schultze (eds) *An American Trade Strategy: Options for the 1990s*, Brookes Institution, Washington D.C.

Krugman, P. (1986), *Strategic Trade Policy and the New International Economics*, MIT Press, Cambridge MA.

Krugman, P. (1994), *Peddling Prosperity*, W.W. Norton, New York.

Kulkarni, M.N. (1995), 'Global Political and Economic Security: Wishes and Horses', *Economic and Political Weekly*, **30**(52), pp. 3343–5.

Kuo, C.T. (1998), 'Private Governance in Taiwan', in S. Chan, C. Clark and D. Lam (eds) *Beyond the Developmental State: East Asia's Political Economies Reconsidered*, MacMillan, London.

Kwak, S. and Lee, H. (1997), 'Conditions of Economic Development in Korea in the First Half of the Twentieth Century', in A. Ikeo (ed.) *Economic Development in Twentieth Century East Asia*, Routledge, London.

LaCroix S.J., Plummer, M. and Lee, K. (eds) (1995), *Emerging Patterns of East Asian Investment in China: From Korea, Taiwan and Hong Kong*, M.E. Sharpe, Armonk.

Lake, D.A. (1983), 'International Economic Structures and American Foreign Economic Policy, 1887–1934', *World Politics*, **35**(4), pp. 517–44.

Lee, C. (1999a), 'On Economic Security', in G. Wilson-Roberts (ed.) *An Asia–Pacific Security Crisis?: New Challenges to Regional Stability*, Centre for Strategic Studies, Wellington, New Zealand.

Lee, C. (1999b), 'The Asian Turbulence: A Case Study of Economic Security', paper presented at the *40th Annual Convention of the International Studies Association*, 16–20 February, Washington D.C.

Lee, C.J. (2000), 'South Korean Foreign Relations Face the Globalisation Challenges', in S.S. Kim (ed.) *Korea's Globalisation*, Cambridge University Press, Cambridge.

Lee, D.H. (1999), 'The Challenges and Opportunities of Economic Diplomacy in the Era of the Ministry of Foreign Affairs and Trade', *Korean Observations on Foreign Relations*, **1**(1), pp. 108–27.

Lee, E.W.Y. (1998), 'The Political Economy Of Public Sector Reform In Hong Kong: The Case Of A Colonial-Developmental State', *International Review Of Administrative Sciences*, **64**(4), pp. 625–41.

Lee, H.K. (1996), *The Korean Economy: Perspectives for the Twenty-First Century*, State University of New York Press, New York.

Lee, J. (1999), 'East Asian NIEs' Model Of Development: Miracle, Crisis, And Beyond', *Pacific Review*, **12**(2), pp. 141–62.

Lee, K.Y. (2000), *From Third World to First: The Singapore Story, 1965–2000*, Times Editions, Singapore.

Lee, W.K.M. (1997), 'Foreign investment, industrial restructuring and dependent development in Singapore', *Journal of Contemporary Asia*, **27**(1), pp. 58–70.

Lee, Y.H. (1997), *The State, Society, And Big Business In South Korea*, Routledge, London.

Lee, Y.S. (1997), 'Globalisation in Korea: Prospects, Problems and Policy', *Korea's Economy 1997*, No. 13, pp. 36–40.

Lee, Y.H. and Kim, H.R. (2000), 'The Dilemma of Market Liberalisation: The Financial Crisis and the Transformation of Capitalism', in R. Robison, M. Beeson, K. Jayasuriya and H.R. Kim (eds) *Politics and Markets in the Wake of the Asian Crisis*, Routledge, London.

Leech, D.P. (1993), 'Conversion, Integration, and Foreign Dependency: Prelude to a New US Economic Security Strategy', *Geojournal*, **31**(2), pp. 193–206.

Leifer, M. (2000), *Singapore's Foreign Policy: Coping with Vulnerability*, Routledge, London.

Leng, T.K. (1996), *The Taiwan–China Connection: Democracy and Development Across the Taiwan Straits*, Westview, Boulder.

Leng, T.K. (1998), 'A Political Analysis of Taiwan's Economic Dependence on Mainland China', *Issues and Studies*, **34**(8), pp. 132–54.

Leong, H.K. (2000), 'Citizen Participation and Policy Making in Singapore: Conditions and Predicaments', *Asian Survey*, **40**(3), pp. 436–55.

LeviFaur, D. (1997), 'Economic Nationalism: From Friedrich List to Robert Reich', *Review of International Studies*, **23**(3), pp. 359–70.

LeviFaur, D. (1998), 'The Developmental State: Israel, South Korea, And Taiwan Compared', *Studies in Comparative International Development*, **33**(1), pp. 65–93.

Li, R. (1996), 'The Taiwan Strait Crisis and the Future of China–Taiwan Relations', *Security Dialogue*, **27**(4), pp. 449–58.

Lie, J. (1998), *Han Unbound: The Political Economy of South Korea*, Stanford University Press, Stanford.

Lim, H.C. (1985), *Dependent Development in Korea: 1963–1979*, Seoul National University Press, Seoul.

Lim, H.S. (1995), *Japan's Role in Asia*, Times Academic Press, Singapore.

Lim, L and Pang, E.F. (1991), *Foreign Direct Investment and Industrialisation in Malaysia, Singapore, Taiwan and Thailand*, OECD, Paris.

Lin, T.C. (1995) ,'The ROC's Foreign Aid and Southward Policy', *Issues and Studies*, **31**(10), pp. 1–20.

Lin, T.C. (1998), 'An Analysis of Taiwan's Investment in Guangdong', *Issues and Studies*, **34**(3), pp. 71–87.

Lipset, S.M. (1959), 'Some Social Requisites of Democracy: Economic Development and Political Legitimacy', *The American Political Science Review*, **53**, pp. 69–105.

List, F. (1841), *The National System of Political Economy*, Longmans, London.

Lorot, P. (1998), 'French Foreign Economic Policy', *International Spectator*, **33**(1), pp. 101–20.

Low, L. (1998), *The Political Economy of a City-State: Government-Made Singapore*, Oxford University Press, Singapore.

Lubbe, A. (1997), 'National Economic Security', *Polish Quarterly of International Affairs*, **6**(4), pp. 59–76.

Luciani, G. (1988), 'The Economic Content of Security', *Journal of Public Policy*, **8**(2), pp. 151–73.

Luttwak, E. (1990), *Disarming the World's Economies*, Centre for Strategic and International Studies, Washington D.C.

Mann, M. (1986, 1993), *The Sources of Social Power, Vol. 1,2*, Cambridge University Press, Cambridge.

Manning, B. (1977), 'The Congress, The Executive and Intermestic Affairs', *Foreign Affairs*, **55**(2), pp. 306–25.

Marsh, P. (1980), 'EEC Foreign Economic Policy and the Political Management of East–West Economic Relations', *Millennium*, **9**(1), pp. 41–54.

Martin, W.G. (1990), 'Introduction: The Challenge of the Semi-Periphery', in W.G. Martin (ed.) *Semi-Periphery States in the World Economy*, Greenwood Press, New York.

Marton, A., McGee, T. and Paterson, D.G. (1995), 'Northeast Asian Economic Cooperation and the Tumen River Area Development Project', *Pacific Affairs*, **68**(1), pp. 9–33.

Mastanduno, M. (1998), 'Economics and Security in Statescraft and Scholarship', *International Organisation*, **52**(4), pp. 825–54.

Mastanduno, M. (2000), 'Models, Markets and Power: Political Economy and the Asia–Pacific, 1989–1999', *Review of International Studies*, **26**(4), pp. 493–508.

Mathews, J.T. (1989), 'Redefining Security', *Foreign Affairs*, **68**(2), pp. 162–77.

Mathews, J.A. (1998), 'Fashioning a New Korean Model Out of the Crisis: The Rebuilding of Institutional Capabilities, *Cambridge Journal of Economics*, **22**(6), pp. 735–46.

McBeath, G.A. (1998), *Wealth and Freedom: Taiwan's New Political Economy*, Ashgate, Aldershot.

McGowan, P. and Walker, S.G. (1981), 'Radical and Conventional Models of US Foreign Economic Policy Making', *World Politics*, **33**(3), pp. 347–82.

McMichael, P. (2000), 'Sleepless in Seattle: What is the WTO All About?', *Review of International Political Economy*, **7**(3), 466–74.

McNamara, D.L. (ed.) (1999), *Corporatism and Korean Capitalism*, Routledge, London.

Mendl, W. (1995), *Japan's Asia Policy: Regional Security and Global Interests*, Routledge, London.

Mengin, F. (1998), 'Trade and Investments Across the Taiwan Strait: Toward a New Type of Regionalism?', paper given at *The Development of Contemporary Taiwan and its Implications For Cross-Strait Relations, the Asia–Pacific Region and Europe* Conference, Institute of National Policy Research, Taipei, 16–17 December.

Mercado, S. (1995), 'Towards a New Understanding of International Trade Policies: Ideas, Institutions and the Political Economy of Foreign Economic Policy', in J. MacMillan and A. Linklater (eds) *Boundaries in Question: New Directions in International Relations*, Pinter, London.

Milner, H. (1992), 'International Theories of Co-operation Among Nations: Strengths and Weaknesses', *World Politics*, **44** (April), pp. 466–96.

MINDEF (2000), *Defending Singapore in the 21st Century*, Ministry of Defence, Singapore.

Moeller, K. (1994), 'Taiwan Between Annexation and Independence', *Aussenpolitik*, **45**(2), pp. 199–208.

Molle, W. and Mourik, A.V. (1987), 'Economic Instruments of a Common European Foreign Policy', in J.K. De Vree, P. Coffey and R.H. Lauwaars (eds) *Towards a European Foreign Policy: Legal, Economic and Political Dimensions*, Martinus Nijhoff, Dordrecht.

Moon, C.I. (1988), 'Complex Interdependence and Transnational Lobbying: South Korea in the United States', *International Studies Quarterly*, **32**(1), pp. 67–89.

Moon, C.I. (1995), 'Globalisation: Challenges and Strategies', *Korea Focus*, **3**(3), pp. 62–77.

Moon, C.I. (1999), 'Political Economy of East Asian Development and Pacific Economic Co-operation', *Pacific Review*, **12**(2), pp. 199–224.

Moon, C.I. and Ko, D.W. (1999), 'Korea's Perspective on Economic and Security Co-operation in Northeast Asia', in T. Akaha (ed.) *Politics and Economics in Northeast Asia: Nationalism and Regionalism in Contention*, MacMillan, London.

Moon, C.I. and Lee, S.S. (1995), 'The Post-Cold War Security Agenda of Korea: Inertia, New Thinking, and Assessments', *Pacific Review*, **8**(1), pp. 99–115.

Moon, C.I. and Mo, J. (eds) (1999), *Democratisation and Globalisation in Korea: Assessments and Prospects*, Yonsei University Press, Seoul.

Moon, C.I. and Prasad, R. (1994), 'Beyond the Developmental State: Networks, Politics and Institutions', *Governance*, **7**(4), pp. 360–86.

Moon, C.I. and Rhyu, S.Y. (2000), 'The State, Structural Rigidity, and the End of Asian Capitalism: A Comparative Study of Japan and Korea', in R. Robison, M. Beeson, K. Jayasuriya and H.R. Kim (eds) *Politics and Markets in the Wake of the Asian Crisis*, Routledge, London.

Moon, C.I and Yoo, H. (1997), 'Embedded Mercantilism and Regional Integration in East Asia', paper presented at the 17th World Congress, International Political Science Association.

Moran, T. (1993), 'An Economic Agenda for Neo-Realists', *International Security*, **18**(2), pp. 211–5.

Moran T. (1996), 'Grand Strategy: The Pursuit of Power and Plenty', *International Organisation*, **50**(1), pp. 175–205.

Moravcsik, A. (1993), 'Integrating International and Domestic Explanations of World Politics: A Theoretical Introduction', in P.B. Evans, H.K. Jacobsen and R.D. Putnam (eds) *Double-Edged Diplomacy: International Bargaining and Domestic Politics*, University of California Press, Berkeley.

Moravcsik, A. (1997), 'Taking Preferences Seriously: A Liberal Theory of International Politics', *International Organisation*, **51**(4), pp. 513–53.

Mosley, M. (1982), 'French Foreign Economic Policy Under Mitterrand', *Fletcher Forum*, **6**(2), pp. 418–34.

Nester, W. (1990), 'The Development of Japan, Taiwan and South Korea: Ends and Means, Free Trade, Dependency, or Neomercantilism, *Journal of Developing Societies*, **6**(2), pp. 203–18.

Nester, W. (1991), 'Japan and the Far East: Neo-mercantilism, Prosperity and Dependence', *Asian Profile*, **19**(6), pp. 505–18.

Nukazawa, K. (1980), 'Whither Japan's Foreign Economic Policy? Straws in the Wind', *World Economy*, **2**(4), pp. 467–80.

O'Brien, R., Goetz, A.M., Scholte, J.A. and Williams, M. (2000), *Contesting Global Governance: Multilateral Economic Institutions and Global Social Movements*, Cambridge University Press, Cambridge.

Odell, J.S. (1982), *US Monetary Policy: Markets, Power and Ideas as Sources of Change*, Princeton University Press, Princeton.

Odell, J.S. (1990), 'Understanding International Trade Policies: An Emerging Synthesis', *World Politics*, **43**(1), pp. 139–67.

OECD (2000), *Economic Survey of Korea*, OECD, Paris.

Oh, J.K.C. (1999), *Korean Politics: The Quest for Democratisation and Economic Development*, Cornell University Press, Ithaca.

O'Hearn, D. (1994), 'Innovation and World-System Hierarchy: British Subjugation of the Irish Cotton Industry, 1780–1830', *American Journal of Sociology*, **100**(3), pp. 587–621.

Ohmae, K. (1995), *The End of the Nation-State: The Rise of Regional Economies*, Harper Collins, London.

O'Leary, J.P. (1979), 'Controlled Dis-Integration: Toward a Strategy For United States Foreign Economic Policy', *Comparative Strategy*, **1**(4), pp. 333–69.

Olson, R.S. (1979), 'Economic Coercion in World Politics: With a Focus on North–South Relations', *World Politics*, **31** (July), pp. 471–94.

Onis, Z. (1991), 'The Logic of the Developmental State', *Comparative Politics*, **24**(2), pp. 109–26.

Onis, Z. and Aysan, A.F. (2000), 'Neoliberal Globalisation, the Nation-State and Financial Crises in the Semi-Periphery: A Comparative Analysis', *Third World Quarterly*, **21**(1), pp. 119–39.

Ooi, G.L. and Koh, G. (1998), 'State–Society Synergies: New Stakes, New Partnership', in A. Mahizhnan and T.Y. Lee (eds) *Singapore: Re-Engineering Success*, Oxford University Press, Singapore.

Orru, M., Biggart, N.W. and Hamilton, G.G. (1997), *The Economic Organization of East Asian Capitalism*, Sage, London.

Park, S.C. (1996), 'Korean High Technology Industries in Intra-Regional Division of Labour and Industrial Change in East Asia', *Korea Observer*, **27**(3), pp. 363–88.

Park, S.H. (ed.) (1995), *Korea in the New World Economic Order: Issues and Solutions for the Future*, Korea Institute for International Economic Policy, Seoul.

Park, S.H. (1997), 'Foreign Direct Investment in Korea: Current Status and Future Prospects', paper presented at *Major Changes for European Corporations in the Globalising Asian Economy* Conference, Macau Institute of European Studies, 3–4 April.

Pastor, R.A. (1980), *Congress and the Politics of US Foreign Economic Policy, 1929–1976*, University of California Press, Berkeley.

Peebles, G. and Wilson, P. (1996), *The Singapore Economy*, Edward Elgar, Cheltenham.

Pempel, T.J. (1978), 'Japanese Foreign Economic Policy: The Domestic Bases for International Behaviour', in P.J. Katzenstein (ed.) *Between Power and Plenty: Foreign Economic Policies of Advanced Industrial States*, University of Wisconsin Press, Madison.

Pempel, T.J. (1999a), 'The Developmental Regime in a Changing World Economy', in M. Woo-Cumings (ed.) *The Developmental State*, Cornell University Press, Ithaca.

Pempel, T.J. (1999b), 'Democratisation and Globalisation: A Comparative Study of Japan, South Korea and Taiwan', in C.I. Moon and J. Mo (eds) *Democratisation and Globalisation in Korea: Assessments and Prospects*, Yonsei University Press, Seoul.

Perry, M., Kong, L. and Yeoh, B. (1997), *Singapore: A Developmental City-State*, Wiley, Chichester.

Pinder, J. (1985), 'European Economic-Security: How Can We Master the Modern Economy?', *International Journal*, **40**(1), pp. 128–44.

Polanyi, K. (1944), *The Great Transformation*, Beacon, Boston.

Porter, M. (1990), *The Competitive Advantage of Nations*, MacMillan, London.

Praet, P. (1987), 'Economic Objectives in European Foreign Policy Making', in J.K. de Vree, P. Coffey and R.H. Lauwaars (eds) *Towards a European Foreign Policy: Legal, Economic and Political Dimensions*, Martinus Nijhoff, Dordrecht.

Prakash, A. (2001), 'The East Asian Crisis and the Globalisation Discourse', *Review of International Political Economy*, **8**(1), pp. 119–46.

Price, T.J. (1981), 'State Development Agencies as International Actors and the Decentralization of United States Foreign Economic Policy, *Publius*, **11**(1), pp. 37–48.

Putnam, R.D. (1988), 'Diplomacy and Domestic Politics: The Logic of Two-Level Games', *International Organisation*, **42**, pp. 427–60.

Putnam, R.D. (1993), *Making Democracy Work: Civic Traditions in Modern Italy*, Princeton University Press, Princeton.

Ra, S. and Gong, Y. (1998), 'Abnormal Utilization of Commercial Paper: A Catalyst of Korean Financial Crisis', paper presented at the *Korean Economic Association Meetings*, August.

Rahim, L.Z. (1998), 'In Search Of The Asian Way: Cultural Nationalism In Singapore And Malaysia', *Commonwealth and Comparative Politics*, **36**(3), pp. 54–73.

Ramesh, M. (1995), 'Economic Globalization And Policy Choices: Singapore', *Governance*, **8**(2), pp. 243–60.

Randall, C.B. (1954), *A Foreign Economic Policy for the United States*, University of Chicago Press, Chicago.

Ravenhill, J. (2000), 'APEC Adrift: Implications for Economic Regionalism in Asia and the Pacific', *Pacific Review*, **13**(2), pp. 319–33.

Regnier, P. (1991), *Singapore: City-State In South-East Asia*, Hurst, London.

Reich, R. (1991), *The Work of Nations*, Knopf, New York.

Reynolds, L. (1993), 'The Future of International Economic Policy', *Management Review*, **82**(3), pp. 30–33.

Richardson, J.H. (1936), *British Economic Foreign Policy*, Allen and Unwin, London.

Risse-Kappen, T. (1995), 'Structures of Governance and Transnational Relations: What Have We Learned?', in T. Risse-Kappen (ed.) *Bringing Transnational Relations Back In: Non-State Actors, Domestic Structures and International Institutions*, Cambridge University Press, Cambridge.

Robinson, T.W. (1998), 'America in Taiwan's Post Cold War Foreign Relations', in D. Shambaugh (ed.) *Contemporary Taiwan*, Clarendon, Oxford.

Rodan, G. (1989), *The Political Economy of Singapore's Industrialisation: National State and International Capital*, MacMillan, Basingstoke.

Rohrlich, P.E. (1987), 'Economic Culture and Foreign Policy: The Cognitive Analysis of Economic Policy Making', International Organisation, **41**(1), pp. 61–92.

Rosecrance, R. (1986), *The Rise of the Trading State: Commerce and Conquest in the Modern World*, Basic, New York.

Rosenau, J. (1969), *Linkage Politics*, The Free Press, New York.

Ross, R.S. (1996), 'The 1996 Taiwan Strait Crisis: Lessons for the United States, China and Taiwan', *Security Dialogue*, **27**(4), pp. 463–70.

Rowley, C. and Bae, J. (eds) (1998), *Korean Business: Internal and External Industrialisation*, Frank Cass, London.

Roy, D. (1996), 'China's Threat Environment', *Security Dialogue*, **27**(4), pp. 437–48.

Sabatier, P. (1998), 'The Advocacy Coalition Framework: Revisions and Relevance for Europe', *Journal of European Public Policy*, **5**(1), pp. 98–130.

Sachs, J. (1998), 'The IMF and the Asian Flu', *The American Prospect*, No. 37, pp. 16–21.

Sandlands, R.J. and Tan, L.H. (1986), 'Comparative Advantage in the Re-Export Economy: The Case of Singapore', *Singapore Economic Review*, **31**(1), pp. 34–56.

Scharpf, F.W. (1994), 'Games Real Actors Could Play: Positive and Negative Co-ordination in Embedded Negotiations', *Journal of Theoretical Politics*, **6**(1) pp. 27–53.

Schein, E.H. (1996), 'Strategic Pragmatism: The Culture of Singapore's Economic Development Board', MIT Press, Cambridge MA.

Schive, C. (1999), 'How was Taiwan's Economy Opened Up? The Foreign Factor in Appraisal', in G. Ranis, S.C. Hu and Y.P. Chu (eds) *The Political Economy of Taiwan's Development into the 21st Century*, Edward Elgar, Cheltenham.

Schreiber, A.P. (1973), 'Economic Coercion as an Instrument of Foreign Policy: US Economic Measures Against Cuba and the Dominican Republic', *World Politics*, **25** (April), pp. 387–413.

Schumpeter, J. (1950), *Capitalism, Socialism and Democracy*, Harper, New York.

Shin, R.W. (1998), 'Implementation of Science and Technology Policies for Global Competition: Korea's Electronics and Telecommunications Industries', *Journal of International Development*, **10**(6), pp. 715–31.

Silvestrov, S. and Filatov, V. (1995), 'Russian Foreign Economic Policy: A Systemic View', *Problems of Economic Transition*, **38**(5), pp. 54–76.

Simon, D.F. (1992), 'Taiwan's Strategy for Creating Competitive Advantage: The Role of the State in Managing Foreign Technology', in N.T. Wang (ed.) *Taiwan's Enterprises in Global Perspective*, M.E. Sharpe, New York.

Simon, D.F. (1998), 'Charting Taiwan's Technological Future: The Impact of Globalisation and Regionalisation', in D. Shambaugh (ed.) *Contemporary Taiwan*, Clarendon, Oxford.

Simon, D.F. and Soh, S. (1994), 'Korea's Technological Development', *Pacific Review*, **7**(1), pp. 90–103.

Smith, D.A. (1997), 'Technology, Commodity Chains and Global Inequality: South Korea in the 1990s', *Review of International Political Economy*, **4**(4), pp. 734–62.

Smith, D.A. (1999), 'Lessons of Global Neo-Liberalism? The East Asian Economic Crisis Reconsidered', *Global Economic Review*, **27**(4), pp. 45–63.

Smith, D.A and Lee, S.H. (1990), 'Limits on a Semiperipheral Success Story? State Dependent Development and the Prospects for South Korean Democratisation', in W.G. Martin (ed.) *Semiperipheral States in the World Economy*, Greenwood Press, New York.

Smith, M. (1994), 'The EU, Foreign Economic Policy and the Changing World Arena', *Journal of European Public Policy*, **1**(2), pp. 283–302.

So, A.Y. and Chui, S.W.K. (1995), *East Asia and the World Economy*, Sage, London.

Sohn, C.H. (1996), 'The Emerging WTO and New Trade Issues: Korea's Role and Priorities', *KIEP Working Paper No. 96–04*, Korea Institute for International Economic Policy, Seoul.

Sohn, C.H. and Yang, J. (eds) (1998), *Korea's Economic Reform Measures Under the IMF Programme*, Korea Institute for International Economic Policy, Seoul.

Sohn, C.H., Yang, J. and Yim, H.S. (1998), *Korea's Trade and Industrial Policies (1948–1998) – Why the Era of Active Policy is Over*, Korea Institute for International Economic Policy, Seoul.

Song, B.N. (1994), *The Rise of the Korean Economy*, Oxford University Press, Oxford.

Soon, C. (1994), *The Dynamics of Korean Economic Development*, Institute for International Economics, Washington D.C.

Soon, T.W. and Stoever, W.A. (1996), 'Foreign Investment And Economic Development In Singapore: A Policy-Oriented Approach', *Journal Of Developing Areas*, **30**(3), pp. 317–40.

Sperling, J. and Kirchner, E. (1997), *Recasting the European Order: Security Architectures and Economic Co-operation*, Manchester University Press, Manchester.

Stiglitz, J. (1998), 'More Instruments and Broader Goals: Moving Toward the Post-Washington Consensus', *The 1998 WIDER Annual Lecture*, Helsinki, 7 January.

Stopford, J. and Strange, S. (1991), *Rival States, Rival Firms: Competition for World Market Shares*, Cambridge University Press, Cambridge.

Stepan, A. (1978), *The State and Society*, Princeton University Press, Princeton.

Story, J. (1988), 'The Launching of the EMS: An Analysis of Change in Foreign Economic Policy', *Political Studies*, **36**(3), pp. 397–412.

Strange, S. (1994), *States and Markets*, Pinter, London.

Stremlau, J. (1994), 'Clinton's Dollar Diplomacy', *Foreign Policy*, No. 97, pp. 18–35.

Suh, J.W. (ed.) (1993), *Korea's New International Economic Diplomacy and Globalisation Policy*, Korea Institute for International Economic Policy, Seoul.

Taylor, M. and Thrift, N. (1981), 'Some Geographical Implications of Foreign Investment in the Semiperiphery: The Case of Australia', *Tijdschrift voor Economische en Sociale Geografie*, **72**(4), pp. 194–213.

Tooze, R. (1994), 'Foreign Economic Policy in the New Europe: A Theoretical Audit of a Questionable Category', in W. Carlsnaes and S. Smith (eds.) *European Foreign Policy: The EC and Changing Perspectives in Europe*, Sage, London.

Tucker, N. (1994), *Taiwan, Hong Kong and the United States, 1945–1992: Uncertain Friendships*, Twayne, New York.

Ullman, R. (1993), 'Redefining Security', *International Security*, **8**(1), pp. 129–53.

Ungson, G.R., Steers, R.M. and Park, S.H. (1997), *Korean Enterprise: The Quest for Globalization*, Harvard Business School Press, Boston.

Ursacki, T. and Vertinsky, I. (1994), 'Long Term Changes in Korea's International Trade and Investment', *Pacific Affairs*, **67**(3), pp. 385–400.

US Council on Competitiveness (1994), *Economic Security: The Dollars and Sense of US Foreign Policy*, US Council on Competitiveness, Washington D.C.

Vernon, R. and Spar, D. (1988), *Beyond Globalism: Remaking American Foreign Economic Policy*, Free Press, New York.

Viner, J. (1948), 'Power Versus Plenty as Objectives of Foreign Policy in the Seventeenth and Eighteenth Centuries', *World Politics*, **1**(1), pp. 1–29.

Viner, J. (1968), 'Economic Thought: Mercantilist Thought', in *International Encyclopedia of the Social Sciences: Vol 4*, Free Press, New York.

Vogel, S. (1996), *Freer Markets, More Rules: Regulatory Reform in Advanced Industrial Countries*, Cornell University Press, Ithaca.

Wade, R. (1988), 'State Intervention in 'Outward-Looking' Development: Neo-Classical Theory and Taiwanese Practice', in G. White (ed.) *Developmental States in East Asia*, MacMillan, London.

Wade, R. (1990), *Governing the Market: Economic Theory and the Role of Government in East Asian Industrialisation*, Princeton University Press, Princeton.

Wade, R. (1996), 'Japan, the World Bank, and the Art of Paradigm Maintenance: The East Asian Miracle in Political Perspective', *New Left Review*, **217**, pp. 3–36.

Wade, R. (1998), 'The Asian Debt-and-Development Crisis of 1997-?: Causes and Consequences', *World Development*, **26**(8), pp. 1535–53.

Wade, R. and Veneroso, F. (1998), 'The Asian Crisis: The High Level of Debt Model Versus the Wall Street-Treasury-IMF Complex', *New Left Review*, **228**, pp. 3–22.

Wade, R. and White, G. (eds) (1984), 'Developmentalist States in East Asia', *Institute of Developmental Studies Bulletin*, special issue, University of Sussex, Brighton.

Wallace, W. (1975), *The Foreign Policy Process in Britain*, Royal Institute of International Affairs, London.

Wallerstein, I. (1978), 'World System Analysis: Theoretical and Interpretative Issues', in B.B. Kaplan (ed.) *Social Change in the Capitalist World Economy*, Sage, Beverly Hills.

Wallerstein, I. (1979), *The Capitalist World Economy*, Cambridge University Press, Cambridge.

Wang, C.N. (2000), *The Asian Currency and Financial Crisis: Did the Twin Liberalisation Matter? – The Taiwan Experience*, Economic Research Department, Central Bank of China, Taipei.

Weber, M. (1922), *Economy and Society*, Bedminster Press, New York.

Weber, M. (1947), *The Theory of Social and Economic Organisation*, Oxford University Press, New York.

Weiss, L. (1995), 'Governed Interdependence: Rethinking the Government–Business Relationship in East Asia', *Pacific Review*, **8**(4), pp. 589–616.

Weiss, L. (1998), *The Myth of the Powerless State: Governing the Economy in a Global Era*, Polity, London.

Weiss, L. (1999), 'State Power and the Asian Crisis', *New Political Economy*, **4**(3), pp. 317–42.

Weiss, L. (2000), 'Developmental States in Transition: Adapting, Dismantling, Innovating, Not Normalising', *Pacific Review*, **13**(1), pp. 21–56.

Weiss, L. and Hobson, J.M. (2000), 'State Power and Economic Strength Revisted: What's So Special About the Asian Crisis?', in R. Robison, M. Beeson, K. Jayasuriya and H.R. Kim (eds) *Politics and Markets in the Wake of the Asian Crisis*, Routledge, London.

White, G. (1988), *Developmental States in East Asia*, St. Martins Press, New York.

White, G. (1998), 'Building a Democratic Developmental State', *Democratisation*, **5**(3), pp. 1–32.

Whitley, R. (1990), 'Eastern Asian Enterprise Structures and Comparative Analysis of Forms of Business Organisation', *Organisation Studies*, **11**(1), pp. 47–74.

Whitely, R. (1992), *Business Systems in East Asia: Firms, Markets and Societies*, Sage, London.

Wilson, P. (2000), 'The Dilemma of a More Advanced Developing Country: Conflicting Views on the Development Strategy of Singapore', *The Developing Economies*, **38**(1), pp. 105–34.

Woo, M. (1993), 'Export Promotion in the New Global Division of Labour', *Sociological Perspectives*, **36**(4), pp. 335–57.

Woo-Cumings, M. (1991), *Race to the Swift*, Columbia University Press, New York.

Woo-Cumings, M. (1996), 'The Political Economy of Growth in East Asia: A Perspective on the State, Market and Ideology', in M. Aoki, H.K. Kim and M. Okuno-Fujiwara (eds) *The Role of Government in East Asian Economic Development*, Oxford University Press, Oxford.

Woo-Cumings, M. (ed.) (1999), *The Developmental State*, Cornell University Press, Ithaca.

World Bank (1993), *The East Asian Miracle: Economic Growth and Public Policy*, Oxford University Press, Oxford.

World Trade Organisation (1996), *Trade Policy Review of the Republic of Korea – 1996*, Geneva.

World Trade Organisation (2000a), *Trade Policy Review of Singapore – 2000*, Geneva.

World Trade Organisation (2000b), *Trade Policy Review of the Republic of Korea – 2000*, Geneva.

Yahuda, M. (1998), 'Some International Dimensions of the Taiwan Problem', paper given at *The Development of Contemporary Taiwan and its Implications For Cross-Strait Relations, the Asia–Pacific Region and Europe* Conference, Institute of National Policy Research, Taipei, 16–17 December.

Yang, U.C. (ed.) (1998), *The Political Economy of Korean Unification: Agenda Preparation*, Sejong Institute, Seoul.

Yang, J.S. and Kim, H.Y. (2000), *Issues in Korean Trade 1999: Trends, Disputes and Trade Policy*, Korea Institute for International Economic Policy, Seoul.

Yeoh, B. and Willis, K. (1997), 'The Global–Local Nexus: Singapore's Regionalisation Drive', *Geography*, **82**, No. 355(2), pp. 183–6.

Yeung, H.W.C. (2000), 'State Intervention and Neoliberalism in the Globalising World Economy: Lessons from Singapore's Regionalisation Programme', *Pacific Review*, **13**(1), pp. 133–62.

Yoon, B.J. (1999), 'The Korean Financial Crisis, the Chaebol and Economic Reform', *Korea Observer*, **30**(3), pp. 411–42.

Yoon, C.H. (1992), 'International Competition and Market Penetration: A Model of the Growth Strategy of the Korean Semiconductor Industry', in G.K. Helleiner (ed.) *Trade Policy, Industrialisation and Development: New Perspectives*, Clarendon Press, Oxford.

Yoon, Y.K. (1995), 'Korea and Regional Economic Co-operation', in Sejong Institute (ed.) *Korea's Economic Diplomacy*, Sejong Institute, Seoul.

Young, S., Lee, C.J. and Zang, H.Y. (1998), 'Preparing for the Economic Integration of Two Koreas: Policy Challenges to South Korea', in M. Noland (ed.) *Economic Integration of the Korean Peninsula*, Institute for International Economics, Washington D.C.

Yuen, F.K. (1999), 'Singapore: A Time for Economic and Political Engagement', in A.I. Johnston and R.S. Ross (eds) *Engaging China: The Management of an Emerging Power*, Routledge, London.

Yun, J.K. (1999), 'Liquidity Crisis in South Korea: A Year After', *Korea Observer*, **30**(3), pp. 371–84.

Yun, M. (1999), 'Case Studies: Doing Business in Korea', *Korea's Economy: 1999*, Korea Economic Institute of America, Washington D.C.

Zyzniewski, S.J. (1958), 'Soviet Foreign Economic Policy, *Political Science Quarterly*, **73**(2), pp. 206–33.

Index